EXPLORING CONSCIOUSNESS

EXPLORING CONSCIOUSNESS:

NON-DUALITY TO NON-LOCALITY

PREFACE BY HIS HOLINESS THE DALAI LAMA

Editors
Côme Carpentier
Anmol Mahajan

MLBD PUBLICATIONS
Motilal Banarsidass Publications

MOTILAL BANARSIDASS
PUBLICATIONS
4741/23, Ansari Road, Daryaganj, New Delhi - 110002 (India)
Email: mlbd@mlbd.com | sales@mlbd.com | exports@mlbd.com
Website: www.mlbd.com

Exploring Consciousness
by
Côme Carpentier
Anmol Mahajan

First Edition Published in 2024

Published in India
by
Motilal Banarsidass Publications
and
India Foundation

ISBN : 978-93-91759-94-0 (HB)

Printed and bound in India

THE DALAI LAMA

PREFACE

I am pleased to provide a preface to this compilation of the proceedings of a conference organised by the *India Foundation* in association with the *National Institute of Mental Health and Neurosciences* (NIMHANS) in Bengaluru, Karnataka, on the theme of consciousness. I understand that more than twenty eminent scientists and philosophers from several countries presented papers that are gathered in this book, 'Exploring Consciousness'.

Drawing on ancient Indian findings, the tradition to which I belong defines consciousness as clear and knowing. Clear here refers to the ability of mental states to reveal or reflect. Knowing, on the other hand, refers to the faculty of the mind to perceive or apprehend what appears.

Many modern scientists assume that consciousness is a physical process that arises through the structure and dynamics of the brain. I have on several occasions proposed that mere thought might effect a change in the chemical processes of the brain. The general scientific response had been that since all mental states have a physical basis, it is not possible for thought or mental states to change the brain; however, the discovery of neuroplasticity has changed this.

I believe that it is possible for contemporary heirs to ancient Indian tradition, particularly followers of the Nalanda tradition, and modern science to engage in collaborative research in the understanding of consciousness. For the time being, they can leave aside the philosophical question of whether consciousness is ultimately physical or not. Such collaborative study will contribute not only to greater human understanding of consciousness, but also to a better understanding of the functioning of the human mind and its relation to happiness and suffering.

I am encouraged to see that the conference was an opportunity to bring together the knowledge of ancient India and modern understandings of consciousness, an exploration all the more crucial bearing in mind the vital role our consciousness plays in determining the course of humanity.

8 January 2024

Foreword

The contents of the book reflect the presentations and discussions held at the first International Conference on Exploring Consciousness, the Man-Machine Debate, From Non Duality to Non Locality held on 22-24 September, 2022 at the National Institute of Mental Health and Neurological Sciences (NIMHANS), at Bangalore, India, at the initiative of the India Foundation, with support from the Ministry of AYUSH, the Indian Council of Philosophical Research and the Federation of Karnataka Chambers of Commerce & Industry.

Consciousness is primary for all the experiences in life. The endeavour to understand the origin and nature of consciousness is becoming a mature science. The latter is showing its immense potential application across human endeavours, ranging from fundamental research to clinical applications, ethnics, business, technology and marketing at large for individual and collective well-being. Thus, exchanging and debating information and ideas in this vast domain is of major importance to the scientific community and to society.

The purpose of this exercise is to bring together some of the most eminent researchers and inventors in the area of physics, biology, neuroscience, artificial intelligence, cybernetics, quantum computing and allied fields as well as scholars and spiritual teachers of the main Indic spiritual and psychological disciplines and doctrines. This book aims to build bridges and work towards a consensus between scientists, technologists, sociologists, spiritual and philosophical scholars from Indian/Asian and Western traditions.

We would like to thank the authors who have contributed to this publication and acknowledge the efforts of all who have dedicated their time and effort to raise the quality of this academic exercise including Ms. Jehanara Wasi, Senior Editor and Mr. Abhishek Dwivedi, LLB Student, Delhi University.

List of Authors

1. **S. R. BHATT**
Ex Chairman, Indian Council of Philosophical Research, India

2. **JULIO OZAN LAVOISIER**
Philosopher, Author of Several Books, Argentina

3. **OSCAR PUJOL**
Sanskrit Scholar; Director, Cervantes Institute Delhi, India

4. **STEPHAN SCHWARTZ**
Distinguished Associated Scholar, California Institute for Human Science and Consulting Faculty, Saybrook University, USA

5. **DEAN RADIN**
Chief Scientist, Institute of Noetic Sciences and Associated Distinguished Professor, California Institute of Integral Studies, USA

6. **SHUGAN JAIN**
Chairman, International School for Jain Studies, India

7. **SURENDRA SINGH POKHARNA**
Managing Trustee (President), Dr. Daulat Singh Kothari Institute for Research and Education, Udaipur; Executive Secretary, Jain Academy of Scholars, Ahmedabad

8. **LORA RYSKELDIEVA**
Professor of Philosophy, Crimean Federal University, Russian Federation

9. **JOHN J. KINEMAN**

Senior Research Scientist, University of Colorado, USA

10. **HARALD ATMANSPACHER**

Emeritus Member, Turing Centre, ETH Zurich, Switzerland

11. **JASON BROWN**

Neurologist, Philosopher, Author of Several Books, France

12. **TOBI ZAUSNER**

Adjunct Professor, Graduate College of Psychology and Integrative Inquiry, Saybrook University, USA

13. **TERRENCE DEACON**

Professor of Anthropology and Member of the Cognitive Science Faculty, University of California, Berkeley, USA

14. **PAUL JOHN WERBOS**

Fr. Director, National Science Foundation Program, Washington DC, USA

15. **KANCHI GOPINATH**

Sr. Faculty, Plaksha University, Professor of Computer Science and Artificial Intelligence (Rtd.), Indian Institute of Science, India

16. **SUBHASH KAK**

Chair of the Taksha Artificial Intelligence and Cyber Security (TAICS) Centre and Regents Professor in the School of Electrical and Computer Engineering at Oklahoma State University, USA

17. **THOMAS BROPHY**

President, California Institute for Human Science, USA

18. **ALEX HANKEY**
Professor Emeritus of Biology, MIT World Peace University, India

19. **SHELLI RENÉE JOYE**
Philosopher, Physicist, Author of Several Books, Italy

20. **GEORG NORTHOFF**
Professor, The Royal Institute of Mental Health Research, University of Ottawa, Canada

21. **SAKETH MALIPEDDI**
Senior Research Fellow, Centre for Consciousness Studies, Dept of Neurophysiology, NIMHANS, India

22. **P.N. RAVINDRA**
Additional Professor, Centre for Consciousness Studies, Dept of Neurophysiology, NIMHANS, India

23. **ARUN SASIDHARAN**
Scientist C (Neuroscience) Centre for Consciousness Studies and Dept of Neurophysiology, NIMHANS, India

24. **RAMAJAYAM G.**
Scientist C (Yoga) Centre for Consciousness Studies, Dept of Neurophysiology, NIMHANS, India

25. **BINDU M. KUTTY**
Senior Professor, Officer in Charge, Centre for Consciousness Studies, Dept of Neurophysiology, NIMHANS, India

26. **ROSALIND PEARMAIN**
Faculty Member and Dissertation Supervisor, The Minster Centre Psychotherapy, United Kingdom

Contents

THE PROBLEM OF CONSCIOUSNESS IN SCIENCE

CONSCIOUSNESS AND HEALTH

Introduction

Everything that was alluded to or understood diversely as spirit, mind, soul, and consciousness, the latter being perhaps the most recent of the designations used in all the world's languages, was till fairly recently confined to the provinces of religion, whether mystical or dogmatic and philosophy, in all its schools. However, in the last century, it was gradually claimed by science once it began to apply its research method to the investigation of a field that had long been regarded as lying beyond the pale of objective experimental knowledge. Prior attempts, going back to antiquity, to detect and map the 'mind stuff' in brain matter and to relate it to the electrical force and other natural phenomena had been only marginally successful at best. The essence of what manifests as awareness, cognition, intelligence, and other related experiential features of living creatures has remained elusive.

A great divide still sets apart those who profess that consciousness is some sort of biochemical or biophysical product of brain structures and neurological processes—a bit like honey is the product of a beehive or oxygen the output of photosynthesis in plants - from their colleagues who see the physical world as arising out of a prior or at least transcendent noetic reality. The latter investigators find support in the fact that, so far, mechanistic theories about the emergence of biological intelligence out of living cells through some biochemical reaction remain unconfirmed by experimentation. On the other hand, several scientific interpretations of quantum physical phenomena, often inspired by ancient metaphysical and philosophical concepts, provide plausible and convincing explanations of the nature and features of what many like to define as an intelligent cosmos, whether they choose to call themselves as pan-psychists like some of the neo-platonic philosophers or prefer to say that the ultimate reality is an undefinable 'zero-point field' whose first emanation is consciousness, of which Time and Space are only interfaces (Donald Hoffman).

Since the origins of languages, the mind has been diversely compared or even equated with breath (*anemos*, the spirit, the soul), fire as in the Sanskrit *Agni* and the semitic *Ruach-Ruh* (the 'Holy Ghost'), and light in general, giving rise to the *lumen sapientiae* and *lumen gloriae* of medieval scholastics. Consciousness as a concept is a latecomer, derived from the Latin *conscientia* (Greek *syneidesis*) which initially meant 'to see the same image or to share knowledge with others', kindred to 'consensus' (feeling with others). We had to wait for John Locke to use it to convey the notion of 'knowing that we know' or being reflectively aware of our (otherwise unconscious) awareness.

Etymologies reveal paradoxes in words. Science as a concept is formed out of the Indo-European root of the verb for the action of splitting or separating. Knowing means discerning by giving separate identities to things. Conscience achieves coherence by relating what we feel or know (no clear difference between the two notions) to the perception/conception of others and eventually to overall common views and subsequent values, maturing as ethics. Consciousness gives us the ability to intellectually triangulate (and hence assess and analyse) thoughts (Old Germanic *p(h)encan*, the equivalent of Sanskritic *dhi*) which are appearances or images in the semantic sense, like the Sanskrit *vedana*-s, and thereby gives us the ability to reflect on them, literally like a pond mirrors the shapes that lie above it.

Reflections, however, are separate from the originating objects although dependent on them. Consciousness in its early context may be taken as a stream of mental activity in an individual or collective sense, as an echo of the traditional *sensum communis* that was often held to be a particular attribute of human beings, as distinct from other living creatures credited with various degrees of sensorial perception, instinct, and reasoning ability but not with consciousness as such. However, that dichotomy appeared artificial to many who kept in mind the Pythagorean and Neo-Platonic adage that '*The Spirit (or Consciousness, Nature or God) sleeps in the stone, dreams in the plant, awakens in the animals and becomes fully alive in man*'.

How indeed can it be concluded that animals are not aware of what they experience, feel, and learn? Even plants seem to share a collective memory that helps them react to external conditions and adapt to changing circumstances. In retrospect, it may be inferred that denying 'consciousness' to non-human animal species was intended to absolve the 'regent of creation' of the sin of enslaving and consuming them, in the Biblical scheme of things. The license to kill all other beings for one reason or another, gave humans added agency and ethical immunity but clearly did not make them stop from slaughtering one another.

There remains a debate about the long-assumed uniqueness of the human faculty of introspection and the deeper, meta-individual inference of a 'silent watching universal self', common to various ancient philosophical traditions and symbolised by the Upanishadic parable of the two birds: the one which eats, enjoys and suffers and the other (the higher self) which remains aloof while observing the first one.

dvā suparṇā sayujā sakhāyā samānaṃ vṛkṣaṃ pariṣasvajāte |
tayoranyaḥ pippalaṃ svādvattyanaśnannanyo abhicākaśīti ||

English Translation:
Two birds, inseparable companions, perch on the same tree, one eats the fruit, the other looks on. The first bird is our individual self-feeding on the pleasures and pains of this world; The other is the universal Self, silently witnessing all.
(In the Mandukya Upanishad)

The second bird might manifest as moral conscience, whether we attribute the latter to an inborn ethical sense or to an imparted system of values and code of conduct but both the birds are sometimes depicted as a single one with twin heads, which tells us that they represent consciousness in its various forms and at different levels. The longstanding debate about whether Aristotle conceived of consciousness might thus find a resolution but there is also a dialogue between those who regard the diverse mental entities described in Indic texts (*atman, buddhi, manas, jiva, chitta*) as separate and those, such as Advaita Vedantins, who see them as emanations of a single essence, a view they share with the Neoplatonics who expounded the theory of outflow (*perilampsis*) from the cosmic mind into the living souls.

The meeting between modern neurophysical research and Indic psychography leads to an attempt to define precisely in Western terms Sanskrit concepts like *prajna* which amounts to an awareness of or an insight into the three fundamental characteristics of reality according to Buddhism: impermanence, dissatisfaction, or suffering caused by the former and lack of self as a separate permanent identity.

Prajna could be described as lucid consciousness and its cognate *Samjnana* is shared or common awareness which thereby acquires social validity. Both compounds include the root *jna* (know) which implies an understanding of what is being seen or perceived while the verb *budh,* the root of Buddhi and Buddha, signifies the act of observing, the fount of comprehension. In the light of these etymologies, consciousness appears to be a faculty and an action comparable to light which is a phenomenon that penetrates and dispels darkness. How light and awareness/intelligence arise in an assumed 'dark and empty' pre-universe is an enigma at the root of David Chalmers's 'hard problem' of consciousness but others who do not follow Searle's Biological Naturalism (1992) prefer to turn the issue on its head by putting consciousness first. Note that neither light nor consciousness are 'elements', in the ancient cosmological sense, nor in the chemical meaning of the word. Light denotes a range of radiation (vibrational wavelength and amplitude) or particles, of which only a small section is visible to the human eye…And what about consciousness?

Allan Watts noted a few decades ago concluding that 'all is consciousness' (or *Brahman*, Mind or God, interchangeably) amounts to the truism that 'all is all' but recently created mathematical models have demonstrated that the theory of evolution through natural selection leaves no chance to sentient (i.e. living) organisms to perceive reality as it is (Hoffman, 2016). In other words, what we and all other animate creatures detect sensorially, and hence logically, is an interface made up of signals selected and coded by the instruments of our physical bodies to enable us to function and help us survive and reproduce. An analogy has been given with the icons on a computer screen, used to indicate and access complex stored electromagnetic files, in themselves invisible to our unaided physical organs and undecipherable through mere observation. This rather disheartening induction echoes the Vedantic and Buddhist teachings about the unfathomable ultimate nature of all things, their suchness: *tathata* which is their invisible transcendent essence (*sat*) or David Bohm's Plenum, but we still cannot give up the pragmatic, impression-based analysis of the inner and outer world if we are to exist in this set of dimensions.

As Leibniz had realised three centuries ago, Space and Time are not primary either in the light of post-Einsteinian physics but they are rather understood as aspects of the aforesaid interface consciousness provides us with to make sense of the Being that encompasses them and all else. We have little choice but to play the game (*leela*) of life, assuming that perhaps Consciousness, through all its appearances, including ourselves, is endlessly exploring its own dimensions and faculties endlessly. Mystics will say that this reflection is akin to their immemorial pantheistic poetic musings.

Comparing perceptible reality to an array of psycho-sensorial icons, albeit metaphorically, raises the question of the mechanical nature of mental activity. Can a 'man-made' contraption think and eventually develop self-awareness eventually? The debate is fed by the exponentially increasing R&D on Machine Deep Learning, Quantum Processing *et al.* Both sides have convincing or at least thought-provoking rationales but if there is no permanent border between the organic and the (externally) built, between naturally evolved genetic structures and so-called artificial ('human built') ones, can there not be a certain kind of 'manufactured' conscious entity? The very name of a computer comes from the Latin *computare*: to think or rather 'to think with'. This is where the argument becomes truly interesting as it expands to new territories.

There is growing evidence that what we call the flow of time is the manifestation of entropy as well as the 'reading order' for the consciousness of the observer—who is in fact a participator and co-creator. According to recently found biological evidence, human (and probably animal) consciousness is not a continuous stream of inputs but a series of 'bits' of up to 400 milliseconds duration separated by 'empty' gaps (Herzog, 2016). This fragmented, sequential form of awareness may be the cause of our natural (and vitally necessary) tendency to see all things as separate and distinct and to break up reality into apparently unconnected events, objects, and actions. One result of this mode of perception is that the world as a whole, looks chaotic and meaningless, contrary to the holistic, 'panoptic' vision which detects order and sense in the cosmos.

The debate that has opposed for centuries the advocates of a mathematically designed and regulated universe to the 'experiential physicalist' proponents of a biologically evolving cosmos has taken a sharper edge because laws of physics may not always be reconciled with organic processes. The universe as a whole is not built on a ladder of rising complexity but instead presents a picture of constant complexity at all levels, as in genetics. The minutest components are as complex as their wholes they are parts of. In physics, this discovery dooms all attempts to detect fundamental particles and confirms the Gödelian axiom that it is impossible to build a true theory of everything since there are only 'fractal truth quotients' (Young, 1991).

In that light, neuro-physicists and cognitive psychologists, sometimes defined as 'analytic idealists', who propose to replace

Space-Time with (Universal) Consciousness as the primary reality admit that this cannot be a definitive conclusion either; it only takes research to the level of a higher frame of reference which will in due course be transcended by a still higher one and so on *ad infinitum*. However, just like Newtonian physics, Evolution through Natural Selection, Special and General Relativity, and Quantum theories have been and remain critically useful in getting us to the level of operational understanding and technical ability we have reached so far.

The substitution of Space-Time by Consciousness should enable us to take a radically new approach in our study of nature and ourselves and to develop new technologies while probably refining and raising ethical standards out of a 'hermeneutics of everything' (Kastrup, 2017, 2019).

The most precious outcome should be the rediscovery of the true purpose and meaning of existence, an essential quest that has been so sorely neglected for the last few centuries of mostly instrumental scientific culture, dedicated to the exploitation of new discoveries in order to 'maximise our utilities', in Bentham's vocabulary.

Some of the eminent experts in the cognitive sciences, whether experiential physicalists (Strawson, 2010) or metaphysical realists, are confident that they have found the most elegant way to cut the Gordian knot of 'the hard problem of consciousness', given that neo-quantic physics cancels out space and time as 'real' dimensions and hence abolishes the need to explain an assumedly gradual 'emergence' of intelligence out of the fundamental matter-energy through a quantum process of objective reduction within the brain, sometimes pictured as an 'orchestrated collapse of nanotubes' (Penrose and Hameroff, 2011 *et passim*).

According to that 'consciousness-based' model which takes as its premise that 'you cannot start with unconscious elements to explain consciousness' (Hoffman, 2022), space-time, matter-energy, and all other things that obey the laws of physics are devices born out of life's evolution to help it adapt to an otherwise unknowable background reality not bound by physical laws—even though they are used to describe it - as it is prior to them. The universe is a substratum of a meta-reality of the information structure (Guillemant, 2015).

Science requires precision and, therefore a mathematical structure which philosophical and spiritual teachings mostly lack. Although the endeavour to build a mathematical equation for consciousness seems overly ambitious and perhaps hopeless, its first stage has been to demonstrate, first by Game Theory computer simulations and then through new equations, that natural evolution cannot succeed by providing organisms with a 'real' perception of things as they are but, instead rewards those which best develop the most useful tools for survival, growth, and reproduction.

The recognition that there is an infinite number of possible (and therefore actually coexisting) universes in an indeterminate number of Kantorian infinities explains that adaptive requirement because the perception of the 'Real' in its infinite complexity would make it impossible to detect and carry out survival strategies. Therefore 'no true perception of objective reality is possible in the language of evolution' (Hoffman, ibid.).

The best of all possible worlds will contain all possibilities
(Leibniz)

In philosophy, there has long been a controversy about the Cartesian contention that knowledge is a mirror of outer reality in the human mind. Rorty (1979), in his critique of Kantian epistemology, is only one of the more recent dissenting voices and in a way, he anticipates Hoffman's definition of physical perception through his concept of epistemic behaviourism. Earlier, Wittgenstein had concluded during his solitary retreat in Norway that the essence of Being is not expressible in mathematical language.

A common assumption is that the Quantum theory only applies to microscopic scales and does not visibly influence the objects and events perceptible to us; However, it has proven implications that affect 'macroscopic objects at room temperature'. The brain operates under quantum laws as Karl Pribram established some decades ago through his discovery of holonomic cerebral electrical fields and functions. We live in a quantic world and, although the physicalist analysis of nature has enabled modern man to build a formidable technological civilisation, it has also led him to ignore or even deny intrinsic meaning to the physical realm, seemingly cancelling out untold centuries of a spiritual and theological quest. The utilitarian *doxa* of the (mostly Western) contemporary culture culminated in Sartre's Existentialism which claims that all things only mean whatever the human mind sees in and thinks of them. To use Bohm's terminology, the sole focus of this anthropocentric approach is on the Explicate Order at the cost of denying the Implicate one. An inevitable consequence of that position is to describe human life as meaningless and eventually condemn us to despair, alone in that self-made predicament among an infinite range of other living beings.

Contrary to Buddhism, Taoism, and Advaita Vedanta which deny the world's outer reality but explore its ultimate meaning, physicalist materialism holds that apparent reality to be the sole truth but deprives it of intrinsic significance.

As if to save us from that hopeless conclusion, a fascinating inquiry into the structure and operational mode of the genome was carried out for decades by the late Russian geneticist Pyotr Gariaev. He discovered that it is a holistic continuum in which amino-acid selection is contextual, analogous to a linguistic structure 'based on the scanning of the entire RNA and not on a codon-by-codon dogmatic mechanical selection'. He explained his findings in *The DNA Wave Biocomputer* and other works that imply intelligent functioning at the genetic level. Consciousness seems to be present at that scale, validating the hypothesis that even subatomic particles, as mind-made symbols of whatever lies beyond, may behave like conscious entities (Hoffman, ibid.)

We can only marvel at the sea change in the scientific discourse which not so long ago held consciousness to be a taboo subject. Nowadays, it has become critical to the pursuit of frontier disciplines of knowledge; the old conceptual borders between the living and non-living have been breached and shown to be porous or to boil down to degrees of perception or apprehension.

At the so-called geological time scale, rocks have a behaviour akin to that of admittedly living organisms while rhizomes and blobs are now acknowledged as neural networks. At yet another scale of magnitude, the 'Gaia' theory about the Earth and other planets being biotic entities finds vindication. J.C. Bose anticipated this scientific realisation in the conclusions he formed from his experiments on the sentience of plants and seemingly inanimate structures.

In his PhD thesis research in the 1940s, David Bohm found that plasmas, which make up close to 99 per cent of all matter in the cosmos, behave in some ways like living organisms when they 'seek homeostasis'. So, is there anything truly non-alive in nature?

We have reached a momentous juncture in the scientific quest to understand the world and ourselves. We continue to build mathematical theories that will account for what we have hitherto qualified as supernatural, miraculous, and mysterious. On the other hand, as some of the frontline researchers in the field have pointed out there is a risk of falling into nihilism once we perceive the intractable and paradoxical nature of what lies behind the perceptible (and misleading) field of appearances we live in. Yet, the final message is to pay due respect to those necessary and inevitable appearances. Some form of panpsychism or panentheism is the best escape from the nihilistic shipwreck.

This book seeks to draw a panorama of the data and insights on consciousness collected along innumerable centuries up to the contemporary period by sages, philosophers, mathematicians, physicists, biologists, neurophysiologists, cyberneticians, computer scientists, art historians, and psychologists in East and

West. Studded with many charts and illustrations, it lays out a review of some of the most advanced research done, according to various methodologies, in this ever-expanding field, and reveals parallels between leading-edge scientific inductions and the mystical insights taught in several venerable schools of wisdom that flourished in diverse regions of the world.

From the cosmologies of the Sankhya and Jain doctrines to the pan-psychic metaphysics of Vedanta, from reflections on the non-local character of mystical revelations in all religions to the integrative approach of Systems Science, from the theory of Dual Aspect Monism to the analysis of human agency and motivation, from the role of trance stages in creativity to the perception of consciousness as the set of constraints that enable life to exist and perpetuate itself, from the emerging technologies that mimic mental functions in artificial structures to the Indian philosophical assessment of AI, from the function of mathematics in building so-called 'intelligent' machines to the Actual Theory of Noetic Fields, from the Bohm-Pribram 'holonomic' model of a granular digital cosmos, pulsating in and out of a hidden implicate order, to the hypothesis of Consciousness being rooted in Quantum Instability, we are led to the study of non-dual and non-local states of being, achieved through various meditation techniques that hold the key to real human well-being, happiness, psychic balance, and intellectual power, liberating the infinite potential of the human mind and soul.

The journey of exploration of 'abstract' sciences thus leads us towards self-discovery at the therapeutic and spiritual levels, from the macrocosm to the microcosm and back.

Côme Carpentier de Gourdon
Distinguished Fellow, India Foundation

PHILOSOPHICAL FRAMEWORKS: EAST AND WEST

Sarvam Khalvidambrahma On Visiting Reality: Enigmas and Certitude

S.R. Bhatt

Indian seers and sages right from the dawn of civilisation have apprehended and affirmed the fundamental unity of all existences. They have realised the fact that the entire multiplicity given to us in our varied and variegated experiences springs from one single source and is sustained by it alone. All existences therefore share the same essence. The ultimate Reality is self-existing and self-sustaining and provides the causal matrix to all existence. It is one and unitary but gets diversified by its own freewill.

This viewpoint is enunciated in the Vedas and its culmination is found in the Vedantic thought. This has been the authentic Indian position which is commonly accepted by most of the people in India both as a mode of thinking and way of living. This has been the cornerstone of the noble and sublime Indian culture.

This position is based on supra-normal experience which is codified as *ṣruti* and justified by *yukti*. So, it has the triple foundation of *anūbhuti*, *ṣruti* and *yukti*. We experience both unity and multiplicity and also that multiplicity issues forth from unity. Both unity and multiplicity are given to us in our concrete experiences. We cannot deny either of the two and per force we have to accept veracity of both. We experience one manifesting itself into multiple and the multiple being potentially contained into one, like a seed and the tree. All genuine experiences evince one appearing as many and many being contained in one. So, it can be said that "all is in One and One is in all."

On the basis of this background a two-level distinction has been drawn between the realm of one and the realm of many which we may call as empirical and transcendental. Both are to be reckoned as real. The only difference is that One has to be regarded independently real and many as dependently real. The two share the same essence and therefore there is *ekātmabhāva*, i.e., self sameness. But they have different modes of appearances. The One is formless and the multiple has varied forms. The formless has the potentiality of assuming multiple forms like a lump of clay may assume different shapes of earthen objects.

There is organic unity between One and many just like a living organism. In an organism there are multiple organs contained within the unitary whole. Each organ has dependent existence with respect to the other organ and ultimately with the whole organism. The total organism is characterised by harmonious co-existence of its parts which function in close coordination for the sake of the entire organism. There is marvellous networking in their functioning and sharing the fruits of cooperative enterprise. This is something remarkably natural but due to external factors this may get disturbed resulting in disharmony and disease.

Reality is thus a symbiotic unity of one and many at different levels, be that the individual, family, community, nation and the cosmos at large. Each one is a whole in itself and is related to other wholes in a concentric manner, that is smaller whole being contained in wider one and ultimately in the widest one which we may call as Brahma or by any other name.

Existence of reality is self-evident and does not require any justification. At least no one can deny one's own existence. Similarly, existence and interrelatedness of different multiple reals, is also undeniable though given inferentially. What is disputable is the nature of Reality.

Right from the dawn of human cognitive enterprise the reflective mind has been concerned about the nature of Reality, proximate and ultimate, empirical and trans-empirical. This has been caused by curiosity as well as practical necessity. There have been varied conceptions and theories in this regard but the demand for some kind of universally acceptable conception is one which a thoughtful mind cannot help making. Unfortunately, no two human minds have ever fully agreed with each other in their pronouncements. The dispute boils down to whether matter or consciousness is the ultimate real .

In the West right from the Greek times the dominant trend has been to distinguish between, and separate, mind (Consciousness) and matter. This position was sharpened by Descartes but this led to severe and serious objections and problems. Darwin tried to reduce mind to matter and put forth materialistic theory of evolution which had a great following in natural and social sciences which were made behaviourist and reductionist. But in the present quantum era this position has been challenged and the idea of consciousness transcending matter has been mooted. However, there is no finality about the verdict of science. In the field of science there cannot be finality of judgement because of the very nature of its methodology and empiricist bias.

In India, on the contrary, barring the materialistic school and some thinkers belonging to it, no one has entertained materialistic hypotheses. Either there is dualistic position or spiritualistic monism. However, there is predominance of spiritualistic stance which is the keynote of Indian culture. A clear distinction is drawn between empirical and transcendental forms of Reality. In a dualistic framework the distinction is between living and non-living but in the empirical state the two are experienced to be conjoined. Here the basic problem is how and why they get conjoined. In spiritualistic monism consciousness alone is the ultimate Reality. Existence without consciousness is meaningless. Consciousness alone is self-existing and self-revealing. It is the presupposition of all experiences. Through consciousness existence as well as non-existence of a thing are cognised.

Consciousness is self-cognising. No doubt at the empirical level existence is a wholesome continuum of animate and inanimate but at the transcendental level inanimate is transformed as pure consciousness. It is a spiritualistic theory of evolution. It can legitimately be argued that matter cannot be sui-generis. It depends upon consciousness for its cognizance and therefore it has been argued that it depends upon consciousness for its existence as well. One of the most striking phenomena revealed in human experience is the indubitable and inevitable availability of consciousness. Of course, we are sure of our own conscious existence and say "I exist" and make a contrast with inanimate objects by saying "I am a living being and they are not" or "I experience" or "I am conscious" etc. We are also aware of other conscious existences inferentially, and say "They are also living beings". The point is that existence of consciousness is most intimately felt, whatever be the form of its nature and mode of its experience. All achievements of culture and civilization, all domains of cognition, volition, affection and conation are its manifestations. Its expressions are varied and wondrous. But in spite of all this precise understanding of its nature and modes of functioning has been enigmatic, problematic and elusive to a rational mind.

A study of consciousness is a reflective awareness of a human being. It is an awareness of awareness, a meta-awareness through ratiocinative and discursive reasoning. To a discursive mind it is to be approached and investigated in a phenomenological reduction or through brain dissection or through laboratory experimentation. Though lively and interesting, it is highly complex and perplexing and defies all these approaches. It is at once a matter of certainty, wonder, doubt and denial. Nevertheless, it is a marvellous phenomenon inviting and absorbing more so since it pertains to one's own self.

However, to a spiritually enlightened person it is most intimately experienced, intuitively apprehended and immediately given. As Ādi Śaṃkarācārya has put it, one who denies its existence is himself/herself the evidence of its existence. Consciousness is only to be experienced and it cannot be reasoned or expressed in language. It cannot be an object of thought or of laboratory experiment.

Now the question is, we experience both matter and consciousness but which one is primary and which one is derivative or both are primary or both come from some higher source. Both cannot be primary as the dualistic hypothesis is fraught with many problems and has not been successful so far in pointing out the relation between the two. In the history of Western thought, we have witnessed many such abortive attempts from Plato and Descartes onwards till modern times. However, the fact remains that matter and consciousness do coexist in organic unity in living beings. It is consciousness which animates the inert matter and controls it as well. So, the reductionist hypothesis where matter is regarded as the primary and consciousness as its epiphenomenon becomes untenable. Physical sciences have tried hard to prove this hypothesis but have failed so far. To regard both as derivative from such a higher source will lead to the fallacy of infinite upward movement unless at some stage the higher source is regarded as *sui generis*. But the law of parsimony would make us believe that consciousness may be regarded as the *sui generis* highest principle. This position is strengthened by the fact that matter does not beget matter but consciousness begets consciousness. Reproduction is the sole prerogative of consciousness. Matter can be conjoined and disjoined but this is not reproduction. On the other hand, one life produces another life. Matter is not self-revealing but consciousness has this property. Matter mutates but consciousness can only be concealed and enveloped. Matter can be split up but consciousness cannot be done so. A comparative survey of the properties of the two would reveal that consciousness has some such properties which provide it primacy. Somehow a behaviouristic mind may not agree to this point.

The pursuits of science have so far resulted in scepticism, or probability or uncertainty. In the realm of spirituality on the contrary there is absolute certainty. This provides succour and solace, peace and beatitude which every living being aspires for.

In Indian cultural tradition a clear distinction is drawn between two levels of Reality, knowledge and values. One is empirical and the other is trans-empirical. The empirical is multiple and the trans-empirical is unitary. The empirical is phenomenal and the trans –empirical is transcendental. The former is amenable to sense experience but the latter is beyond the ken of senses and mind and is to be experienced intuitively only. The former is the realm of matter and the latter is the sphere of consciousness. The former provides the stepping stone to transcend to the latter. The two constitute the base and the apex. The material world is the base and has initial significance and value. But it is ephemeral and mutates. It cannot be final. Only consciousness is experienced as permanent. This has been aptly analysed in the Māṇḍukya upaniṣad in terms of four states of existence and in the Taittirīya Upaniṣad in terms of five sheaths covering the Real. These are well known views and need not be discussed here.

Any approach to Reality has to be holistic and should not be partite to understand it fully in its entirety. For this purpose, inner experience which is immediately and intimately realised should be relied upon. It is free from conditioning and limiting influences of senses, mind, language and external surroundings. This is the realm of spirituality which is available in yogic state of equipoise. Different from this is the outer experience which is mediated by several factors like object, circumstances, subjective limitations etc. That is why it is partial, and sometimes faulty and deceptive. It is contingent and conditional and therefore stands in need of verification. This is the area of empirical science. Both spiritual experiences and verdicts of science are valuable in their respective spheres and must be resorted to with judicious discrimination. As stated earlier, there are two levels of Reality—the immutable and mutable, the permanent and changing, the eternal and ephemeral. In a holistic approach both need to be attended to. So, science and spirituality have to join hands together. Just as pursuit of science presupposes certain training and skill so also spiritual experience requires practice of sādhanā, rigorous discipline and deep meditation.

The above stated approach alone can solve the riddle and controversy between science and spirituality. This is the message of the Īśāvāsyopaniṣad, Kaṭhopaniṣad and Mūnḍakopaniṣad. It is hoped that this ancient wisdom will dawn upon us and resolve the tangle for the benefit of humanity and the cosmos.

About Consciousness

JULIO OZAN LAVOISIER

Asking about consciousness implies reaching a philosophical plane, I will try to explain why. The world always presents itself to us as multiple, and in this multiplicity, we can prove with evidence that it is full of intelligence, at least where there is life. By this, I mean that the beings that we identify as individuals are endowed with intelligence. We know that in the face of a simple injury a kind of organised army of lymphocytes, plasma cells and other agents of the immune system immediately try to close the wound; regardless of our will and consciousness. The Intelligence of Flowers (Maeterlinck) has been written about, and their relationship with insects, which in turn demonstrate their ingenuity for survival.

We could talk about consciousness in humans or higher mammals, but we would inevitably fall into generalities because each consciousness has its particularities, depending on its character and acquired knowledge; each consciousness is a world of ideas and feelings. We can, in a general manner, speak of degrees or levels of consciousness, but never of consciousness as a single thing or spirit; we always find ourselves forced with an infinite multiplicity of consciousnesses, although some are more "aware" than others; according to our particular criteria.

Surrounded by, immersed in, and built out of intelligence, we wonder if there is an intelligent Being behind everything that exists, and the majority ultimately believe in its existence. But the inevitable result is that each consciousness has its own idea of this universal Intelligence. The most common idea is of a Supreme Being who has thoughts, feelings and will, that are all too human faculties, to which are added all the attributes of perfection that our minds can conceive, among others the power to create the universe. This anthropomorphic and mythical vision is too simple, which is why it has led many to profess scepticism or simply declare themselves agnostic.

Both have a point, those who believe and the agnostics, but belief, whether by itself or not, does not settle the matter; from a philosophical point of view, it is sterile. However, it is worth exploring the cause of these beliefs, to find out if they have a real basis. Unbelief is easy to explain: an almighty Person who creates and decides on the destiny of creation, from a rational, scientific point of view, does not hold, but is this reason enough to judge a metaphysical reality, since the evidential proof is a faculty intended to apply only to the physical or phenomenal world?

The limits of reason have been precisely drawn by Kant: any rational demonstration of what transcends reason enshrines antinomies and turns out to be sterile, in other words, the sciences can only attend to the relative, the variable, and the dependent on time and space; the metaphysical is the domain of philosophy.

Now, is this God as a Person really metaphysical? Strictly speaking, it is nothing more than a human projection towards the metaphysical and it is also, to a great extent, an invention of reason to explain something that consciousness latently intuits but does not fully understand. And this is how humanity has remained divided between the followers of reason and the followers of faith, and only a tiny minority has realised that it is necessary to overcome these two options, since both respond to the same perspective.

In effect, what has happened is that the human being has become aware of his individuality, and it is this alone that apparently differentiates him from the other animals (see my work Origin and Destiny of Man), but he is still, unfortunately, very far from becoming aware of his universality, that is, of awakening to universal Consciousness.

My proposal is to awaken this Consciousness, and all

my work is directed towards that end. While it is true that this proposal must seem like a fantastic utopia, considering the current state of the human being, in whom materialism reigns supreme and has led to a general alienation of the spirit, it is also true that the general opinion does not in any way alter the intangible truths.

The said universal Consciousness, I will clarify in advance, is not an invention of mine, a philosophical postulate, but is Reality itself, which is common to everything that exists. Proof of this is that it has manifested itself in the mind in various ways since ancient times: mythology, religion, philosophy, morality and art, in their highest expressions, are all inspired by it. I have dedicated a treatise to each one of these branches of philosophy because they are paths of transcendental knowledge. In The Search for Universal Consciousness, I have followed the trajectory of Western idealists, in the Evolution of the Spirit the path chosen by the Buddhists and in Parallel Civilisations charted by Hinduism. I have tried to make this set, which constitutes what I have called Universal Idealism, converge; although everything converges, in truth, in universal Consciousness.

We can appreciate in the Universus, i.e., in the totality of spirit and matter that constitute Reality, a centrifugal force that tends to expand and generate the multiple, and also a centripetal force that tends towards concentration and original unity. Both are emanations of the primordial One, of universal Consciousness. These forces are spiritual in their origin but in their projection, they interact with matter. We can observe these forces in the expansion of the stars and in mutual attraction in the cosmos. But since this material aspect of the Universe falls in the domain of the natural sciences, we will turn to the spiritual sciences.

Many mythologies speak of an original chaos on which order was eventually established; this is not my experience. The original Unity is the absolute Order and on expanding it disintegrates and multiplies, and it is then that chaos can generate itself. On becoming matter Consciousness is no more in its Essence, nor is it purely spiritual; nevertheless, it projects itself into the whole cosmos and fills it, and thus, strictly speaking there are not two realities but one Universus.

The first things that emanate from universal Consciousness are the primary manifestations, which are unitive and of a spiritual nature, i.e., they tend towards unification and reintegration in the original Unity. From what has been said it is clear that between the manifest centripetal and centrifugal forces in the Universus, there has to be an equilibrium that is maintained through contact with the unitive forces, if this were not so the chaos would prevail immediately.

These unitive forces, these primary manifestations of the One are a priori the forms of time and space, that reason uses (Kant) in order to understand the material world. The mental faculties that are connected to the concrete world are external, utilitarian or speculative and generate cumulative knowledge. These faculties are the mental or spiritual aspect of the centrifugal force found in the Universus, which tends towards expansion and multiplication. They are also a projection of the One, but they are mediate or secondary manifestations, already interdependent with matter.

The immediate or primary manifestations are purely spiritual and respond to centripetal forces that tend towards the reabsorption of the Universus in its original Unity, they tend to the absolute Order that is found in the Unity of Consciousness. The Universus, the spiritual and material whole, I repeat, is thus maintained by the equilibrium of the aforesaid forces; hence man's need to maintain contact with the unitive faculties, as disconnecting from them, that is alienation, leads to chaos.

Time and space are not only the conditions for knowledge, but also the conditions for the existence of beings. They are found between two realities, on the border between the Transcendent and Nature, they are the infrastructure of the Universe.

The primary manifestations of universal Consciousness come before time and space: Order in itself, as an ordering energy; Good in itself, as an aspiration towards the perfection of action;

Love itself as an integrating energy; Life in itself which is the energy of life; Beauty in itself, which is the aspiration towards the perfection of forms; and the intuition-instinct that is its intelligent manifestation. These are the guiding principles of everything that exists; all of them emanate from Unity and make creation possible and maintain it; all things tend, according to their possibilities, towards Unity, which is perfect Order, the Absolute.

All the intuitions about universal principles are refracted in Unity, and are inspired by its perfection, by its total Order, by its exemplary integration, harmony, correspondence and, naturally, uniformity. The Good and the Beautiful emanate from Unity, which illuminates moral and aesthetic consciousness; man extracts his morals, his ideals of justice and his sciences from the perception of Order; Love makes him integrate it harmoniously; his élan vital moves him to live. I am speaking here of the most essential, decisive and intimate elements of human nature.

Firstly, the Good and the Beautiful, Love and Order are the a priori ideas indispensable for knowledge in general, without them we would have no capacity for judgement, they are the references without which we would not know which road to take; they are like the compass of reason. We only have to reflect to see that they are implicit in each decisive and ascendant choice; because, of course, capricious and decadent choices seem to lack these parameters. All morality without the Idea of Good, all art without the Beautiful, all relation without Love, all sciences without Order in our mind and without the premise that there is an order in Nature would be impossible. God and the religions would be inconceivable without the attributes that these ideas suggest to us. But these are not just ideas that occur to us, (those who think this way surely forget why they occur to us); they move us and they push us to act, they are forces at work in Nature, they accompany life and drive it in its rising path.

Intuition-Instinct is, in a manner of speaking, in order to make it clearer for human understanding, the intelligent manifestation of universal Consciousness, but it is a priori to all intelligence, it is the pristine aspect, essential to it. I believe that the instincts of all animals have the same origin, except that they cannot process them like human intelligence does, i.e., they cannot apply reason to them. Intuition puts us in direct contact with the Creative itself, for this reason it is the creative aspect of intelligence, that can a posteriori build around original intuition, but this construction obeys another mental mechanism that I have called cumulative knowledge, while the former, like all primary manifestations, is unitive.

The human being ignores the origin of his intuitions because it is not he who creates them, they come to him, and he receives them from the universal Consciousness. The same happens with the animals through instinct; it is for this reason that we humans do not understand from where they get this kind of intelligence, which at times seems more ingenious than ours.

The primary manifestations of universal Consciousness are spiritual and overflow on to the Universus and by extending to all spiritual reality they are in the human mind and for this reason they are paradigmatic par excellence, i.e., they are obligatory and priority references and they are in a priori to all human thought and action. They are a priori to all moral idealism and they are the sources of the same. Man does not create moral, aesthetic, religious or philosophical ideals; he interprets them according to his understanding and tries to apply them.

The primary manifestations are the indispensable references for all 'ascendant' (uplifting) knowledge. They are elementary forces that are expressed as energy in matter, as instinct in animals and as instinct, sentiment and intelligence in higher mammals. The final knowledge is Consciousness of these forces that flow over the world. A clear example is the effect of Order understood as practical reason, like a moral code applied in society. It is no coincidence that all those who intuit that Reality, such as mystics, feel compelled to preach and establish a moral order.

The ultimate objective, the Unity that is absolute Order, can only be realised by the spirit or higher mind, and this is not an inference but an experience that can be acquired by any sensitive person with a capacity to love above and beyond particular objects or people. Various philosophers have observed that Love is a universal force. For Plato it is "a great and admirable god who extends his power over all in the human as well as divine order" (Symposium 186) "in such a way that the whole is connected with itself" (Symposium 203). Are we not speaking about the same unitive energies? They are impalpable forces that work on the most subtle and lightest elements, leaving Nature free to create in keeping with its potential.

A moral universal Order can be intuited; Taoism, Buddhism and Hinduism take it as a premise, so do Plato, Fichte in his own way and I in my thoughts, as expressed in The Roots of Morality. Almost all men experience a unitive force on a personal plane that we call love and many suspect that it transcends this plane. We all intuit that there is a vital force in action that nurtures our lives. Everyone, at least at some point in life has been enraptured by the beauty of Nature; the aesthetic phenomenon is capable of transporting us beyond the matter that we contemplate; as Schopenhauer believed. These suspicions and inklings are real and can be experienced on higher planes of consciousness. Where do these manifestations come from? From the Essence of the World which is not a postulate as we can have immediate awareness of it.

The specific function of philosophy and of the spiritual sciences is to stimulate the centripetal powers of consciousness, whose final objective is reabsorption in the Unity of universal Consciousness, where the spirit attains freedom, not just from matter but also from its dependent faculties: the utilitarian ones.

It will be understood how my project differs from philosophies that wanted or tried to be "scientific," as speculative or utilitarian faculties do not respond to this objective of unification and liberation. My proposal is to make philosophy and the sciences of the spirit more independent of the natural sciences, not to oppose them but to complement them in order to establish the necessary equilibrium, with a view to maintain coherence in human activity.

It is evident that in our times centrifugal forces are so predominant in man that they occupy all his mind and his actions. If one considers the aforesaid on alienation and the consequent chaos, it will be admitted that the situation is alarming. For this reason I have insisted on knowledge of the mechanisms of the mind in a general theory of knowledge, explained in my Psychosophy, and in the need to awaken and activate unitive faculties.

The paths of transcendental knowledge, which are unitive, have unification as their objective i.e., to make us more real. We are real as long as we participate in and manifest our Unity; we are universal, because reality is the Universus. As individuals we are effectively an illusion. In other words, as we near the ideal, our universal Consciousness, we are real, i.e, the ideal is the real. To the common man this could seem to be a play on words by philosophers, but religious beliefs, moral motivations, the urge for justice and the wish to perfect ourselves, to order our ideas, to become better, and so on, which are part of the daily routine of a normal human being, all obey this natural, universal urge to unify our beings with the under being. To give just one example, morality, which is one of the paths of transcendental knowledge, makes us more real, the immoral act disintegrates us, it scatters and alienates us, it drops us into the chaos of the multiple and it leaves us hurling blindly like a meteorite in infinite space.

When the mind is concentrated, it approaches its own essence, the Creative, when it expands it creates (inspired by the Creative consciousness) and grows as an individual, society or species. Individuals and societies expand in such a way that they forget their systole, i.e., their inner life, are left with no foundation and fall apart, and they are projected like fireworks that will fall after having been displayed, and disintegrate.

It is my aim to bring to people's attention this diastole and systole of universal Consciousness in which all beings will participate, the Unity that underlies diversity and plurality, this need to maintain a permanent relation with the Unity which is our real self. When aware of this Unity and of the harmonious pulsation of its Soul, men can develop, avoiding the extremes of thesis and antithesis, walking on the zone of equilibrium; they will find the adequate speed for their creative and dynamic evolution (See *The Spirit in History*).

There is only plenitude of life in the experience of totality, which is the totality of consciousness; there is only plenitude of love in the experience of Love in itself. It is the apperception of these emanations in all beings that gives fullness of life to this existence. The human being is part of universal Consciousness, he is part, consequence and extension of it; hence he has the motivation to create, to love, to order and also to philosophise, which leads to the comprehension of the Origin whereby he closes the Cycle of Life and fulfils his destiny.

Mind and Consciousness in the *Yogasutra*

OSCAR PUJOL

To speak on the concept of the mind means to conceptualise on the very same tool that produces concepts. It is not hard to understand, therefore, that the study of the mind has been considered one of the most difficult subjects in the history of philosophy. How to think thought? It is not perhaps an impossible task. Something like trying to jump on our own shadow.

A typically Indian way of approaching the problem is to establish a distinction between mind and consciousness. Often, consciousness has been understood as a property of the mind, itself a *res cogitans* that can be on, in a conscious mode, or off, in unconsciousness. From a very earlier time Indian thought distinguished between consciousness and mind, mind being an instrument of consciousness. This is the reverse of the earlier stated position. Consciousness is not a simple property of the mind, but it is the mind which somehow becomes subordinated to consciousness by becoming its instrument. Often this instrument was considered as a material substance in contradistinction to consciousness held to be a non-material entity.

For some philosophical schools of ancient India consciousness was the only existing think, the true ground of physical reality. In this case, we would speak of a pure form of consciousness, devoid of content, but able to project the material creation, both in its subtle and gross aspects. Matter would then be a specially condensed mode of consciousness. This ability to project the material creation would imply the capacity of consciousness to take some form, to adopt a diversity of shapes and volumes.

Other philosophical schools like the *sāṃkhya/yoga* preferred not to go beyond dualism and considered consciousness and matter as widely divergent principles, that are interconnected, but that cannot be reduced to the other.[i] One should recognise a certain kind of intellectual honesty in the advocates of dualism, even if dualism has a host of detractors from many different perspectives. The world that we encounter clearly shows this duality, as we tend to consider things as conscious: living beings, including ourselves, or as unconscious: inert objects that apparently do not show any form of sensibility. Dualism appeals to common sense and goes beyond the temptation to identify consciousness with matter or matter with consciousness. In the first case we will fall for materialism or physicalism. In the second case we will end up in some form of idealism.

Today the first option is the favoured one, both in sciences and in the philosophy of mind. As Peter Carruthers stated: "For my purpose here is just to remind the reader of the considerations which make physicalism the default option in the philosophy of mind. Unless there are very powerful arguments to the contrary, we should believe that all mental states and events are physically constituted".[1]

The advantage of materialism and idealism is that by reducing both principles to a single one it is much easier to explain how they can interact. The classical problem of dualism is how to describe the relation between two diametrically opposed principles. This has been also a classical problem for sāṃkhya/yoga: how to explain the relation between *puruṣa* (spirit) and *prakṛti* (matter), especially if there is not an actual point of contact between both and the *puruṣa* is considered to be an immutable principle, beyond and above any kind of modification. How can an unchanging principle interact with an ever-changing flux of matter?

To get a picture of the difficulties it would be useful to mention here the distinction made by David Chalmers regarding the "easy" and the "hard" problems regarding consciousness.[2] The easy problems are those that can be explained by the standard methods of cognitive science, basically in terms of computational or neural mechanisms. These problems include:

- The ability to discriminate, to categorise, and react to environmental stimuli.
- The integration of information by a cognitive system.
- The reportability of mental states.
- The ability of a system to access its own internal states.
- The focus of attention.
- The deliberate control of behaviour.
- The difference between wakefulness and sleep.

According to Chalmers these phenomena can be easily explained away in computational and neuronal terms. The true problem of consciousness lies in explaining how and why experience takes place, especially the subjective aspect of it. What does it mean to feel the redness of red or the sweetness of an apple? How do we explain the existence of organisms that constitute subjects of experience? What is experience in itself? How can it be explained without resorting to the very same experience? How is it possible for the mind to always take a step backwards and contemplate its own thoughts and emotions?

What is interesting is that the distinction made by Chalmers applies also to the Yogasūtra. From the point of view of the Yogasūtra it is relatively easy to explain the earlier mentioned phenomena from a materialist perspective, as they are functionally definable. On the other hand the consciousness of the *puruṣa* is not functionally definable: it does not perform any function. For Chalmers consciousness poses the same problem. We can explain perceptive discrimination, internal access to information and the possibility of verbal communication through a description of their functional mechanisms, but we will not explain why the performance of these functions brings in the concomitant of experience.

The most intricate problem lies in explaining how the *puruṣa* becomes a bhoktṛ or the subject of experience. A description of the functioning of the mind following the theory of *vṛttis* will suffice to solve the first kind of problems, the easy ones. The Yoga system deals with the "hard problems" of consciousness in terms of *saṃyoga*, *sārūpya*, *darśitaviṣayatā*, *pratisaṃveditva*, *anuveditva* and *pratibimba*.

The separation between mind and consciousness is not sufficient to solve the problem of the relation between consciousness and matter, but it is a way of distinguishing between the functional aspects of consciousness and the experiential factor. There is no difficulty in attributing the performance of functions to a material entity called mind; however, the force behind these functions is not a material entity, but the proximity of consciousness (*puruṣa*), which is capable of activating the functionality of the mind that culminates in the experience of the subject.

A metaphor will help us to better understand the relations between a material mind and consciousness. The mind is like a diamond. A diamond does not shine in complete darkness, but when a ray of light touches it, it is able to break the beam of white light into different colours. The polychromy of the diamond is the polychromy of the world. The diamond does not shine with its own light, but it shows the diversity of matter through its reflections. The mind is like a diamond, because it is translucent and has the capacity to fill with content the neutral conscience of the *puruṣa*, like the diamond breaks the beam of white light into a rainbow of colours. Therefore, the mind simultaneously operates a diversification of the homogeneous consciousness of the *puruṣa* and induces a limitation, by binding the freedom of consciousness into the contingency of matter. In fact, these are the two truly objective properties of primordial matter: to allow the experience of diversity (*bhoga*) and to liberate spirit from matter (*kaivalya*).

It is worth considering the interdependence of matter and spirit. *Puruṣa* needs materiality in order to be able to survey the diversity of creation. Matter needs the gaze of the spirit to be able to undergo change. Without it, primordial materiality would not find its meaning, that of unfolding and withdrawing. Figuratively speaking we could refer to the descent of the spirit in matter or the incarnation of consciousness into the materiality of the mind. This descent or incarnation takes place only at the level of the intellect (*buddhi*) and does not produce any modification in consciousness, but it does generate transformations in the intellect, which shines with the light of consciousness and begins to function with this twofold objective.

It does so in order to first unfold the very diversity of the material world. This diversity is not intrinsic to the *puruṣa* but constitutes a specific quality of materiality. The second objective is to reveal the distinction between spirit and matter, a distinction obscured by the mind, when it absorbs the luminosity of consciousness. This distinction, termed discerning vision (*viveka-khyāti*), unveils the false identification between consciousness (*cit*) and the mind (*citta*). The discerning vision will make it possible for the *puruṣa* to definitively free itself from Nature.

One has to note that the plenitude of liberation entails the prior perception of materiality. This means that first the *puruṣa* has to get involved with matter. He or it has to observe the spectrum of an ever-changing reality and enjoy the perception of a material world essentially different from himself. This enjoyment of the world culminates in the experience of the ubiquity of pain (*duḥkham* eva sarvaṃ *vivekinah*), the result of change and the constant friction in the functioning of the three constituents of nature (*guṇa*).[ii] From now on, an inversion takes place at the very centre of the intellect, which will perceive the distinction between mind (*sattva*) and consciousness (*puruṣa*). When the liberation or isolation (*kaivalya*) finally takes place, the *puruṣa* is "liberated (*mukta*), because, figuratively at least, it was earlier "bound" (*baddha*). Of course, as the Sāmkhyakārikā[iii] says, one should not forget that in reality the unchangeable *puruṣa* is never bounded nor liberated. It is nature that is, although these qualities are figuratively (*upacara*) attributed to the *puruṣa*.

According to Larson a double negation takes place.[3] On the one hand, pure consciousness devoid of content seems to arrogate content for itself. In other words, although the three primordial energies of nature carry out all the actions, the agent is really the *puruṣa*. This seems to be quite natural, as the *puruṣa* is conscious, while the energies are not. They cannot have the subjective experience of the agent. On the other hand, the unconscious mind appears as infused with consciousness. The tripartite process of the guṇas seems to be conscious till the very intellect realises that consciousness is the radical absence of material content.[iv]

What is interesting in the dualism of the sāṃkhya/yoga it is that the mind is postulated as a material category, a kind of intermediary between the purely physical objects and the inaccessibility or aloofness of pure consciousness (*puruṣa*). The mind, or better the subtlest part of it, the intellective principle (*buddhi*), is the most refined form of matter. It is translucent matter, able to reflect the light of the consciousness, able to trap the light of consciousness within the opaque, but substantial embodiment, of inert matter. This translucent or transparent matter can act as an intermediary, because it is able to simultaneously partake of the nature of the perceivable object (*dṛśya*), of matter (*prakṛti*) and of the percipient subject (*draṣṭṛ*), that is consciousness (*puruṣa*).[v]

How can a non-material consciousness perceive material objects? If consciousness is unchangeable *(apariṇāmin)* and non-transferable (*apratisaṃkrama*) it will never be able to perceive these objects, as this perception would entail a performative consciousness to assume the shape of these objects (*tadākārāpatti*). The proposed solution hinges around two forms of distinct knowledge: mental knowledge or *vedana* (at times also *saṃvedana* or *anuvedana*) and the knowledge of the *puruṣa* or *pratisaṃvedana* (also at times *saṃvedana*). In *vedana*, the intellect assumes the shape of external objects perceived through the senses and it creates mental representations of those objects. The *puruṣa* nevertheless does not come directly into contact with the objects through the senses, but does so indirectly through the reflection of those objects in the intellect. The *puruṣa* is thus a reflective knower (*pratisaṃvedin*) of the intellect, which shows him the objects already represented (*darśita-viṣaya*). Consequently, the *puruṣa* is spared from contact with the objects and does not undergo any kind of transformation. This reflected knowledge does not change the consciousness of the *puruṣa*, just as a crystal seems to be red due to the proximity of a flower, although it is not really affected by the flower's redness.

To put it in another way, it is not the *puruṣa* who identifies with the intellect. Identification is produced at the level of the vision of the *puruṣa* reflected in the intellect. Vision is identification. The *puruṣa*, like the crystal, does not change even though it looks red due to the proximity of the flower. Besides, the redness of the crystal is only visible from a particular angle of vision, from a given perspective. From another perspective, away from the axis that joins the crystal with the flower, one can see the crystal completely translucent. Thus, it is the perception by itself, depending on a particular angle that constitutes identification.

The proximity of the *puruṣa* and the *buddhi*, like the proximity of the crystal and the flower, transfers the mental processes to the *puruṣa*. This transference is a function of the *buddhi* and not of consciousness, which, as we have said, is by itself non-transferable. Therefore, it is the *buddhi*, and not the *puruṣa*, which by this process of transference ends up appearing as a conscious subject of experience, when in reality consciousness is an exclusive property of the immutable *puruṣa*. The *buddhi*, by apparently acquiring the qualities of the *puruṣa*, becomes an experimenting subject who attributes to himself the properties of pleasure, pain or confusion. It is in this figurative sense that one can talk of the functions or processes of the *puruṣa* (*puruṣa-vṛtti*). Truly the *puruṣa* is not bound by any process (*vṛtti*). It is "non-processual" (*vṛtti-rahita*). The so-called "functions of the *puruṣa*"[vi] are simply functions of the intellect falsely attributed to the *puruṣa*. In this state the *puruṣa*, although it is not a subject of experience (*abhoktāpi*), appears as one (*bhokteva*).[vi]

How does this attribution take place? Is it not a contradiction in terms, a kind of non-transferable transference? In other words, how can the non-transferable consciousness of the *puruṣa* be present in the intellect without undergoing some kind of change or modification? The first answer, given by Patañjali, is in the terms of *sārūpya*. *Sārūpya* literally means "con-formity" or "correspondence in form" and can also be understood as a "correlation between the witness, the *puruṣa*, and the functions of the mind (*vṛtti*)". Vyāsa in his commentary does not clarify what it is the meaning of this "correspondence in form". He seems more concerned to explain its origin. The mind is like a magnet. By its ability to represent and show objects (*darśita-viṣaya*) and by its mere proximity to the spirit, is able to present itself as a visible object (*dṛśyatva*) to the testimonial consciousness of the *puruṣa.* Then conjunction (*saṃyoga*), which does not involve any contact between the *puruṣa* and the intellect, takes place. *Vyāsa* makes haste to affirm that this conjunction is innate. It has no beginning (*anādi*). For this reason, the initial and natural state of each *puruṣa* is his conformity with the functions of the mind. The isolation of the *puruṣa*, on the contrary, seems to require a prolonged cognitive effort exemplified in the practice of yoga. This "correspondence in form" enables, on one hand, the kindling of the mind with the light of consciousness. As a result, the mind appears as a conscious entity. On the other hand, the illuminated mind makes possible for the spirit to witness the mental processes (*citta-vṛtti-bodha*).[vii]

Conjunction (*saṃyoga*) is in reality a distribution of roles, in which nature assumes the role of a visible and changing object and the spirit that of the passive observer. For this reason, Patañjali says that conjunction is "the constitutive cause that makes up the powers of the subject and the object".[viii]

That is, conjunction enables the subject and the object as members of a property relationship between the possessor (*svāmin*) and the possessed thing (*sva*). Conjunction itself creates the subject and the object. They do not exist as such without conjunction. There are neither objects nor subjects previous to the conjunction, nor do they remain after their isolation from each other.

Vyāsa seems to closely follow Patañjali, when he states that the capacity of experience of the *puruṣa* is apparently transferred to changing objects, because it falls in line (*anupatati*) with the functions of the mind.[ix] The verb used by Vyāsa is *anu-pat* which literally means "fly behind, fall behind, follow'. According to Patañjali and Vyāsa a correlation is produced between the functioning of the mind and the consciousness of *puruṣa*. Thanks to this correlation, pure consciousness, although it is not qualified by the functions of the intellect, seems to imitate these functions. On its part, the intellect is characterised by its capacity to arrogate to itself a consciousness that is not innate but acquired from the *puruṣa* (*prāpta-caitanyopagraha-svarūpa*).[x] Vyāsa quotes a well-known verse that says that one should not look for *Brahman* in remote places, nor in the nether world or in a deep cave, nor in the depths of the ocean. *Brahman* manifests itself in the light of our mental perceptions.[xi] *Brahman* is light without content, while perceptual content is a material process produced by the mind.

From Vācaspati onwards however, the theory that becomes most relevant to explain the interaction between the *puruṣa* and the intellect is the theory of reflection (*pratibimba*), a theory that surely seems to have its origins in the Vedānta. The consciousness of the *puruṣa* is reflected in the mirror of the intellect, in the same way that the light of the moon, without requiring any action, is reflected in the water of a pond. The moon reflected in the pond will be subjected to all kinds of fluctuations in keeping with the motion of the water. We will see the tremulous reflection of the moon on the water, although the moon is not shaking nor is it affected by the ripples of the water.[xii] The metaphor tries to illustrate a few finer points. The fact that a transference is produced from the moon/consciousness to the pond/intellect without any action on the part of consciousness and also the fact that consciousness seems to arrogate content for itself, the trembling movement, without being really affected by it.

We know however that light cannot be reflected on a surface without a real transfer of photons. Thus, the idea that a thing can enter into contact with another without any activity on its part remains unexplained. We cannot unduly force the metaphor, as its explicatory power is analogical and not rational. Larson asserts that it is unsurprising that the sāmkhya, and also other Indian schools, use metaphors to illustrate some of their fundamental principles. Those are images that are useful in facilitating intuitive comprehension of an idea that cannot be easily explained in rational terms.[xiii]

Taking into account the importance of the intellect as a mediator between the *puruṣa* and *prakṛti*, it is not surprising that for sāmkhya/yoga the first product of the evolution of primordial matter is the intellect. It has to be remembered that this evolution of matter is the result of the proximity of the *puruṣa*, capable of activating the three primordial constituents or *guṇa*. The proximity of the *puruṣa* should not be understood in terms of physical or spatial nearness as there is no contact between the *puruṣa* and the *prakṛti*. Proximity here means a kind of empowerment or ability (*yogyatā*), which enables matter to present the diversity of its objects to the light of consciousness.

The separation between mind and consciousness lends a special character to the dualism of sāṃkhya/yoga. Everything that we usually catalogue under the label of mental phenomena (perception, hallucinations, rational thought, error, emotions, memory, etc.) would be reducible to pure materiality. What cannot be reduced to matter is precisely the fact that these phenomena give rise to the conscious experience. They are not merely an unconscious mechanism, as they are enkindled by the reflective light of consciousness.

Non-local Consciousness and the Anthropology of Religions and Spiritual Practices

STEPHAN A. SCHWARTZ

Most discussions of religion and spiritual practices centre on dogmas and beliefs, either of a particular religion or a comparison across faiths. I would like to look at religions and the spiritual practices that are an integral part of every religion from the perspective of a consciousness experimentalist, setting aside the dogmas and beliefs.

When I look at religion, any religion, as an experimentalist, what I see is a cohort of people consensually holding a world-view. The process by which that worldview emerges seems to me very much like Thomas Kuhn's description of the paradigm process.[1] The paradigm in a religion is defined by scripture and dogma, not research and theory, and unlike science there is not one religious paradigm but superficially several. The paradigms differ in many ways, but they all have one thing in common. All are centred on the aspect of consciousness that in science we call non-local, and that is now being explicitly researched in several disciplines using a variety of protocols such as near-death studies, therapeutic intention work, and remote viewing.

In religion the individual experience of non-local awareness is called spirit. The eternal aspect of the self, religion's soul. It is a concept amenable to objective verification. We see one aspect in the near-death studies. Thanks to the research at the Division of Perceptual Studies at the University of Virginia School of Medicine, we also know something about the continuity-of-consciousness. This extraordinary decades-long project led by two generations of physicians, first Ian Stevenson and then, when he retired in 2002, taken over by Jim Tucker, has studied reincarnation in the most methodical and rigorous manner.[2] The data from this research, like that on NDEs, presents a compelling objectively measured case for the continuity of consciousness. And while I am on it, I think it is notable that although consciousness is often conceived of in physics terms, some of our most important insights about consciousness have come from medicine—the research on NDEs, therapeutic intention, and reincarnation being examples.

As a researcher, enduring religions seem to me examples of empirical science. I use the term enduring religions to distinguish from transitory cults. All the enduring faiths over generations and millennia developed a kind of empirical neurobiology involving opening to non-local consciousness.

There is an innate recognition of the reality of non-local consciousness in all religions. A small group of materialist scientists, another small cohort of atheists and a few other small factions, may think otherwise, but for the bulk of humanity across time, geography, and culture, within the religious spiritual context the reality of non-local consciousness has been foundational.

Across all religions, rituals are designed to the same end: to train a person to attain and sustain intentioned focused awareness. The mechanism to do this is grounded in the rituals, the religious equivalent of a scientific protocol. That is why the cultures of martial art dojos, Buddhist temples, and Christian monasteries are all based on a life-style of attaining and sustaining intentioned focused awareness, though it is expressed in many different ways.

In consciousness research we confirm the wisdom of that religious anthropology. We know from the experimental data that meditators routinely do better at non-local tasks than non-meditators, whether it is remote viewing, expressing therapeutic intention, or any other non-local task.[3,4] Why? Because meditators can attain and sustain intentioned focused awareness better than random people who lack this training, and intentioned focused awareness is how one opens to the non-local, whether it is in a religious or scientific context. What differs is not the process of the experience, but the assessment we make of the experience through the culture of our worldview. In science we assess non-local consciousness not through faith, but in objectively verifiable ways. We have protocols and measurement, and the shared world view that facts matter. In religion the measurement is orthodoxy and adherence to dogmas and beliefs. Facts hardly enter into it. But whether it is science or religion, experiencing non-local consciousness is the fundamental experience.

Non-local consciousness experiences are faith's birth cradle. Regardless of denomination, dogma, or belief, all religions begin with a single individual who experiences a non-local consciousness event. Siddhartha Gautama, the Buddha, whose birth is dated between 578 and 447 BCE, awakens in the hermitage of Arada Kalama, a teacher of meditation who shows him how, through meditation, he can attain the "state of non-existence"; and he does experience this state of intentioned focused awareness. There are several versions of his awakening. I will use the description of the scholar monk Thanissaro Bhikkhu, (Geoffrey DeGraff) an American Buddhist monk of the Thai forest *kammatthana* tradition whose books and videos have had a major impact on the modern understanding of Buddhism.

He writes, "The Buddha described the Awakening experience in one of his discourses, first there is the knowledge of the regularity of the Dhamma — which in this context means dependent co-arising — then there is the knowledge of *nibbana*. In other passages, he describes the three stages that led to insight into dependent co-arising: knowledge of his own previous lifetimes, knowledge of the passing away and rebirth of all living beings, and finally insight into the four Noble Truths. The first two forms of knowledge were not new with the Buddha. They have been reported by other seers throughout history, although the Buddha's insight into the second knowledge had a special twist: He saw that beings are reborn according to the ethical quality of their thoughts, words, and deeds, and that this quality is essentially a factor of the mind. The quality of one's views and intentions determine the experienced result of one's actions."[5]

Jesus, at the beginning of the Common Era, at the age of 30, experiences his opening of consciousness when he is baptised and goes to meditate in the wilderness.[6] In 610 CE, at 40, Muhammad experiences a revelation in a cave called Hira where he had gone to meditate. The archangel Gabriel appeared to him and told him he would be a messenger of God.[7] It should be noted, I think, that in all of these accounts, so different in their details, that the one constant is meditation, the practice of attaining and sustaining intentioned focused awareness, exactly what is required in the scientific exploration of non-local consciousness.

Those individual revelations only become the basis of a religion, however, if they are recognised by others. Revelation is an individual experience, but religion is a group consensus; that is what separates cranks from prophets. The latter must have personalities charismatic enough to attract people to come and listen to them.

Everything after that is the product of human thought and action. From the accounts of the teachings arise scriptures and the institutions that grow up around those teachings, manned by individuals who commit themselves to maintaining the dogma and their perception of its orthodoxy. But it all begins with one person's non-local consciousness experience or experiences. And that person's experiences of the non-local becomes the path.

With that foundation it is not really surprising that the rituals of religions all seek to give practitioners a measure of focused control over mind and body, holding out the promise that they, too, may be able to open to the non-local aspect of consciousness. Inevitably the paths incorporate some model of non-local unity promising it as the path or the way, and the rituals to attain this state of consciousness develop by empirical observation across millennia.

In Christianity the spirit of the Lord is the creative power of life.[8] It is an incorporeal feeling of connecting with a greater conscious unity. In the New Testament spirit is described as that aspect of consciousness wherein a direct relationship with God is possible.[9] It is the spiritual aspect that enables continuing conversation with the divine Spirit.[10] Totems like rosaries, prayer beads, religious statues, and structured prayers help the follower to develop intentioned focused awareness, which research has shown is the key to opening to non-local awareness.

The sixteenth century Christian saint and Carmelite mystic, St. Teresa of Avila, counselled: "This magnificent refuge is inside you. Enter. Shatter the darkness that shrouds the doorway. Be bold. Be humble. Put away the incense and forget the incantations they taught you. Ask no permission from the authorities. Close your eyes and follow your breath to the still place that leads to the invisible path that leads you home. Follow your breath."[11] It is a statement from a Medieval Roman Catholic that a Buddhist or Hindu could comfortably have made, and one did.

Patanjali, considered to be the author of the famous Yoga Sutras, is one of those mysterious figures from the ancient past. We have only the single name, have no idea where exactly he was born, or even when he lived. The best both Eastern and Western scholars can do is say that it was some time between the fourth and second centuries BCE. Almost certainly born a Hindu, he apparently studied a number of spiritual traditions, in his own personal quest, as indicated by the fact that he wrote his famous sutras in a hybrid Buddhist Hindu Sanskrit. It is clear that he understood spirituality as a matter of consciousness, something not restricted to any one religion, because the sutras speak at length about moving into non-local awareness through meditation. Psychologist William Braud, who made a particular study of this, noted: "The sixth, seventh, and eight 'limbs' of ashtanga Yoga are dharana (concentration), dhyana (meditation), and samadhi (profound absorption), respectively."[12] Patanjali refines this further, Braud explains, saying, "The repeated continuation, or uninterrupted stream of that one point of focus is called absorption in meditation (*dhyana*), and is the seventth of the eight steps" (*tatra pratyaya ekatanata dhyanam*). When these three are practised together, the composite process is called *samyama*. *Samyama* might be translated as constraint; thorough, complete, or perfect restraint; or full control; it might also be translated as communion or mind-poise. *Samyama* conveys a sense of knowing through being or awareness through becoming what is to be known. Through mastery of *samyama* comes insight (*prajna*), and through its progressive application, in stages, comes knowledge of the Self and of the various principles of reality (*tattvas*). With increasing yogic practice come a variety of mystical, unitive experiences, states, conditions, or fulfilments — the various samadhis — along with the attainments or powers (*siddhis*)."[13]

The linkage with the non-local and the creation of sacred space is another manifestation of consciousness threaded throughout religions across time, geography, and culture. There is always a dedicated place to meet, whether it is a temple, a cathedral, a synagogue, or an Etruscan oak grove. Why does this place issue seem to matter so much? Is there something objectively verifiable about "sacred" space beyond the obvious psychological emotional importance? The non-local consciousness research suggests there is. It is more numinous.

Carl Jung described numinosity thus, "We should not be in the least surprised if the empirical manifestations of unconscious contents bear all the marks of something illimitable, something not determined by space time. This quality is numinous.... numina are psychic entia"- Jung says "numina are psychicentia."[14] I think the research confirms that. Numina, I believe, should be thought of as non-local information. Numinosity is a kind of non-local informational architecture that can be detected by consciousness, and to some degree manipulated through intentioned focused awareness.

The more frequently attention is focused on anything the more it develops numinous qualities, which may be of positive or negative valence. The more numinous the object, the easier it becomes for others to unconsciously sense this quality. Numinous constructs excite a stronger psychophysical response than mundane objects, and as such they can be unconsciously discriminated from less-numinous objects.

In remote viewing research we know that targets of greater numinosity are easier to perceive than targets that may have similar physical characteristics but are less numinous. Functionally, that means that Chartres cathedral is easier to see than a warehouse of the same size. Why? Because Chartres, from the moment of its conception and for all the centuries since that moment, has been the focus of unnumbered acts of intentioned awareness experienced in a heightened state of emotion. In contrast nobody pays much attention to warehouses, nor do they evoke much emotion even when they are noticed.

This non-local intention effect also extends to the substances we associate with religious rituals: water and wine. This linkage of water, wine and the sacred is so ancient its origins are lost in deep time. Why should such a linkage exist? The obvious answer in the case of water is that human life is not possible without it. Perhaps that is the reason it is the primordial element in most creation myths.

Examples of this: The Assyro-Babylonian gods that arose from the melding of salt, Tiamat, and sweet potable water, *Apsu*. The Egyptian Sun-God Atum arose from the world ocean, Nun. The Judeao-Christian Bible begins with God dividing the waters (Genesis 1:1-6). The story of humanity is dotted with sacred rivers, springs, and lakes. It has been a fundamental belief in many religions that praying, focusing therapeutic intentioned awareness on water, transforms it in some way, making it "sacred." It is an idea that dates back into deep time and yet continues down to the present day. The Christian faiths of Roman Catholicism, Eastern Orthodoxy, Coptic and Oriental Orthodoxy hold to this as dogma, as does Anglicanism. It is a cultural aspect of water that is well-recognised and widely discussed in anthropology, history, and theology, but almost never from the perspective that something objectively measurable is actually happening.

But is this only a belief, an article of faith, or is it another example of an insight concerning non-local consciousness gained through close empirical observation evolving across generations? Does anything actually change in water that is the focus of intentioned awareness, something that can be measured? Is this change physical, or subjective and aesthetic; or both? It is this second aspect to sacred water that I wish to focus on here.

There are a number of studies directly addressing the first question: Is there a physical change that can be objectively measured? The answer through replicated spectroscopy studies, using well-established protocols employed in laboratories around the world, appears to be: Yes.[15,16,17,18]

Here is an example: "Through standard techniques of infrared (IR) spectrophotometry, sterile water samples in randomly selected sealed vials evidence alteration of infrared (IR) spectra after being proximate to the palms of the hands of both Practising and Non-Practising Therapy Practitioners, each of whom employed a personal variation of the Laying-on-of- Hands/ Therapeutic Touch rituals. This pilot study presents 14 cases, involving 14 Practitioners and 14 Recipients. The first hypothesis, that a variation in the spectra of all (84) Treated spectra compared with all (57) control spectra would be observed in the 2.53.0 mm range, was confirmed (p = 0.02). Ten per cent (15) of the spectra were done using a germanium Internal Reflection Element (IRE). Ninety per cent of the spectra (126) were done with a zinc selenide IRE, and the difference in refractive index between the two IREs skews the data. The zinc selenide IRE spectra alone yield p = .005. The authors believe the most representative evidence for the effect appeared in the sample group of Treated vs. Calibration Controls using the zinc selenide IRE (p = 0.0004). The second hypothesis, that there existed a direct relationship between intensity of effect and time of exposure was not confirmed. This study replicates earlier findings under conditions of blindness, randomicity, and several levels of controls. Environmental factors are considered as explanations for the observed IR spectrum alteration, including temperature, barometric pressure, and variations dependent on sampling order. They do not appear to explain the effect."[19]

Similarly, the second question: Is there an objectively measurable subjective aesthetic effect that can be objectively measured, can also be answered in the affirmative. Beginning in 1994 an independent Japanese researcher, Masaru Emoto, had the idea to freeze double-distilled water, freeze snow crystals from the water and observe through a microscope the snow crystals that formed.[20]

Emoto's general idea was to see if various stimuli to which the water was exposed would change people's aesthetic experience of snow crystals made from the water. He showed alphabet letters to water. He presented pictures. He played music to water. He then froze the water and had people look at the snow crystals, comparing their aesthetic experience of the treated water with identical water that was not the focus of such intentioned awareness. And he saw differences.[21] The pictures of the snow crystals make it obvious.

Emoto also directly addressed the question as to whether intentioned focused awareness using the ritual of prayer caused a change, and once again found that it did. The water upon which intention had been focused produced crystals that were judged to be more aesthetically appealing when compared to control snow crystals.

These experiments, although they produced fascinating results, were very controversial, and many critiques of the protocols were advanced. It was not even clear who was the agent of action, whether the effect observed was the result of the intention of the influence used, or the researchers' intentions.

Dean Radin, Chief Scientist at the Institute for Noetic Sciences, took up the question and created a variation of Emoto's protocol that in my view dealt with all the issues advanced about the earlier forms. In 2006 Radin's team reported their results: "The hypothesis that water 'treated' with intention can affect ice crystals formed from that water was pilot tested under double-blind conditions. A group of approximately 2000 people in Tokyo focused positive intentions towards water samples located inside an electromagnetically shielded room in California. That group was unaware of similar water samples set aside in a different location as controls. Ice crystals formed from both sets of water samples were blindly identified and photographed by an analyst, and the resulting images were blindly assessed for aesthetic appeal by 100 independent judges. Results indicated that crystals from the treated water were given higher scores for aesthetic appeal than those from the control water (p = .001, one-tailed), lending support to the hypothesis."[21]

The oldest archaeological evidence of wine dates to ca. 7000- 6600 BCE, and involves a fermented beverage made of of rice, honey, hawthorn fruit and grape. A joint American Chinese research team led by archaeologist Patrick McGovern from the Pennsylvania Museum, recovered residue in pottery vessels found in Jiahu, China, in the Yellow River Valley during the excavation of a Neolithic village. This find predates by more than 500 years the earliest prior evidence of wine found in the Middle East.

In their paper McGovern's team reported, "Based on the oracle inscriptions from the late Shang dynasty," (circa 1200-1046 BCE) "the earliest tests from China. . . three beverages were distinguished: chang (an herbal wine), li (probably a sweet, low-alcoholic rice or millet beverage), and jiu (a fully fermented and filtered rice or millet beverage or 'wine,') with an alcoholic content of probably 1015 per cent by weight." [23]

Perhaps because from the beginning of its history alcohol has been recognised for its psychoactive properties, across all of human history there has always been an association of wine and consciousness, but there are differences from the linkage of consciousness and water. The drinking of water made holy through intentioned awareness is not common. For millennia people have known that drinking what today we are calling "Raw Water" could be dangerous. Wine, however, did not suffer that limitation. From earliest times there has been the cultural recognition that there are two distinct ways in which wine is used. One is secular, what might be thought of as entertainment drinking and cooking, while the other is spiritual or religious.

It is this second aspect that is of concern here, because as with "holy" water, sacramental wine has always been perceived as having been created through some kind of alteration achieved by an individual or group trained in some technique for attaining and sustaining intentioned focused awareness. There are many variations of this belief, from the religious convictions of the followers of Dionysus, son of Zeus and Semele, who was seen as the god of fertility and wine, to the Christian belief in transubstantiation, a matter of dogma still maintained today by whole branches of that faith.[24]

As with water, when one puts aside the particulars of the various faith-beliefs one is left with the realisation that for much of humanity something happens to substances like water and wine when they are the focus of intentioned awareness. With water, as described, there is a physical objectively measurable effect. Whether there is a similar change in the spectra of wine is unknown; there is no equivalent infrared spectrum analysis. The experiment has yet to be done. But in the experiment that follows we do see a commensurate aesthetic effect, different from the snow crystal experiments of Emoto and Radin, but similarly a subjective aesthetic experience.

The protocol was a series of 12 experiments to assess whether there was some aesthetic difference between wine treated by intentioned awareness and control wine, physically identical but unexposed to intentioned awareness.[25] Three party-giver hosts, blind to the existence of the others and blind to the experiment's purpose and protocol, independently, once a year for four years, gave the parties where the tasting was done. Eighty-four unpaid volunteer participants, seven at a time, of both genders, acted as the tasters, at each party, participating only once.

The intender group consisted of ninety-three individuals all belonging to various metaphysical study groups who shared an interest in non-local consciousness and a belief that intentioned consciousness could produce non-local perturbation. All of the intenders were regular meditators with long established daily meditation practices and a history of meditating together as a group at their meetings, which took place anywhere from once a week to once a month. As groups they tended to be made up of a mix of married couples and single people. Ages ranged from late 20s to early 70s. They met in each other's homes under some mutually agreeable arrangement.

The researcher purchased a single 750 ml bottle of wine for each session. The wines were all mid-price range California Cabernet Sauvignons of the quality one might serve at a dinner party amongst good friends, pleasantly palatable but not lastingly memorable. The day of the intention meditation session the bottle was decanted into two identical sealable carafes, 375 ml in each carafe. A pair of dice was thrown to assign the carafes as either A or B. An even number throw was an "A" and an odd number throw as a "B." This first throw determined the first carafe's label. The carafes were each put into separate Styrofoam wine carriers, and a second throw of the dice was carried out. An odd throw determined the B carafe would be the treated carafe for the evening's meditation session. An even throw would make the "A" bottle the treated carafe. The two carafes in their Styrofoam carriers were both driven to the site of the evening's meditation group. Except for the intention session, each carafe had the same timeline history.

Upon arrival at the meditation site, the group had their discussion period. When it came time for the group mediation with which they closed their meeting, the researcher would go out to the car and bring back the carafe designated as "treated" for the subsequent taster session. The carafe was taken out of its Styrofoam sleeve and put on a table or chair placed in the middle of the room where the group was gathered. They were asked by the researcher to, "Please dedicate your meditation to holding the intention that this bottle of wine is improved during the course of the meditation." The meditations lasted between 20-30 minutes.

The meditation sessions typically took place on a Wednesday or Thursday, and the tasting sessions on a Friday or Saturday. The two carafes were taken into the house and put in different rooms. The morning of the tasting session the carafes and 14 identical red wine glasses were taken to the location for the tasting session, usually the home of the party host, and given to them. The party host was not told about the meditation sessions and was blind as to which was the "treated" carafe and which was the "control." In his mind it was a question of tasting two different bottles of wine to determine which to buy.

The party host arranged for seven people to come in to ostensibly taste two wines and then have a party. The story the tasters were told was that a friend was considering buying several cases of wine and had winnowed it down to two candidates. Before spending several hundred dollars he wanted to see which was the preferred one. It was explained that he was not present, and all labels and other quality hints had been removed to avoid any possible cueing, so the tasting would be unbiased and just a matter of taste. The party host measured out seven equal portions of wine from each carafe into the identical glasses. Each glass was numbered A1 and B1, A2 and B2 and so on. The tasters tasted each wine and then marked on a card they were given which glass of wine they preferred. They also noted their gender and handed the card back to the party host, were told the group's assessment, and had a social evening.

The scientific question being tested was: which wine was preferred? Given that the tasters were all in the same room, it could not be assumed that their responses were independent of one another. Therefore, the analysis was based on the consensus of the majority at each party. The parameter p was the probability that the treated wine would be preferred by a majority in a group of seven tasters, and 1p was the probability that the untreated wine would be preferred. A tie could happen if one (or three or five) tasters had no preference. In the case of a tie, the data from that party would not be used in the analysis because neither wine was preferred by a majority of the tasters. A one-sided hypothesis test was appropriate, because the research hypothesis was that the treated wine would be preferred. Therefore, the hypotheses to be tested are: H0: $p = 0.5$ Ha: $p > 0.5$

For the 12 parties, 11 resulted in a majority preferring the treated wine and one resulted in a tie. Using an exact binomial test, the p-value is (0.5)11 = 0:00049. This result is similar to the probability of flipping a fair coin 11 times and getting heads each time. Therefore, the null hypothesis could be rejected for any reasonable significance level, and it could be concluded that the probability that a majority would prefer the treated wine was greater than 0.5. With 95 per cent confidence it could be said that the probability that a majority would prefer the treated wine is at least 0.76.26

This experiment of itself, of course, does not prove that focused intention can alter the subjective aesthetic perception of a substance. However, this experiment is not "of itself." As with the water spectroscopy experiments, the issue of intentioned awareness affecting the aesthetic experience of individuals partaking of a substance, compared to controls, has been addressed from a number of angles.

In 2007, Dean Radin led a team that did something similar to the wine study in which chocolate was the focus of the intention. As they describe their protocol, it is easy to see the parallels. "Individuals were assigned to one of four groups and asked to record their mood each day for a week by using the Profile of Mood States. For days three, four and five, each person consummed a half ounce of dark chocolate twice a day at prescribed times. Three groups blindly received chocolate that had been intentionally treated by three different techniques. The intention in each case was that people who ate the chocolate would experience an enhanced sense of energy, vigour, and well-being. The fourth group blindly received untreated chocolate as a placebo control. The hypothesis was that mood reported during the three days of eating chocolate would improve more in the intentional groups than in the control group."[27]

The results they reported closely align with what was found in the wine study. "On the third day of eating chocolate, mood had improved significantly more in the intention conditions than in the control condition (p = .04). Analysis of a planned subset of individuals who habitually consumed less than the grand mean of 3.2 ounces of chocolate per week showed a stronger improvement in mood (p = .0001). Primary contributors to the mood changes were the factors of declining fatigue (p = .01) and increasing vigor (p = .002). All three intentional techniques contributed to the observed results."[28]

Six years later, in 2013, Yung-Jong Shiah at National Kaohsiung Normal University in Taiwan and Radin carried out another study paralleling the wine study. As they reported, "Each evening, for seven days in a row, volunteers recorded their mood using the Profile of Mood States (POMS) questionnaire. On days three, four, and five of the test, each participant drank 600ml of oolong tea in the morning and again in the afternoon. One randomly assigned group blindly received tea that had been intentionally treated by three Buddhist monks; the other group blindly received untreated tea from the same source. On the last day of the test, each person indicated what type of tea he/she believed he/she had been drinking."[29]

Once again, the change was a subjective aesthetic judgement. How did it come out? As with the wine study there were significant subjective differences. "Those who drank treated tea showed a greater increase in mood than those who drank untreated tea (Cohen's d 1=4 0.65, p 1=4 .02, two-tailed). Change in mood in those who believed that they were drinking treated tea was much better than those who did not believe (Cohen's d 1=4 1.45, p 1=4 .00002, two-tailed)."[30]

We now have two related bodies of research. One is described here: the ability of intentioned focused awareness to produce a non-local perturbation effect on what are thought of as inanimate systems, specifically water and wine, so often associated with religious ritual and practice, augmented by the results of similar research involving chocolate, and tea.

There is a far larger corpus of research on another category of studies reporting on the effects of intentioned focused awareness on living organisms, what religions call healing prayer or curses, and science calls therapeutic intention (TI).

Before going any further, though, I want to bring attention to this observation: As with the inanimate systems previously described, from the beginning therapeutic intention research produced significant and successful results. It is not a large effect, but it is remarkably consistent. If we restrict ourselves to studies with no issues concerning placebo effects, researcher cuing effect, or any of the other critiques of human therapeutic intention research, and focus only on the non-local consciousness essence of the effect, it becomes easy to see. We can do this by considering non-human studies involving laboratory conditions and simple organisms, specifically fungus and bacteria studies.[31,32,33,34]

In this category perhaps the earliest therapeutic intention study, done to standards that would be accepted today, is this one. In 1968, research physician Jean Barry of l'Institut M'etapsychique carried out an experiment using Violet Tooth fungus cultures which had been cultivated under optimal conditions: ten petri dishes with the culture for each participant, in all a total of 195 dishes. Of that total, 151 of the cultures in the dishes showed inhibited growth. There were 10 participants, each of whom carried out nine sessions expressing TI. Their task was to inhibit the growth of fungus cultures. To do this they concentrated for 15 min from a distance of about four feet (1.2 M) away, never touching the cultures. Of 194 dishes 151 showed retarded growth.[35]

But what makes this study particularly interesting is that while most Therapeutic Intention studies are focused on improving the health of the organism that is the target of the therapeutic intention, this early Barry study already recognized a very important distinction, one that is also a factor in spiritual practices: therapeutic intention works both ways. Perhaps because it is something you could never formally test in humans, although it has a strong religious history involving curses, hexes, and "evil eyes", it is not widely considered, nor often discussed today, but a number of these simple organism studies have confirmed this two-way effect.[36] I picked the Barry study for that reason and because of its primacy.

In 2010, Larry Dossey, Bravewell Fellow, physician, and author, and I explored this in detail, and found a study done by biologist Carroll Nash of St. Joseph's College, Philadelphia, particularly compelling because it was so explicit in this regard. As we reported, "Nash carried out a therapeutic intention study involving bacterial colonies, cultured in common, and then split into three independent subpopulations.[37] His purpose was to replicate earlier studies by nun and biochemist Sister Justa Smith[38] and nursing pioneer Dolores Krieger who along with Dora Kunz would later develop the non-sectarian approach to therapeutic intent known as Therapeutic Touch.[39] Smith's studies had shown significant differences between treated and controls measuring changes in haemoglobin and enzyme activity, which were the focus of the expressed intention. But Nash had a second question. He asked, 'Could intention alone not merely affect the cell colonies, but could it do so both positively and negatively, when compared to controls?' The results showed that it could, although positive intention produced a more significant result than negative intention."[40]

What is the conclusion here? On the basis of the evidence, I think we have to say that when at least some individuals attain and sustain intentioned focused awareness, whether in a religious or scientific context, they open to a part of themselves that is essentially non-local, that is, it is not physiologically based nor limited by spacetime. In this altered state of consciousness, they can both acquire information, formally non-local perception, as well as produce small measurable effects on spacetime, non-local perturbation.

It is, I think, a notable distinction that both inanimate substances and living organisms can be affected in ways that can be objectively measured. Changes that are both physical, and that produce subjective aesthetic reactions in individuals who have a sensorial interaction with such substances, Anthropologically, the wine study I report here, along with the other studies I have cited, should also be understood as examples of empirical science. I see this process echoed in acupuncture, which developed over 6,000 years ago, although where is unclear,41,42 and ayurvedic medicine, which began with the Indus Valley Civilisation (3300-1300 BCE) in India and "is based on the belief that health and wellness depend on a delicate balance between the mind, body, and spirit."[43]

All these arose from close observation passed down generation-to-generation. The answer to the question, does intentioned focused awareness, whatever ritual is used to employ it or dogma is attached to it, actually produce a measurable effect? Is it belief or is there evidence? The answer is: there is evidence. The dynamics of numinosity even extend into the letters of the languages in which scriptures are written. Can that be possible? It is such a radical idea that I want to present eight experiments carried out in different places, at different times, by different researchers. Five of them involved a prediction of improved memory, one involved improved confidence, and one involved a greater sense of "spirit" for real vs. fake words. They all focused on a model of consciousness reported by British biologist Rupert Sheldrake that he called Morphic Resonance,[44] a model that is closely resonant with the idea of numinosity.

The first test involved memorisation of a nursery rhyme in Japanese by non-Japanese speakers, one a real nursery rhyme and two that were meaningless. Then participants in the UK and the USA were asked which they could remember better, predicting that the real nursery rhyme would be easier to remember because of morphic resonance. Rupert Sheldrake, who formulated the idea upon which the study was based, reports "that this was indeed the result, to a statistically significant degree."[45]

A second test was reported by Gary Schwartz, then a Yale professor of psychology, currently Director of the Laboratory for Advances in Consciousness and Health at the University of Arizona. Schwartz used 48 three-letter Hebrew words from the

Old Testament, of which 24 were common and 24 were rare words. From each of those words he produced a meaningless anagram by scrambling the letters, thus producing a total of 96 "words." Participants who did not know Hebrew were shown these words one by one and asked to guess their meaning by writing down the first English word that came to mind. They were also asked to estimate their confidence in their guess. He found on average that the group of 90 participants were significantly more confident about their guesses when viewing real words than scrambled words, even though they did not know some of the words were real and others false.[46]

The third test was reported by Alan Pickering, a psychologist specialising in cognitive psychology. At the time he was a lecturer at The Hatfield Polytechnic (now the University of Hertfordshire) in England. Like Gary Schwartz, Pickering used real and scrambled words. In this study they were drawn in Persian script. Participants were shown a word for 10 seconds then asked to draw it. Independent judges evaluated the reproductions without knowing which words were real or scrambled. The judges assessed that the real words were reproduced significantly more accurately than the false words. This finding was later successfully repeated in student projects using Persian and Arabic words.[47]

A fourth study was carried out by Arden Mahlberg, an American psychologist at the Integral Psychology Center. Mahlberg took a slightly different tack; instead of language as that term is usually understood, he used a code. In 1836, Samuel Morse, inventor of the telegraph, assisted by Joseph Henry and Alfred Vail, created a code that permitted messages to be sent as a series of electric signals. The code consisted of a sequence of dits, a short signal, in written form represented by a dot, and dash, a long signal, represented by a dash. Mahlberg created a series of real Morse code messages and a similar-looking but fake code. His participants were all people who did not know Morse code, a rather specialised skill. The protocol was a comparison of the ability to learn the fake and genuine Morse code. On average, participants learned real Morse code significantly more accurately than the new code.[48]

The fifth and sixth studies were carried out by German psychology professor Suitbert Ertel, at the University of Gottingen. Ertel tested recognition of hiragana, a phonetic form of Japanese writing, and predicted that these characters would be recognized better when they were the right side up than when upside down, since right side up would correspond to the "morphic form" known by Japanese writers. This is what he found.[49] In another experiment, he compared memory for fake vs. real hiragana characters, and found that real characters were remembered better than fakes.[49] Ertel then ran additional, more complex tests, which resulted in ambiguous outcomes.

Robert Schorn, Professor of Psychology at the Department of Psychology and Medical Sciences, University for Health Sciences, Medical Informatics and Technology (UMIT), Hall in Tyrol, Austria, Gottfried Tappeiner, professor in the Department of Economic Theory, Economic Policy and Economic History at the University of Innsbruck in Austria, and statistician Janette Walde, Department of Statistics also at the University of Innsbruck, conducted a seventh study relevant to the anthropology of religion. They used symbols such as flags, emblems or trademarks that were once well known but were now forgotten, or symbols that are very familiar to some people but not others, such as the Chinese Coca-Cola symbol, or Far Eastern religious symbols. For each real symbol a fake symbol was created using similar patterns and complexity. Participants were then shown pairs of symbols, one real and the false, in a random order, and they were asked to judge which of each pair had more "spirit." They selected real symbols significantly more often than the fake ones. In a follow up test this group compared real Russian words written in Cyrillic along with meaningless anagrams. Again, real and false words were presented in pairs, and participants judged which word had more "spirit." As before, real words were selected significantly more than the anagrams.[51]

Kimberly Robbins and Chris Roe, both part of the Psychology Division at the University of Northampton, Park Campus, in Northampton England, designed an experiment similar to the one used by Ertel, this time using real and fake Chinese characters. Sixty participants, who knew nothing of the Chinese language or the characters used to write it, were shown five real and five fake Chinese characters in a random sequence. Then on a sheet with 20 characters they were asked to circle the 10 they had just seen. They recognised the real characters significantly better than the false ones.[52]

What is all this data telling us? The forms of the rituals of religion, the places where these rituals are conducted, even down to the letters in which the scriptures cited there are written, are founded in consciousness.

Finally, let me turn to the elements of the rituals themselves because they too, I think, were all designed through empirical observation across generations with non-local consciousness in mind. Although the dogmas and culture of each religion are very different, the rituals are remarkably similar and constitute protocols for opening to non-local consciousness in the same way that a research protocol supports individuals opening to non-local consciousness in a remote viewing experiment. The only real difference is context and intent. In religion the context is a religious service or practice, and the intent is to have a sense of spiritual connection. In science the context is a laboratory experiment, and the intent is to describe a target the viewer will be shown in, say, an hour.

When the faith-believers gather in their "sacred" space their collective intent expressed through the recitation of the words in the language similarly make the rituals numinous, and it begins with a statement of intention. In Christianity it is often the Nicene Creed, in Judaism it is the Shema, Buddhists do not pray to a deity conceived as the Creator, as is the case in the Abrahamic religions. Buddhists use mantras, recognising them in much the same way that science does. As the Buddha Dharma Education Association explains it, "Tibetans pray in a special way. They believe that when certain sounds and words, called mantras, are repeated many times, they arouse good vibrations within the person. If a mantra is repeated often enough it can open up the mind to a consciousness which is beyond words and thoughts."[53]

Through all the rituals there are prayers, sermons and homilies, all oriented towards creating common intention, and this is accompanied by singing, chanting, dancing, drumming to further augment this linkage. Brain entraining ensues in which the congregation's brains become synched. Gabe Turow at Stanford University describes this: "...ritual technologies like chanting, drumming, mantra recitation, and prayer, all utilise repetitive sounds to help induce a wide variety of states of consciousness that correspond to the tempo or rate of the repetition."[54]

Studying this has been a significant research effort of radiologist Andrew Newberg at the University of Pennsylvania. He has used standard imaging technologies focused on monitoring the brain activity of spiritual practitioners as they exercise their practice, scanning the brains of nuns, Sikhs, and Buddhists. His research has detected changes in their brains, and reported, "Meditation involves attentional regulation and may lead to increased activity in brain regions associated with attention such as dorsolateral prefrontal cortex (DLPFC) and anterior cingulate cortex (ACC)."[55] From Newberg's work and that of other researchers has arisen the subdiscipline of Neurotheology.

For me what is perhaps most interesting of all in studying both religions and science is that this is one of history's great confluences. The practices of religion and the practices of science, although very different, have found common ground and reached the same conclusions.

Is There a Collective Consciousness? The Global Consciousness Project and an Assessment by Artificial Intelligence

DEAN RADIN

The philosophy of dual-aspect monism states that reality consists of an undifferentiated psychophysical realm that Carl Jung called the *unus mundus*, the one world[1]. This holistic reality is said to split into different aspects, two of which we perceive as mind and matter. These splits are proposed to be triggered by "deep meaning," although the exact nature of this type of meaning is not entirely clear.

Despite the lack of clarity around the splitting process, dual-aspect monism suggests that aspects of mind and matter emerge and interact with the neutral psychophysical realm in a recursive relationship, suggesting that this recursion may represent the sought-after meaning. Importantly, the proposed mind-matter correlation does not involve causation, but is instead said to be related acausally, in a manner akin to the correlations of quantum entanglement, or to Aristotle's notion of *final cause*.

Dual-aspect monism can be contrasted with the philosophy of dualism, which considers reality to consist of two fundamentally different "substances" (mind and matter). Dualism does not provide a satisfactory answer to the question of how two such dramatically different substances could interact, and as such it is not taken seriously today within the context of scientific metaphysics[16]. Dual-aspect monism differs from the philosophy of idealism, which asserts the primacy of consciousness (or more generally, mind) over the physical world. That philosophy begs the question of how physicality can arise out of something which is non-physical[5]. And dual-aspect monism also differs from materialism, which proposes that everything, including mind, is fundamentally physical. That philosophy begs the question of how subjective awareness – the only reality that we can ever know first-hand, with everything else necessarily being an inference – can arise out of presumably non-conscious matter[9]. Of greater interest for the present discussion, dual-aspect monism's concept of an intimate correlation between mind and matter suggests a testable "metaphysical hypothesis," namely that when minds collectively move into a coherent, focused state, then matter too should collectively reflect that coherence.

This idea suggests two kinds of experiments: One would predict that if a group of meditators came together to create a period of collective mental coherence, then that action would influence the physical environment in ways that ought to have measurable effects. The second would predict that during periods when collective mental coherence emerged as a result of millions of people watching live media broadcasts of important world events, then during those periods there should again be measurable changes in the physical environment.

Meditation Experiments

Regarding the first type of experiment, the best known studies of the effects of meditation on environmental conditions is by practitioners of Transcendental Meditation, and in particular the advanced TM-Sidhi programme[6]. Some four dozen such experiments have been reported, and the results are said to indicate that reduced individual and collective stress resulting from meditation also has a stress-reducing effect on the collective consciousness of society, which leads to reduced violent crime at both individual and societal levels. While the mind-body effects of meditation practice are now reasonably well established, the societal effects are more controversial.

Analysis of one long-term meditation experiment suggests that these interventions significantly reduced violent crime, homicide, and murder in the United States from 2007 to 2010, which coincided with the start of the TM-Sidhi programme intervention in 2007[4]. An alternative explanation proposed for this outcome was attributed to changes in economic conditions, like the increase in unemployment in the United States in the late 2000s. However, increased unemployment is usually associated with increased crime, and not a reduction in crime. Another proposed alternative is associated with changes in incarceration rates. However, prison admissions and releases from 2006 to 2009 showed a reduction in the growth of the US prison population, which would presumably predict an increase and not a decrease in violent crime. Other alternatives, involving an increase in the proportion of youth aged 18 to 25, and a trend towards warmer temperatures, would also not predict a reduction in violence during the experimental period.

Overall, these findings, when combined with dozens of similar experiments reported by Transcendental Meditation researchers, suggest that while it is impossible to entirely rule out other factors, reductions in crime and violence indices do seem to be related to collective consciousness interventions. However, additional replications by other groups representing different meditative traditions, and resulting in similar outcomes, would be desirable to increase confidence that the observed correlations are really due to a collective consciousness effect.

Global Consciousness Project

Regarding the second kind of experiment, the Global Consciousness Project (GCP), which started in 1998, was designed to test the notion that large-scale coherent "movements" in mind would correlate with measurable aspects of the physical world[11]. The project employed an Internet-based network of truly random number generators (RNGs) around the world. These RNGs were all based on quantum indeterminate random processes, such as electron tunnelling. This experiment had an advantage over the meditation experiments because it did not have to rely on complex sociological metrics about crime and violence, but rather on straightforward statistical metrics based on random physical processes.

On the "mind side," the GCP focused on events that drew worldwide attention through live broadcasts on the world's media. Such events included reports of terrorism, deaths of celebrities, celebrations like the open ceremonies of the Olympics, and so on. The experimental hypothesis was that during these globally significant events, the collective attention of people worldwide would "cause" the RNGs to produce outputs that were not as random as they "should" be. In other words, the GCP expected to find a correlation between events of mass interest and deviations from randomness in the RNG data.

Over the course of 500 formally defined events from 1998 to 2015, all of which involved first defining the time-period of interest for each event and only then retrieving and analysing the data from the RNG network using a predefined method, the result was a 7 sigma correlation between the RNG data and global events[2,10]. That outcome was associated with odds against chance of over 3 trillion to one, and as such it provided unusually clear evidence in favour of an anomalous correlation consistent with the prediction of dual-aspect monism. The magnitude of the correlation was quite small on a per-event basis, but the effect was consistent enough over all 500 events to accumulate into a statistically unambiguous outcome.

One question often asked about this experiment, given that it only considered 500 attention-capturing events over nearly two decades, was what else was happening during periods that were not selected for this study? There were undoubtedly many other events that would have captured the attention of millions of people that were not part of the formal study events, so wouldn't those events have also influenced the RNG outputs? That is, would there not be a continuous relationship between mind and matter that should be reflected in the GCP output? To explore this possibility, the investigators analysed correlations between RNG data and daily news events[14], and with global stock market indices[7,8], and significant correlations were found in both cases.

In addition, the researchers proposed that the random walk generated by the RNGs would not consistently follow the expectations of a truly random system because collective focused attention is always fluctuating, and that, according to the hypothesis, ought to inject periods of non-random structure into the data.

To investigate this idea, they use a multiscale entropy (MSE) complexity index to analyse the original RNG data. This technique is used to measure the degree of temporal complexity of time series data. The idea is that if there was non-random structure arising in the GCP data, then that should result in different entropic values at different timescales, suggesting a complex, multi-scaled process.

The investigators compared this complexity index metric with the results of two other sets of data: one set where the original data sequence was randomly scrambled (thereby preserving the distribution of values but altering their temporal order), and another set generated by a pseudorandom algorithm (specifically, the Mersenne Twister algorithm). They also developed a second analytical approach based on the concept of deconvolution. This method is commonly used in signal processing to separate a complex signal into its constituent parts. Both these approaches resulted in highly statistically significant evidence of temporal structure appearing in the real GCP RNG data as compared to the same data that was randomly scrambled, and to newly generated pseudo random data[13].

Discussion

Both the experimental approaches discussed here produced results in alignment with the predictions of dual-aspect monism, which postulates an inextricable correlation between mind and matter. The first class of experiments predicted that collective coherent mental states associated with the practice of meditation would produce similarly coherent mental and physical influences in the environment, which would in turn be reflected by reductions in crime statistics. The GCP experiment predicted that collective mental coherence evoked by millions of people paying attention to the same live media broadcasts during important world events would influence the environment, as reflected by unexpected negentropic changes in the behaviour of random physical systems.

Both types of experiments have naturally attracted criticism because the underlying hypotheses of these studies strongly challenge the materialistic assumptions largely adopted by modern science. Thus, the debates continue as arguments and counter arguments are proposed on both sides.

Achieving a genuinely neutral assessment of this debate, given the controversial nature of these studies is not easy. But there is a relatively new approach that can be used to help inform the debate. Modern artificial intelligence (AI) systems, like chatGPT[12], have become remarkably adept in assessing evidence in scientific articles. To find out what chatGPT "thought" about the ongoing debate, two articles were given to the AI to evaluate and then compare. The two articles both appeared in *American Psychologist*, the high-impact flagship journal of the American Psychological Association. One article, published in 2018[3], reviewed the experimental evidence for parapsychological phenomena. The other, published in 2019[15], was a sceptical counterpoint. ChatGPT's evaluation of the abstracts of the two articles was as follows, reprinted it its entirety:

The two abstracts present contrasting perspectives on the field of parapsychology. The [2019] abstract presents a strongly critical view of the entire field and dismisses claims made by parapsychologists as inherently flawed. The language used is strongly opinionated and lacks specific evidence to support its claims. The [2018] abstract, on the other hand, presents a more balanced and evidence-based view of the field. The language used is neutral and scientific, and the abstract presents recent theories and meta-analyses that suggest psi [psychic] phenomena are at least plausible. The authors also acknowledge the controversy surrounding the field and provide recommendations for further progress. Overall, the [2018] abstract appears to be more credible due to its evidence-based approach and neutral language. The [2019] abstract may be biased and may not be a credible source[12].

In sum, using chatGPT as a neutral AI observer without an emotional stake in this debate, it concluded that the empirical evidence for phenomena consistent with the mind-matter hypotheses discussed in this article is more persuasive than the opposing contention. Whether that assessment will continue to be reached in the future remains to be seen but given that one side of this debate can offer empirical evidence, while the other side can only offer polemics, it seems increasingly likely that not only does a collective consciousness exist, but it also plays an active role in the physical world.

The Jain View on Consciousness In the Perspective of Contemporary Physics and Neuroscience

SHUGAN C. JAIN

Before we address soul or consciousness in Jain philosophy, it is important to have an idea of two basic concepts of existence in Jainism, namely *anekānta* (non-absolutism) theory of existence and *Syādvāda* (conditional dialectic) theory of judgement or expression of the truth, along with reality itself, as in the light of these notions further discussions will take place.

Anekānta not only talks of the sum of many parts of an existent but also of a continuum with affirmation of equally real opposites. Thus, both absolute permanence or momentariness are only denied as independent and as the only feature of existence[i]. We shall use this doctrine of non-absolutism during our study of consciousness and the physical world, called cosmos (*loka*) and Conditional dialectic as its representation, in writing or speech, to avoid absolutism.

Reality (sat)

All existents are real, i.e., everything that exists is real. Reality from four different views is shown in Appendix 1. Reality is termed as substance (*dravya*). Substance is characterised by origination destruction and permanence simultaneously, i.e. it is both permanent and impermanent or changing continuously. This is also similar to Parker who states "to make identity real there must be some substantial core which persists, despite its continual change".[1] Substance is also an amalgam of attributes and modes (instant states of existence or *paryaya*)[ii]. Substance finds its expression in the successive states (modes) of its attributes and is a link which connects them with each other. Attributes are found inheriting in the permanent substance, i.e., substance can never be found without the diversity of attributes which undergo change from minimum to maximum and never disappear, they are something in the structure of the substance[3]. With this, the absolutist view of creation of the universe and its destruction is also denied. Substances are infinite in number and broadly divided into living beings / sentient beings / *jīva* and insentient beings / *ajīva,* i.e., Jainism talks of duality of existents. Characteristics of six types of substances are given in Appendix 3.

Jīva /Living Beings are Sentient Beings

Jīva and the soul are concomitant but these names are used in different contexts. Similarly, the soul and consciousness are concomitant as the soul cannot exist without consciousness and consciousness cannot exist anywhere except in the soul. Thus, *jīvas* with consciousness and its manifestation[iii], are active i.e. they perform some activity to achieve their objective, though non-concrete (cannot be cognised by sense organs). There are infinite numbers of living beings, each with its independent soul and they retain their independent existence forever. The four infinites, i.e. infinite vision/perception, knowledge, energy and bliss are the primary attributes of pure soul[iv]. It is different from *asuci* (dirt), *anidāna* (free from desire for future), and different from *deha* (body)[v]. For practical purposes, living beings are called as *prāṇīs* i.e. with four *prāṇas* or vital attributes, namely life span (āyu), breathe (*ucchvāsa*), sense organs (*indriya*) and energy (*bala*) of mind body and speech[vi]. Living beings are classified in different manners but the most popular is: i. immobile (soul with a material body and classified as air, water, earth, plant and fire-bodied living beings) with touch sense only and ii. mobile (soul with two to five senses from ants to animals, birds and human beings) which can move from one place to another[vii]. This is contrary to Descartes who claimed that only human beings are living while all others are machine-like.

Ajīva / non-living beings (insentient). These are further sub-classified in five categories as follows:

Four types which are supporting and non-perceptible:

- *Dharma* (principle of motion). Non-concrete. Supports motion of *jīva* and *pudgala*. One continuum pervading the entire cosmos (*loka*).
- *Adharma* (principle of rest). Non-concrete. Supports the rest state of the *jīva* and *pudgala.* One continuum pervading cosmos (*loka*).
- Ākāśa (Space). Non-concrete and infinite. It is also a continuum but has two divisions, *loka* and *aloka*. *Loka* provides space for *jīva* and *pudgala*, *dharma* and *adharma* to exist. It is one continuum pervading the cosmos (*loka*) and *aloka* where nothing else surrounds it. The total volume of cosmos is 343 cubic *rajjus* where 1 *rajju* = $1.84*10^{21}$ kms. Our earth is a very small part of the cosmos that is located in the part of *loka* known as the middle world (*madhya loka*).
- *Kāla* (Time): Non concrete. Support change in *jīva* and *pudgala*. Conceptual, it consists ofindependent small particles called *kālāṇus* pervading each space point of the cosmos.

Appendix 2 shows the cosmos (*loka*) in the shape of a human being standing with his palms on hips and legs apart) and surrounded by space called *aloka*. Thus, *loka* is co-extensive with *dharma, adharma* and *kāla* and filled with innumerable independent *jīvas* and *pudgala* of different types and forms. This is similar to the Quantum model which says 'all physical reality is primarily energy existing in a vast web that is interconnected across space and time. This web, the quantum field, holds all probabilities, which we can collapse into reality through our thoughts, observations, feelings and state of being'[1]. However, the cosmos according to Jainism has many different types of constituents and not just one *Pudgala* (matter) as an active and perceptible substance type.

Pudgala/Matter: Only Active and Perceptible Type of Ajīva

Fusion and fission are a primary characteristic of nature. All existents which can be cognised by sense organs fall in this category. It exists as *paramāṇu* (smallest indivisible particle 'SIP') and /atoms, molecules and lumps or aggregates as collection of SIPs which are Infinite in number. SIP is highly unstable and is capable of moving at 14 *rajjus* per time-instant; it acts randomly in all directions. SIP does not occupy any space, nor does it obstruct other SIPs in sharing the same space. Various modes in which *pudgala* can exist are sound, bondage, subtle matter (ness), gross matter (ness), physical structure, division in parts, darkness, shadow, together with brightness and heat, fineness and grossness, shape and size. Thus energy (heat, light and sound), matter (solids, liquids and gases as subtle, gross) and invisible waves travelling throughout the cosmos are all matter. Matter and energy are interchangeable, thereby giving the common understanding that matter and energy are convertible to each other. Thus, the entire visible *loka* appears to be matter only.[viii]

It is the only active category of insentient/*ajīva* which affects jiva and is affected by it as well. Matter attracts *jīva* and is also attracted by it. Our body, organs of speech, mind and respiration, thoughts, knowledge and karma also matter. Similarly matter contributes to feelings like pleasure, suffering and to the life and death of living beings. SIPs combine with each other to give a special type of aggregates of use to jīvas, called *vargaṇās*, which develop certain additional properties and consequently can give rise to not only the material universe, but also to all the mental and psychical faculties of living beings, like thought (*mano-vargaṇā*), speech (*bhāṣā-vargaṇā*), breath (śvāsocchvāsa vargana), karma body (*karmaṇa vargaṇā*) etc. besides different types of bodies like the physical (*audārika*), celestial (*vaikriyaka*), astral (*tejas*), communication (āhāraka) bodies of use to living beings and responsible for all physical, physiological and psychical processes going on in the universe.

According to Narendra Bhandari[ix], a *paramāṇu* / 'SIP' is considered to be the primary, smallest, indivisible, dimensionless particle of *pudgala* (commonly termed as matter). An Infinite number of SIPs can coexist (termed *apratighātī* in Jain texts) in a single space unit (*pradeśa*), similar to the behaviour of bosons. SIPs are much finer (subtler) than all the known particles (e.g., photons, electrons or neutrinos, etc.). In other words, every SIP is eternal, never gets destroyed, only becomes part of an aggregate and so loses its identity as an independent SIP but regains its identity when aggregates disintegrate. The whole *loka* (universe) is fully packed with SIPs, i.e., there is an infinite number of SIPs in the *loka*. Matter is cognisable by our sense organs due to certain properties possessed by SIPS. Matter has eight types of touch (4 pairs of opposites of which only one can be present at a time), colour (5), taste (5) and smell (2) giving a maximum of 200 different basic elements types.

'$E = mc^2$' by Einstein implies energy and matter are completely interchangeable, or the most fundamental components of our physical world, both as waves (energy) and particles (physical matter), depending on the mind of the observer[1]. The quantum model says 'Atoms are mostly empty space; atoms are energy, i.e., everything physical in our life is not solid, rather all fields of energy or frequency patterns of information. All matter is more 'nothing' (energy) than something (particles)'[1]. Further, at the subatomic level of matter, it does not obey the laws of classical physics the way that larger objects did, (like SIPs moving randomly associating and dissociating according to Jainism). Quantum physicists also discovered that a person observing or measuring the tiny particles that make up the electron (component of atom which is a collection of several SIPs) affect the behaviour of energy and matter. Only when an observer focuses his attention on any location of a sub-atom (commonly indicated as electron) does that electron appear, i.e. a particle cannot manifest in reality until it is observed—a phenomenon called collapse of wave function or the observer effect[x] This premise has been questioned by some scientists and even Jains, as it means that the world does not exist unless observed. Perhaps concepts of influx (āsrava), stoppage (*saṁvara*) and dissociation (*nirjarā*) of the Jains are similar to this hypothesis.

Jīva or Living Beings

Broadly *jīvas* are classified either as empirical i.e., consciousness/soul bonded with matter bodies or liberated soul/ pure-consciousness. Nine characteristics of both types of *jīvas* are depicted in Appendix 5. Soul and consciousness are concomitant as soul cannot exist without consciousness and consciousness cannot exist anywhere except in the soul. This property, as per Jain definition of substance, of the structure of a *jīva* / living-being is indicative of the empirical souls embedded with matter which must be existing from eternity side by side. From a philosophical viewpoint *jīvas* or empirical souls can be understood from the following picture.

Figure 1: ***jīva***

- White is pure soul/consciousness (ps). Non-concrete
- Scarlet is psychic-material karmas like delusion, attachment, emotions (pb)

- Blue is matter karmas storing past actions to yield experiences and store new actions (kb)
- Yellow, the outermost is the physical body, termed as no-karma or nkb. On death this combination (ps + pb + kb) leaves nkb and is born in a new nkb. In the end when pb and kb are also extinguished, then ps stays in this state (*nirvāṇa* or liberation) for ever and does not interact with anything.

Thus, my soul is my consciousness and my consciousness is my soul. It appears that energy (*vīrya*, and bliss attributes of soul) makes my consciousness surge within me and my soul is a sphere of energy that is encased in my body (*svadeha parimāṇa* characteristic of soul). Further, it appears that my soul dwells within me until my bodily death and my soul makes me conscious of my existence and experience of all that exists around me. We may be able to introduce some of the qualities of the soul in non-living beings by evoking consciousness artificially, but these beings may never experience the soul or consciousness that I experience, hence the term Artificial Intelligence.

Manifestation of consciousness as knowledge can be of two types, pure knowledge which stays within the pure soul (immaterial and used to enjoy its own nature by pure soul) and impure material knowledge (information, intelligence) affected by both psychic and past karmas, and external activities induced by the body due to its own state and external stimuli.

The soul extends itself into the body with five sense organs (*indriyas*) and mind (quasi-sense organ). This definition also supports the concept of two types of each organ, namely physical sense organ (for accomplishment and protecting from the environment) and the corresponding psychic (*bhāva*) organ (for attainment/*labdhi* concerning knowledge-obstructing karmas). There are other body parts like the brain, central nervous system, heart, stomach, and kidneys etc. that are parts of nkb.

The mind in Jainism, is accordingly classified as of two types, namely:

- The psychic mind (*bhāvamana*) indicating the purity of soul arising on the destruction cum subsidence of energy obstructive and quasi-sense-covering karmas that manifests from moment to moment. It pervades the whole body along with consciousness.
- The physical mind (*dravyamana*) which is momentary and assumes the shape of eight-petalled lotus near the heart, due to the rise of primary and secondary limbs and body making karmas (*aṅgopāṅga-nāmakarma*) [xvi]. The manifestation of the physical mind depends on the thinking activity (psychic mind), with one thought moment at a time, and as a fast-flowing stream as knowledge[3] where sense impressions and mental (psychic mind) phenomena are constantly changing. Thus, knowledge may be held as manifestation of an attribute, an ever-changing series of cognitions, a process or an activity or an entity itself.[3]

The mind is a set of cognitive faculties including consciousness, imagination, perception, thinking, judgement, language and memory, that affects and is affected by the brain, and the central nervous system. It is responsible for processing feelings and emotions that result in attitudes and actions.

The structure of *jīva* can be compared to the architecture of computers with a central processing unit performing computations as per standard logic, application and system software, memory like karma body comprising storage of actions, software, triggers, electronic circuitry as a central nervous system and the sympathetic and parasympathetic networks carrying emotions, actions originated in consciousness and impact of other body parts as information and energy, and external devices for receiving information from external sources and sending results back to them in the form of information (electronic signals). The difference between a computer system and *jīva* is that the intelligence as software of all types and the architecture/design of computer hardware is provided by the *jīva*.

Function of Consciousness and Matter

Sentience (consciousness and its manifestation as awareness/perception and knowledge) is the differentia of the soul.[xi] That which arises from both internal and external causes and is concomitant with the soul is *Upayoga* (manifestation)[3]. Kundakunda[xii] talks about consciousness with a feeling quality too. This distinguishes the soul from the body, though it is one with the body in regard to its bondage. *Upayoga,* like mental activity, is of two types, namely: vision/perception/conation (awareness or detail-less knowledge) and knowledge /cognition[xii] Jain scholars like Kundakunda and Aklaṅka also associate energy (*vīrya*) and bliss (ānanda) attributes of soul to manifestation of consciousness thus including the four infinites (*ananta darśana- jñāna-vīrya* and ānanda) in the manifestation of consciousness. This combined with nine characteristics of *jīva* (Appendix 5) can be clubbed as understanding (conation and cognition), energy (action and enjoyer), feelings of pain and pleasure or conation cognition and affection(impulse) as synonymous with consciousness[3] making it as the basis of studies of psychology[xiv].

Umā Svāmi[xv] talks of *Upayoga* as states/ dispositions (thought activities) arising from subsidence (of deluding karmas), destruction (of eight types of *karmas*), subsidence cum destruction of the four obscuring karmas, rise of eight types of karmas and the inherent nature of the soul (free from *kārmika* association). Vibrations in the space points of soul are caused by the activities of the molecules of body, speech and thought activities of the physical mind, with one thought moment at a time, as a fast- flowing stream, where sense impressions and mental (psychic mind) phenomena are constantly changing substances or their attributes but one by accepting the virtual action (*upakāra*) of another undergoes transformation in its own constitution (supported by consciousness being present throughout the body (*svadeha parimāṇa*) and two types of sense organ, namely psychic and material (Appendix 3). Their effects are carried back as molecules of emotions (tainted and otherwise) to body and speech as well and cause the psychic mind to affect structure and function of the physical mind and flow of associated emotions (e.g., tainted like anger, arrogance, deceit and greed or pleasant ones like love forgiveness etc.)[xvi] I think these emotions are primarily carried by *leśyā*, and not the mind throughout the body. These emotions and vibrations flow throughout the body and the resulting experience is enjoyed by the soul. Conation and knowledge are sequential in the case of the empirical soul while they are simultaneous in the pure soul as there is only one *upayoga* i.e., of its inherent nature and hence no knowledge is transmitted anywhere else.

The manifestation of consciousness is shown on the next page as a flow chart.

Jain psychology is ultimately based on the joint effect of the powers of the soul and the reactions due to karmic energies and body activities. The doctrine of karma holds that every activity, whether physical or mental, produces, besides its perceptible consequences, also an imperceptible effect known as karma (subtle matter particles). Being a force, the karma must be inherent in some substance.[3] Therefore, the actions and desires to affect any change in us must transform themselves into a medium of homogeneous nature with our physical constitution itself, i.e., matter. This is supported by psychology that says that no desire, no feeling or conation passes the threshold of our mind, without in some way, modifying the neural process, thereby explaining the information exchange between the soul and matter in the human body.

This is similar to researchers and proponents of Artificial Intelligence 'AI' saying that Intelligence and consciousness are different. Intelligence involves an ability for problem solving which increases with the increase of the computing power and availability of vast streams of data while consciousness is the ability to feel things such as pain, joy, anger, ego and goes hand in hand with intelligence[xvii], they are both degraded states of the four infinites of pure soul. Is intelligence not a manifestation of consciousness? Do AI scientists recognise souls? These are the ongoing topics of discussions amongst scientists.

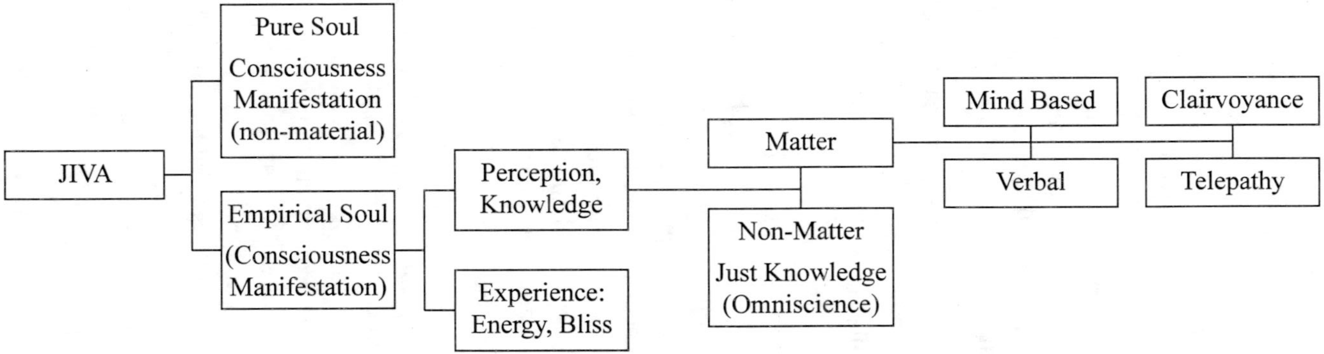

Figure 2: Manifestation of Consciousness

In 1975, Prof. Robert Ader (a psychologist) and Nicholas Cohen (an immunologist) at the University of Rochester, demonstrated that a signal via the nervous system (taste) was affecting immune function. 'Their research led to further works on the ways the central nervous system and the immune system communicate - biological pathways that make the mind, the emotions.[xviii] The mind and the body are not separate, but intimately entwined'[2]. Further, the chemical messengers that operate most extensively in both brain and immune system are those that regulate emotions.

In 1985, research by the neuro-pharmacologist, Candace Pert[xix], of the National Institute of Health at Georgetown University, revealed that

- The nervous and immune systems (both with memory and capacity to learn) were clearly in communication with each other[4]. A number of brain loci, many within emotion mediating brain areas are enriched with many types of neuropeptide receptors, suggesting a convergence of information processing at these nodes. Thus, neuropeptides and their receptor join the brain, glands and immune systems in a network of communication between brain and body, probably representing the biochemical substance of emotions.
- The mind is the flow of information as it moves among cells, organs, and systems of the body. One of the qualities of information flow is that it can be unconscious, occurring below the level of awareness (manifestation of consciousness or psychic mind, a nonphysical non-material substrate that has to do with flow of that information). This psychic mind is immaterial, yet it has a physical substrate which is both the body and the brain. It may also be said to have the mind-body connection in a widely distributed psychosomatic network of communicating molecules where the mind holds the network together, often acting below our consciousness, linking and coordinating the major

systems and their organs and cells in an intelligently orchestrated symphony of life[4].

- Our internal chemicals, the neuropeptides and their receptors, are the actual biological underpinnings of our awareness, manifesting themselves as our emotions, beliefs, and expectations and profoundly influencing how we respond to and experience the world. The body is not a mindless machine, the body and mind are one. —- The mind is non-local. This information exchange takes place over a network linking all of our systems and organs, engaging all our molecules of emotion, as the means of communication. What we see is a mobile brain that moves throughout the body, located at all places at once and not in the head. This body-wide information network is ever changing and dynamic.

The research of PNI and later Candace Pert also supports the Jain doctrine of function, structure and characteristics of the soul (like the *svadeha parimāṇa,* action and enjoyment characteristics of the soul associated with the four infinites of soul; psychic mind and physical mind communicate (material and efficient causes and as the *upakāra* of one on the other).

These discussions reflect the flow of information (a material manifestation of consciousness of the empirical soul) within the body where the soul exists. A stand-alone computer also follows a similar structure and functioning, but the flow of information is in the form of electronic impulses rather than chemical in nature. [XX] However, in pure consciousness (liberated souls), there is no information flow as manifestation of consciousness as conation and knowledge by the soul is simultaneous and just meant to enjoy its own nature.

The flow of consciousness external to the body the soul owns is not possible due to the *svadeha parimāṇa* or soul as the size of the body it owns (Appendix 3) thus clearly supporting that consciousness cannot travel out of the body. Further, the soul has a tendency to move up and in a straight line. However, manifestation as awareness and knowledge of the empirical soul can travel outside the body the soul owns as these are matter (*mati, śruta, avadhi and manaḥparyaya jñānas*) for the empirical soul (*vibhāva guṇa)*[xxi] Also the first, third and fourth types of knowledge discussed here are mind-based and for use by the knower (*jñātā*) while the second is in the form of word/signals to convey this knowledge to others. Knowledge here infers to information, as seen earlier in discussions by Adler and Pert and can be processed by other *jīvas* or can impact matter designated by consciousness/soul and vice versa. Realities like Influx (*saṁvara*), bondage (*bandha*) and dissociation (*nirjarā*) (appendix 1) can be understood by this reasoning. For the pure soul, this knowledge/ information is internal to enjoy its nature as it has no material bodies associated with it and does not travel outside the soul itself (*kevala jñāna* or *svabhāva guṇa*).[xxii] The Gītā (verse 7.12) also differentiates between pure consciousness and its manifestation as material energy thereby sharing the Jain view of consciousness and its manifestation.

Leśyā, a unique concept in Jain metaphysics denoting light or radiation that links the dynamics of the soul (consciousness) and the karmic body with the psycho-physical activities performed by the physical body, and is believed to be associated with every empirical soul due to the association of the soul with matter. *Leśyā* relates to the stream of psychic karmas like delusion, anger etc, and the rise of matter-karmas bonded with the soul and psycho-physical activities (*yoga*). *Leśyā* is further classified as *dravya* (matter) and *bhava* (psychic). *Dravya-leśyā*, the material form can be viewed as colourations reflecting the state of the soul while *bhāva leśyā* attracts corresponding karmic particles affecting activities of mind, body and speech as well as other living and non-living beings (matter primarily), thus allowing scope for the modification of behaviour and diluting karmic determinism. Pure soul has no *leśyās*.

Viney Jain relates *leśyā* with biophotons and says, 'Studies of the interaction of coherent electromagnetic fields with living systems and biological materials suggest that living systems produce a characteristic pattern of frequencies of electromagnetic radiations as an expression of their electrochemical activities. The coherent emission of biophotons is associated with the bioenergetic as well as the bio-cybernetic processes and thus closely correlated with the functioning of the living systems. Behaviour dispositions and the spiritual progress of living systems are characterized by 6 different types of *leśyās*, denoted by different colors: 1. *Kṛṣṇa* (black), 2. *Nīla* (blue), 3. *Kapota* (grey), 4. *Taijas* (red), 5. *Padma* (yellow) and 6. Śukla (white)'. He further refers *leśyā* as similar to aura, DNA being an important source of biophotons and the coherent biophotonic; field of the DNA provides the basic communication network regulating the functioning of the living organism, indicating a possible relation of biophotons with *leśyā*.

Energy

Our physiological vehicle, i.e., the body is made of the same stuff as the rest of the physical world /universe, and what animates the body seems to be a form of energy that constitutes the physical universe.

As we have seen earlier, Jainism talks of three different of forms of energy, namely

- *Vīrya* or energy as an attribute of the soul which helps conscious elements to stay conscious and develop feelings of pain, pleasure etc. It is also the energy which lets consciousness manifest as conation and knowledge. This form of energy is non-material. Gītā (verse 7.12) also differentiates the energy of pure consciousness and its manifestation as material energy. When we talk of transport of consciousness, we talk of transport of its manifestation as knowledge (information/ intelligence) due to the impact of karmas, and internal/ external factors which are matter i.e., consciousness embedded with matter, as the empirical soul does not travel outside its body till death (destruction of physical body), known as *vigraha-gati* to acquire a new body. Pure consciousness without a physical body travels in a straight line till the end of cosmos (summit) beyond which it cannot travel due to absence of *dharma* and *adharm* (*aloka*). However, we are not discussing very special cases (treated as exceptions) of a highly spiritual being (said to be in the sixth stage of 14 stages of spiritual purification) who generates a special body, called āhāraka (projectable) body which transcends the body to either acquire knowledge from a highly spiritually purified person (a *tīrthaṁkara*) and then returns to the old body or of an ascetic tainted with emotions who creates a similar body which goes out of the original body to harm someone and return to its original 'body'. Similarly, pure soul still bonded with non-obstructing karmas expands to the limits of cosmos to shake off remaining karmas and moves up at the time of its liberation from the body (*nirvāṇa*).

- Energy due to the rise of karmas; activities of mind body and speech and state dispositions of the soul cause vibrations in the space-points of the psychic mind transmitted as instant states of the physical mind resulting in information molecules or electronic signals that are material and transmitted throughout the body. This is in the form of matter-energy, depending on the type of karmic energy arising from emergent karmas resulting in manifestation of consciousness as conation and knowledge (information) and state dispositions of the soul discussed earlier. These information particles in the external space travel as discussed earlier as *leśyās* (radiation). Further movements of body parts caused by such molecules cause vibrations in the space surrounding the body in different directions. This flow of information, as energy can be in the form of omnidirectional waves getting affected by other similar but different information flows taking place till it reaches the designated *jīva* / matter and affects the same.

- Energy in the form of *dharma, adharma* as constituents of the cosmos; there are similarities to water for the fish to move (*dharma*) and gravitational force or tree shade (for *jīva*) in the desert to support transfer of information or *jīva*/matter. This form of energy is non-material and inert.
- Energy of matter generated by its nature of fusion and fission or conversion of matter from one state to other that is material in nature and researched by scientists.

Thus, we see the presence of energy everywhere but of different types and sources and it is different from consciousness which is immaterial.

Conclusion

Consciousness and soul are concomitant in Jainism. There are infinite independent souls in this cosmos. Pure consciousness has infinite conation, knowledge, energy and bliss as its primary attributes. It is just aware of itself and its attributes. When this soul is associated with matter, it becomes aware of its field and manifests as conation and knowledge (in the form of information or intelligence) which are matter. It gets affected by matter and other souls embedded with matter as well as affects them. It is this knowledge which travels both within the body in which it exists and outside the body. Matter is another type of reality which is devoid of consciousness, with fusion and fission as its nature. Its smallest form of existence is called *paramāṇu*. Matter and energy are interchangeable but consciousness which is immaterial is not interchangeable with matter.

Ātmā, Soul in Jainism Described as a Hologram

Surendra Singh Pokharna

The concept of ātmā is the foundation of Jain philosophy. Extensive literature is available in Jain āgamās and other literature in Shwetāmbār and Digambar traditions. It is observed that although āgamās also discuss the concept of ātmā at great length, the details are available in *Samayasār* of Acharya Kundakundā which has a unique position in Jain literature. In his Sanskrit commentary *Ātmakhyāti*, Āchāryā Āmritchandrā composed verses of great spiritual value and mentioned forty-seven *Shaktiyān* (Powers) of ātmā, out of infinite *shaktis*. Extensive details of these *shaktis* are available in *Pravachan Navneet*, in Hindi with Gujarati script, based on the lectures delivered by Sadguru Pujyaniya Kanji Swamy of Songadh (Gujarat) in the last century. It is observed that although forty-seven *shaktis* are mentioned for a pure ātmā. However, knowledge is treated as the most important shakti of ātmā. This is in complete agreement with the *Consciousness as an Informational Phenomenalism* of Anton P. Zeleznikar (1997), who has laid great emphasis on the informational aspect of consciousness. Also, a pure ātmā is considered to be non-physical and formless. It is a distinct property of living beings which is not present in non-living substances. However, it is mentioned that a worldly soul is in association with matter from an infinite past. This matter is known as karmās which are small particles of matter. But through spiritual processes, one can get rid of these karmās and can acquire a pure ātmā through fourteen stages of evolution.

A scientific analysis of these *shaktis* was carried out by the author and it has been observed that these *shaktis* indicate a holograph-like configuration of ātmā[1]. Nandi Ghoshji[2] Maharasahab (Acharya) on the other hand has conceptualised that ātmā as defined in Jainism is a hologram. Michael Talbot (1991) has extensively analysed the current science in general and quantum mechanics in particular and showed that non-locality and quantum entanglement strongly indicate that not only the brain acts as a hologram, but the whole Universe is a hologram. It is based on David Bohm's concept of implicate order and concept of non-local information. He argues that parapsychic phenomena like telepathy, clairvoyance, out of body travel, near-death experience and other mystic experiences might be explainable with the assumption that the whole Universe is a hologram. Similarly, Brahama Kumari Pari, a disciple of the Brahamakumari sect was so impressed by the concept of holography that she has written a book entitled *Holographic Universe* (2015). Devesh Mehta[3] in an article in *Gujarat Samachar* mentioned that like the Upanishads, the theory of Hologram of physical sciences also implies a total, complete, unbroken reality. Recently Rulin Xiu[4] has revived the concept of holography through the string theory. Very recently Anil Anantswamy[5] has documented the twenty-fifth anniversary of the concept of the Holographic Universe in *Scientific American*. On the other hand, Marcer Peter J. and Schempp Walter[6] have discussed the quantum hologram-like property of a neuron. Hence there are strong indications that hologram-like structures exist in nature at various levels, including universal levels.

The ātmā is treated as a multidimensional image of the whole Universe and so it has complete knowledge of all substances of the Universe (known as *loka* in Jainism) including their past, present and future. In addition, an ātmā is assumed to have small constituents known as ātmā pradeshās such that each ātmā pradesha has partial knowledge of all substances of the Universe. These attributes strongly indicate holographic properties of the Jain concept of ātmā.

It is argued that the holographic aspect of ātmā and hence consciousness can explain the possibility of viewing microscopic particles of matter through clairvoyance as claimed by ancient

Jain scholars[1] and Annie Besant and her team[7] (to be noted by ABC for Annie Besant and C.W. Leadbeater and C. Jinrajdas for future in this paper) with its further analysis by Phillips[8].

Why Study of Consciousness is Required

Darwin's principle of "survival of the fittest" of evolution versus the spiritual principle of "Live and Let Live" of spiritual evolution

If we look at the state of our planet today, we find that half of the animals in the world have disappeared since the last 50 years, that is after 1970. It is because of uncontrollable expansion of human activities[i]. A report by the World Wildlife Fund (WWF) has found that populations of mammals, birds, reptiles, amphibians and fish have declined on average by 52 per cent in the last 40 years. And for freshwater creatures the situation is even bleaker, with a population collapse of more than three quarters over the same period. Almost the entire decline is due to human activity, through habitat loss, deforestation, climate change, over-fishing and hunting. If this is not adequate enough to shock the human soul, there is another heart burning news, and it is that every year, we are losing almost 25,000 biological species[ii]. But this is only one side of the coin. We also observe a large increase in terrorist activities and wars among countries and senseless violence in daily life in many countries in recent times, including attacks on women and children.

An increase in ill feelings towards competitors and fellow beings can be observed these days with cut-throat competition in all walks of life. It is due to Darwin's principle of evolution expressed through the famous expression of "survival of the fittest". However, Darwin's ideas are based on analysis of past data and developing correlations among them to establish his hypothesis. Goldsmith[9] finds that there are no goals for species in this principle. They only look at the near future and attempt to survive. Goldsmith[9] feels that it is due to too much emphasis on Darwin's principle of evolution that so much damage has been done to the environment. This work is supported by Daniel

Dennett's book entitled *Darwin's Dangerous Idea: Evolution and the Meanings of Life*[10]. Hence there is a need to compare Darwin's principle of evolution with the spiritual principle of evolution described as "Live and Let Live". These two principles will have totally different impacts on the definition of the concept of development and evolution. However, to understand these topics more precisely, we have to go to the roots of these problems and look at the methodology of modern science itself.

Limitations of physical sciences as they are applied to study living systems in light of the General Systems Theory (GST)

Our approach consists in studying the problems faced in the current methodology of physical sciences which are used to study biological and human systems and review them in light of the General Systems Theory. In particular the concept of scientific knowledge is examined critically in the light of GST. To fill in the gap created in the knowledge system due to these limitations, the concept of knowledge as mentioned in Jainism is explored to find out if that system of knowledge and its evolution can provide new ideas about the very concept of knowledge.

All living systems are essentially irreversible in nature, that is, they grow and decay and they are also open systems compared to the physical systems which are virtually closed systems. The living systems constantly interact with the environment like human beings, who take oxygen from the atmosphere and release carbon dioxide. So, the biological and social systems cannot be strictly subjected to the process of measurement and hence they are not exactly describable in the strict terminology of the physical sciences. In addition, human systems and many animals and insects have memory, free will, creativity, a tendency to interact strongly with other fellow beings and the environment. Also, there are micro-controls in the form of thought processes which cannot be easily adjusted in any planned "scientific experiment".

So, it is impossible to perform experiments on human systems and predict events about them from a purely scientific point of view. Hence such systems are studied in a different way by using statistical procedures. In such methods only some rough trends or patterns can be found.

Therefore, to handle these problems, we look for a new discipline which has recently become very popular (1978) and is called General Systems Theory (GST). It has been developed to handle such complex systems and their behaviour. This concept takes into account both physical systems and biological as well as social systems. Actually, systems properties depend on their domain. The domain of systems is the field over which they extend. It can be classified as to whether: (a) Systems are living or non-living, (b) Systems are abstract or concrete, (c) Systems are open or closed, (d) Systems exhibit a high or low degree of entropy or disorder, (e) Systems display organised simplicity, unorganised complexity or organised complexity, (f) Systems can be ascribed a purpose or not, (g) Feedback can exist or not, (h) Systems are ordered in hierarchies and/or Systems are organised.

In this analysis pure physical sciences are categorised as hard systems and subjects like sociology, religion, psychology, biology etc. are classified as soft systems. GST[11] has been developed to handle such diverse systems and is a serious attempt to reconcile physical sciences with social sciences. As per this theory, all systems are characterised by transfer of information, knowledge and entropy/order which are much more important than any other attribute. Even energy comes next to them.

Limitations of Scientific Methodology Due to Conservations Laws

Any phenomenon is called scientific if it can be verified in a laboratory under a given set of controlled conditions and is reproducible at any other point of time and at any place. This condition is called space-time invariance condition in science. In addition, we define conservation laws in physics which are the foundation of all scientific measurements. Thus, we have conservation laws for energy, linear momentum and angular momentum. Now all these conservation laws are defined for isolated closed systems, thus approximating nature. For example,

Energy is defined as that variable of a closed isolated system which does not change over time. But in principle we can never treat a biological system as a totally closed isolated system. Similarly linear momentum is defined as that property of a closed isolated system which remains invariant with any spatial displacement and so on. Hence the mere definitions of conservation laws are not proper because they first divide the world and then try to define it. The interactions among these systems are then studied by considering the nature and magnitude of the interaction among them (four interactions of nature viz. Gravitation, Electromagnetic, Weak and Strong). For biological systems which strongly interact with each other, this type of formalism cannot be applied in a satisfactory way.

Limitations of scientific knowledge due to Gödel's incomplete theorems

The most attractive aspect of scientific knowledge is its mathematical basis. We generally feel that this mathematical representation of various scientific facts makes our knowledge more precise and accurate. However, from two theorems which have been put forward by the great mathematician Kurt Gödel, we find that any mathematical representation of any physical reality limits our knowledge of that reality. Not only this but the theorems also imply that none of the languages or representations can express the reality of nature with perfection. Complete knowledge must necessarily have its foundation in an unexpressed, unmanifest field of intelligence[1].

We need to realise that scientific knowledge is only a subset of the total knowledge system and actual knowledge is structured in consciousness:

With the advent of science and the resulting technology, a misunderstanding and misconception has developed among the masses that scientific knowledge is the only ultimate knowledge. Not only this, it is also presumed that only the knowledge which is experimentally verifiable and repeatable at any place and at any time alone is the actual knowledge. This is far from the truth.

The fact is that the so-called modern science is just around three years old and the concept of knowledge existed much before that for several centuries. The Vedas, Upanishads, Puranas, Agamas, Mahabharata, Ramayana, Koran and Bible have extensive knowledge about life and the rules to be followed. But they do not fall in the domain of modern science.

Actually, the recent developments in computer science and neurobiology clearly show that knowledge is nothing but information organised in some way[9]. And in turn, information is just organisation of data in some fashion. It is also accepted that human consciousness (and even animal consciousness) is capable of organising these data and can generate information and hence knowledge in some way. Therefore, what we call scientific knowledge is just a subset of this grand concept of knowledge, which can exist in the human consciousness. In addition, all interpretations of scientific experiments are ultimately done by human consciousness. Also since knowledge is another crucial concept associated with the brain or consciousness, it is equally important to understand the concept of knowledge associated with the brain and consciousness. This is in complete agreement with the "Consciousness as an Informational Phenomenalism" concept as formulated by Anton P. Zeleznikar[12].

As the forty-seven *shaktis* in Jainism are quite similar to the quantum hologram (QH), I will first briefly describe classical and quantum holograms and related topics of nilpotent quantum mechanics (NQM).

Holograms and Nilpotent Quantum Mechanics

There are two different types of holograms discussed in modern science. They are described in what follows. In addition, I briefly describe the Universal Rewriting System and Nil-potent Quantum Mechanics.

Classical Hologram

In a classical hologram, a coherent laser beam splits into two parts. One part directly falls on a photographic plate, and the other part is reflected from the object whose hologram is to be created. These two beams interfere with each other, producing an interference pattern on a photographic plate such that each fraction of the interference pattern has partial information about the whole object. When the photographic plate is exposed to laser light, the three-dimensional image of the object is produced again[iii].

Quantum Hologram

Every material body emits and absorbs quantum radiations into or from the zero-point field (ZPF). These quanta contain quantum information that is non-local and has all the history of the quantum states of the system stored in the ZPF. For living beings, these radiations are very coherent. Because of information's non-locality, the instantaneous transfer of information is possible, and this information is not attenuated over time. This information, its storage, and its recall are called the quantum hologram[13]. The information is stored in terms of frequency, amplitude, and phase[14]. The Quantum Hologram is also described for a neuron by Marcer and Schempp[6]. Bousso (2002) gives a good review of a hologram.

Universal Rewriting System and Nilpotent Quantum Mechanics

The universal rewriting system is based on the assumption that "zero" is the foundation of reality. Hence, if one starts writing any alphabet, then its inverse is automatically and simultaneously written in the rest of the universe such that the total "sum" is zero again. This writing system has been used to study a fermion and the corresponding quantum vacuum such that the total sum is zero. It has led to a new branch of quantum mechanics known as nilpotent quantum mechanics[14]. If the fermion is described using a vector space "A," then its dual vector space "D" is an exact mirror image and will describe the inverse of it. Yet the information content of the two vector spaces is exactly the same (but in different forms), and both can contain local and non-local information. I have extended this formalism to the constituents of the whole Universe. So, a pure ātmā has information of all the constituents of the Universe, but is not physically observable.

Is the Universe a Hologram

In the case of a simple hologram, two coherent beams of light interfere such that one is reflected from an object and the other acts as a reference beam. The two interfere and an interference is produced on a photographic plate. When this two-dimensional plate is exposed again with the coherent beam then the original holographic wave pattern of the original object is produced. Thus, information about the original three-dimensional object is stored in a two-dimensional plate. Extending this idea further, attempts have been made to explain the basic structure of our three-dimensional universe from a two-dimensional plate like structure which is more fundamental than the actual Universe[15] . However, a straightforward study of this problem has been done by Xiu Rulin[4]. According to her:

> *Grand unification theory is to use one mathematical formula to derive all laws and phenomena. Currently, the String theory is the prime candidate for the grand unified theory. However, the principle and symmetry that lead to the string theory remain unknown and predictions from the string theory are limited. To find the grand unification theory, we need to know the fundamental constituent and the principle that creates all the observed phenomena. In this work, we propose that holographic principle is the fundamental principle that leads to the formulation of the grand unified theory. We suggest that elementary information, the pure, abstract, and universal information, is the essential element underlying and creating all physical phenomena. We show that two-dimensional spacetime encodes the elementary information and is the hologram from which all phenomena and laws of physics emerge. We derive the minimum spacetime needed to encode one piece of elementary information. From this we obtain the holographic action which describes the maximum amount of information for a system ingrained on the hologram and is proportional to the area of*

the 2-dimensional elementary information spacetime. We find the holographic action is similar to the string action. This new derivation of string action gives a new way to understand, interpret, and apply String Theory. We point out that holographic action derived here is also a natural extension of the action appearing in quantum physics and general relativity. We demonstrate how to use the holographic action to calculate the black hole entropy and the cosmological constant from it. We find the cosmological constant calculated in this way is consistent with current experimental observation. It can solve the long-standing cosmological constant problem. We show how the observed physics phenomena, such as elementary particles, gravity, gauge interaction, dark matter and dark energy emerge from holographic action. We find that the observation of elementary particles is due to the Poincaré symmetry.

The existence of gravity and gauge interaction including electromagnetic, weak, and strong interaction, is due to the diffeomorphic symmetry. We point out how holographic action provides a possible solution of the large hierarchy problem between the Planck scale and electroweak scale. John Wheeler has proposed "It from Bit", meaning all phenomena come from information. This work provides the basic principle and mathematical formulation of "It from Bit". It is a grand unification theory that includes the string theory, quantum mechanics, general relativity, and all physics laws in principle. It also has the power to make specific predictions and solve difficult problems in physics and philosophy. In the past work, we have shown that spirit and consciousness are related to the information existing in our body and vibrational field. This work reveals mathematically how our spirit and consciousness manifest all physical phenomena.

Details are not available but the point to be noted is that the holographic model of the universe is now being taken very seriously in fundamental physics.

Michael Talbot[15] has written a very interesting book entitled *The Holographic Universe* in which he has strongly argued that the Universe is a hologram. He has started from the brain being a hologram and has discussed David Bohm's implicate order and an interconnectedness at a very fundamental level. He claims that this concept of reality can also explain many parapsychic phenomena. Mehta D (2022) and Brahama Kumari Pari (2015) have also argued along these lines.

Concept of Consciousness and Knowledge in Jainism

Let us now look at the concept of knowledge in Jainism. In Jainism, the world is assumed to consist of six elements. They are: *Dharmāstikayā* (Medium of Motion), *Ā̲dharmāstikayā* (Medium of Rest), *Ā̲kāshāstikayā* (Space), *Pudgalastikāyā* (Matter), *Jeevāstikāyā* (Living beings having a soul) and *Kāla* (Time). Jainism has defined the soul as the basic constituents of all living beings. According to the conception of Jainism, a perfect soul has infinite knowledge, infinite intuition, infinite bliss and infinite power. The perfect soul has other characteristics but knowledge has been regarded as the chief characteristic of the soul. Kundakundā[16] has stated that although, from the empirical point of view, there is a difference between soul and knowledge yet from the transcendental point of view it is sufficient to say that the soul is the knower and nothing else. He further said that there is no difference between the knower and his knowledge. From an empirical point of view an omniscient (*Kevali*, i.e. a perfect soul) perceives and knows the whole of reality and from the transcendental point of view he perceives and knows nothing. Therefore, what we call scientific knowledge appears to be just a subset of this grand concept of knowledge, which can exist in the human consciousness.

All species may be physically different but are existing in the world from a past which does not have any beginning. It is due to their attachment to material particles known as karmās that they continuously take birth in the world again and again. The direction of evolution should be towards a goal of liberating the soul from all material attachment that is all karmas. A process of selection by oneself is involved in spiritual evolution as certain rules and principles have to be followed and are described separately for ordinary humans and for enlightened souls like acharyas and sādhus, sādhvis, etc. It appears that Jain practices like chanting of *navār mantrās*, *loggus*, doing *sāmāyik*, *pratikramana ekāsna* and *upwās*, āymbil, *varshi tap*, *mās khaman*, *updhān*, *siddhi tap*, *nanyānu yātrās*, and several other practices lead to very stable life, increased self-confidence, recognition of inner strength of soul, and ultimately evolution of one's soul. It is preached that one should reduce one's requirements in such a way that even if there is scarcity of resources, lower consumption will guarantee survival of all in a cooperative way. A state of highest orderliness is defined as a pure soul, towards which, everyone has to evolve. This is compatible with the General Systems Theory in which definite goals are defined.

The Jain concept of the Soul has some kind of "Order" built into it

The spiritual path suggested in Jainism and the properties of a worldly soul as it evolves towards a state of perfection have many interesting features which appeal to scientists. Several attributes of such an ordered soul are enunciated and are found in many monks. Thus, for example *shatāvdhanis* who demonstrate several powers of the brain not commonly found elsewhere. Such practices lead to recognition of inner strength of the soul and a highly ordered mental state.

Forty-Seven Characteristics of Ātmā

I will now describe fortyseven shaktis of ātmā as mentioned in Pravchan Navneet.

1. **आत्म-द्रव्य-हेतु-भूत-चौतन्य-मात्र-भाव-धारण-लक्षणा-जीवत्व-शक्ति**

(Ātmā-Dravya-Hetu-Bhut-Chaitanya-Mātra-Bhāva-Dhāran-Lakshnā-*Jeevatva-shakti*): The *jīvatva shakti* is responsible for distinguishing a living being from a non-living being. It has four attributes: *jñāna* (knowledge), *dārśan* (intuition), *ānand* (bliss), and *vīrya* (power).

2. **अजड़त्व-आत्मिका-चिति-शक्ति**

(*A-jadtva-Ātmika-Chiti-Shakti*): This second shakti is *a-jadtva* (non-material) *chiti shakti*; in contrast to the *jīvatva shakti*, it has only two attributes: *dārśan* and *jñāna.* It can be treated as similar to consciousness.

3. **अनाकार-उपयोग-मयी-दृशी-शक्ति**

(*Anākar-Upayog-Mayee-Drashi-Shakti*): This is a power through which formless, non-physical ātmā has an initial or preliminary view of reality that is further knowable. Through it, one sees ātmā dravya, oneself, all *paryāyās* (orders or manners of being), and everything else. It indicates the structure of a hologram.

4. **साकार-उपयोग-मयी-ज्ञान-शक्ति**

(*Sākār-Upayog Mayee- Jñāna-Shakti*): This is a power through which one has detailed knowledge of the self and all other substances like the size, shape, colour, taste, smell, and touch of *pudgal* and other five substances (that are knowable like *Ākastikāya*, *Jivāstikayas*, *Dharmāstikāya*, *Adharmāstikāya* and *Kāla*). This again indicates a holographic structure.

5. **अनाकुलत्व-लक्षणा-सुख-शक्ति**

(*Anākultva-Lakshna- Sukh-Shakti*): This is a power that has *anāku-latva* (absolutely no worry). Hence, one is always happy, and there is a state of bliss in all three-time domains, because one has full knowledge of reality.

6. स्वरुप-निर्वर्तन-सामर्थ्य-रूपा-वीर्य-शक्ति
(*Swaroop-Nirvartan-Sāmarthya-Roopa-Vīrya-Shakti*): The ability of ātmā to create and retain its state is due to spiritual energy, known as *vīrya shakti*. This term has nothing to do with the Hindi word *Virya*, which means semen and manliness.

7. अखण्डित-प्रताप-स्वातन्त्र्य-शालित्व-लक्षणा-प्रभुत्व-शक्ति
(*Akhandit-Pratāp-Swātantrya-Shālitva-Lakshana-Prabhutwa-Shakti*): The ātmā is almighty, free, and independent and does not require the support of any external substance for its existence; it is unbroken and nobody can divide it.

8. सर्वभाव-व्यापक-एक-भाव-रूपा-विभुत्व-शक्ति
(*Sarvabhāv-Vyāpak-Aik-Bhāva-Roopa-Vibhutwa-Shakti*) Due to this power, ātmā dravya pervades all the other infinite *shaktis* (powers) and their *paryāyas*.

9. विश्व-विश्व-सामान्य-भाव-परिणत-आत्म-दर्शन-मयी-सर्व-दर्शित्व-शक्ति
(*Vishwa-Vishwa-Sāmanya-Bhāva-Parinat-Ātmā-Dārśana-Mayee Sarva-Darshitva-Shakti*): This power is such that, through it, one perceives all substances of the lokākāsha (cosmic world) in totality; that is, as a whole, that is existing but without its details. It again shows a holographic-like structure.

10. विश्व-विश्व-विशेष-भाव-परिणत-आत्म-ज्ञान-मयी-सर्वज्ञत्व-शक्ति
(*Vishwa-Vishwa-Vishesh-Bhāva-Parinat-Ātmā-Jñāna-Mayee-Sarvagyatva-Shakti*): Through this power, there is a capability of knowing *dravya, guna*, and *paryāyas* of all substances in the *loka*. In a state of omniscience, it perceives all these aspects together, including their past, present and future. This again shows a hologram-like structure, but in this case, it also contains information about time, which needs further investigation.

11. **नीरूप-आत्म-प्रदेश-प्रकाश-मान-लोक-अलोक-आकार-मेचक-उपयोग-लक्षणा-स्वच्छत्व-शक्ति**

(*Ni-Rupa-Ātmā-Pradeśa-Prakāsh-mān-Loka-Aloka-Āakār-Mechak-Upayoga-Lakshanā-Swachhatva-shakti*): The ātmā is a formless, self-illuminating, clean power having many forms (*Mechak)*. All attributes of *pudgal, dharmāstikāya, adharmāstikāya*, *ākash*, and *kāla* are reflected in this mirror-like power. However, the ātmā does not have any property of a *pudgal*, like taste, smell, touch, form, or colour—yet the ātmā dravya still has *pradeśas*-like structure known as ātmā pradeśas. This further asserts a hologram-like structure, with a *pradeśa* as an element of the hologram.

12. **स्वयं-प्रकाश-मान-विशद-स्व-संवित्ति-मयी-प्रकाश-शक्ति**

(*Swayam-Prakāsh-man-Vishad-Swa-Samvitti-Mayee-Prakāsh-Shakti*): This is self-enlightened power through which one has self-knowledge and self-realisation (*Swa-Savedan*). Therefore, it is sensitive to itself and can also experience itself in all its aspects. Everything is direct (*pratyakṣa*) and clear (*spashtha*).

13. **क्षेत्र-कालान-अवच्छिन्न-चिद्विलास-आत्मिका-असंकुचित-विकासत्व-शक्ति**

(*Kṣetra-Kālān-Avchinna-Chid-Vilāsa-Ātmika-Asankuchit-Vikāsatva-Shakti*): Due to this power, the ātmā can expand across both space and time (leading to *atindriya jñāna*).

14. **अन्य-अक्रिय-माण-अन्य-अकारक-एक-द्रव्य-आत्मिका-अकार्य-कारण-शक्ति**

(*Anya-Akriya-mān-Anya-Akārak-Aik-Dravya-Aatmika-Akārya-Kāran-Shakti*): This is the power through which ātmā paryāya is neither the cause of other *dravyas* nor is it the effect of other *dravyas*. This shows the independent nature of ātmā.

15. पर-आत्म-निमित्तक-ज्ञेय-ज्ञानाकार-ग्रहण-ग्राहण-स्वभाव-रूपा-परिणम्य-परिणामकत्व-शक्ति

(*Par-Ātmā-Nimittak-Gyeya-Jnānākar-Grahana-Grāhana-Swabhav-Roopa-Parinamya-Parinama-katva-Shakti*): Due to this power, an ātmā can absorb knowledge of knowable entities and can also help others (living beings) in absorbing that knowledge.

16. अन्यून-अतिरिक्त-स्वरुप-नियतत्व-रूपा-त्याग-उपदान-शुन्यत्व-शक्ति

(*Anyun-Atirikta-Swaroopa-Niyatatva-Roopā-Tyag-Upadan-Shunyatva-Shakti*): Due to this power, the *dravya ātmā* and its *shaktis* and *paryāyas* are unchanged and constant. They appear to be analogous to the independent frequencies which are fixed.

17. षट-स्थान-पतित-वृद्धि-हानि-परिणत-स्वरुप-प्रतिष्ठत्व-कारण-विशिष्ट-गुणात्मिका-अगुरू-लघुत्व-शक्ति

(*Shat-Sthān-Patit-Vriddhi-Hāni-Parinat-Swaroop-Pratishthatva-Kāran-Vishista-Gunātmika-Aguru-laghutva-shakti*): Through this power, six types of attributes increase and simultaneously six other types decrease during one *paryāya* of one *samay*. The six attributes are *anant-guna-hani* (infinite power loss); *asankhyaat-guna-haani* (innumerable power loss); *sankhyaat-guna-hāni* (finite power loss); *anant-bhāg-hāni* (infinite parts loss); *asankhyāt-bhāg-hāni* (innumerable parts loss); and *sankhyāt-bhāg-hāni* (finite parts loss). Simultaneously, there are six complementary attributes that cause all these to increase; that is, they are gained.

It appears that these attributes describe all sorts of possibilities that can exist in one *samay.* Therefore, a *paryāya* in one *samay* contains everything. This attribute appears to be close to the quantum entanglement of quantum physics, in which everything is interconnected. This also supports a holographic-like structure.

One microscale oscillation involves three types of increases and three types of decreases of parts and attributes at macroscale (all occurring in one time unit

Type	Infinite	Innumerable	Finite
Losses of Parts	Infinite parts Losses	Innumerable parts Losses	Finite Parts losses
Gains of Parts	Infinite parts are gained.	Innumerable parts are gained	Finite parts gain
Losses of attributes	Infinite attributes Losses	Innumerable attributes Losses	Finite attributes losses
Gains of attributes	Infinite attributes are gained.	Innumerable attributes are gained	Finite attributes are gain

Mathematical definition of quantum entanglement or more than that???

Figure 1: Increase and Decrease involved in Microscale Oscillation

18. क्रम-अक्रम-वृत्त-वृत्तित्व-लक्षणा-उत्पाद-व्यय-ध्रुवत्व-शक्ति (*Krama-Akrama-Vritta-Vrittitva-Lakshana-Utpād-Vyaya-Dhruvatva-Shakti*): This power is such that

Simultaneous and sequential *paryayas* of infinite *shakties*.

Shakti	Samay 1	Samay 2	. . . . . .	Samay ∞
Shakti 1	Paryaya1,1	Paryaya1,2	. . . . . .	Paryaya 1,∞
Shakti 2	Paryaya2,1	Paryaya2,2	. . . . . .	Paryaya 2,∞
.	.	.	. . . . . .	.
.	.	.	. . . . . .	.
Shakti ∞	Paryaya ∞,1	.	. . . . . .	Paryaya ∞,∞

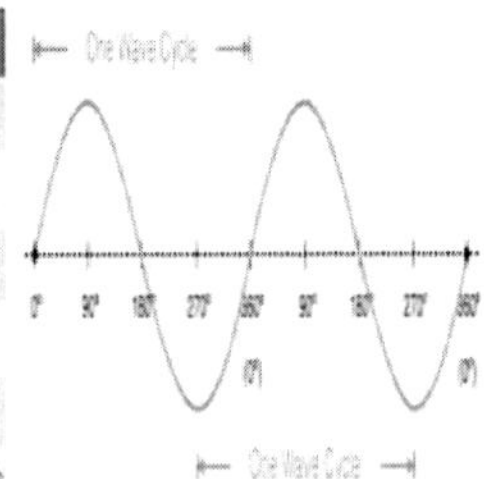

This type of representation has been termed as an Aayat (rectangle)

Figure 2: Simultaneous and Sequential *Prayayas* of Infinite Shaktis

there is simultaneous movement of all infinite *shaktis* at the same time—that is, in parallel—but each power has its own *paryāyas*, which are all sequential. Every *shakti* has a *roop* (form) of *utpād* (production), *vyaya* (destruction), and *dhriuva* (conservation).

19. **द्रव्य-स्वभाव-भूत-ध्रौव्य-व्यय-उत्पाद-आलिंगित-सद्दश-विसद्दश-रुप-एक अस्तित्व-मात्र-मयी-परिणाम-शक्ति** (*Dravya-Swabhāv-Bhut-Dhrauvya-Vyaya-Utpād-Aālingit-Sadrisha-Visadrisha-Roop-Ai-k-Astitva-Mātra-Mayee-Parinām-Shakti*): Due to this power, *dhrauvya, vyava*, and *utpād* are connected with each other. This differs from the eighteenth shakti in which they were connected but in a different sequence: first we had *utpād*, then *vyaya*, and finally *dhrauvya*. Here the sequence is reversed: *dhrauvya* comes first. then *vyaya*, and then *utpād*. These two attributes show some complementarity or inverse relationship and thus show some type of symmetry.

20. **कर्म-बन्ध-व्यपगम-व्यंजित-सहज-स्पर्शादि-शुन्य-आत्म-प्रदेश-आत्मिका-अमूर्तत्व-शक्ति** (*Karma-Bandh-vyapagam-Vyanjit-Sahaj-Sparshādi-Shunya-Aatma-pradesha-Aatmikā-Amurtatva-Shakti*): Owing to this power, there is a formless *parinaman* of *paryāyas* of *shaktis* that do not have any *karma bandhan* and so are free from *sparsh* (touch), *gandh* (smell), *swād* (taste), *rang* (colour), etc.: this *parinaman* is there even at the ātmā pradeśa level. This further indicates two vector spaces, with one physical and other non-physical but having the same information.

21. **सकल-कर्म-कृत-ज्ञातृत्व-मात्र-अतिरिक्त-परिणाम-करण-उपरम-आत्मिका-अकर्तत्व-शक्ति** (*Sakal-Karma-Krita-Gyātratva-Mātra-Atirikta-Parinam-Karan-Uparam-Aatmika Akartatva shakti*) Due to this power, ātmā is not a cause of *shubh* and

ashubh bhāvas (good and bad states of being), which are totally due to karmas, but ātmā is just a knower of them. In addition, ātmā is not responsible for *parinams* of *raga* caused by eight types of karmas. This further establishes a hologram-like structure.

22. **सकल-कर्म-कृत-ज्ञातृत्व-मात्र-अतिरिक्त-परिणाम-अनुभव-उपरम-आत्मिका-अभोक्तृत्व-शक्ति**
(*Sakal-Karma-Krit-Gyātratva-Mātra-Atirikta-Parinaama-Anubhav-Uparam-Ātmika-Abhoktratva-Shakti*): Due to this power, an ātmā is not *bhokta* (enjoyer) nor *karta* (doer) of *karma*. So ātmā is neither a sufferer nor an enjoyer of the impact of all eight types of karmas. This supports the concept of two vector spaces.

23. **सकल-कर्म-उपरम-प्रवृत्त-आत्म-प्रदेश-नैष्पंध-रूपा-निष्क्रियत्व-शक्ति**
(*Sakal-Karma-Uparam-Pravratta-Ātmā-Pradeśa-Naishpandh-Rupa-Nishkriyatva-Shakti*): Through this power, inactiveness (no vibration) is realised in all ātmā pradeśa when there are no karmas. But a part of this shakti is realised even say, in the fourth guṇasthāna of a samayakdarshi, and this part is partially realised in all innumerable ātmā pradeśas. This firmly establishes a hologram-like structure.

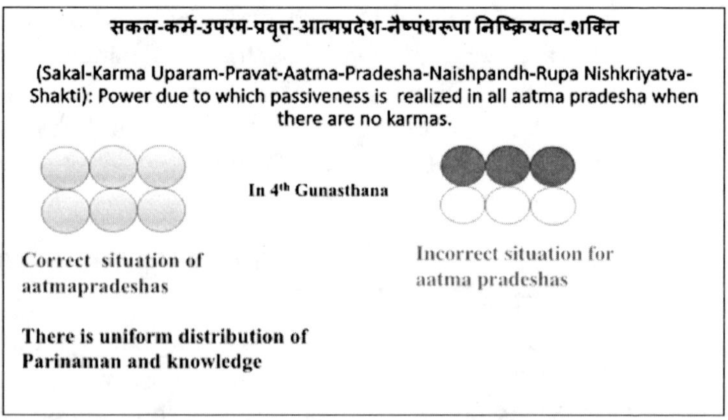

Figure 3: Correct and Incorrect Distribution of Ātmāpradesha

24. आसंसार-संहरण-विस्तरण-लक्षित-किंचित-न्यून-चरम-शरीर-परिमाण-अवस्थित-लोकाकाश-सम्मित-आत्मा-वयवत्व-लक्षणाः

(*Aa-Sansār-Sanharan-Vistaran-Lakshit-Kinchit-Nyuṇ-Charam-Sharir-Parimāna-Avasthita-Lokākāsha-Sammit-ātmā-Vayavatva-Lakshanā*): Due to this power, ātmā can expand and contract. Actually *a-sankoch-vistar shakti* can result in the ultimate realisation of complete *dravya*, complete *kṣetra*, complete *kāla*, and complete *bhāv* without any obstruction. Thus, a body of an elephant also has the same number of ātmā pradeśas as the body of an ant. This is due to the expandability property of a group of ātmā pradeśas, but each ātmā pradeśa does not expand. It appears that the *pradeśas* are linked through "spring-like" entities; they can change their total size depending on the size of the physical body. Strangely, the apparent size of ātmā, as enclosed in the living being, is slightly smaller than the size of the body occupied. Ultimately from one point of view, it can occupy the whole *lokākāśa* in a state of *Kevalajñāna*. This again strongly establishes a hologram-like structure.

25. सर्व-शरीर-एक-स्वरूप-आत्मिका-स्वधर्म-व्यापकत्व-शक्ति

(*Sarva-Sharir-Aik-Swaroop-Aatmika-Swa-dharma-Vyapaktva-Shakti*): *Ātmā* is confined to itself, even in a living body, thereby keeping its own separate identity; that is, it does not interact with any cell or its parts or their groups. Ātmā is not *vyāpak* (spread) in the body of living beings nor in the *raga* of them: ātmā is *vyāpak* in its own form. The ātmā and body are just two independent entities, which again supports the two vector spaces of a hologram.

26. **स्व-पर-समान-असमान-समानअसमान-त्रिविध-भाव-धारण-आत्मिका-साधारण-असाधारण-साधारण-असाधारण-धर्मत्व-शक्ति**

(*Swa-Par-Samān-Asamān-SamānAsamān-Trividh-Bhāv-Dhāran-Aatmikā-Sādhārana-Asādhāran-Sādhārana-Asādhāran-Dharmatva-Shakti*): Ātmā has three types of attributes with respect to other substances. They are identical *dharmas*, non-identical *dharmas*, and both identical and non-identical *dharmas* simultaneously. These attributes are also known as ordinary, special as well as ordinary and special simultaneously. Thus *swa* (self) and *par* (other five substances) are *sāmān (*similar) in the sense of *astitva* (existence), *vastutva* (substance-like), and *prameyatva* (knowable by others). Yet, *jñāna* (knowledge) is there in ātmā only and is *a-sāmān (*not present) in the five other substances. The *a-sāmān* (dissimilar) is also called *a-sādhāran* (not-normal). Finally the non-physical attribute exists of ātmā as well as Ākāshtikaya and *dharmastikāya* and *adharmāstikāya* but this is not an attribute of matter (*pudgal*). Therefore, this attribute corresponds to *SādhāranaAsādhāran* type.

27. **विलक्षण-अनन्त-स्वभाव-भावित-एक-भाव-लक्षणा-अनंत-धर्मत्व-शक्ति**

(*Vilakshan-Anant-Swabhāv-Bhāvit-Aik-Bhāva-Lakshanā-Anant-Dharmatva-Shakti*): Ātmā has infinite *shaktis* with different characteristics, but there is one *chaitanya* (consciousness) root that has all these *dharmatva shaktis*.

28. **तद-तद्रूप-मयत्व-लक्षणा-विरुद्ध-धर्मत्व-शक्ति**

(*Tad-Tadrupa-Mayatva-Lakshnaa-Virudhha-Dharmatva-Shakti*): Ātmā has the property to know but does not have knowable entities. There are two *shaktis* that are contradictory to each other: *tad-Tadroop-mayatva* and *a-tadrup-mayatva. Tad* refers to ātmā that has *gyayak swabhav* (one which wants to know), and *a-tad* means that it does not have anything *gyeya* (which needs to be known by others). This again strongly supports the holographic model of ātmā because a hologram only has information and does not have any of the five substances.

29. **तद्रूप-भवन-रूपातत्त्व-शक्ति**

(*Tadroop-Bhavan-Roopa Tattva-Shakti*): Due to this *tadroop* power, ātmā is *tadroop* in its own *dravya-kṣetra-kāla-bhāva* (substance-field or place-time essence). Its *parinaman* is defined through these four parameters. It does not contain any *raga* (passion). Again, this property shows that an ātmā has its own structure, and functions. Thus, it has its own identity.

30. **अतद्रूप-भवन-रूपा-अतत्व-शक्ति**

(*Atadroop-Bhāvan-Rupā-Atatva-Shakti*): Due to this power, ātmā cannot be another *atma's dravya-kṣetra-kāla-bhāva roop* or inanimate *roop.* This also shows that an ātmā does not have other substances in it. This further clearly establishes shakti number twenty-nine quite clearly.

31. **अनेक-पर्याय-व्यापक-एक-द्रव्य-मयत्व-रूपा-एकत्व-शक्ति**

(*Anek-Paryāya-Vyāpak-Aik-Dravya-Mayatva-Roopa Aikatva-Shakti*) Although there are infinite *paryāyas* of infinite *shaktis* associated with ātmā dravya, but only one single ātmā dravya is present in all infinite *paryāyas* of all infinite *shaktis.* This further supports the holographic structure because there is only one single hologram, but it has infinite attributes.

32. **एक-द्रव्य-व्याप्य-अनेक-पर्याय-मयत्व-रूपा-अनेकत्व-शक्ति**

(*Aik-Dravya-Vyāpya-Anek-Paryāya-Mayatva-Roopa Anekatva-Shakti*): Due to this *shakti, ātmā dravya* pervades all infinite *paryāyas* of all infinite *shaktis.* Again, this property shows the other side of the thirty-first property. It means that all the infinite attributes have the same holographic content.

33. **भूत-अवस्थत्व-रूपाभाव-शक्ति**
(*Bhuta-Avasthatva-Roopa-Bhāva-Shakti*): Due to this *bhāva shakti*, some *nirmal paryāya* (without any physical form) in a current pure form is always there in all infinite *shaktis* at any time. This again confirms the oscillatory nature (*nirmal paryāya*) of the infinite *shaktis* in all time domains at a very fundamental level.

34. **शून्य-अवस्थत्व-रूपा-अभाव-शक्ति**
(*Shunya-Avasthtva-Roopa-Abhāva -Shakti*): In ātmā, when *nirmal paryāya* is there, then it has no *bhāva karma* or other *paryāyas.* This further establishes the holographic structure, because ātmā does not have any attribute that may lead to its having anything else in it (of the universe).

35. **भवत्य-पर्याय-व्यय-रूपा-भाव-अभाव-शक्ति**
(*Bhāvatya-Paryāya-Vyaya-Roopa-Bhāva-Abhāva-shakti*): There is a power in the ātmā known as *bhāva-abhāva shakti,* which causes a *paryāya* that is *bhāv-roop* at present will become *abhāv-roop* in the next instant (*samay*). This clearly indicates the wave nature of *shaktis* due to which the current oscillation disappears in the next instant (*samay*) and a new oscillation appears.

36. **अभवत-पर्यायोदय-रूपा-अभाव-भाव-शक्ति**
(*Abhavāt-Paryayodaya-Roopā-Abhāva-Bhāva-Shakti*): A pure form (*nirmal paryāya*) that is not present at a given *samay* (whose *a-bhāva* is there at a given time) will exist in the next *samay*: its *bhāva* will be there in the next *samay*. This again indicates the wave nature of *shaktis*, due to which an oscillation that is not present at a given instant (*samay*) will appear in the next *samay.*

37. **भवत्पर्याय-भवन-रूपा-भाव-भाव-शक्ति**
(*Bhāvat-Paryāya-Bhawan-Roopa-Bhāva-Bhāva Shakti*) Due to this power, a *paryāya* of one type will remain the same throughout the time domain. This property indicates the independence of waves. It means that these *paryāyas* of one type of wave will remain the same over time (all three-time domains).

38. **अभवत्पर्याय-भवन-रूपा-अभाव-अभाव-शक्ति**
(*Abhāvata-paryāya-Bhavan-Roopa-Abhāv-Abhāva Shakti*): Due to this power, the ātmā's parinaman is without any *vikar swabhav*, and its *parinaman* will remain without *vikār* in the future also. This doubly confirms the independence of ātmā from other substances of the universe.

39. **कारक-अनुगत-क्रिया-निष्क्रान्त-भवन-मात्र-मयी-भाव-शक्ति**
(*Kāraka-Anugata-Kriyā-Nishkrānt-Bhawan-Mātra-Mayee-Bhāva-Shakti*) Due to this power, a *nirmal paryāya* of a *shakti* of ātmā will never have any *bhāva* of a *paryāya* of *raga* (*vikar-paryāya*), which involves six *kārakas*. Details of *kārakas* are given later. Any *vikrit paryāya* of one *samaya* with rāga has six *kārakas* contained in it. This *malin paryāya* is itself a *kriya* (activity) of this *paryāya;* this *paryāya* is itself karma (action) for this *paryāya*; *this paryāya* itself is *kartā* (doer) of this *shubha-ashubha paryāya;* this *paryāya* is itself kāran (reason) for this *paryāya*; this *paryāya* is also *sampradan* (giver of this *paryāya*); and this *paryāya* is also itself *apadan* (taker of this *paryāya*) for this *paryāya.* Hence, it appears that this concept of *paryāya* is an ultimate and final entity that has all the attributes required for describing its own total attributes. It implies some kind of a cyclic process so that no further reductionism is possible. This ultimate entity moves around and around ad infinitum, which seems to be a self-organised dynamic structure that may

also involve some topological structure. Similar kārakas would be there for a *nirmal paryāya* as well. They could be similar to closed strings.

40. **कारक-अनुगत-भवत्ता-रूप-भाव-मयी-क्रिया-शक्ति** (*Kārak-Anugat-Bhavatta-Roop-Bhāva-Mayee-Kriyā Shakti*): Due to *shath kārakas* of *dravya,* a *paryāya* that is having *parinaman* is *kriya (activity) shakti.* The thirty-ninth *shakti* holds that a *nirmal paryaāya* is completely free from *vikrit paryāya* of *raga* containing six *kārakas.*

41. **प्राप्य-माण-सिद्ध-रूप-भाव-मयी-कर्म-शक्ति** (*Prāpya-Maan-Siddha-Roopa-Bhāva-Mayee-Karma-Shakti*): *Karma* (here it means action and not pudgal karma) like power through which a *nirmal paryāya* of ātmā dravya is acquired.

42. **भवत्ता-रूप-सिद्ध-रूप-भाव-भावकत्व-मयी-कर्त्तृ-शक्ति** (*Bhavatta-Roopa-Siddha-Roopa-Bhāva-Bhāvakatva-Mayee-Kartri-Shakti*): *Kartritva* (*or Karta that is doer*) *shakti* induces *bhāva-mayee bhāva*, resulting in the *nirmal paryāya* of all *shaktis*. Once one attempts to acquire *nirmal paryāya*s, then the corresponding *bhāvas* are produced by a *kartritva shak*ti.

43. **भवद-भाव-भवन-साधकतमत्व-मयी-करण-शक्ति** (*Bhavad-bhāva-Bhavan-Sādhak-Tamatva-Mayee-Karan-Shakti*): Due to this *shakti*, ātmā alone is responsible for *nirmal pariniti-roop kriya*. The action going on in the current *nirmal paryāya* is due to the *karana (cause) shakti*, which is a result of continually focusing on the *nirmal bhāva* (*bhāva bhana*). This *karana shakti* is *sādhaktam karana shakti* (*shakti* proceeded by focused intent or discipline).

44. **स्वयं-दीयमान-भाव-उपयेत्व-मयी-सम्प्रदान-शक्ति** (*Swayam-Deeyamān-Bhāva-upayetva-Mayee-Sampra-daan-Shakti*): *Sampradan shakti* is such that due to this

shakti, an ātmā is the giver as well as taker of the *nirmal paryāya* in the same unit of *samaya.*

45. **उत्पाद-व्यय-आलंगित-भाव-अपाय-निरपाय-ध्रुवत्व-मयी-अपादान-शक्ति** (*Utpād-Vyaya-Ālangit-Bhāva-Apāya-Nirpāya-Dhruvatva-Mayee-Apādān-Shakti*): Due to this *shakti*, new *nirmal paryāya* is produced from the *dhruva* (immovable or permanent) portion of ātmā dravya. This *apadan shakti* is such that it is a source of both *dhruva upaadan* and *kṣanik* (momentary) *upādan*, and both are produced by this shakti. This kārak implies some kind of separation from something. The *trikālik guna* (tri-temporal feature) is *dhruva upādan*, whereas a current *nirmal paryāya* (present during a given *samay*) has *utpad-vyaya* and is ālangit (embraced) with *Dhruva* (permanence), but is a *kṣanik upādan.*

46. **भाव्य-मान-भाव-आधारत्व-मयी-अधिकरण-शक्ति** (*Bhāvya-Mān-Bhāva-Adharatva-Mayee-Adhikaran-Shakti*): It is due to this *shakti* that ātmā dravya produces *nirmal paryāya* and all other six *nirmal kārakas*. Therefore, this is the *bhāva* that is *bhāvne-layak* (a feeling that is worth adopting).

कारक-अनुगत-भवत्ता-रूप-भाव-मयी क्रिया शक्ति:
(*Karak-Anugat-Bhavta-Roop-Bhava-Mayee Kriya Shakti*):
Six types of karkas associated with karmas and aatma.
They indicates a topological like structure at basic level

SN	Karaka Type	Equivalent word in English	Meaning in Hindi
1	कर्ता	Doer	ने
2	कर्म	Work	पुरुषार्थ
3	करण	Resource	से, द्वारा (साधन)
4	सम्प्रदान	For whom or to whom	को दिया या के लिये किया
5	अपादान	From where	से
6	अधिकरण	Support	आधार
7	क्रिया	Total Action	किसी भी क्रिया में छहों कारक शामिल होते है

Figure 4: Structure of *Karkas* Associated with *Karmas* and Ātmā

47. स्वाभाव-मात्र-स्व-स्वामित्व-मयी-सम्बन्ध-शक्ति (*Swabhāv-Mātra-Swa-Swāmitva-Mayee-Sambandh-Shakti*): Due to this *shakti, ātmā dravya* is of *shudha parinati* (pure blossoming, fulfilment or manifestation) and not the *swamy* (master) of *shubh-ashubh parinati*. It emphasises the realisation of oneself that is *swabhāv-mātra* (only one is oneself). This again strongly supports the hologram-like structure because *shubh* and *ashubh bhāvas* are all associated with the vector space "A", whereas the vector space "D" has only information about these *bhāvas*. Therefore, it is advisable to focus only on this *shuddha bhāva* (vector space "D"), and not *shubh* and *ashubh bhāvas* (vector space "A").

Universal Rewriting System, Nil-Potent Quantum Mechanics and Jain Concept of Ātmā

The universal rewriting system is based on the assumption that "zero" is the foundation of reality. Hence, if one starts writing any alphabet, then its inverse is automatically and simultaneously written in the rest of the universe such that the total "sum" is zero. This writing system has been used to study a fermion and the corresponding quantum vacuum such that the total sum is zero. It has led to a new branch of quantum mechanics known as nilpotent quantum mechanics[14]. If the fermion is described using a vector space "A," then its dual vector space "D" is an exact mirror image and will describe the inverse of it. Yet the information content of the two vector spaces is exactly the same (but in different formats), and both can contain local and non-local information. However, the vector space "D" is not observable. I have extended this formalism to the constituents of the whole Universe because this formulation of electron and its vacuum is scale free. So, a pure ātmā has all information of all constituents of the Universe, but is not physically observable. As we shall see this scientific formulation of physics is very close to Jain philosophy and both formalisms use the same word "mirror" for the two states of reality "say electron and its corresponding vacuum" and "ātmā and the corresponding Universe", which is being described. Both "electron's vacuum" and ātmā have significant information about the corresponding electron (in the first case) and Universe (in the second case). Details are given in the following Figures 5 and 6.

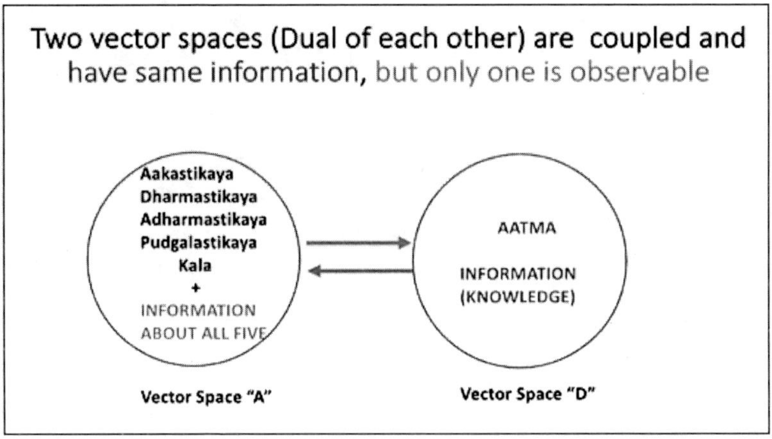

Figure 5: Vectors Depicting Local and Non-Local Information

Universal Rewriting System and Jain Concept of Aatma

- Vector space "A" will consist of Akashastikaya, Dharmastikaya, Adharmastikaya, and Kala along with all information about their movements and dynamic nature.
- Vector space "D' which is dual of vector space "A' will consist of just aatma only and will not have any of substance contained in vector space "A".
- The two vector spaces will have exactly the same information but in a different format. Information-wise the two will be exact mirror images of each other.
- Information or knowledge is nothing but patterns of movement or changes in states of all five substances (parinaman) in vector space "A".
- Both local and non-local information will be contained in two vector spaces.

Figure 6: Difference in Format of Local and Non-Local Information Vectors

Quantitative Evidence that Ancient Jain Acharyas Tried to Estimate the Size of Smallest Particles of Matter which is Quite Close to Modern Scientific Measurements of Atoms and Nuclei

This model of Jainism has remarkable parallels with the Relativistic Quantum Holographic (RQH) model of consciousness developed in modern science. The infinite *shaktis* are almost independent but are weakly coupled non-linearly and may correspond to infinite frequencies of a hologram. The concept of dual vector spaces of topology with zero sum developed for nil-potent quantum physics helps in distinguishing ātma from all other substances including pudgal (matter). *Keval jnana* and *samudghat* are then explainable on the basis of non-local information due to quantum entanglement whereas a worldly ātma will always have local and non-local information.

One of the most important aspects of the Jain concept of ātman is its parapsychic capacity for telepathy and clairvoyance, known as *avadhi jnana* (clairvoyance) and *manahparyaya jnana (telepathy)* in Jain literature. They are also known as *pratikshya jnana* in contrast to *paroksha jnana* like *mati jnana* and *shruta jnana*. We have found important evidence of this *pratyaksha jnana* from *Triloya Pannati*, which concerns the possibility of directly observing the microscopic particles of matter like atoms and nuclei. The rough estimates of sizes of these particles made by ancient Jain ācharyas are remarkably close to the size of atoms and nuclei as estimated in current physics.

This example is taken from ancient Jain scriptures[iv], which indirectly indicates that direct observations of microscopic particles of matter like atoms, nuclei and even quarks are possible through clairvoyance. Table 1 gives a list of measurement of length. It starts from the smallest particle of matter (known as a *paramāṇu* in Jainism, a term which is different from *paramāṇu* defined in modern science) and goes up to one Yojana (a commonly used unit of length, prevalent in India even now). It indicates that ancient Jain ācharyas made an attempt to develop a table for measurement of length in twenty steps. There is an octal system till step twelve.

S.No.	Measure of First Length	Measure of Second Length
1	Infinitely many *paramāṇus* =	1 *Avasannasanna skandha*
2	8 *Avasannasanna* units =	1 *Sannasanna* skandha
3	8 *Sannasanna* units =	1 *Trutreṇu*
4	8 *Trutreṇu* units =	1 *Trasareṇu*
5	8 *Trasareṇu* units =	1 *Rathareṇu*
6	8 *Rathareṇu* units =	1 *Uttama bhogbhūmi bālāgra* (U.b.b.)
7	8 U.b.b. units =	1 *Madhyama bhogbhūmi bālāgra* (M.b.b.)
8	8 M.b.b. units =	1 *Jaganya bhogbhūmi bālāgra* (J.b.b.)
9	8 J.b.b. units =	1 *Karma bhūmi bālāgra* (K.b.b.)
10	8 K.b.b. units =	1 *Liksā*
11	8 *Liksā* units =	1 *Yūkā*
12	8 *Yūkā* units =	1 *Yava* (Barley com)
13	8 *Yava* units =	1 *Angula* (Finger breadth)
14	6 *Angula* units =	1 *Pāda* (Barley com)
15	2 *Pāda* units =	1 *Vitasti*
16	2 *Vitasti* units =	1 *Hasta* (Forearm)
17	2 *Hasta* units =	1 *Rikku* or *Kisku*
18	2 *Kisku* units =	1 *Daṇda* or *Dhanus* (Bow)
19	2000 *Daṇdas* units =	1 *Krosa*
20	4 *Krosa* units =	1 *Yojana*

Table 1: Measurement of Length as Found in Jain Literature

Here a *paramāṇu* has been defined as the smallest particle of matter, having no length, no breadth and no height. This is defined as a particle which can be only thought of but is not practically perceivable. This is similar to a parton (a point-like particle in momentum space, introduced in modern physics). The particle which is perceivable is a group of *paramānus*. The smallest *skandha* (division) is an *avasannasanna skandha*. Let us therefore estimate its size by roughly taking the average width of a finger to be equal to 2 cm. We can therefore write the following simple formula:

- Size of an *angula* is = 8^{12} of the size of an *avasannasanna skandha*.
- So size of an *avasannasanna skandha* is = 8^{-12} cm
- Which is equal to 2.9×10^{-11} cm.

This estimate of 2.9×10^{-11} cm is the size of the smallest particle of matter in Jainism; it lies between the size of an atom which is of the order of 10^{-8} cm. and the size of a nucleus, which is of the order of 10^{-13} cm. It is very clear that the estimate made for the smallest particle of matter by Jain Ācharyas through clairvoyance is most remarkable and it shows the power of clairvoyance. This possibility is also supported by the capability of *avadhi jñāna* in general and *Vardhman avadhi jñāna* and *Apratipati avadhi jñāna* in particular as they are very stable types of clairvoyance and are probably used in seeing the smallest particles of matter. Looking at the limitations of the tools which were available at that time and used for developing this table, one can say that this result is statistical in nature, but even this agreement with the size of an atom and size of a nucleus is striking. At least it cannot be ignored. The mere fact that it was arrived at from the *Avadhi Jñāna* (clairvoyance) at advanced level through which one can see even up to the smallest particle of space known as a *pradeśa* in Jainism, should be a very exciting observation. This again shows that the Jain concept of knowledge should be taken seriously by the scientific community and should be further explored.

Possibility of Direct Observations of Atoms, Nuclei, Quarks and Sub-Quarks Through Clairvoyance: Occult Chemistry Developed by Annie Besant and Her Team Provides More Evidence of a Holographic Structure of an Ātmā

This has further motivated me to take this result to search for similar studies being done by some other investigators. In this section, I describe another example of directly viewing the microscopic particles of matter through clairvoyance by Annie Besant. C.W. Leadbeater and her team (1908) about a century ago. To my surprise, it has been found that Annie Besant, and her colleagues tried to use *anima siddhi* to see the structure of atoms and nuclei as early as 1895 and until about 1932, that is around one hundred years ago. They saw the structure of ninety-two elements of the periodic table, that is from hydrogen to uranium which were available at that time. The description of these structures is available in the report by Annie Besant, Leadbeater and C. Jinarajdas[v].

Summary of Work of Annie Besant and Co-Workers

Particles which can be considered as the ultimate, smallest constituent of matter have been a subject of prime importance in modern physics as well as in ancient philosophies. Ancient Greeks, using logic as the basic tool, visualised atoms as the primary constituents of all matter and Democritus proposed the atomic theory, which later, in the early Nineteenth century, was developed by a British scholar, John Dalton and is known as Dalton's atomic theory[vi]. Indian seers, especially Jains, using meditative techniques, described *paramānus*, extremely small, indivisible, dimensionless particles as the primary particles of matter, and developed the *pudgal* theory of aggregation and dissociation to explain all physical matter in the universe[vii]. The standard model of particle physics considers quarks as the smallest constituent of hadrons, whereas electrons are the smallest constituents of leptons. Particles smaller than quarks, termed as sub-quarks have been also conceptualised and studied[viii, 17] but have not yet been observed.

Annie Besant and co-workers, over a hundred years ago (around 1908: 1895 to 1932) used the clairvoyant technique of *Anima Siddhi* described in Patanjali Yoga sutra[ix] to 'see' the smallest particles of matter, present in 92 elements and many molecules. These particles were named as *Anu-s*[v]. This work was published in the book *Occult chemistry*[8], and in a series of papers and journals of the Theosophical Society. In spite of the fact that several predictions of their work came true as scientific techniques developed, still the work of Annie Besant, Charles Leadbeater and C. Jinrajdas (ABC in short for later use) was largely ignored, being regarded as a hoax or fraud (Yale University, 1999).

Anima Siddhi Technique of Yoga

"*Anima Siddhi* is the ability to reduce one's conscious body to the smallest possible size. This *siddhi* offers the practitioner the practical knowledge and understanding of the most delicate interconnections of matter, space and energy, and the ability to manipulate it. A psychic power associated with this *siddhi* is the ability to control the density of an object or of one's body, such that one could walk through solid matter"[x]. According to the Jain philosophy a living being has three permanent and two transient bodies. The permanent bodies are *audarak* body, i.e., the physical body, *tejas* or energy body (responsible for metabolic activity) and *Karman* body (which possibly has records of all physical and mental activities of an individual). The transient bodies are conscious bodies, that is *aharak sharir* and *vaikriyik sharir*. It appears that clairvoyance developed through *anima siddhi* involves *vaikriyik sharir*. *Vaikriyik sharir* may be an astral body-like entity. The size of this *vaikriyik* body can be reduced or enlarged and it can be transported to distant regions also with one's wishes or intention.

Brief Details of the Work of Annie Besant and Her Team

We will now discuss the work of Annie Besant et al (1908, described in *Occult Chemistry* and related publications during 1905-1932). The way ABC saw the constituents of atoms is described in detail in *Occult Chemistry*[V]. We quote here the method of observing the atoms from this book:

> *The method is unique and difficult to explain. Many have heard of the word "clairvoyance" ("clear seeing", connoting the cognition of sights and sounds not perceived by ordinary people). In India, the term Yoga is sometimes related to faculties that are beyond ordinary cognition. It is stated in the Indian yoga system that one who has trained himself (say with anima siddhi), "can make himself infinitely small at will". This does not mean that he undergoes a diminution in size of physical body, but as mentioned earlier, (most probably), it is his vakriyik sharir (astral body) only that can be reduced to very small size. So relatively his conception of himself can be minimised so that objects which are normally small, appear to him/her as quite large. The two investigators have been trained by their Eastern Gurus to exercise this unique faculty of Yoga so that when they observed a chemical atom, it appeared to their vision as highly magnified.*
>
> *When using this method, the investigator is awake and not in any form of trance. He/She employs his/her usual faculties for recording what he observes; he/she maps out on a piece of paper as sketch and may describe his impressions so that a draftsman-cum-stenographer can take down his remarks. Just as a person, looking into the microscope and without removing his eyes from the slide, can describe what he observes so that it can be recorded. So the clairvoyant investigator watching an atom or molecule can describe what he sees in front of*

him. What he sees is not subjective, in the sense that it is not a creation of imagination.

The object examined, whether an atom or a compound is seen exactly as it exists normally, that is to say, it is not under any stress caused by an electric or a magnetic field. As each object is in rapid motion, the only force brought to bear on it is a special form of will-power, so as to make its movement slow enough to observe the details." It means using the power of concentration, one can control the motion of these particles which move almost with the velocity of light or so.

ABC claimed that through the power of clairvoyance, they had seen the smallest particles of matter for the hydrogen atom, to begin with[v]. They found that the hydrogen atom consisted of 18 constituents (Fig.7) known as *Anu*, name of the smallest physical particle of matter in Hinduism. They have actually seen six subgroups having a spherical shape, each of the spheres containing three *anu-s*. These six spheres are distributed in two triangular structures (Fig.7). Similarly, they saw the *anuic* structures of ninety-two elements of the Periodic table, which were known at that time. In today's terminology, they can be tentatively compared with quarks or even sub-quarks, but more work is required to understand their status and significance in modern physics. They also observed micro-structure of *anu*, known as strings and even their sub-components. Thus, the *anu* was enlarged by more concentrated clairvoyance and was found to be consisting of vortex-like structures having 10 strings, interwoven in complicated ways (Fig. 8). The circles shown in this figure (Fig. 7) are actually spheres and are in constant motions of different types, and groups of *anu-s* are interconnected and also have motions of different types. In the process of observation, clairvoyants could slow down the speed of the *anu-s* quite significantly through their will power of consciousness. Now this group of six spheres is enclosed in a shell, surrounded by some type of matter. The positive and negative signs on the *anu-s* do not represent charge but are supposed to indicate clockwise and anticlockwise movements. A very detailed description of structures of atoms of 92 elements is available in the book *Occult Chemistry* (2003)[v]. Based on their work spanning nearly 30 years, ABC made several predictions, many of them were verified later as scientific research progressed. We list some of them below:

- ABC predicted the existence of some elements which have isotopes, a fact not known at that time, and were discovered decades later.
- They visualised Helium, whose structure was not discovered by that time. ABC found that it has three nucleons (9 anu-s). Soon thereafter when the structure of helium was determined, it was found to consist of four nucleons. Initially the claims of ABC were considered erroneous. but, subsequently, another (though less abundant) isotope of helium, i.e. He3 was discovered, substantiating the structure seen by ABC. Similar is the story of Krypton-81 (Kr81). The stable isotopes of krypton in order of their abundance are 84, 86, 82, 83, 80 and 78, and the mass given by ABC was 81. Kr81 was not known at that time. Discovered subsequently in 1950[xi], Kr81 was found to be radioactive with a half-life of 0.23 million years and thus there is truth in what ABC could see.
- Besides atoms of various elements, ABC also observed structures of many molecules and anu-s of ether which fills the universe. Actually, they observed four types of ethers, made up of various types of complex structures of anu-s, which probably correspond to dark matter and dark energy[1].

Critical Investigation of ABC Work by Prof. Stephen Phillips and Others

This work was first studied by Stephen Phillips, an English particle physicist from London who found it amazingly accurate. We have critically examined this work and found that what ABC have seen are quarks and their constituents which were impossible to even imagine a hundred years ago as the concept of quarks was introduced in 1960 by Gellman. Prof. Stephen Phillips[18,19] studied this work in great detail and found in it support for his theory of sub-quarks also. But his assumption that two nuclei collided to produce a microscopic psi atom does not appear to be correct as it is observed that what Clairvoyants had seen were individual atoms. This assumption of Stephen Phillips was criticised by Y.H. Dobyns[20] who also reviewed the paper of Stephen Phillips[19]. Otherwise his attempt is admirable. His argument that the circular rings around *anu-s* might be similar to superstrings of particle physics is a very powerful argument. A similar study was carried out by Prof. J. Michael McBride of Yale University (1999), but it was not conclusive, as no explanation was given as to where the number 18 for the hydrogen atom had come from. Some more studies were also carried out by Arnikar[3] and Billimoria[21] and Jawaharlal Shah[22] also mentioned the *anu* like structure in his thesis for PhD submitted to Gujarat Vidhyapeeth, Ahmedabad.

Comparison of Predictions of ABC Using Quark's Rest Masses and Quantum Units of the TDVP Model

Hence Pokharna et al[23,24] have reexamined the work of Annie Besant and co-workers, along with the arguments of Stephen Phillips, in the light of Jain Agamas and the model of Neppe and Close[25]. In the TDVP model, Neppe and Close[25] have used the masses of up quarks and down quarks and normalised them with respect to the mass of the electron and called them Quantum Units (Table 2). As per the studies carried out in the Large Hadron Collider and other sources, it is found that rest masses of electrons, up quark and down quark are respectively found to be 0.51 Mev/c^2, 2.01 Mev/c^2 and 4.79 Mev/c^2. If the mass of an electron is taken as 1 then dividing the masses of two quarks by this value of 0.51 Mev/c^2 and making the result equal to the nearest integer, one finds normalised mass/energy values as 4 for up quark and 9 for down quark respectively. These values of 4 and 9 are treated as multiples (integers) of the smallest quantum unit, required to generate a stable proton. As a proton has two up quarks and one down quark, so their total normalised mass/energy values in whole numbers is 17 (4x2 + 9). Thus, for a proton, a value of 17 is the normalised mass. By similar analysis, the normalised mass values for neutrons have been found to be 22. For Hydrogen if this value for proton is combined with normalised mass value of 1 for electron, then one finds a total value of 18 for hydrogen (Table 2 in this study and Table 13 (A-H1), page 65 in Close and Neppe[22]. Hence 18 units in the case of a hydrogen atom can be taken as 18 quantum units for mass.

These masses are actually in terms of electron mass units but we prefer to call them as quantum units (QU), a term used by Neppe, Pokharna and Close[25]. Thus rest masses of particles like quarks (Table 2) and elements (Z = 1 for hydrogen up to 92 for uranium), depending on the number and type of quarks they contain, can be expressed in terms of quantum units. We can also find the number of anu-s in different elements based on clairvoyant data of ABC, which are available in the Appendix of Annie Besant et. al.[v]. It has been found that the number of *anu-s* observed by ABC for 92 elements is remarkably close to the number of quantum units for these elements. The correlation coefficient calculated by Neppe et al[25] is found to be 0.9996 (Fig. 9), which is astonishing.

Constituent	**Number**	**Rest Mass in Mev/c^2**	**Normalised Mass**	**Quantum Units**
Up quark	1	2.01	2.01/0.51=3.94 ~ 4	4
Down quark	1	4.79	4.79/0.51=9.37~ 9	9
Electron	1	0.51	1	1

*Mev = Million electron volts and c is velocity of light in meters/seconds

Table 2: Rest Masses of Constituents of Hydrogen Atom-Proton (Two Quarks) and Electron Along with Their Normalised Rest Masses with Respect to Electron Rest Mass

Constituents	Number	Total Quantum Units
Up Quarks	2	8
Down Quark	1	9
Electron	1	1
Total Quantum Units of Hydrogen	1	18

Table 3: Exact Structure of Hydrogen Atom and its Normalised Rest Mass

Average percent in difference was computed using the following formula:

- Average percent difference = Sum over number of atoms of (Quantum Units – Number of *Anu-s*) × 100/ (Quantum Units)

Pokharna et al[23,24] have shown that for twenty elements, the number of *anu-s* seen by clairvoyants and the number of quantum units calculated from the normalised rest masses of up quarks and down quarks were closely related and there was only an average normalised difference of 8.80 per cent. The average percentage of difference between the *anu-s* and quantum units for 92 elements is found to be +8.64 per cent when electrons are not taken into account. Details of data and Tables are given in Pokharna[1]. The positive sign implies that the number of quantum units is always higher. In the case of hydrogen these two are equal (=18), since electrons are included. In electron free calculation, quantum units will be 17, ~ +6 per cent less than the number of *anu-s*. This low percentage error is most remarkable in view of the fact that these data come from two entirely different sources. However, one should be careful about equating these numbers of quantum units and corresponding number of *anu-s*. The comparison is meaningful in the sense that the *anu* in the ABC model is known as the smallest physical particle, whereas in the TDVP model, the quantum unit is the smallest physical unit of normalised rest mass for quarks. Hence, they look similar and one can say that a quantum unit corresponds to the smallest physical particle and it could be just a part of a quark. The close match between *anu* and the number of QU in various atoms gives credence to clairvoyance technique. A detailed statistical analysis of the difference of these parameters has been presented by Neppe, Pokharna and Close[25].

The numbers of *Anu-s* and quantum units in various elements have been clearly obtained by unrelated, and independent approaches, the first by clairvoyant techniques and the second by a theoretical physical model. This has huge implications. This agreement can be taken as a proof of the correctness of the clairvoyant technique with *anima siddhi*, unknown to scientific methodology, and gives credibility to the work of ABC. It also implies that an *anu* has a mass quite close to that of an electron.

A Possible Explanation of this Avadhi-jñāna (Clairvoyance) Using the Concept of Quantum Hologram

The observation made by ABC can be explained through the theory of Quantum Hologram. As we know, in quantum hologram, each material particle has its own quantum hologram in the zero-point field. Hence the *anu-s* and their groups also have their own quantum holograms in the zero-point field. These Quantum Holograms will have all histories of their source particles and systems, that is all the quantum states that ever existed in them and this does not attenuate with time. Simultaneously observers like Annie Besant and Leadbeater also have their quantum holograms present in the zero-point field. It appears that using the *anima siddhi*, when attention is being focused by an observer on the *anu* then the two quantum holograms interact in such a way that they can influence each other and they will develop resonance (Phase Conjugate Adaptive Resonance = PCAR[13]) because of which transfer of information can take place through the quantum hologram of the observer to the quantum hologram of the *anu-s*, atom or quark and also vice-versa that is transfer of information from the anu-s, atom or quark to the observer. As the living being will have more coherence, the observer will be able to influence the quantum hologram of the object (*anu-s* atom or quark here). So, the claim made by the ABC team that they could control the speed of the *anu-s* through focusing is correct as this can be done by influencing the QH of anu-s atoms or quarks through this PCAR. As the QH contains all history of the quantum states of the corresponding system, all details can be extracted through the PCAR. This is what appears to be a mechanism for getting information from the sub-quarks-like particles to the human consciousness. The information involved is non-local but there seems to be another mechanism through which the information gathered is transferred to the physical brain also and hence it is ultimately transferred to Annie Besant and Leadbeater and finally to the draftsman Jinrajdasa, through oral communication, and he finally draws pictures on the paper. It is also mentioned that Annie Besant and Leadbeater could even retain the structure of anu-s in their minds like a film for some time. This is also possible as one can always have access to one's hologram for a fairly long time, till some decoherent factor arises and disturbs it or attention is taken away from this.

The concept of 47 *shaktis* of Jain ātmā has another similarity in the concept of the two-vector space concept of Nilpotent Quantum Mechanics[16] also. As their formalism is scale free, we straight away extend it to the whole Universe and its contents. The corresponding vacuum state could be the zero-point field. The two vector spaces are dual of each other and both have the same information. So, it appears that the dual vector space "D" has knowledge of all atoms and quarks in the Universe whose description is there in vector space "A". The vector space "D" is under control of the observer who can influence the motion of anu-s, atoms and the quarks. Further investigation is in progress.

The concept of *avadhijnana* can be explained as the storage of non-local information in the vacuum field or zero-point field.

Jainism Strongly Supports This Possibility

Jainism strongly supports this possibility in view of extensive description of different types of *avadhijñāna* and their capabilities to see even the smallest space regions of ātmā that is an aatma-*pradeśas* as well as the whole *lokaakash*. Through the Vardhman *avadhijñāna* and *apratipati avadhijñāna.* Hence the observations made by Jain Ācharyas and Annie Besant are also vindicated by this claim.

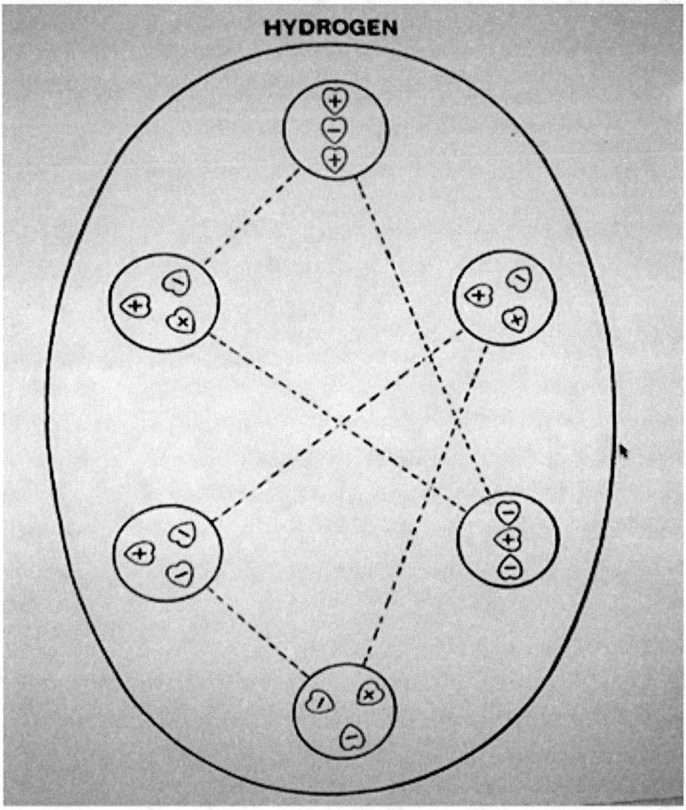

*There are six big spheres each having three small spheres viz. three *anu-s,* 18 in all, nine are of positive type and the other nine are of negative type [from ABC, 2003)].

Figure 7: Structure of Hydrogen Atom as Seen Through Clairvoyance

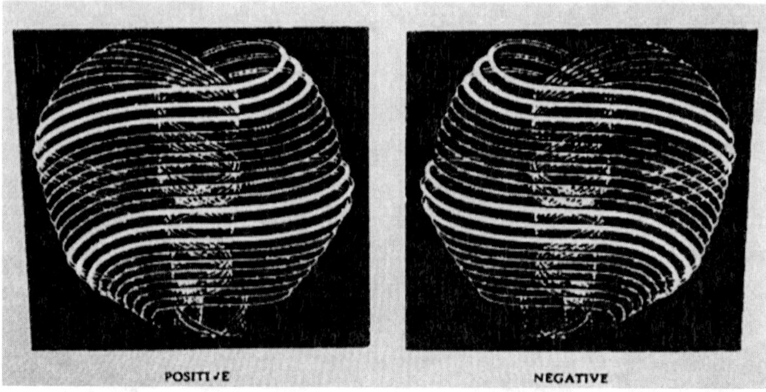

*The 10 lines (3 thick and 7 thin lines) are strings, similar to the strings of the strings model [reproduced from ABC, 1907].

Figure 8: Two Different Types of Vortices Moving in Opposite Directions

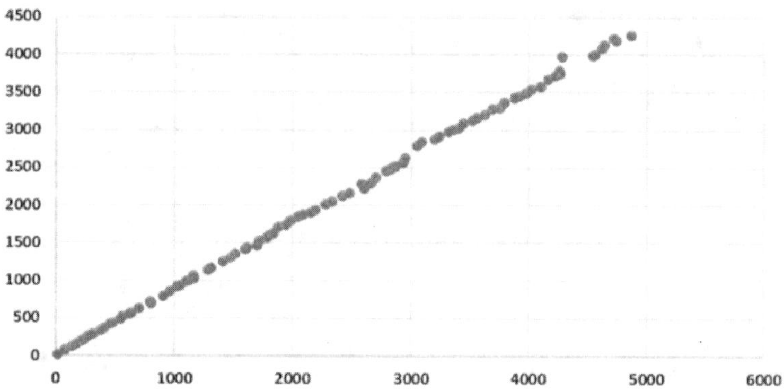

Figure 9: Scatter Plot Between Number of Quantum Units (X-axis) and Number Anu-s (Y-axis) for 92 Elements

Some Inferences and Hypotheses

From these results, the following inferences and hypothesis may be formulated:

1. Clairvoyance of microscopic particles is a hard reality and the concepts of *avadhi jñāna* of attributes of matter

at *pradeśa* level (discrete unit of space) developed by Jain Ācharyas is confirmed by Annie Besant, Charles Leadbeater and C. Jinrajdas.

2. Claims made in the Patanjali Yoga Sutra about *Anima siddhi* are correct and confirmed by this high correlation found between number of *anu-s* and quantum units computed for 92 elements of the periodic table of chemistry.

3. The fact that the ABC team could not only "see" the microstructure of atoms and nuclei but could even control the speed of group of *anu-s* and individual *anu-s* shows, that consciousness not only possesses knowledge or a mechanism to see *anu-s* but also power to control the speed of these *anu-s*. It is similar to what one finds in the large hadron collider and other accelerators, where speeds are controlled by electric and magnetic fields. The mechanisms involved in the former case may require deep studies of *siddhis*. However, a very good hint comes from the TDVP model which discusses the impact property of consciousness through which it can influence matter and so may even influence the speed-like property of matter. Yet this does not agree with the Jain model according to which a pure ātmā cannot influence a material particle.

4. However, the other mechanism involving quantum holograms appears to work even better for explaining the whole process of these observations. Hence this should be further pursued. It may be mentioned that Edgar Mitchel and Robert Staretz[13] have argued that their concept of quantum hologram does not involve higher dimensions nor does it involve any concept of planes or another type of energy or *prāna* or anything of that sort. The whole concept works in the four dimensions (3s,1t) only. But their concept of consciousness is still meaningful in the sense that it is a total combination of all holograms present in the zero-point field and these holograms and their union represent the whole knowledge of reality.

5. This is very preliminary work and further investigations are required about the mechanism involved in the whole process which is at an exploratory stage.

Chalmer' Hard Problem Has a Solution in This Jain Holographic Model

In this Jain holographic model of ātmā, lies a reasonable solution to Chalmer's hard problem of consciousness which is having difficulty of reconciling the objective and the subjective experiences. Since ātmā has knowledge of both the external world as well as the internal world, both the objective knowledge of the external world through modern science as well as the subjective knowledge of the internal world are explained with the help of this Jain hologram which contains both these kinds of knowledge.

Discussion and Conclusion

A summary of this paper will now be given and conclusions are given as under:

1. The situation of the world has become very bad in the last fifty years because of large-scale problems in the environment like emission of greenhouse gases, overexploitation of resources (land, water, air etc.) and disappearance of thousands of biological species every year and several others. This seems to be a result of too much focus on economic development, accelerated by advancements in science and technology. The condition of the earth is worsening every day and it is moving towards what is now known as a sixth extinction. The recent attack of the coronavirus pandemic has taught us another lesson by forcing us to make a major change in our perspective on science, technology and on policies for economic development. It is also necessary to mention that although science has brought many great concepts, technologies and products, unfortunately it is not able to make an ordinary insect like an ant or even a blade of grass because they are biological conscious

entities. Hence a basic paradigm shift is required in our perspective of reality.

2. The conservation laws of physics which constitute the foundation of modern science are defined for isolated closed systems, but living systems are open, highly dynamic and strongly interacting with the surroundings and the environment. So, the space-time invariance condition generally applicable for the verifiability of a scientific hypothesis may not exactly work for studying biological systems. Hence new approaches are required for better understanding of biological systems in general and human systems in particular. The General Systems Theory is one such possible candidate which has some similarity with Indian philosophy in general and Jainism in particular, because all three of them discuss the concept of a higher goal such as *moksha* in one's life, which is a teleological notion, attributed to irreversible biological system in the General Systems Theory.

3. There are many mystical phenomena which are rare and do not fall into the domain of modern science. Thus, telepathy and clairvoyance, out-of-body travel, near death experience, living without food and water for several years and others are not recognised in modern science and appear to be beyond limitations of space and time and hence ordinary experiments in which space and time invariance is necessary may not apply. However, these phenomena do exist and so it implies that the basic concepts of science itself needs to be updated.

4. It appears that all parts of nature and reality are interconnected at various levels. This attribute is close to the concept of quantum entanglement of quantum physics at a fundamental level. Hence some kind of "order" is inbuilt in nature through this interconnectedness. The scientific approach of reductionism has distorted this point of view, broken nature into parts and is neglecting the concept of wholeness present in nature. Hence a total view of reality is required where reductionism and wholeness

are given equal importance. Many problems of the world today are directly related to this reductionist approach which has resulted in a large increase in entropy or disorder in all walks of life including, the environment and the society resulting in people becoming more and more self-centred.

5. In view of these problems and issues, many scientists now feel that there is an urgent need to understand the concept of consciousness among human beings, animals and even insects. Thousands of scientists from different disciplines are now working to understand consciousness and ātmā from different perspectives. However, extensive details are available in Jainism about an ātmā and *cetanā* which are required to understand reality. These details are very appealing and can provide new avenues of thoughts.

6. Forty-seven *shaktis* of ātmā described in Pravchan Navneet by Sadguru Pujyaniya Kānji Swamy, imply wave-like behaviour of matter as well as *shaktis* of ātmā through *utpād* (production), *vyaya* (destruction) and *dhrovya* (conservations). The Jain model of ātmā has many similarities with neuro-physiological observations also, because different types of oscillatory phenomena like breathing, heart-beat, many cellular processes, biological rhythms, alpha, beta, gamma, delta and theta waves emitted from the brain have some similarities with oscillations (*parinaman*) of different *shaktis* of ātmā and matter. The importance given to such oscillatory processes by Jain saints and Ācharyas strongly indicate that they had significant knowledge about these processes at a fundamental level. Similarly, the large number of parallel processes going on in the living bodies are similar to infinite *shaktis* of ātmā, which also appear to be operating in parallel.

7. The property of *agurulaghutva* seems to be quite close to the concept of quantum entanglement of quantum physics, which is again a very profound result of this study.

8. The concept of ātmā in Jainism that it is non-physical and has infinite properties including knowledge is a profound concept. This seems to be more general than scientific knowledge. It involves telepathy and clairvoyance and also deals with infinite knowledge as compared to scientific knowledge which appears to be finite and limited by space and time. This integrated view is a totally new concept for science and it will have far-reaching consequences.

9. The recent theory of the universal rewriting system which starts from the concept of "*shunya*" is a very attractive innovation and scientists are recognising this as the starting point of reality. This concept has been further developed to explain the properties of a fermion (an electron for example) and the corresponding quantum vacuum by one single formalism coming from "zero". This is based on what is now termed as nilpotent quantum mechanics (NQM). This formalism is based on dual vector spaces. Here, one vector space is the fermion, whereas its dual vector space concerns the corresponding quantum vacuum. The interesting point is that the information content in the two vector spaces is exactly the same but in different formats. Not only this, one of the vector spaces has physical content (fermion), whereas the dual one has only information (of the fermion) but is completely non-observable. In addition, this involves both local and non-local information. It may be mentioned that although NQM talks of electron and its vacuum state, this formalism is scale free and can work at any other scale. Hence this formalism is found to be very similar to the concept of *lokākāsha* and ātmā and its forty-seven *shaktis*, as explained in Pravchan Navneet. Not only is the concept of non-physical and non-observable ātmā explained by this formalism, but even the term "mirror" used is exactly the same in both formalisms. The corresponding term used in Jainism is "*Darpan*" (A Hindi name for mirror).

10. Therefore, the most outstanding result of this study is the recognition of remarkable similarity between the concept of quantum hologram of modern science and the concept of the Jain hologram emanating out of forty-seven *shaktis* of a pure ātmā.

11. With this formalism, it is possible to explain the clairvoyant observations of *avasanāasannā skandha* mentioned in *Triloy Pannati*. An important table for measurement of length is found in it, which starts from the smallest particles of matter and goes up to a *Yojana*. An estimate of the size of this *avasanāasannā skandha* shows that its size lies between the size of an atom and the size of a nucleus. This indicates that clairvoyance does exist and one can directly see the microscopic particles of matter through it.

12. The above hypothesis is strongly supported by the independent observations of finer structures of ninety-two elements of the periodic table through clairvoyance using *anima siddhi* by Annie Besant and her team a hundred years ago, when there was not much knowledge about the atomic structure of elements. The claim made by these occult chemists that even particles smaller than quarks could be directly seen through clairvoyance developed by *anima siddhi* and *vaikriya sharir,* is a major challenge to modern science. Such observations provide another support to the *Vardhman* and *Apratipati avadhi jñāna* mentioned in the list of six types of clairvoyance in Jain *agamas*. Details are available in Surendra Singh Pokharna (2022).

13. *Anima siddhi*-like concepts can take science to deeper levels of reality and need to be further examined.

14. Concepts of knowledge and order should be criteria of evolution in contrast to Darwin's empirical principle of evolution.

15. Several mystical phenomena might be now explainable due to this formalism of the hologram and should be further explored.

On Conscience and Smysl (Sense) or Lost in Translation

LORA RYSKELDIYEVA

Introduction

The problem of consciousness in general is one of the most relevant in modern science. Are there any specialists in this field? Does the science that studies it as a subject exist? Can psychology be considered this type of science or is a combination of sciences within the framework of cognitive research needed? I assume that I will not be mistaken if I say that there are no satisfactory answers to these questions. What do philosophical reflections on consciousness in this case come to?

At first glance, these reflections yield nothing. The word "consciousness" is understandable to any layman, it is believed that all people "in their right mind" (common sense) possess consciousness, are aware of their actions. However, European philosophy has always been attentive to consciousness (*conscience*) and everything that is associated with it: thinking, cognition, reason, intellect, etc. Moreover, successive upheavals and revolutionary changes in Western philosophical culture can be seen as shifts in metaphysics, in the ways of thinking about thinking, being aware of consciousness, carrying out higher level reflection. The details of interpretation of the correlation between consciousness and being, determine the difference between different types of philosophy and philosophers: between empiricists and rationalists, monists and pluralists, agnostics and fideists, etc. However, anything related to consciousness has acquired particular relevance in different fields of knowledge in modern days when it comes to Artificial Intelligence (AI) and

General Artificial Intelligence (GAI), when the possibility of modelling and creating programs that completely duplicate the activities of human and even public consciousness is presupposed.

Optimists of this field are waiting for breakthrough solutions and unexpected clues from the philosophy of consciousness, but their optimism is not always justified. Two main features of the modern version of metaphysics of consciousness have determined two main theses:

1. Consciousness must be reviewed in an effective/active context. This is inevitable, firstly, in view of a practical or pragmatic turn in European philosophy, and secondly, in light of the principle "the same in the other way" that corresponds to the modern interest in diverse cultural ways of thinking.
2. The activity of consciousness (awareness) must be compared with the activity in the meaning-sense sphere (comprehension). This is inevitable, firstly, in view of the "turn towards language" in European philosophy, and secondly, in light of the need to take into account the discursive specificity of the language in which thinking is carried out.

These features determine the following difficulties of thinking in this subject area:

1. Essentialism of European philosophical culture. European metaphysics is originally substantial and the problem of consciousness in its context is raised as a question of "What is consciousness?" It has no solution in this form; perhaps that is why the problem has been transferred to the experimental plane and translated into the practice of modelling or programming.
2. The connection of thought with language leads to the fact of a fundamental difference in the formation of meaning in different cultures. An example can be the difference between the European culture, where the

formation of meaning is well illustrated by Euler's circles, and the Arabic culture, that does not think in sets but in processes, as well as the Buddhist culture, where the understanding of thinking is in no way connected with the familiar function of reflection and duplication of reality in consciousness.

Consciousness is Not a Thing (Res) But a Fundamental Problem of European Philosophy

Neither the term nor the problem of consciousness are known to antiquity, however this problem is quite traditional for European philosophy: New European metaphysics originates in the Cartesian "Cogito" (I think) as the basis for asserting the reality of the world. Surprisingly, the term *conscientia* is used by Descartes rarely, on average once or twice in one work. At the same time, the main term that became specifically Cartesian is the famous Cogito and its derivatives, having meanings associated with "to think". How are these terms associated with *conscientia*?

"... *adeoque actus cogitativi, ut intelligere, velle, imaginari, sentire, omnes sub ratione communi cogitationis, sive perceptionis sive conscientiæ conveniunt, atque substantiam, cui insunt, dicimus esse rem Cogitantem*" - Descartes writes in "Reflections on the First Philosophy. Objection VII"[i]. Here is the Cartesian union of *cogital* acts of intelligence, will, imagination, and feelings (*intelligere, velle, imaginary, sentire*) in the substantive subordination to thinking (*Res Cogitans*): "whether it is perception or consciousness" meaning that any act of thinking can be either passive perception, or active consciousness. Who carries out such acts?

For Descartes the scientist the answer is obvious since he is engaged in the study of his own inner world given to him directly in the obviousness of the inner experience—the experience of the Self (Ego). The unity of this experience for Descartes is beyond question, reflecting that Ego does exist and the fundamental presumption of Cartesianism is about the dynamic activity of the Ego, available for study that is actually consciousness. Thus was born the main feature of the New European philosophy – reflective, perceptive Ego. How does it work, how does Ego think, how does consciousness work?

It is clear that the problem of consciousness sets the beginning of the entire philosophical discourse and compels us to start from the very origin, "the before" thinking, up to the realisation of the contact of the thinking with the thinkable, up to the establishment of connection between the subject and the predicate in the judgement, for it is the establishment of meanings, connections of "that" and "this", "what" and "which". Philosophical Oriental studies show the mechanism for establishing this connection is not identical in different philosophical cultures. "*The Logic of Sense*" is the name of two works: the iconic manifesto of postmodernism by J. Deleuze "*Logique du Sens*" where he leads the reader to the surface in search of depth without seeing the fundamental difference between sense and nonsense, and the philosophical work of the Arabist (expert in Arabic culture) A.V. Smirnov "*Logica Smysla*", who put forward the principle of the "same as different" or "the same in the other way" as the main principle of a translation faced with the task of finding the meaning of "this" in another language and culture: in a different culture this same sense will be expressed differently. At the same time, only options are possible, there is no invariant! There is no unified and paradigmatic sense-generating procedure for a person in general, just as there is no unified human in general.

European culture is based on the intuition of existence. It thinks substantively, essentially, in generic relations, its essence is conveyed by Euler circles and the set theory. At the same time, European thinking allows many subjects with one predicate and vice versa. Arabic-speaking culture is based on the intuition of the flow, establishing a connection between the actor and the object of action. Its logic is procedural[1], and the normative structure of the Arabic speech allows you to associate only one subject with one predicate. The logic of sense-generating procedure in Indian and European cultures is not unified but the study of ways to separate it into branches of one Indo-European root[2] and the allocation of different types of meaning formation can be considered promising. One of the main signs of detection of this challenge is the presence of "untranslatability", the search for which, according to B. Cassien[3], is a proper tool in the fight against linguistic and ideological globalisation. The success of this approach is shown by the fact that Indian philosophy has already "forced" the world culture to learn such words as *Karma*, *Nirvana*, *Samsara*, *Samadhi*, etc.

How can consciousness be conceived by means of the European logic of meaning? How can it be made into a subject of reflection?

Consciousness is the Activity of Appropriation

The main intellectual "intrigue" in the process of answering these questions is outlined in the development of self-reflection: Descartes - Kant - Husserl. Here "reflecting Ego" is the existing Cogito as a premise, as a noun term - the Ego as the centre of decision-making, the subject of self-centred reflection, the subject of responsibility towards itself. That is why D. Dennett's argument about the "Cartesian theatre" is serious: the affirmation of reality of the Self is inevitably associated with dualism and "bad infinity". From a substantialist point of view, it is impossible to define it.

The substantialist optimism and "cogital realism" of R. Descartes regarding the existence of an active reflecting Ego, might be considered a fatal blow for the transcendentalism of I. Kant in the eighteenth century. Within its framework, Cogito ceased to exist – either as a thing or as a phenomenon. If for Descartes Ego is a kind of bridge between reflection and extension, when "reflecting Ego" and "extended Ego" are one, then since the time of Kant, Cogito has become a unity of self-consciousness as a transcendental condition for the implementation of categorical synthesis, that is, the formation of concepts. "Therefore it is only because I can combine a manifold of given representations in one consciousness that it is possible for me to represent the identity of the consciousness in these representations itself, i.e., the analytical unity of apperception is only possible under the presupposition of some synthetic one" - he writes in CPR (B 133)[4]. Based on the obvious and seemingly simple unity of self-consciousness of the thinking individual, Kant cannot claim that it is given to us, it is the result of my activity ("spontaneity"), when I, perhaps not always consciously associate all representations as mine (analytical unity), which is possible only if I realise that all these representations are mine (synthetic unity). That is, Cogito (I think, *Ich denke*) has become such an addition to everything that happens in my inner world, in the mind (in *mente*), thanks to which it is one and whole, and I am "in my mind" and everything that I find in it is guaranteed to me with the obviousness of "my" world.

In the early twentieth century, E. Husserl in his transcendental phenomenology made an amazing and bold attempt to reconstruct the Cartesian Cogito but in post-Kantian conditions. In his efforts he was aided by the expansion of the then budding science of empirical psychology. However, he saw danger in it (psychologisation of philosophy!) and emphasised that his phenomenology is fundamentally anti-psychological, since it is engaged in a kind of extraction of pure, transcendental Ego-structures from a series of acts of perception. He believes it is possible if natural perception is redirected and modified: "there is the fact that certain modifications of the original mental process are possible which we characterise as a free turning of "regard" — not precisely nor merely of the physical, but rather of the "mental regard" ["*geistigen Blickes*"][5]. Only such purified cogitation reduced to "*geistigen* view", "a mental process of consciousness"[ii] is given. If we ask why? "For the sake of truth", E. Husserl would answer. The founder of phenomenology can be called its last *Knight of Truth*, since the ultimate goal of his amazing meditations was supposed to be comprehension of the essence of things, "thing-givenness" the knowledge of which, as he assumed, should eliminate nihilism, scepticism, relativism and other painful points of modern science that is no longer able to serve as a life guide because it cannot indicate the meaning of life.

It can be added within parenthesis that the destiny of Husserl's pure phenomenology and rather stunning truth deserves a separate work since in our days of post-truth dominance the possibility of countering nihilism, relativism and cynicism remains as relevant as in the early twentieth century.

Just as psychology was popular in Husserl's time, in modern days a special stimulus for the study of cogital processes is provided by a new science for the twenty-first century – cognitive science and the project to create a "strong" AI, a computer capable of carrying out everything that happens in the human mind. We already realise that to think "like a person" means to have not only a decision-making centre but also to pose problems, not only to execute commands, but also to learn self-study, not only to process data, but also to be aware of them, to think in the first person. In this regard, the question of consciousness as the desired "addition" to the process of data processing acquires particular practical relevance, and the analytical philosophy of consciousness actively responds to it, perfectly understanding the difficulties of reproducing phenomenal consciousness. However, it remains in general in the position of naturalism and dualism, where naturalism in our days has become a modern form of what we used to call materialism just a while ago.

However, the analytical philosophy of consciousness has a great problem solving potential, it does a lot for the search for paradoxes, aporia and other difficulties while translating a philosophical problem into a scientific problem; everyone knows numerous metaphors like "brains in a bank", "millions of Chinese", etc., still, retained the original Cartesian attitude and understands consciousness as an essential, at the same time complicating the program before the appearance of something that has not happened yet, and when and if the program acquires this X, the computer will begin to realise and then the programmer will no longer face analytical problems but rather ethical problems. What kind of X are we talking about?

The X is easily detected in the process of human mental

activity, and in language—verbal formations. In the Russian language there is a verb "to be conscious of" —from "conscience". In English, its meaning cannot be conveyed by the expression "*to conscience*" (perhaps "to aware" would be an equivalent if aware were a verb, but it has a different etymology). Yet if we could translate it, what is its significance? We say "I need to be conscious of this" when we get new data from the outside, when we need to let in the result of some experience or, as they say now, information, make it our own, give it meaning. *I, My, Me, Mine*—this series of pronouns serves to indicate the results of such appropriation, the transformation of information or data into knowledge. The universality of this appropriation as "making mine" extends to what can not seem to be mine—the Other, who has long and "by default" been perceived as Alter Ego: it is either the flip side of myself or another one just like me. Either way, Me or Ego is the basis of perception, knowledge and understanding of Another or Alter! It is obvious that *with such a view*, real and essential Otherness of Another can never be comprehended[6]. It is this process of appropriation that is quite natural for human nature, that forms the basis of European psychological egotism and socio-cultural individualism.

Without a reason to be optimistic about a "strong" AI, I will say that even if we assume such an infinite complexity of the program, in which all the operations as well as all the elements involved in them, receive the desired recursiveness, there will be another obstacle in creation of a machine that will think in a human way. It is associated not only with the action of awareness ("to conscious"), but also with the action of comprehension ("to sense"). This point needs to be clarified.

Awareness is Opposed by Comprehension, Untranslatability

Awareness as expansion is a complex reflexive activity that distinguishes the human way of thinking, the intelligent activity of Homo sapiens. However, what am I doing currently when contemplating this activity? What gave Kant the opportunity to "see" the transcendental unity of self-consciousness and where is it "seen" from? How is it possible to realise consciousness? What kind of activity gives me the opportunity to not stop trying to objectify it?

We can call this activity second-level reflection – reflection on thinking, meta-reflection or metaphysics. What is causing it? Aristotle would have said that nothing is causing it since pure θεωρῐ́ᾱ must be the result of "*disinterested*" and autonomous contemplation of the essence.

Nowadays we can say that the presence of philosophy in the "body" of European culture is a fact guaranteed by the irreversibility of the history of philosophy and the presence of philosophers, who do not abandon attempts to comprehend our thinking from century to century. What kind of data is used then and do we receive information meanwhile? Obviously not. Then what does our mind do in this case?

Along with the verb "to be conscious" ("to *conscience*") in the Russian language, there is another verb that is completely untranslatable into English, this is a verb formed from the noun *smysl* ("to sense"?). This word comes from the well-known European philosophy of the pair "meaning – sense", which in the conditions of a "turn towards language" becomes the basis for the current socio-cultural discourse, and the difficulties of translating the iconic German text of G. Frege and L. Wittgenstein into English produced tremendous confusion and frequent substitutions of one word and meaning for another. A large number of works about the problem of sense or significance in the twentieth century made it elusive, it became similar to the smile of a Cheshire cat. At the same time, there is often a psychologisation of the metaphysical problem of meaning. I will name two popular works: a book by Victor Frankl *Man's Search for Meaning: An Introduction to Logotherapy*, where the need for sense is presented as the foundation of psychotherapy, and the work by Benno Hübner *Sinn in SINN-loser Zeit: Metaphysische Verrechnungen – eine Abrechnung*, where the author declared sense to be another illusion, and his current search is another way to get away from boredom, which inevitably accompanies the state of satiety and comfort of an average modern West European.

Since the time of Frege, the approach to the problem of "meaning vs sense" on the part of *analytical philosophy* has had nominalist roots and has been focusing on working with meanings, with the subject sphere; and working with meaning is understood as working on the correlation of subject with the thought about it. The pragmatic formulation of the question, in line with "making the Sense" is no stranger to it; that addresses the formation of the ability to construct the whole from parts, of a completely conventional procedure of acquiring the skill (more precisely, competence) to correlate the whole and its parts, to understand text.

Hermeneutic philosophy has dissolved meaning in language, making language the force of nature, replacing traditional philosophy of Being, and the entire culture, including philosophical one, has become a text. The result has been a strong philologisation of philosophy and the thesis that it is nothing more than science of literature. It is significant that Russian (Soviet) science of literature turned out to be especially sensitive to the nuances of meanings of the term "sense" and to the problem itself, and the philosopher-literary critic M.M. Bakhtin (1895-1975), who wrote extensively about these ideological nuances, became the founder of a particular school of hermeneutics. Numerous studies as well as a separate journal "*Bakhtiniana*"[iii] are dedicated to him.

However, if we try to preserve the specifics of philosophical reflection and avoid extremes (and the risks) of psychologisation and philologisation, it is essential to highlight the main features of the work of our mind in connection with meaning.

Firstly, meaning always points to a boundary, a limit to what is being talked about and in this respect, it is always marginal. This limit exists not only to linguistic expressions and the texts, but also to life, to culture, to the world. Therefore, in the process of comprehension, it is impossible to master; the main thing here is to stay "on edge" and continue to think. A thinking human in such circumstances is not a lyrical hero in the manner of the "Fool on the Hill" of Paul McCartney and not an affective person in a trance, but a thinker who, by virtue of his vocation, continues to think where the average person can no longer do it. Indeed, to see your mind is possible only being out of your mind, and therefore the famous philosopher of the late Soviet era M. K. Mamardashvili (1930-1990) called philosophical thinking "going crazy full of sense", 'when I am crazy, but in my whole mind - I go crazy for a reason'. He also called the philosopher a "spy of an unknown homeland" referring to his ability to be a stranger among his own, to be and not to be in this world at the same time. Inasmuch, secondly, as such "thinking on the edge" points out the prerequisites and prejudices of my judgments, their roots and cultural foundations, it shows me in my thinking what was thought by me and not by someone else and what I have learned from the world and culture, that is, from the Other. Then who is this "spy"? Who sees the foundations, prerequisites and initial intuitions of his own thinking?

Not only the answer, but the question itself will not be clear if we do not take into account the fundamental "elusiveness" of consciousness from "grasping" even in the immediacy and obviousness of self-consciousness. Precisely because consciousness conscious per se as such cannot be defined by no means can become object, but never can be objectless, it is always an action or a process of awareness ("to conscious"). And since European philosophy does not give us any other way to think about consciousness except with the help of the Self, its main character, the special exertion of my efforts to overcome the objectivity of thinking makes it possible to see its edge or limit. The totality of these efforts as a process that takes place in the present, here-and-now, was called by a famous Russian-British Buddhologist A.M. Piatigorsky (1929 – 2009) "fighting against the consciousness". It is this edge or limit that is expressed by the Russian term *Smysl* (sense) and by the inaccurate English equivalent verb "to sense".

What is the main nuance of the Russian word "*smysl*" and why is it not translated? This sense-*Smys*l, unlike the analytical interpretation, is not reduced to a set of meanings and unlike its hermeneutic understanding points not to the whole (text), but to the wholeness, which is always greater than the whole. It is more than the sum of all its parts, we cannot "put It together" or add to it, it requires other efforts for its understanding. And those efforts are not only about the thesis of neuro-culturology, it is to the possibility of opposing the analytical/European/rational holistic/Asian/intuitive way of thinking and solving problems, not only about the possibility of the holistic trend in modern science because of the logicians' interest to teleology and goals, this is also about the efforts to re-evaluate the purpose of science as a type of discourse and the philosophy of sense (Philosophy of *Smysl*) as the context of the philosophy of consciousness fits well into the framework of this reassessment, the possible cultural implications of this philosophy. They are as follows:

1. *The mode of existence of Meaning-Wholeness is deontological*. However, we would like to know Cogito as "pure" a priori or "purified", as a phenomenological reduction in the process of thinking itself, in its activity and actuality, the wholeness of the world, language and culture is Datum only in a transcendental way, it defines my type of thinking, my "logic of sense". Wholeness according to A.V. Smirnov is revealed within the correlation of subject and predicate, it is the guarantor of the coherence of all the acts of my consciousness. There is no world without such wholeness, that is without *Smysl*, but I can not take it for granted, for Its being in absence of Me is not guaranteed. *Smysl* is not given, but it definitely ought to be." "No *Smysl* – no World" (M.M. Bakhtin), but if It exists or, so to say, is given (*Datum*), it is given only deontologically and always takes Me for its being Datum.
2. *Comprehension is the opposite of awareness.* Correlation with Wholeness-Smysl is the work of consciousness

contrary to the direction of "to conscience" since it is revealed that everything that I consider my own, everything "Mine", does not really belong to me, and the whole world that is significant for me unfolds, is revealed from *Smysl*, the carrier of which is Ego. To what extent does our *Smysl* play the role of Ālaya-vijñāna of Vijñānavādins? Is it then possible to begin the exposition of the problem of consciousness—Cogito and the ways of its comprehension not with the doubts of Descartes, but with the Fourth Truth of Gautama Buddha—Ārya-Mārga? If pure Cogito is an artificial, constructed product, then everything that I have embraced, everything that has come to my attention, everything that means something and has sense to me is determined by my language, culture and the world. So, on one side, the limit of the possibilities of thinking can lead me to the boundary of my language, my world, my culture and force me to look for the same in another, and, on the other hand, the study of another culture driven by the desire to understand its structure can lead me to the ultimate foundations of mine. Then it becomes clear that there are other ways of thinking.

3. *There are other logics of Sense.* The main condition for the accuracy of this thesis—"hermeneutically disciplined consciousness" developed by Gadamer, is the presupposition that *Smysl* is every type of meta-reflection in every culture, and every culture that processes such philosophical reflection is a Big Culture for him, where *Smysl* and Wholeness is unravelled. That is why European metaphysics of meaning nowadays is impossible absent the efforts to comprehend the true otherness of Another, i.e. an ability to overcome all stereotypes of Orientalism and Occidentalism, without philosophical oriental studies, on the basis of following the principle of "the same as different" or "the same in the other way". For the implementation of this

principle there are no strict rules, the "logic of sense" as philosophy gives the point of view and from this point one can see the way to peace, where it is not universal-eurocentrism that governs, but where voices of all the cultures are heard.

Conclusion

Lost in Interpretation is important:

(a) for the study of alien or "exotic" cultural phenomena, the untranslatability of *Smysl* is another "contribution" to the treasury of arguments against Orientalism and Occidentalism and in support of the fundamental principle of openness of the hermeneutics of culture "the Same as Different"- towards the real Other, but not only Alter Ego. Paradoxically, "*intraduisibles*" give a positive effect and contribute to the mutual understanding of people of different cultures with their diverse logic of sense generating procedures.

(b) for understanding the difficulties in working on AI I really don't understand how it is possible to program the process of sensing (*Smysl*)? Does this mean that only the "Russian mind" is not subject to programming? Obviously not. If every culture with developed reflection and self-reflection is able to find a number of "untranslatabilities" in its language, then what should we do with that untranslatability, when and if programming is applied to these problems ?

The Conscious Whole: Healing the Post Truth Psyche

JOHN J. KINEMAN

As most people are not familiar with this holon framework that I will be using throughout this paper, I need to give a brief explanation of the theory. The ideas are well researched, but it is not standard thinking, so it may help if you imagine that you're attending a play where you suspend disbelief for now and accept the characters and story at face value.

The "holon" is a mathematical category analysis of cyclical causality representing the order and organisation of nature. These four causal archetypes are the main actors, working together as

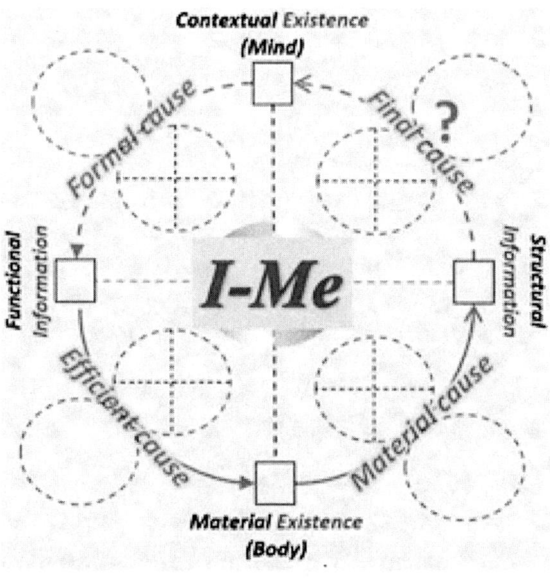

Figure 1: Representation of the Holon Theory

a whole "system attractor". They relate mind-body existence (vertical axis) with complex structure-function information (horizontal axis) as a whole system with an identity (in the middle). They are open to infinite relations with other holons in a universal holarchy (indicated by the red circles). This is non-traditional science because we are including the final cause (upper-right), which modern science leaves out.

Figure 2 shows a holon with the essential functions for life in the internal quadrants. It turns out that this analysis predicts four types of life that are confirmed by taxonomy. It also shows essential elements of science in the outer circles, suggesting that the holon is a causal pattern that underlies science, life, and perhaps everything. But this is a "top-down" view of meta-system organisation. It does not tell us about the mechanisms in each quadrant, which can be studied by other modelling methods.

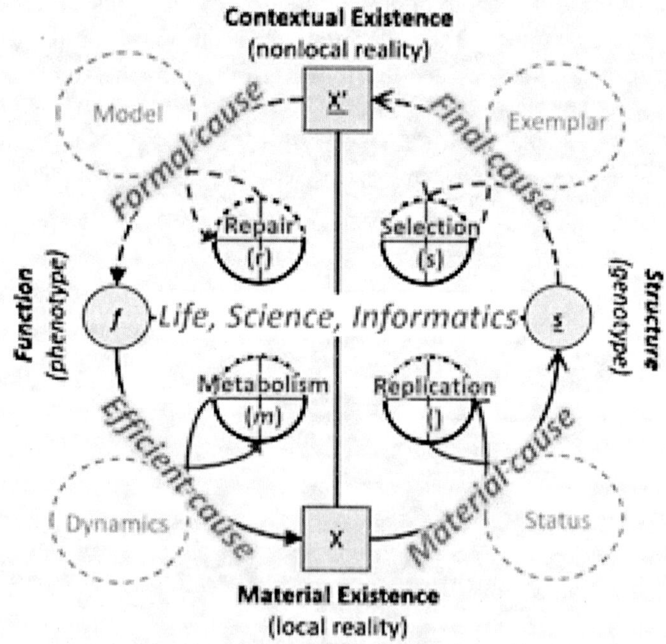

Figure 2: Life, Science, and Informatics (Eukaryote Type)

The invocation to the Isha Upanishad paraphrased here, "*Nature is whole, We are whole, taking whole from whole, or adding whole to whole, the result is whole*", captures the fractal nature of holons, as 'whole within whole'.

As such, the holon implies a general framework for coupling four kinds of models to describe nature in terms of whole systems, and to build better informatics. In any case, working out relations in a holon network is a fun puzzle. In fact, I'd love for someone to create the "Game of Holons".

Aristotle's terms for the four causes – final, formal, efficient, and material – four ways of answering questions, but a complete answer requires all four.

Aristotle's "Aitions" (Of Vedic Origin)

The whole—Fifth Essence (Quintessence): The transcendent cycle unifying the four

1. Conceptual world
   (a) Final: Meaning or potential of example in context
   (b) Formal: Model or design encoding meaning
2. Material world
   (a) Efficient: Dynamics expressing model, in physical actions
   (b) Material: Existence resulting from dynamics, as example

The four ways were called "aitions" in Greek. I believe they are the four "feet" or "faces" of Brahman in Vedanta. They are four quadrants of the dancing Shiva in a wheel of fire and they appear in hundreds of four-part cycles in the Rig Veda and Upanishads.

These will be our main 'actors', which together describe a whole system and give it an identity that generally points towards consciousness as a fundamental principle. We can try to define the four causes, but that is difficult because they are "archetypes", which are best defined by their effect. Like stage actors, they can play a type of character, but they will have different faces and names in each play, that is, in each system we analyse.

For this reason, examples are the best way to explain holons, which is how cycles of creation were explained in the Vedas and Upanishads. So here is a holon example for building a house (Figure 3):

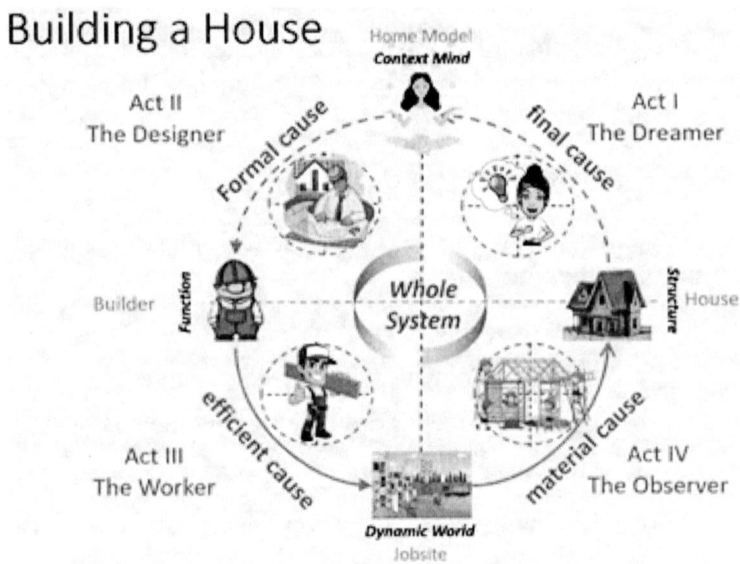

Figure 3: Holon Example for Building a House

The main actors are in the quadrants. There are two supporting actors telling the story in terms of function and structure (horizontal axis), and establishing the mind-world drama (vertical axis).

So now, the Play:

- In Act I we see the Dreamer imagining a home while remembering a house she once saw. A house becomes a home when it has one's anticipated meaning.
- In Act II we see the Designer, who is translating the

home model into plans that specify what functions the Builder will have to perform to get the intended result.

- In Act III we see the Worker, who takes the builder's instructions to perform the right actions at the jobsite.
- In Act IV we see the Observer, who sees the results, manifesting as a house.

The builder communicates what was intended to the workers and the results communicate what actually happened in various contexts, thus iterating the cycle for improvements, corrections, or other related systems.

This kind of analysis can be applied to any system. With that basic understanding of holons, let's look at post-truth.

The Oxford English Dictionary defined it in 2016 as: "Relating to or denoting circumstances in which objective facts are less influential in shaping political debate or public opinion than appeals to emotion and personal belief."

Notice this is about systemic imbalance. It does not say that emotions and opinions are unimportant compared to facts, but that the systemic balance between the two is crumbling. We will look at that balance in terms of holons.

For centuries, we expected a benevolent cycle of human improvement from the diffusion of science and technology into society. The World Wide Web was no exception, but the big challenge was to build in "meaning". The failure of the "semantic Web" reinforced a negative cycle that formed in society.

What we got instead was a four-cause 'perfect storm' disrupting global civilisation – a pathological cycle instead of a beneficial one. Here's how I think it played out:

- Our drive towards "pragmatism", thought to be constructing useful human knowledge, made all contexts relative to each other, abandoning the idea of ultimate truth. This created the opportunity for a radical increase in intellectual disinformation.

- Free Speech and the Semantic Web were supposed to provide more and better information, but instead they opened the opportunity to spread self-serving memes and media disinformation.
- Social Relativity, which we thought would increase multicultural understanding, facilitated the spread of fake news in "artificial" contexts, expanding geopolitical disinformation instead of containing it.
- The combination of these trends resulted in physically disruptive agents at the material level—a biological pandemic, but also an institutional one reinforcing the cycle.

This is a "causal loop" like the one we saw for creating a home, except this one is pathological, destroying our home – maybe leading us to World War III.

Figure 4: Post-Truth Crisis

The above resulted from Post-Truth were the four kinds of insanity:

- Pragmatism (intellectual supremacy)
- Moralism (righteous supremacy)
- Nihilism (viral supremacy)
- Populism (autocratic supremacy)

Figure 5 shows the five traditional human values described in Vedanta. They can also be described by associating them with the thumb and fingers on the hand. Ahimsa is associated with the thumb, which is the only digit that can unify the hand as a functional whole. We can interpret non-violence as harmony, especially harmony of the other four.

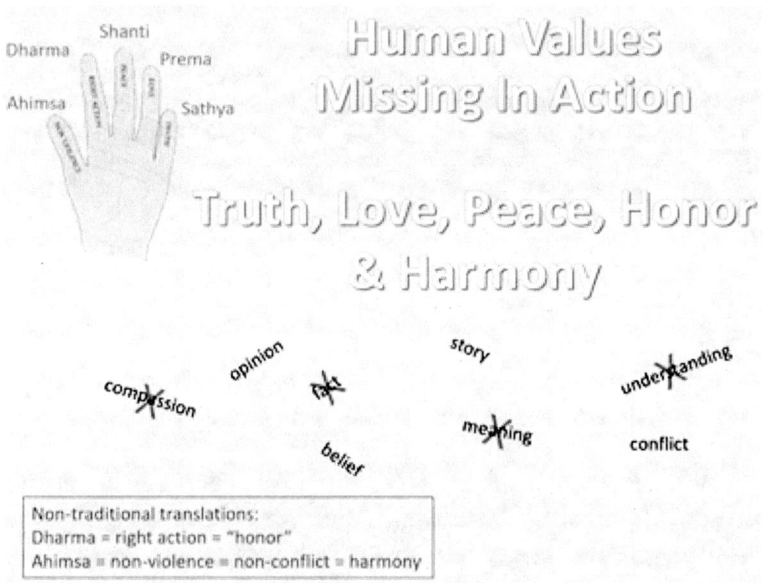

Figure 5: Five Traditional Human Values in Vedanta

Post-truth eliminates human values that would otherwise create a beneficial cycle. Truth becomes relative, love becomes utilitarian, peace is negotiation, honour is pride, and harmony then becomes chaos.

Figure 6 shows the five human values as a holon cycle. Truth, in the lower right quadrant, means what actually exists. Entering the divine mind, existence evokes love. As the basis for a plan, that becomes peace. "The peace that surpasses understanding". That, in turn, guides honourable actions which then add to truthful existence. When these harmonise, the whole is self-sustaining, as in the quote on the right. It then reflects the ultimate cosmic order.

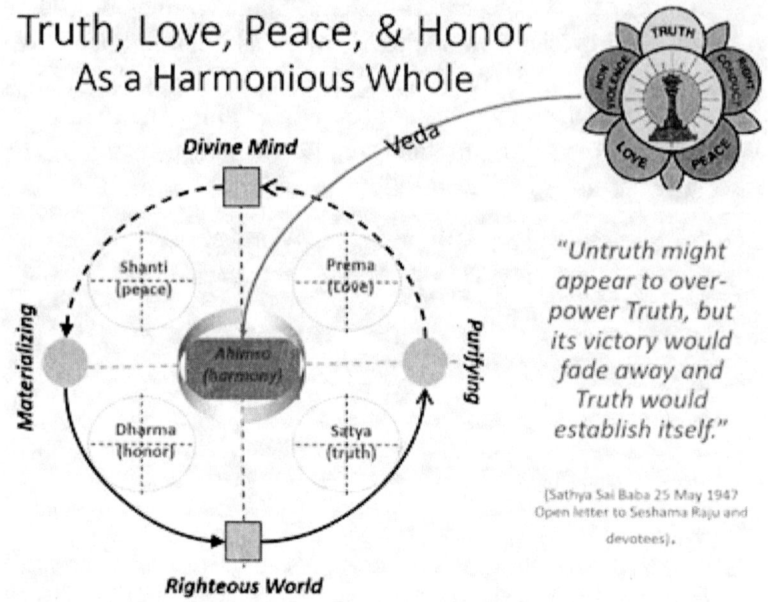

Figure 6: Five Human Values as a Holon Cycle

Whole self-sustaining systems can be beneficial or disruptive. Creative and disruptive aspects are also part of the cosmic cycle itself, like Shiva's "wheel of birth and death". But if systems are related only to each other, they will normalise polarities and become destructive. This is the post-truth dilemma. Systems reflecting a universal attractor will be drawn to balance constructive and destructive aspects, sustaining agility for overall benefit. "Good" therefore means that 'birth' and 'death' are kept in balance with other systems, timescales, and cosmic order (Rta).

We can thus state criteria for a beneficial system:

1. A universal attractor balances preservation and renewal.
2. Causal isolation polarises systems and is generally disruptive.

Figure 7 shows a holon diagram of post-truth consciousness.

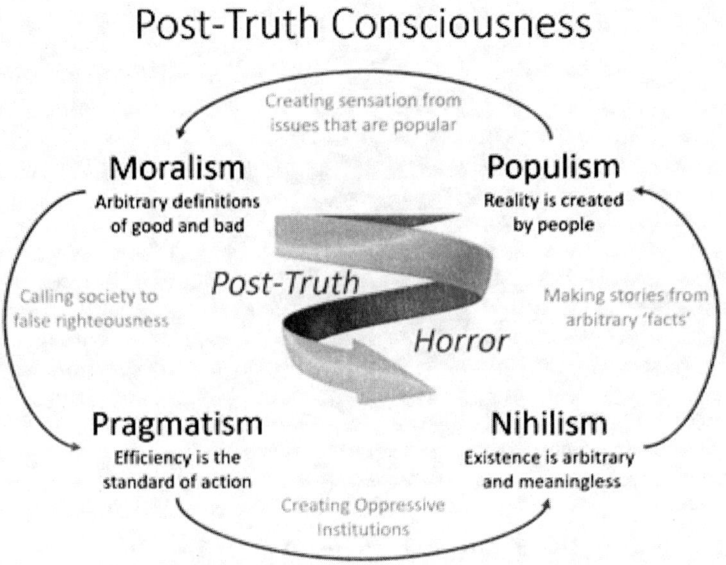

Figure 7: Holon Diagram of Post-Truth Consciousness

The nature of the loop is a downward spiral that can destroy everything it relates to except those systems that sustain it. Eventually it destroys those systems too. The cycle continues till it too is disrupted, or it sets the system back to some original status where creation begins again to build a new system; perhaps a new person, new society, new government, or new civilisation.

So, we can predict a harmonious future, but the question is what components of current civilisation it will retain. That could be nearly everything, if we learn how to re-balance the system, or nothing if we do not.

This shows the mutually supporting causes of the post-truth crisis on four levels. The strategic type is viral, corresponding to the proto-life type. All it knows is how to infect a host, and all critical organic functions are then supplied by the host, which also becomes a viral agent infecting others.

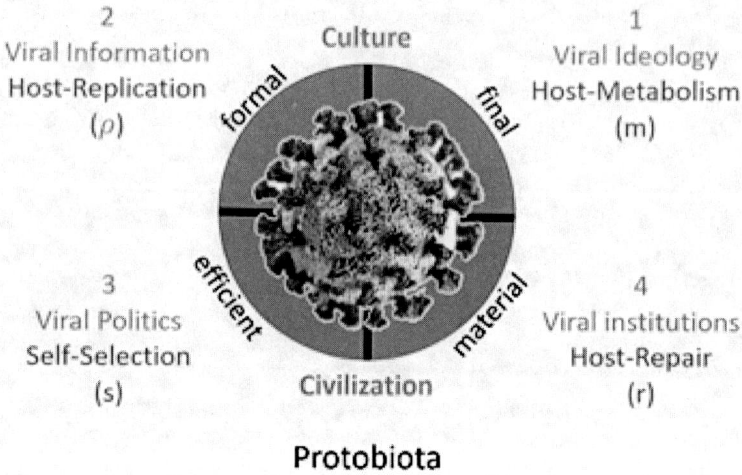

Figure 8: Viral Strategy on Four Levels

We can talk about a viral strategy in politics, science, society, or biology. It provides no meaningful functions of its own other than to induce its own selection by re-defining the system. Elements of this strategy have been used in human conflicts throughout history. But it came together now as a "perfect storm" on four levels of civilisation. The world's poor global response to the pandemic was only one result. I think we have yet to see others.

As Disney's Captain Barbosa said in the movie *Pirates of the Caribbean*: "You'd better get used to horror stories, because you're in one." The effect of this strategy, if played out on a global level, would be to dissolve and then regenerate civilisation in a "new global order". The degree of destruction depends on when it is itself disrupted, and what we get, depends on what disrupts it. If it isn't stopped, it could be a real horror story taking us back to primitive life.

But by understanding how this works it is also possible to disrupt the destructive cycle and reestablish a creative system. The key is the truthful flow of information in a self-reinforcing cycle.

All systems are unified only by information. The viral strategy works by destroying valid contexts for truthful information. Restoring information integrity is key because, with that one correction, the system will become self-sustaining in harmony with natural wholeness, just as it becomes disruptive without it.

The US Constitution was based on these ancient Vedic principles implementing a balance of the four causes, with its constitution as the moral centre. It is currently being challenged by a "constitutional crisis" created by viral disinformation and disruption. Ancient Harappan and Vedic civilisation had a similar order and was self-sustaining for thousands of years. The moral centre was a stronger constitution: the immutable Veda. But it was disrupted by physical environmental changes that forced migration. Dualism took over and dominated ever since, as the ancient knowledge was preserved in texts and monastic orders.

Figure 9 depicts a holon for governance as an organic whole. Note the balance of powers centred on a constitutional core that reflects the cosmic order, and also the opposite cycles of governance and review.

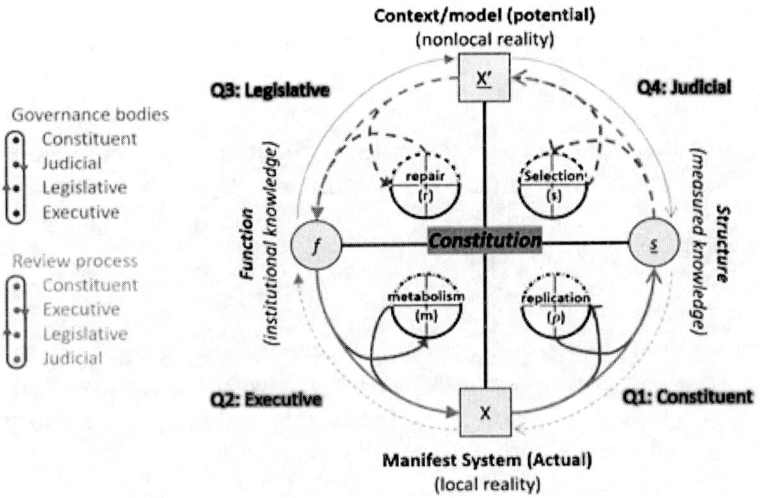

Figure 9: Governance as an Organic Whole

There are implicitly three kinds of stable government system types corresponding to strategic organism types. The metabolic type shown here emphasises enterprise, the replicative type, colonisation, and the repair type, tradition.

From what we know of ancient civilisation in India it followed perhaps a repair type emphasising tradition, constitutionally centred on the Vedas as divine knowledge. That produced a self-sustaining cycle that was highly resistant to disruption.

Holon symmetry is fundamental to life, consciousness, and to the benevolent operation of interrelated whole systems. Systems are held together by information symmetry represented in the holon. Broken symmetry is caused by viral disinformation. The only way I see to fix the post-truth disruption is to retain the original context of information in holistic structures at every level (including ourselves), building greater systemic harmony. New information systems can be built using the holon model and AI technology to realise these principles. The key is how they are designed. Holistic governance can be established on the same basis, and with the aid of better informatics, to restore information integrity.

Garret Hardin famously wrote that there is "no technical solution" to the Tragedy of the Commons, that only a moral solution will work. Thirty years later he confirmed that opinion, with the caveat that higher order management could prevent it. I think an understanding of cosmic order disseminated through educational institutions, and intentional efforts to rebuild information integrity could bring such higher-level management about.

But here's the bottom line. Even if we do all that, for it to work, the essential ingredient is our own personal introspective context – higher awareness through forms of yoga as essential knowledge. Only seeking a greater whole will align these efforts for overall benefit – science itself is reaching this conclusion.

Mind-Matter Relations in Dual-Aspect Monism

Harald Atmanspacher

Dual-Aspect Monism came as a reaction to Discartes interactive dualism that avoids both physicalist and idealist leanings. Spinoza (Ethics 1677) and Schelling (Freedom Essay 1809) were among the pioneers of dual-aspect thinking, where the mental and the physical are regarded as epistemic aspects of an underlying reality that is psychophysically neutral. Ernst Mach, William James and Bertrand Russell on the other hand, followed the philosophy of neutral monism. Quantum-inspired versions of dual-aspect thinking can also be seen in the works of Wolfgang Pauli and Carl Gustav Jung; Arthur Eddington and John Wheeler as well as David Bohm and Basil Hiley. An in-depth review of the literature can be found in the 2022 monograph by Atmanspacher and Rickles which covers Dual-Aspect Monism and the deep structure of meaning.

There are two modes of Dual-Aspect Thinking:

1. Composition of psychophysically neutral elements leads to configurations that are either mental or physical. This mode is reductive and inspired by classical system theory (Mach, James, Russell, Chalmers).
2. Decomposition of a psychophysically neutral whole leads to partitions, one of which is that of the mental and the physical. This mode is non-reductive, inspired by quantum holism (Pauli/Jung, Eddington/Wheeler, Bohm/Hiley).

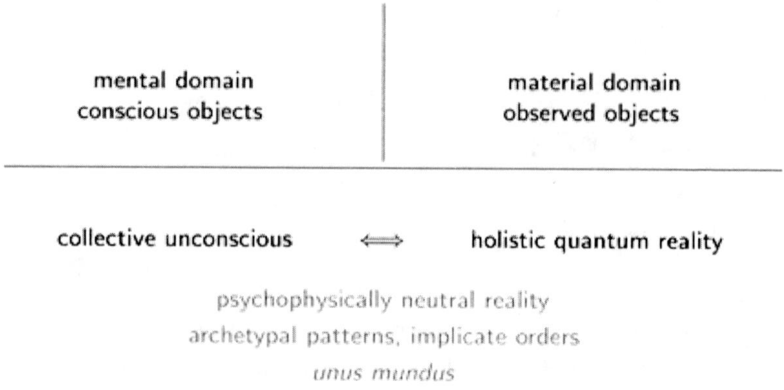

Figure 1: Mental and Material Domain

Figure 1 depicts the following key features of the interrelations of mental and physical domains with an underlying psychophysically neutral domain:

- Unus mundus as one fundamental psychophysically neutral domain without distinctions such as mind-matter, subject-object, self-world.
- Mental and physical emerge as dual epistemic aspects due to partitioning of the holistic psychophysically neutral domain.
- Archetypal patterns provide a hierarchy of psychophysically neutral order elements between unus mundus and mental/physical aspects.
- Psychophysical correlations (e.g., synchronicities) reflect lost holism of archetypal patterns (inspired by quantum holism).
- Psychophysical correlations are substantiated neither causally nor by chance, but rather by meaning!
- Meaning (not syntactic information) is posed as a basic relational ingredient of the fabric of reality

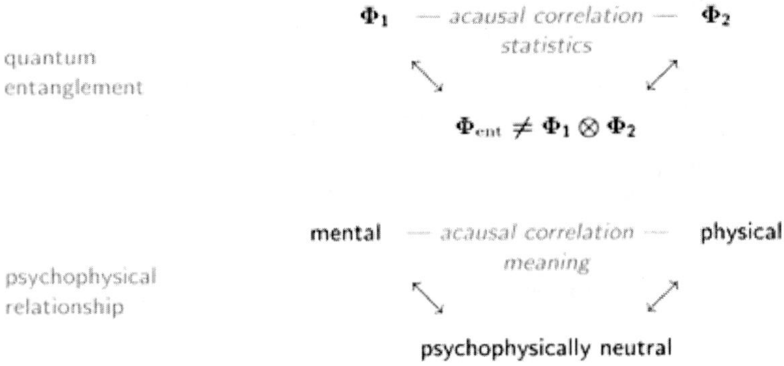

Figure 2: Analogy with Quantum Theory

There are two types of psychophysical correlations namely, structural psychophysical correlations which are persistent as well as robustly reproducible and induced psychophysical correlations which are only occasional, evasive and irreproducible.

Structural psychophysical correlations provide a baseline from which induced psychophysical correlations deviate.

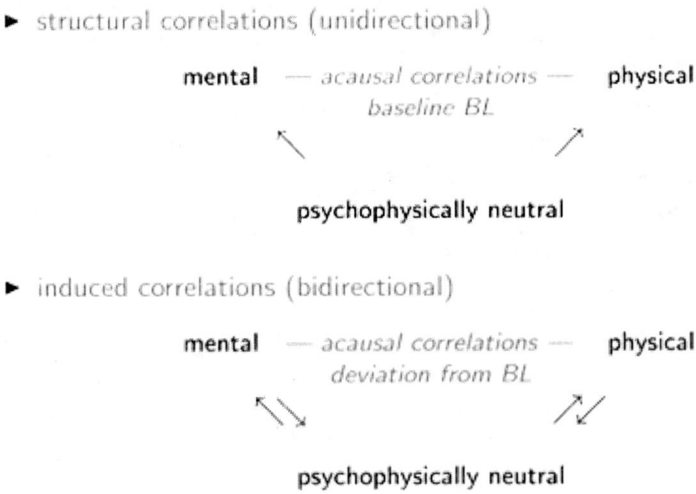

Figure 3: Structural and Induced Correlations

In this context, positive and negative deviations are possible where excess correlations lead to the experience of "coincidence" and deficit correlations lead to the experience of "dissociation". Both circumstances are experienced as meaningful because they deviate from the baseline of ordinary correlations. The scale goes from "numinosity" or extreme deviation to "ordinary case" or no deviation.

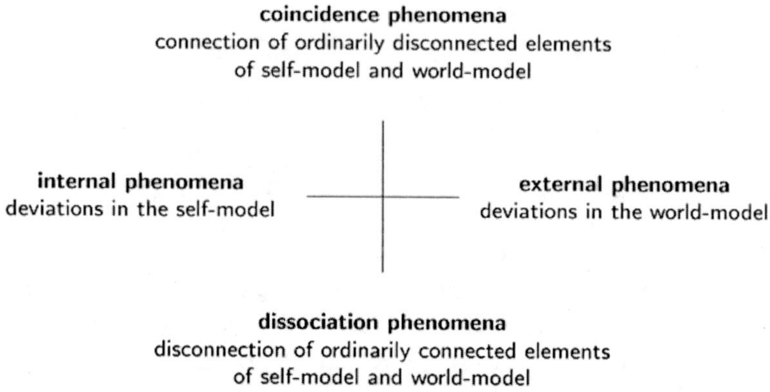

Figure 4: Experience of Psychophysical Correlation

Psychophysical studies provide more selective information, for instance allowing the identification of individuals with coincidence disposition. More than 2300 reports of exceptional experiences were collected at the Institute for Frontier Areas of Psychology at Freiburg and elsewhere (see also Luhrmann et al. 2021, Taves et al. 2021). Analyses support the four-pattern taxonomy shown in Figure 4 as suggested by the dual-aspect model. Distribution over patterns is comparable for different subsamples.

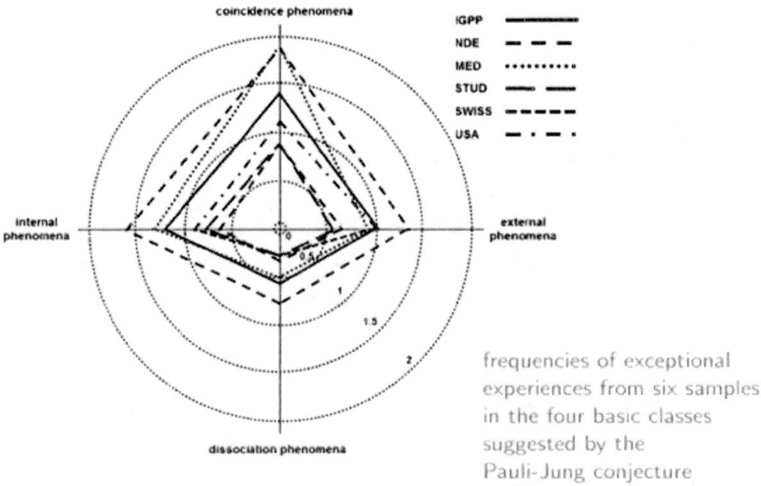

Figure 5: Frequencies of Exceptional Experiences Suggested by Pauli-Jung Conjecture

Some of the leading thinkers in the field of psychology, physics and philosophy have theorised along these lines since the early nineteen hundreds and even before. Some quotes are as follows:

> *On the one hand, many psychologists, originally those of the behaviourist school, tend to adopt what is essentially a materialist position as a matter of method if not of metaphysics. They make psychology increasingly dependent on physiology and external observation, and tend to think of matter as something much more solid and indubitable than the mind. Meanwhile the physicists, especially Einstein and other exponents of the theory of relativity, have been making matter less and less material. ... Whoever reads, for example, Professor Eddington's Space, Time, and Gravitation, will see that old-fashioned materialism can receive no support from modern physics.*
>
> *—Russell 1921*

The ordering and regulating factors must be placed beyond the distinction of "physical" and "psychic" – as Plato's "ideas" share the notion of a concept and of a force of nature (they create actions out of themselves). I am very much in favour of referring to the "ordering" and "regulating" factors in terms of "archetypes"; but then it would be inadmissible to define them as contents of the psyche. The mentioned inner images ("dominant features of the collective unconscious" after Jung) are rather psychic manifestations of the archetypes which, however, would also have to put forth, create, condition anything lawlike in the behaviour of the corporeal world. The laws of this world would then be the physical manifestations of the archetypes. . . . Each law of nature should then have an inner correspondence and vice versa, even though this is not always directly visible today.

—Pauli to Fierz, 7 January 1948

The development of "microphysics" has unmistakably led to a remarkable convergence of its description of nature with that of the new psychology: While the former, due to the fundamental situation known as "complementarity", faces the impossibility to eliminate actions of observers by determinable corrections and must therefore in principle relinquish the objective registration of all physical phenomena, the latter could basically complement the merely subjective psychology of consciousness by postulating the existence of an unconscious of largely objective reality.

—Pauli to Jung (likely in 1954)

As soon as a psychic content transgresses the threshold to consciousness, its synchronistic byproducts disappear. Space and time resume their accustomed sway, and consciousness is again isolated in its subjectivity. This is one of those cases which can best be captured by the term "complementarity", known from physics. When an unconscious content trespasses into consciousness, its synchronistic manifestation ceases and, conversely, synchronistic phenomena can be elicited by putting a subject into an unconscious state (trance). The same relation of complementarity can be observed in those frequent medical cases in which particular clinical symptoms disappear when their corresponding unconscious contents become conscious. We also know that a number of psychosomatic phenomena, otherwise outside the control of volition, can be induced by hypnosis, i.e. by an attenuation of consciousness.

—Jung, On the Nature of the Psyche, 1954

At present, dual-aspect monism is the only metaphysical framework offering a natural and parsimonious explanation for psychophysical correlations. This framework looks at mind and matter as two (epistemic) aspects of an underlying undivided, psychophysically neutral reality. There is empirical support of a taxonomy of exceptional experiences which can be derived from the dual-aspect model.

Action-Feeling and Self-Conscious Mind

JASON BROWN

The Lord: How many Tathagatas have you honoured, Mañjuśrī?

Mañjuśrī: As many as there are the mental actions which have been stopped in an illusory man.[i]

Introduction

Philosophical speculation on action focuses on conscious choice and interaction with the world, and has not, for the most part, taken into consideration the immediate ancestry of conscious phenomena and the patterns of dissolution which, in relation to isolates in the conscious stream, drop out once their outcomes are secured, while the symptoms of disruption, which are the basis for a reconstruction of the process, are perceived as anomalies in the normative state.

As a result, two main components of voluntary action have been distinguished. One is that of agency and the implementation of an act such as grasping a cup or pulling the trigger of a gun. The other concerns the reasons and justifications for the action, such as the desire for a sip of coffee or wanting to use the gun to kill someone. The former is the feeling of willed action, the latter involves decision and self-object relations. The implementation of the action and its rationale are intra-personal though there is an extra-personal aim, while the effect of the action on objects is extra-personal. Action as bodily movement is conceived as physical output, mechanical and governed by the laws of nature; reasons, which relate to conscious choice, judgement and awareness of consequences, may or may not be causal or deterministic.

To claim that the conceptual drivers of an action are physical effects of the brain and causally determined, whether or not it is correct, applies to the mind the paradigm of empirical science and implies that causation is invariant in mind and world. It also raises the question whether necessity is (or is not) incompatible with free will, or if agent-causation is essential to a free act. Philosophical studies tend to dismiss action as an irrelevant, to-be-clarified physiology, a causal output with little impact on the understanding of associated mental events. Here I explore some of these questions in relation to a theory of the micro-temporal transitions that underlie the action process[1,2].

Micro-Temporal Structure of Action

Because action and perception involve widely distributed regions in the brain, speculation on the succession of segments in the mental state, and specifically in the action-process, is possible only at a level of considerable generalisation. Yet, given the speculations to follow, the microgenetic account, as a plausible theory based on clinical study, deserves the same consideration as the groundless replacement of an organic system by computational theory. After all, central processors, buffers, inputs and outputs, and mind as software are pure abstractions with little or no psychological reality. Microgenesis has the value of a theory of the mental state grounded in growth and brain evolution; it is not a model that simulates cognitive function. However, a problem for psychological theory is that structural components in an underlying *Bauplan* have, in the course of evolution, so individuated that their uniformity of organisation is concealed in their complexity. A hierarchic organisation in evolutionary layers leading through limbic and mesolimbic structures to neocortex and asymmetric action in the world entails a progression from bodily space and axial motility to neo-cortical motor areas for discrete innervation and distal limb action.

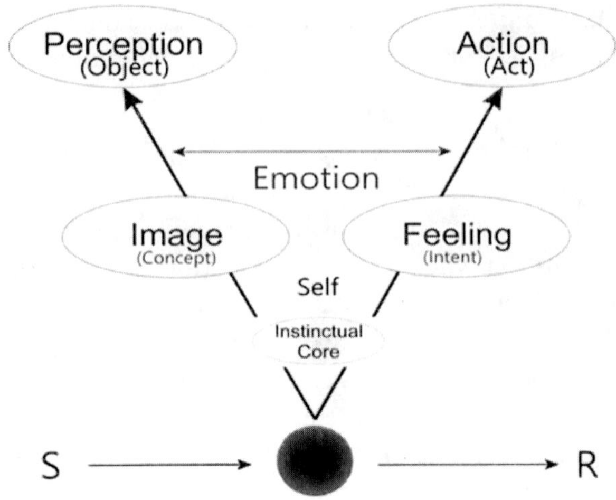

Figure 1: Behind the Scenes for the Psychology and Physiology of Stimulus Response

In figure 1, Acts and objects develop in parallel out of an instinctual core, traversing substrates of imagery and emotion. There is a shift from the serial chain of stimulus/response (SR) of reflex to a simultaneous development of action and perception. The percept-development transports drive-categories through concepts to objects. The act-development transports drive-impulse through feeling to acts. Concepts give the quality of emotion. Feeling gives intensity.

The corresponding process in perception leads from the upper brainstem through a limbic transition of experiential memory to externalisation and object space. The transitional series can incline to motility or perception depending on the dominance of feeling or concept. In both, the process leads from a deep midline source in drive-based systems of brainstem, hypothalamus and/or diencephalon, through limbic formation to neocortex. The common transition through limbic segments accounts for the reciprocal influence of action-derived feelings and perception-derived concepts, the conceptual modulation of action and the affective and intentional bias in thought. Rather than a top-down transition, act and object begin at an archaic source and develop "upward" to final externalisation; importantly, they are not products but endpoints that incorporate a cycle of successive phases.

The fundamental shift in the origin of drive is from the circularity of reflex to a synchronous act-object (Fig. 1). In reflex, a stimulus elicits a response that serves as a stimulus for another S-R reaction[3]. The argument here is that action and perception arise as multi-tiered representations out of the seriality of reflex. In this process, rhythmic systems of axial motility, such as human and animal gait, develop out of oscillatory systems such as the periodicity of circadian, biologic, respiratory and other cycles. A series of nested oscillators leads from earlier stages in evolution that support the gait and respiratory cycle to recent formations that underlie the "breath group", prosodic contour and the fine temporal pattern of digital and articulatory movement. Early music and dance are also invented through rhythmic phases. Evidence for the oscillatory foundations of action comes, *inter alia*, from the observation that purposeful finger movements appear at the crest of the rhythmic wave in resting tremor. Kinetic rhythms peel into bodily action[4]. The pattern is one of a hierarchic series of rhythmic oscillators discharging at multiple levels.

In this derivation, objects develop through concepts out of drive categories; actions through feeling out of drive energy. That is, pre-terminal segments in perception are concepts or images; pre-terminal segments in action are feelings. The act-development transports drive-impulse through feeling to action. The fusion of feeling with concept gives emotion. Concepts give the quality of emotion, feeling gives the intensity. Action provides the feeling that infuses concepts with emotion, as well as the intent to act and the forward momentum that brings aims and ideas to satisfaction. In this process, the dynamic of action (feeling) is the becoming of the epoch and the relative stasis of perception (concept) is the being, with their coincidence translating as a becoming-into-being.

In sum, the co-temporal development of act and object gives conceptual-feeling, with arousal of concepts or images on the pre-perceptual side and, on the action side, an intensity of feeling at phases prior to discharge. Act and object go on to completion but the activation of earlier segments of thought and feeling combine to give an emotion in which the quality or category of feeling—what emotion it is—is related to perceptual imagery and the quantity or intensity of feeling – how strongly it is felt—is related to phases in action discharge. The category gives the specificity of the emotion; the action-feeling gives direction and intensity to what is felt. The unity of act and object, or feeling and concept, is a process of becoming into being, which passes from archaic strata in the mind through intermediate stages to actualise in the world.

Thus, with regard to intra-psychic process, the transition from potential to actual – the specification by elimination – gives the feeling of contingency and possibility behind every act. Action arises in drive and carries through to desire, which retains the binary quality of approach and avoidance. In desire, action specifies a feeling of intent directed to choices uncovered in the object-development. The arousal of phases prior to objectification produces ideas in the perceptual series and conscious feelings in the action series. The self is a precipitate of knowledge, drive and experience at the floor of the mental state, and is felt as an agent of the forward surge in action.

Agency and Choice

This account opens up a new way of thinking on some fundamental problems in action theory. To begin, actions discharge in the body at a phase which, in perception, corresponds to pre-object concepts. An early phase in action is characterised by will or impulse; an intermediate phase by feeling and intent. The action is partly intra-psychic and, unlike an object which belongs to the world, is felt as belonging to the actor. The ownership of action is part of agency, the feeling of willed activity and the intuition of a self that can instigate or cause an action to occur. The central phenomenon of conscious action—the core experience—is a self that can deliberately cause an action or mental image to occur. This can be a thought, a vocalisation, a decision or an emotion. The action is purposeful, such that aims are felt as implemented by movements. Specifically, the feeling of agency stops with the action but its aim is for the outcome. It would be absurd, though not contradictory, to substitute an action such as combing one's hair instead of pulling the trigger if the aim is to shoot someone but the action would still be agentive, and even purposeful though intended for a different aim. Such displacements of action occur in apraxia, when they are still, it would appear, felt as purposeful.

With agency comes the problem of mental causation and the freedom of will. Agency is subordinate to volition, which implies freedom of thought or action. A voluntary act is willed and psychically unhindered. Volition is knowing that an act is freely decided, while freedom is generally approached in terms of options, not open-ended possibilities. As agency is feeling and commitment, choice is experienced as open and not simply mechanical or causal. The freedom of choice is not resolved by chance, probability or randomness, which loosen the grip of causation but do not explain the feeling of willed activity. Similarly, a common assumption is that freedom of action, if it occurs, is infrequent and requires contingency and/or quantum indeterminacy, but this leaves self-initiation unexplained. A relaxation of constraints does not explain voluntary action but merely expands its range. Regardless of how one interprets a freely willed act, conscious intent is required. The problem of whether the self can cause an act to occur and whether, though caused, that event is freely caused, are separate problems. The self might underlie or precede an act that is felt to be freely-decided even if, going back to arguments by Aristotle, the act is necessitated by circumstance, character and the experiential history of the individual.

We do not know how character and experience lead to action though this is the basis of volition and self-determination since any action, however unexpected, can be attributed to experience and would thus not be entirely free. On the other hand, the "ability to do otherwise" (see, *inter alia*, discussion in Pears[5] and O'Connor[6]) has, in my view, no explanatory weight, for it boils down to the psychology of choice and decision. Since every act materialises in the suppression of alternatives, for whatever act occurs there is always a "what if" for an act that does not occur. An outcome that is predictable even if the choice is not to act, or with awareness of the possibility to act otherwise, or if, in a gesture of freedom, a rational person should choose an irrational or self-destructive act, could still lead one to conclude that the act would be the only act that could occur, given the sum of conditions at the point of decision. On the other hand, it is difficult to conceive of a voluntary action in the absence of all experience. Kant noted that a person free of attachments and without bias is someone without a history, without experience, loyalties, interests and without the knowledge to make an informed rational choice.

Another relevant feature is that choice usually boils down to two or three options. Most possibilities die still-borne. Once an option arises, it may fade and/or be replaced, or gain strength and sap the force of others. Options trace to the drives as preferences, which spill largely into opposing vectors, such as fight or flight[7]. This might explain the usual binary nature of choice. Thought tends to settle on polarities, not gradations, for example, good and bad, mind and nature, universal and particular. These stabilities anchor transitions which are ignored, sublimated or imperceptible. There may also be a limit on attention to more than two or three ideas in the same or alternating states. Of course, not every choice is between polar opposites. Most decisions are this or that, better or worse, not right or wrong. Everyday choices would overwhelm an individual without preferences, or with apathy, indifference or weakness of will. Agency depends on predispositions to strip away a plenitude of possible actions leaving a few to surface to conscious choice.

A person unable to choose a meal from fifty entries on a menu, or a movie from a library of films, has a weakness in the capacity to decide, and with it an erosion of the feeling of agency, but not a loss if the individual can still peruse options and feel that choice is possible. Such a person resembles the memory prodigy described by Luria[8] who was unable to select a thought from a flood of memories, much as in the short story of *Funes the Memorius* by Borges. Someone with too many options has a weakness of agency, though the freedom to choose remains. A person without options does not, for that occasion, have the ability to choose, and can be said to lack volition. This means that a person can have a sense of freedom to choose though unable to make a choice, or have a feeling of agency without the freedom to choose. A person is an agent even if forced to climb the steps to the gallows. An intra-personal impulse, not outer conditions, underlies the feeling of agency, but the purposefulness of agency must include the aim towards which the action is directed.

Volition

Decision-making can feel willed, but choice, though it accompanies intent, is not an ingredient in agency, which is a feeling of willed activity in the production of images or bodily movements. The primary event is the action, not the contact of body and object. The feeling that the mind acts directly on objects is telekinesis. The relation to the body is internal though the action has external consequences. Thus, in writing, it is the innervation of the hand that is holding the pen and the idea behind it, not the words on the page, though the pen feels like an extension of the hand as the words flow through it. There is a similar feeling in the baton of a conductor. In conversation the effect of one's words is not the basis of causal feeling but an extension of mental- to object-causation. The spoken or written word is a nexus of agentive feeling to the object (paper, reader, listener) on which it acts. One can speak of a writer causing the words on a page, or causing a reaction in a reader, but this chain of events has long left the writer. The endogenous feeling of agent-causation passes, deceptively, for the perception of object-causation. Indeed, it has been argued that the source of necessity in object-causation is the infant's reach for a (moving) target. Agency is a felt mental experience that begins with intent and ends in purposefulness[9].

Obstruction magnifies effort but not agentive feeling. A person feels he is an agent whether lifting a heavy weight or a needle. In cases when resistance is futile, as in a hanging, the impact is on volition, not agency, since the will does not depend on external conditions. In Tolstoy's *War and Peace*, Peter, imprisoned, still feels an agent in thought, thus, he "cast his eyes upon the firmament, filled at that hour with a myriad of stars. 'All that is mine,' he thought. 'All that is mine is in me, is me. And that is what they think they have taken prisoner.' What is lacking is not agency but the volition or freedom to do what one wants, and being conscious that, were the action to be permitted, the actor could carry it out.

Volition and agency are in conflict when the selection of one act voids the possibility of others; options are foreclosed even if new possibilities arise. The freedom to act without restrictions exists as a potential that embraces a multitude of possible acts, while commitment precludes all acts except that which occurs. More precisely, volition is the ability to select from a range of options; freedom is conceptual possibility; agency is the active feeling in the selection. Put differently, volition applies when an action is not coerced; agency applies when an action is (felt to be) instigated by the self; and freedom is self-determination and the expectation that a broad range of actions can be implemented. The concurrence of segments in act-development and object-development aligns agency with becoming as feeling delivers the idea to motility (Fig. 1).

Self and Decision

Drive arises from an energetic feeling as the initial manifestation of will and is refined over segments as conscious feeling and intent. Will is felt as a forward surge of the action-impulse arising out of instinct at the onset of the mental state, passing through the self as a coalescence of drive categories in relation to knowledge and experience. Instinctual drive lays down the self which precipitates out of experience and character. Action develops in concert with perception. The subjective in thought becomes the objective in perception. A subliminal action in every object corresponds to a tacit object in every act. Various writers have argued that thought develops in the delay before action, a delay that permits an expansion at segments within the forming act or object. The retreat to interiority permits a consciousness of feeling as an impetus to thought and the ground of intent. We can act without thinking or think without acting but every mental state inclines to feeling or concept.

Through feeling, action is resolved to definiteness. The feeling in agency propels decision to finality, while reason is the adaptive quality of what is decided. Commonly, a focus on two or three alternatives accompanies a conscious assessment of the relative value of what is possible. In thinking, one or more ideas are rejected (vetoed), often implicitly, to arrive at the one that is chosen. Relating to Libet's[10] work (see below), the idea of a conscious veto can be interpreted as a continuation into consciousness of the parsing – the selection-by-inhibition – that occurs at antecedent stages. Sub-surface proclivities are trimmed to uncover final specifications. Though acts are interpreted as the endpoints of a causal sequence, exposing an outcome is not the same as producing it. If decisions are uncovered, not selected, wherein lies the causal effect? The finding that action begins prior to consciousness of decision, along with studies of the readiness potential, are consistent with the unconscious origin of acts and objects and imply a duration that concurs with that implied by the perceptual moment hypothesis[11] and temporal lag.

Intent

As agency is the feeling of an active exertion of will, intent is the conscious desire to do something that anticipates or substitutes for an act. One might say that intention is knowing what one wants to do—the purposefulness of an act—while agency is the feeling of doing it. Intent is a weak feeling of agency, a desire to act in which a decision is made to do something that is not yet carried out. In one instance, there is an emphasis on the object of the action, in the other, on the preliminary feeling. Agency is the conscious implementation of intent, as intent is a tributary of will. Intentions do not inevitably lead to actions but they do imply preferences or decisions. Intention can accompany agency, as when I intend to say or do something but fail in the attempt, say, finding the right word, or when I "change my mind", yet there is a feeling of agency in the effort. Agency may pass through intention as it spills into an act. However, unlike agency, which is restricted to bodily or mental activity, an intention, say to lift a book, entails the knowledge that I can lift it. I do not intend to do the impossible. Intention requires knowing what I want to do even without the capacity to do it. I intend to (try to) win the race though I may not be fast enough, but I would not intend to have a race with a horse. Knowledge participates in decision, with intention as a combination of knowledge and desire[12]. Perhaps intention is less the knowledge that inspires an action than the feeling of knowing what to do, with desire as an accompaniment, a rationale or justification for the decision.

The desire to lift a book has a trace of the directionality and self-initiation that are more strongly felt in agency when the book is actually lifted. We see the forward direction as an inclination to act. The 'futurity' of intention distinguishes it from agency and emotion which entail present feeling. Agency is a more bodily feeling than intention. The closer to the world surface, the less the feeling is grounded in the body. Intention entails a conscious if implicit choice that can resolve indecision even if its aim is ill-defined. It may even be that intention arises in the making of a decision rather than being a forecast of its selection or implementation. One can think of intention as a specification of desire that expresses a wish or objective biased towards action more than to objects, and directed to future satisfaction. A thing desired is valued and the impulse to act is an expression of a desire. Perhaps we could say that desire is feeling directed to things (events, etc.) of value, and agency is feeling directed to acts that achieve desired or valued ends. The distinction concerns the distribution of feeling into concepts or actions.

Freedom and Agency

Free will is a conflation of volition and agency, making an appearance when freedom of action is appended to the exercise of agency. One might say that freedom is for the many, action for the one, with free will combining adventure in the world with the mind's imaginative reach. Freedom is a catalogue of potential; agency is a dynamic of forward-directed activity, a manifestation of will in relation to action as drive-energy flows into movement or mental content. In sum, *agency is inner activity in relation to purposefulness; volition is the menu of possible actions, and free will is their unholy alliance*. Ultimately, freedom must be tested if it is to be more than theoretical, and action must be rational to merit the freedom that volition requires. To paraphrase the poet, lack of freedom is more than 'vague longings bred by want of power'; freedom is the capacity to act in accordance with rational desire.

One aspect of free will is the ability to do otherwise; another is the ability to freely decide. With respect to the former, even if a decision is conditioned at unconscious phases, given the postulate of a conscious veto, there is a potential to arrest the action if not done otherwise. If the choice is a film or concert, or something better or worse, the individual is always free to do nothing. In fact, the necessity of choice can itself be an obstacle to freedom. Inaction is no less a decision than action; to not make a choice is also a choice. In an occasion of decision, choices are like competing tendencies within or between categories with the potential for further elaboration. Preference becomes priority as recurrent traversals establish a relative dominance of one path over another. Feeling as intent "nudges" an idea to finality.

If we set aside agency as inner feeling, and concentrate on the freedom of choice, we can ask whether decision is effected in consciousness or imported to consciousness by submerged predispositions and, if the latter, what accounts for the belief that thoughts, plans and actions are freely chosen? What role in the origination and implementation of ideas is played by consciousness? If options are derived from presuppositions, inherent bias and the growth of preference over an iterated series of mental states, deliberation is a sideshow, yet still we believe that informed conscious intent is central to decision. Further, for an actor to state the reasons for an action, when those reasons are the analytic endpoints of the presuppositional biases that underlie them, is to accept surface justifications as inciting factors.

In simple actions such as purposeful finger movement, studies show that the onset of action is prior to conscious decision. The decision is primarily when to move the finger, not whether to move a finger or make a fist, since the choice is fully constrained by the experimental conditions. The subject can, and implicitly does, decline to move the finger till it actually moves. Could one say that since the action is pre-decided, the duration up to movement is that from generalised activation to specific intent? Further multiple mental states would be required for a single act or object. It also has to be noted that finger movement is not that simple, but likely develops out of axial and postural motor systems through the proximal to the distal musculature, which requires some duration. The quota of feeling that accounts for intent is what is felt to impel the act. Other studies of unconscious cognition (masking, priming, etc,) show unconscious activation. These studies provide a strong challenge to the claim that volition arises in consciousness, and they are consistent with a before/after traversal from the archaic (unconscious) to the recent (conscious) in brain structure.

With deliberation, choice is less likely to be fully specified before it becomes conscious. The act must traverse instances in which the quality of feeling and the persuasiveness of ideas, regardless of their unconscious attribution, are options unique to the individual. While an informed rational person usually makes informed rational choices (are we to say unconscious decision is rational?), freedom is not necessarily in selecting the most rational choice but in the license to be who you are to make it. This includes the emotion that carries value to commitment. The individual is not a calculator that computes an objective outcome, but a person who brings a history to every decision. Decisions that are not the most rational may be a sign of ignorance, egoism or impulse, but they are also expressions of personhood or personality, namely, the freedom to decide in conformity with one's feelings and character. Freedom owes to the dispositions of the agent, asserting the freedom to act according to personal desire, interest, bias and experience.

Feeling, not thought, is what drives and consolidates choice. What sways the decision are feelings applicable to that individual. Given the primacy of feeling in an organism, the will or the impulse to action is, as many philosophers have maintained, of all mental phenomena the most likely to be a direct experience of reality or the least likely to be illusory. A will is not free of ancestral claims, but the sense of free will or unhindered choice, leaving aside what constitutes a limitation on freedom, is too powerful to be dismissed without an account of how the phenomenon comes about. I would argue that the self, and act or object, occur as ingredients of the same epoch. In the mental state, the self is antecedent to act and idea, a predecessor, not necessarily a cause. The relation of self to object or image stages a private play that is the basis for consciousness. The epochal nature of the state entails simultaneity of phases until the state actualizes, at which point the agent becomes conscious of the succession, or the relation of self to image gives consciousness. This depiction of the mental state does not preclude the possibility of causation, especially in the replacement of one state by another, since the replacing state overlaps earlier phases in the preceding one. A causal effect across epochs would reinforce and supplement the base of the state prior to its actualisation.

With regard to free decision, given a choice between two conscious options, does agency occur when the individual makes the final choice or when the option not selected fades away? Does the person feel like being an agent to an act unaware that alternatives have been eliminated? A final choice occurs when options are disempowered by the surviving course of action, which occurs implicitly even if the person feels that a displaced option has been intentionally rejected. The feeling of agency arises in the implementation of an intended act or event as well as in the final selection when other options have been discarded.

The question of causal necessity arises in relation to agency. If one conceives an action as the outcome of a transition that begins with instinctual drive, not as a circulation in consciousness of competing reasons or an externalism that ignores the action structure, the momentary pre-history of an action is critical. Early phases associated with (animal) drive that give rise to instinct-driven acts cannot be said to be freely decided, while acts with a dominant focus on phases that correspond to emotion, and consequent limitation of choice, may not have the rationality to justify being described as free. The label of freedom then applies largely to conscious acts that require a reasoned decision.

In a choice between competing options, if one option is reinforced over recurrent states such that its competitor is gradually replaced, how are we to describe the selection process? The dominant content arising from unconscious experience has a conceptual and emotive bias. The accrual of dominance over repeated volleys can be described as causal but is this true of the final choice if there is no actual selection but a dropping out of alternatives? The self is an ingredient in decision but cannot be said to cause it. The actual cause is the resolution of one line of thought or intent by a reinforcement of the axis of its growth.

On this account, the self "stands behind" a decision but most likely does not cause it to occur, yet the final decision is conditioned by past and present experience. Agent-causation is an uncovering of the selection and the feeling of its causal effectuation. Unlike the passage of drive into action, which in animals is more or less direct, choice is a realisation of the potential for multiple outcomes. Individual freedom can be construed as the self-actualisation of one's own character including personal experience, knowledge and emotion, along with the ability to act without extracorporeal constraints. It is useless to ask if an act would be the same at another time if conditions were identical since there is novelty in events and in growth of personality. Novelty makes room for freedom but is not itself the freedom we are looking for. Self-expression will differ according to the individual life-experience out of which the self consolidates, but the individual must take responsibility for who he or she is, as others in using their moral judgement have a responsibility to consider his or her formative history and circumstance.

Creative Consciousness: Its Neuroscience, Non-Linear Dynamics and Trance

TOBI ZAUSNER

Creativity, diverse and inclusive, is an aspect of human life, intrinsic to people of all cultures and different abilities. Its consciousness, creative consciousness, can be investigated by neuroscience, modelled by non-linear dynamics, and contains a multitude of altered states of consciousness that collectively can be called a creative trance.[1]

Multiple States of Consciousness

Inherent in all of us, are many possibilities, and among those possibilities are multiple states of consciousness. Some of these are altered states intrinsic to the creative process that comprise the multiple aspects of creative consciousness. As William James[2], said "Our normal waking consciousness, is but one special type of consciousness, yet parted from it by the filmiest of screens, are entirely different forms of consciousness ... but apply the requisite stimulus, and ... they are there in all their completeness".

In my research, I found that creativity is one of the most pervasive stimuli allowing us to enter altered states of consciousness. I collectively call these altered states of creative consciousness a creative trance. Their manifestation is such a widespread phenomenon that I have written a book about it, *The Creative Trance: Altered States of Consciousness and the Creative Process*[1] which forms the foundation for this paper.

Although waking consciousness is fundamental to daily living, the altered states of consciousness, intrinsic to the creative process, are part of all cultures throughout time. Manifesting across domains in the arts, the sciences, sports, and practices of self-transformation, these multiple aspects of a creative trance range from the reveries of everyday life to plans that alter civilisations. They can appear in daydreams, night dreams, visualisations, meditations, focused attention, remembering, planning, absorption, immersion, and flow.

We will look at the multiple aspects of creative consciousness across domains, then examine its neuroscience and nonlinear dynamics, and finally, investigate the subjective experience of multiple localities of consciousness during the creative process.

Daydreams That Have Changed Our World

There are instances of a creative trance during daydreams that have changed our world. At age sixteen, Albert Einstein (1879-1955) imagined that he was riding a light beam.[3] While this daydream later became a basis for his work in relativity theory, Einstein's daydreaming caused him trouble in school.[4] A teacher told his parents that the boy was slow, constantly daydreaming, and would never amount to anything.

The Nobel Prize winning physician and pharmacologist James Black (1924-2010) said about his creative process, "I daydream like mad,"[5] and described his thinking as "an imaginative sense, entirely open-ended and entirely pictorial." Through his research, Black developed the beta-blocker propranolol that calms the heart and Cimetidine to treat gastric ulcers (Nobel Prize, 2022).

When Worlds Seem to Come Alive in a Creative Trance

Sometimes in a creative trance, a person's inner world may seem to come alive, causing a temporary lapse in consensual or shared reality. While studying the genetics of corn cells, the Nobel Prize winning cytogeneticist, Barbara McClintock (1902-1992), imagined she was transported into the interior of the cells that she studied. From this vantage point, McClintock was able to clearly discern the mobility of their genetic elements.[6]

At other times during a creative trance, the outer world seems to become more alive. Then, instead of lessening, stimuli from the environment appear to intensify and enhance the altered state. This happened to the primatologist Jane Goodall (b. 1934), who recalled a sense of awe while working with chimpanzees in Tanzania's Gombe National Park. The pouring rain had suddenly stopped, and Goodall remembered[7], "I could smell the wet hair on the chimpanzees, and I could hear the insects singing loudly, and I just felt absolutely at one."

Three Levels of a Ccreative Trance

The American Psychological Association (2020) has designated three levels of depth to the hypnotic trance, and there appear to be three levels of depth in a creative trance[1]. A light trance would correspond to Csikszentmihalyi's (1990, 1996) concept of flow, while a medium trance has more absorption. In a deep creative trance, immersion and focus on work obliterates all distractions, and the entire universe seems to consist only of the creative person and the work in progress. Examples of a deep creative trance are evident in sports. Jack Snow (1943-2006) played football for the Los Angeles Rams and described this experience as self-hypnosis and intense concentration, saying that "If a plane crashed in the stadium, I don't think I'd notice it till the play was over."[8]

When Roger Bannister (1929-2018) was running to break the barrier of the four-minute mile, he said,[5] "There was no pain... and the world seemed to stand still or did not exist. The only reality was the next two hundred yards of track under my feet." This analgesic or pain suppressing aspect of the creative trance helped the folk artist Maud Lewis (1903-1970), who had multiple disabilities and pain from severe juvenile arthritis that continued throughout her life.[9,10,11] Her hands were very affected by the illness, which had twisted her fingers. Yet Lewis said, "As long as I've got a brush in front of me, I'm all right."

Illness and its resulting resilience can intensify a creative trance as it did for Itchiku Kubota (1917-2003), who called his experience of acute hepatitis, the most important time "in my life as an artist."[12] Afterwards, he redesigned an ancient tradition of Japanese textiles and kimonos and gained international recognition.

Dreams and the Creative Trance

For some individuals, it is dreaming and the related hypnagogic and hypnopompic states that are the sites of a creative trance. Elias Howe (1819-1867) dreamt the solution to his invention of the sewing machine in a nightmare where he was surrounded by angry warriors.[13] In the dream, Howe noticed their spears looked like sewing machine needles, but with holes at the tip, not the middle where he had placed it. Lucidly realising this during the dream state, Howe woke up, made a needle with the hole at the tip, and his sewing machine finally worked. It changed civilisation through mass-produced garments and employment possibilities for women.

Inspirational dreams and associated altered states are acknowledged across cultures. The Benin people of Africa believe the deity Olokun inspires creativity through dreams and states of reverie[14] and Australian Aborigine artists depict Dreamtime,[15] an altered state containing a divine parallel world of spirits and ancestors. In Hinduism, the sleeping god Vishnu is associated with creativity. He gives birth to Brahma, creator of the phenomenal world, and is also creative through his connection with vegetation, specifically the sacred medicinal plant tulsi (basil) and the lotus that springs from his navel.[16]

The Hypnagogic and Hypnopompic States

The hypnagogic and hypnopompic states between wakefulness and sleep, can also be times of a creative trance. Mary Shelley's idea for the novel *Frankenstein* came to her in a hypnagogic state. Shelley recounted[17] that during a restless summer night, unable to sleep, she had vivid images, with her eyes completely closed, of a scientist bending over his strange creation.

The contralto Marian Anderson (1897-1993) said the time before sleep was when she lived in "mood of the music" and became "lost in the spirit of the song."[18] Anderson described music as elusive, and revealed that after a long struggle with a song, "suddenly, there is a flash of understanding." Anderson's flash of sudden insight has now been mapped by neuroscience. Kounios and Beeman,[19] found that when a creative solution erupts into conscious awareness, it may be accompanied by a burst of gamma waves in the right temporal lobe of the brain, specifically in the anterior superior temporal gyrus.

Neuroscience and Non-Linear Dynamics of the Creative Trance

Although Kounios and Beeman[19] identify a specific location associated with insight, they acknowledge that creativity is a complex process engaging many parts of the brain. Cognitive neuroscience reveals the heterogeneity of creative trance states through activation of different brain regions, such as the medial temporal lobe memory network, the prefrontal cortex, both brain hemispheres, and significantly the default mode network, which is associated with divergent thinking and daydreaming. There can also be activation of the visual cortex and the auditory cortex, evidence of activity in the mind's eye and the mind's ear. One of the reasons that creativity may be enjoyable is because it is associated with the release of hormones that stimulate positive emotions, such as dopamine, endorphins, serotonin, and oxytocin.

As a time of multiple interacting variables, the creative trance can be modelled as a creative chaos through the lens of nonlinear dynamics.[1] Unlike the clockwork universe of Newtonian dynamics limited to two variables, the multiple variables in a creative process combine in a three-body or n-body way that Poincaré demonstrated[20] would be a deterministic chaos. As a result of multiple variables, there are many possible trajectories and potential bifurcations to new activity and the possibility of personal transformation. With its disciplines of chaos theory and complexity theory, nonlinear dynamics can explain processes like creativity that do not progress in a straight line, are not predictable, never exactly repeat themselves, and yet have the capacity for originality and revolution.[21]

Experiences of External Inspiration: Secular and Divine

One of the more dramatic aspects of consciousness during a creative trance is the experience of a seemingly external source of inspiration. As the poet Percy Bysshe Shelley (1792-1822) said, "One after another, the greatest writers, poets, and artists confirm the fact that their work comes to them from beyond the threshold of consciousness."[13] The inventor Thomas Edison insisted, "People say I have created things. I have never created anything. I get impressions from the Universe at large and work them out, but I am only a plate on a record or a receiving apparatus."[ii.]

Edison experienced his external inspiration as secular. Yet for spiritual people like the mathematician Srinivas Ramanujan (1887-1920), outside sources of inspiration may appear to come from the divine.[13] Ramanujan said that the Goddess Namagiri came to him in dreams at night, giving him mathematical formulas.[13] Ramanujan would write them down in a notepad by his bed, and then laboriously work out the mathematics supporting the formulas so that he could present them to the world.

Speaking to the musicologist Arthur Abell, Giacomo Puccini (1858-1924) revealed that the music for his opera, Madame Butterfly "was dictated to me by God. I was merely instrumental in putting it on paper and communicating it to the public."[22] Yet Abell insisted, "but to do all that, you had to have knowledge and technical skill of a high order." "Of course, that is self-understood," agreed Puccini, who said the composer should "acquire by laborious study and application the technical mastery of his craft." Then he added, "but he will never write anything of lasting value unless he has Divine aid also."

The singer, songwriter, and musician, Stevie Wonder (Stevland Hardaway Morris, b. 1950), is also spiritual and sees his music as coming from a divine source. He says, "I'm only being used as a vehicle, through which comes encouragement, inspiration, hope, and some clarity…It is an honour to do it and I never forget the honour." [23]

Religious traditions have ritualised the phenomenon of divine inspiration, which can be seen in the practice of sacred dance. The Bharatanatyam, one of the sacred Hindu dances of India, which derives its lineage from the worship of Shiva, is performed to manifest a divine source through human form and movement.[24] In the Islamic Sufi tradition, dancing whirling dervishes perform an act of harmony with the cosmic order.[25] Their circular movements convey the generative energy of the spiral with expansive energy radiating outwards from the centre.

Multiple Localities of Consciousness with Seeming Autonomy

Locality and non-locality have become familiar concepts in consciousness.[26,27,28] Yet during a creative trance there may be the subjective experience of multiple localities of consciousness.[1] The creative person is one locus of consciousness, while the work in progress can feel like a seemingly separate consciousness. These multiple consciousnesses may form a hierarchy with the work in progress assuming an executive function. In this case, the ego willingly relinquishes conscious control, and the work, assuming a seeming autonomy, appears to dictate its own creation.

As the pianist Rosalyn Tureck (1913-2003) insisted, "I do what Bach tells me to do. I never tell the music what to do."[29] It was obviously very successful, because the Tureck International Bach Competition is named in her honour. This seemingly autonomous locus of consciousness appears to be a projection of the unconscious mind, what I call an artistic projection. When erupting into conscious awareness, it manifests as a formerly unconscious, now conscious imperative.

As a result, work is more directly created by the unconscious mind and often better, because the unconscious is a vast parallel processor compared to the smaller sequential conscious mind. Artists seem to realise this intuitively and willingly allow their conscious mind to take a secondary role. As the visual artist Joan Mitchell (1925-1992) said, "I sit and look at the painting, sometimes for hours. Eventually, the painting tells me what to do."[18]

Is it advisable or even possible to go against the directives of a work in progress? I can attest from personal experience that for me, it is neither advisable nor possible if you want the best results. My work tells me what to do, even if I don't agree.

I tried in vain to fight against the directives of a painting while working on this large oil on canvas, called The Pilgrim (Figure 1). The figure in the work represents all of us, with our loads to carry and our paths to travel. Although I repeatedly pushed back against the will of this painting, in the end, the painting won.[30] I wanted to paint a nice garden in the foreground where the figure could rest, his journey over, but the painting kept insisting on a road, so he could keep walking. This made me very angry, but none of the gardens I painted were acceptable. Finally, I gave in and painted the road. It was the best and only solution.

Further indication that the creative trance is an altered state of consciousness, comes from its instances of expanded awareness. One of these instances happened while I was struggling to paint the stone walkway that the figure is traversing. After painting many different types of walkways that didn't suit the image, I saw in my mind's eye, a path of white stones that looked like they might suit both the meaning and the visual aspect of the work.[31] I painted them, and then six months later, on a trip to San Francisco, I saw the exact stones that I had painted months earlier in New York.

Another unusual event occurred during my painting called Memories (Fig. 2). It was very late at night, and I was extremely frustrated by not being able to paint the structure of the clouds across the top of the canvas.[31] After hours of trying and failing,

Figure 1: The Pilgrim, Oil on Canvas, 82 × 57 in. and Archival Print on Paper, Multiple Sizes © Tobi Zausner 2002

Figure 2: Memories, Oil on Canvas, 50 × 73 in. and Archival Print on Paper, Multiple Sizes © Tobi Zausner, 2002

I couldn't stand to look at the painting anymore, nor was I able to stop working. So, I turned my head away from the canvas and painted without looking. Finally, when I turned around to face the canvas, there was the underlying structure of the clouds that I could not paint during conscious control. When dry, they would be ready to receive the layers of glazes that bring depth to the finished work in Fig. 2. Perhaps, in a creative trance, with its pronounced dominance of the unconscious mind, we have greater access to implicit muscle memory. As Jung (1927, CW-8:180) wrote, "Often the hands know how to solve a riddle with which the intellect has wrestled in vain."

Aspects of a Work in Progress Can Appear to be Alive

Sometimes in a creative trance, the work not only dictates its progress, but may also seem to come alive as a fully autonomous presence. This can result in a sense of exteriorisation of consciousness along with an experience of otherness in the creative elements. In this state of consciousness, authors may find that the fictional characters in their writing seem to come alive with preferences of their own that may differ from the author's intentions. This experience appears to be a frequent occurrence during the writing of fiction.

When Alice Walker (b. 1944) was working on her novel, *The Color Purple*, she related that its characters complained to her that they didn't like living in Brooklyn – too many tall buildings they said.[18] So, she moved to San Francisco, but they didn't like it there either. Finally, after renting a small cottage in Boonville, northern California, which was more like the rural setting of the novel, they became friendly and talkative again. Walker recounted[18] that "They were very obliging, engaging, and jolly."

Sometimes, it is the seemingly inanimate that appears to have an independent existence in a creative trance. Nicola Tesla (1856-1943) could imagine the machines he was creating so vividly, that he was able to set them running in his mind, and then check on them later to see if they showed signs of wear or needed adjustments.[32,33]

Figure 3: The Eternal Present, Archival Print on Paper, Multiple Sizes, © Tobi Zausner, 2010

While I was working on a pastel drawing that eventually became an archival print called The Eternal Present (Fig. 3), the little Buddhist nun came alive for me as an internal vision. I was having difficulties with her hands, especially the fingers. Finally, in frustration, I lay down, closed my eyes, and then suddenly, either in a hypnagogic or meditative state, I saw the little nun as a gentle, smiling, spiritual, and completely real person. Sitting under a diffuse light, she was opening and closing her hands to show me how her fingers worked. After this, I was able to accurately draw her hands.

The Liminal Boundary Between Psychological and Spiritual

Yet what are these seemingly real, outwardly autonomous entities generated through creativity? According to Alexandra David-Neel (1868-1969), Tibetan Buddhism might identify this outwardly autonomous figurative entity as a type of thought form called a Tulpa.[34] She describes them as manifestations of concentrated mental energy, and recounts seeing a Tulpa thoughtform behind a painter that resembled one of the figures in his work. By regarding them as manifestations of the mind, contemporary neuroscience might seek to uncover the underlying neurological patterns. Mapping the brain activity of fiction writers in this altered state of consciousness, neuroscientists may discover whether different fictional characters have specific individual neural signatures.

There is a liminal boundary between the psychological and the spiritual. The writer and philosopher Raja Rao (1908-2006) speaks of this liminality through the metaphysical aspects of words as connections between the ephemeral and the eternal. He says[35], " I am a man of silence. And words emerge from that silence with light, of light, and light is sacred." Rao believes that a writer must forget himself in the process of creativity and "go back to the light from which words come."

In summation, when we examine the multiple altered states of creative consciousness, we can begin to realise how vast and varied they are, shaped by culture, time, and individuality, and how much the musings of our inner life have changed the workings of the outer world.

THE PROBLEM OF CONSCIOUSNESS IN SCIENCE

Consciousness: The Hole at the Wheel's Hub

TERRENCE W. DEACON

Despite being non-material in nature, consciousness feels substantial and is proven to be physically efficacious.

Figure 1: Self as Constitutive Absence

"Thirty spokes converge at the wheel's hub to an empty space that allows it to turn. Clay is shaped into a vessel to take advantage of the emptiness it surrounds. Doors and windows are cut into walls so that a protected space can be occupied. Though we must work with what is there, use comes from what is not there"

—*Tao Te Ching #11*

Matter and energy, according to the first law of thermodynamics, can neither be created or destroyed. In other words matter and energy cannot cease to exist. In contrast, the existence of a living being is constantly at risk. Take any organism for instance. Even as the organisation of the organism persists, its materiality changes. However, according to the second law of thermodynamics, organisms can be created or destroyed. It can even spontaneously degrade. This is why organisms are at risk and require work in order to exist.

"To be is to do" —Hans Jonas

Therefore the *work of being* must ultimately be directed to maintain this same capacity to do work.

Figure 2: Function as Absence Instead of Material

Simply put, it must be self-directed. In machines the designs are external imposed constraints and the work performed is also externally directed work. Their function is determined by the constraints on the dynamical excursions their parts can assume, i.e., that which is prevented. Loosening these constraints to include degrees of freedom beyond a given threshold results in loss of function.

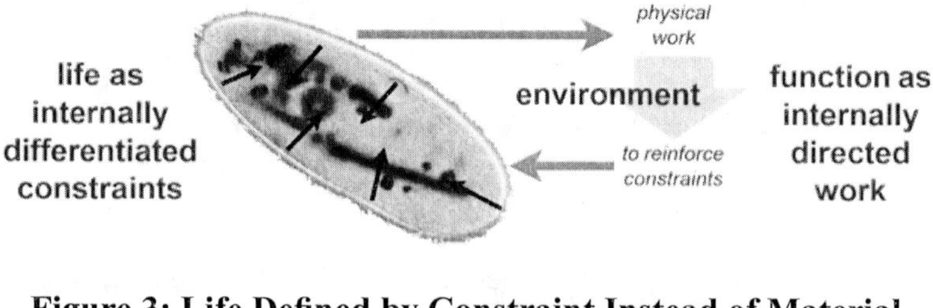

Figure 3: Life Defined by Constraint Instead of Material

Life is also defined by constraints that are intrinsic to the organism; but what is absent or prevented in this case, is not some part of the organism, instead, it is the information embodied in a negative sense. A living organism consists of a vast and complex system of reciprocally synthesised molecules, where the stability of this organisation depends on the possible molecular interactions being highly constrained. Though we think of death as a loss of something, what is lost is this constraint, as many degrees of freedom of chemical interactions become possible.

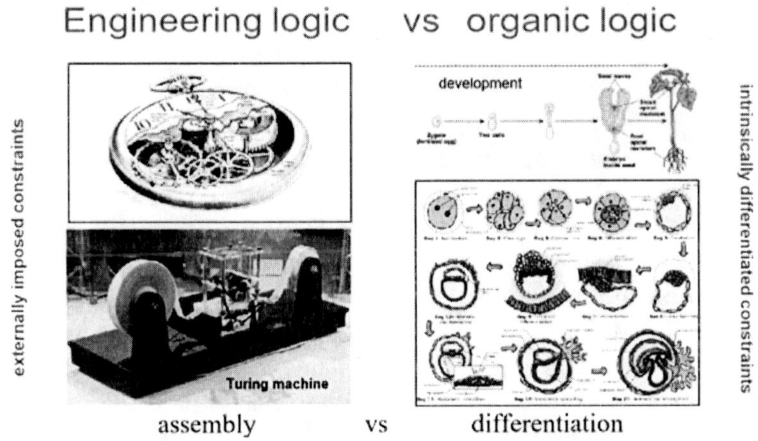

Figure 4: Engineering vs Organic Logic

Another major distinction comes in the form of organic logic, where the whole precedes the parts and these parts differentiate from each other via interaction in a way that continuous functioning never stops versus engineering logic, where the parts precede the whole in a process of step by step additive assembly such that the function can only be initiated after completion. The only relation that parts of a machine have to one another is their fitted interactions, but because parts of an organism differentiate out of a functional whole, they contain a trace of the whole within them. Kant, who is a well known critique of technological judgement, notes that a machine has solely motive power, whereas an organised being has self-forming power.

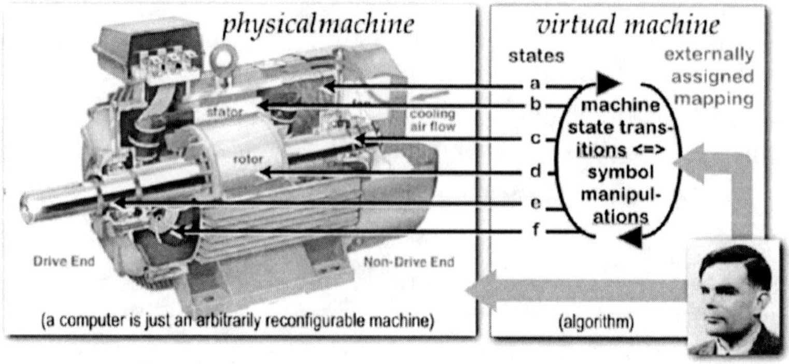

Figure 5: Lack of Computational Qualia

The lack of computational qualia is a result of the way a machine functions in the first place. Computing involves assigning a symbolic interpretation to each of a set of distinct machine states (tokens), and constraining the operation of the machine so that running the machine will traverse states in a way that parallels states in the operation of performing a formal or mental inference using those tokens. Computing here plays no role in producing or maintaining the physical basis that its dynamical activity depends upon. In contrast, mental activity is both dependent on and constantly modifies the material basis of its dynamical activities. In this way neural activity is intrinsically entangled in its own materiality.

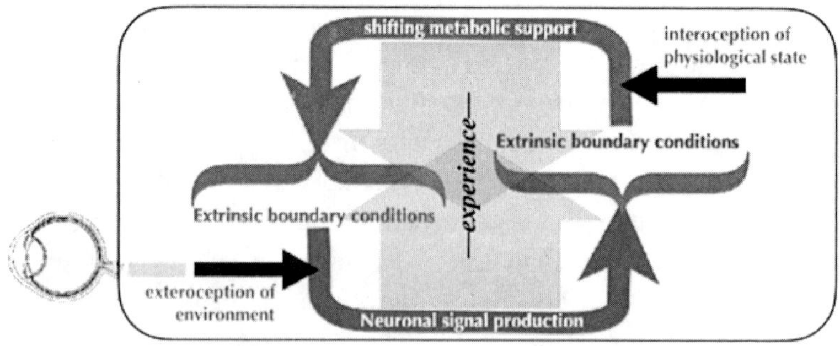

Figure 6: Mental Experience - Function of the Entanglement of Neural Signalling with its Material-Energetic Support

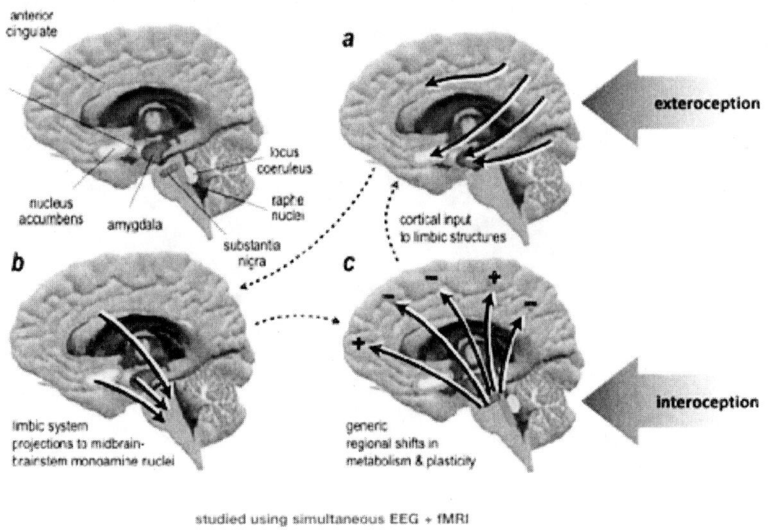

Figure 7: The Circular Causality of Feeling

As cortical activity indirectly modulates the metabolic constraints affecting its own activity, there exists a circular causality of feeling. The assessment of a signal's importance by limbic structures modifies how midbrain-brainstem systems redistribute metabolic support to different cortical regions. Neural activity levels are modified by shifting metabolic support. This means that there can be changing differentials between metabolism and neurological activity. The greater this differential, the more intense the qualia.

Cogito ergo sum ("I think therefore I am") should rather be *"I feel therefore I am real"*

Feeling is not perception. It is a representation of the brain's own conditions of existence, and especially of the deviations from its basic homeostasis, which requires incessant metabolic work. Perception, action and cognition are modulations of this "feeling" of doing neurological work. Machines do no self-generative work and so lack both feeling and thought.

Consciousness is not found in the matter of energy that we are made of, but in the constraints that organise this constantly changing material substrate. Since here the constraints are themselves in the form of absences, consciousness is neither material nor energetic but an expression of the physical influence of how absence shapes what is present.

New Breakthroughs in Understanding Consciousness: From Brain to Internet to Soul

PAUL J. WERBOS

Overview and Summary

Thanks to recent breakthroughs in science, and thanks to new efforts by sincere mystics all over the world, a new understanding of consciousness has begun to emerge, with huge potential benefits both to human health and to our hope of surviving massive changes appearing in the global internet. Old delusions and apparent contradictions now need to be dispelled, urgently, because the changes in technology will overwhelm us if we do not elevate our understanding soon enough.

Changes in Technology which Demand Deeper Consciousness

The website build-a-world.org posts a few of the extensive new materials already available in 2022 from IEEE, NSF and other deep scientific efforts on:

- Four Great Fears ("Existential Threats") SURVIVAL:
    - Internet/AGI (Artificial General Intelligence)/ IOT (Internet of Things) if we fail to reach Sustainable Intelligent Internet (SII)
    - Climate extinction, all of our species and many others
    - Misuse (1) of nuclear tech[i] and (2) biotech, e.g. "Borg"

- Two great Hopes GROWTH:
  - Quantum leap in attaining human potential, including our connections to each other and our noosphere.
  - Economically sustainable settlement of space (e.g., National Space Society).
- SITUATIONAL AWARENESS FOR HUMANS IN COSMOS:
  - Quantum leap in attaining human potential, including our connections to each other and our noosphere
  - Economically sustainable settlement of space (e.g., National Space Society
  - Use of AGI and new constellation sensing technology (from electromagnetics to new force fields such as axial Higgs) to observe the sky and better understand the place of our species in the larger cosmos

This paper cannot go deep into all these complex issues, but this list should be enough to wake us up to the fact that better understanding and expression of consciousness is a matter of life or death for all humans. The issues to be discussed here play an important role in the larger US and UN discussions of how to address these challenges better than anyone has in the past[ii].

Human Health and Consciousness

Better understanding of consciousness and soul are also essential to a more effective, integrated science-grounded approach to holistic healing as illustrated in Figure 1.

For reasons of length, this paper will not discuss the full set of connections between consciousness and human health, important as they are. It will focus more on the mundane nervous system and on the soul, both of which play crucial roles and must work together for optimal human health, as well as sanity or zhengqi[1].

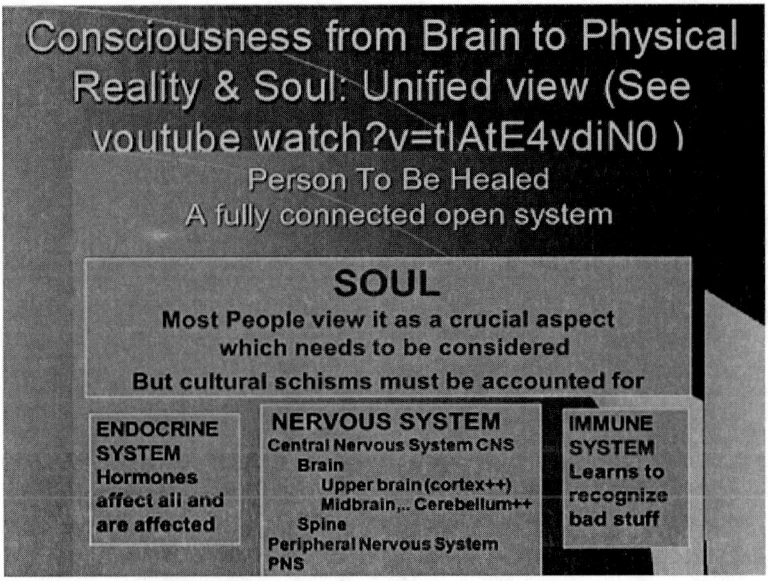

Figure 1: How Consciousness Fits into Healing

What is Consciousness?

There are many definitions of the English word "consciousness". In fact, one test of our personal level of consciousness, or "sanity"[1], is whether we do not get confused by empty issues of semantics. Following my spiritual ancestor, John Von Neumann (Von Neumann and Morgenstern), I will start from a definition of an important word, without wasting time on insane debates about which is the "proper" definition. For "consciousness", there are many different but useful definitions, and many definitions which fuzzify or confuse the mind of those who support them[1]. This paper will define the word "consciousness" as "consciousness qua mind", as an emergent property of an intelligent system such as a brain or a soul or a new type of intelligent computer system which a few of us now know how to build[3].

Certainly the ability to pass the classic Turing test is one of the signs of a kind of intelligent system, but there are many others, and many levels of intelligence or consciousness[2].

Three Types of Substance or Hardware Platform for Consciousness

Most of us now understand that any modern design or architecture for a digital computer, such as a Turing machine, is a general design built up from components which could be implemented on many different physical hardware systems. The Turing capability is defined by higher level properties. It is an example of what Aristotle would call "form," not substance, not just one specific type of matter. Brain-like intelligence is much more than simple digital Turing designs, but it too can exist on many different physical platforms. Sections 2, 3 and 4 of this paper will discuss three important choices — organic brain, internet, and soul or noosphere. Belief that mind is just a kind of substance, rather than form, is an obsolete belief, similar to ancient beliefs in phlogiston

Consciousness at the Mundane Brain Level

(Organic brains are one very important example, to be discussed in section 2)

There have been enormous breakthroughs since 2016 or so[4] in understanding how mammal brains actually attain higher order capabilities, like those described in the National Science Foundation research challenge "COPN"[5], illustrated in Figure 2.

"Telos" or Purpose are central to the new understanding. NSF[6] is now extending that approach further, though the most interesting new results have not yet been released to the public. Section 2 will summarise what some of us now understand about how consciousness emerges in the brain, rising far beyond older, more mechanical models of the brain. In 2015/2016, we drew on the very best real-time brain data then available, but are now working on extensions to exploit new data from sources such as crcns.org, DANDI and the Allen Brain Institute. In a way, this is only a first landing on a whole new continent, but we can now see the whole thing in front of us, with implications for health, for sanity, and for Brain-Computer Interface (BCI).

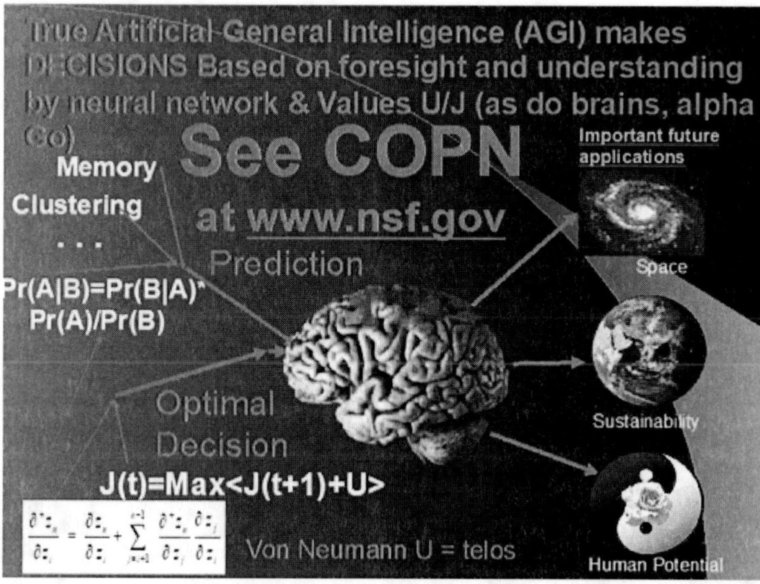

Figure 2: Elements of the NSF COPN Research Strategy

Artificial General Intelligence (AGI)

Can we actually build "computers"—artificial information processing systems—which exhibit the same level of consciousness-qua-intelligence as mammal brains do, or higher? Because this topic excites the public, and "experts" who are experts in exciting the public, most of the public literature on this subject today is woefully ignorant, uninformed by the current frontier of real research.

In my plenary award talk at the World Congress on Computational Intelligence (WCCI) 2022, I said to that audience:

> *If you find an authoritative expert who tells you that AGI will destroy humanity, or that it will make our lives much better, you have identified a very common species of*

psychopath or liar. It is a lie because none of us humans here on earth knows, because it depends on what you and other people like you actually choose to do.

I will not describe the mathematical details of the choices here, because I have already presented them elsewhere in more detail than can fit in this paper,[iii,7] and because they include additional equations and details on how to implement Quantum AGI (another whole level of intelligence or consciousness) which would exceed the limits for a chapter in this book.

In general, the new mathematics gives us a new picture of the levels of consciousness possible, beyond what I knew in the past:

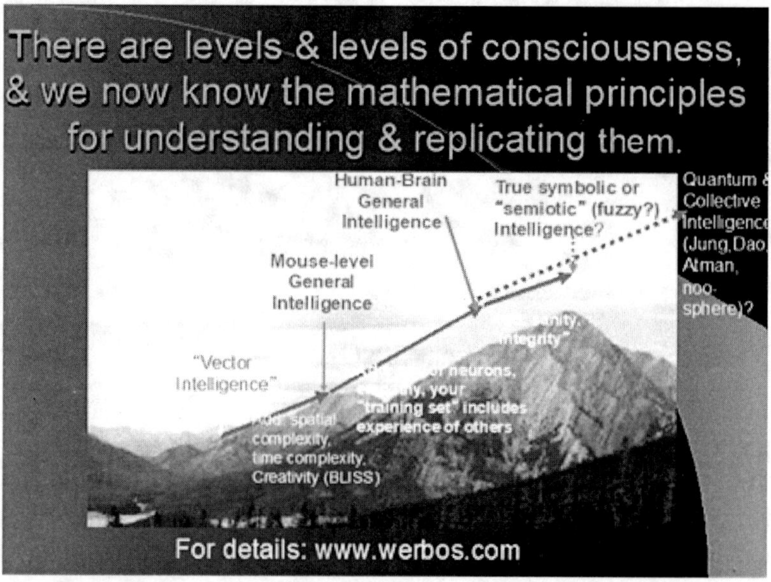

Figure 3. Levels of Consciousness Understood in Broad Terms in New Neural Network Mathematics

There are many philosophers educated in ancient beliefs — now obsolete in this aspect — which tell them that we could not possibly build AGI that could replicate aspects of consciousness which they view as sacred and nonmechanical — like qualia (sensations like "red" or "pain") or emotions or will or telos. Yet all of these exist at the level of the basic mundane mammal brain, which we can build on mathematical principles that we understood back in 2014, which have been taken further and implemented in a major research effort based in the Chinese Academy of Sciences and NSFC[7]. (This gave China superiority over the West in some technologies like hit-to-kill missile interception, after parallel US efforts in this level of technology were discontinued in 2014.)

I would urge such philosophers to study the play and preface of Shaw's *Back to Methusaleh*[iv] which presents a brilliant, clear and precognitive account of how that actually can play out. Two of the characters in that play, called Romeo and Juliet, are advanced but mundane AGI, illustrating how such AGI can reflect all the angst, qualia and emotion that certain gentlemen are so proud of, all in mundane mechanical form. But Shaw goes on to describe how there exist levels of consciousness beyond what such people are proud of, which section 3 will discuss.

Because world government and economic processes will be implemented more and more via internet networks, it will be important to design networks which better reflect Karl Deutsch's idea of mirroring lessons learned from studying the brain[8]. These need to include "immune system" mechanisms to prevent many types of Conflict-of-Interest problems, which can be fatal in AGI systems[9].

See ICCSI[ii] for a link to an IEEE international conference focusing on the first great fear listed at the beginning of the chapter, with plans to post keynote talks both from their global organiser and from me, urging us to account for this great hope as part of how we address the first great fear, and build stronger international cooperation and peace.

Brains with Telos: A Revolution in Systems and Computational Neuroscience

Modern science has become so huge and diverse that many factions have emerged, which often fail to keep up with each other. This exacerbates the challenges described by Thomas Kuhn

(Kuhn 1970). That book is one of the great classics on what science really is. When I worked for NSF, we had directors who cited that book as a kind of Bible. They emphasised the need to work hard to open the door to the new revolutions we need in scientific thought — especially in building new connections between disciplines[5,6], supported by one of those Directors).

Now, as tens of thousands of people attend annual conferences of the Society for Neuroscience, and very diverse groups attend the two main annual conferences on consciousness, the challenge of fragmentation across subgroups demands attention more than ever in the past, to prevent the ever-present threat of people unable to "see the forest for the trees".

Figure 4 illustrates how some people think about consciousness in the human brain, and how some build computational models.

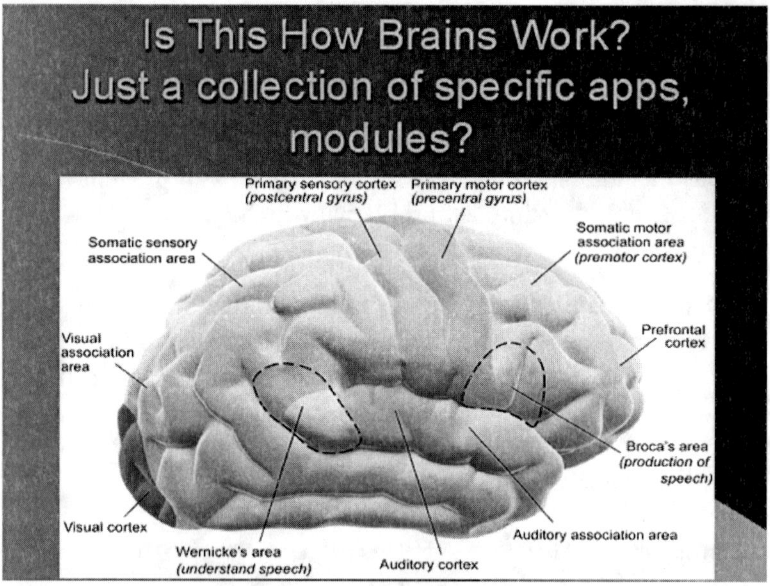

Figure 4. The Most Common But Obsolete Mental Model of Human Brain Consciousness — A Collection of Specific "Modules."

This problem of fragmentation already began decades ago, when people began creating maps like this. These maps remain important and useful, but they mask the most important aspect of human intelligence — our ability to learn new things[5,6], which results in changes in what task is located where, and variations between people. This challenge resulted in the creation of a whole new school of thought in systems neuroscience, illustrated in Figure 5.

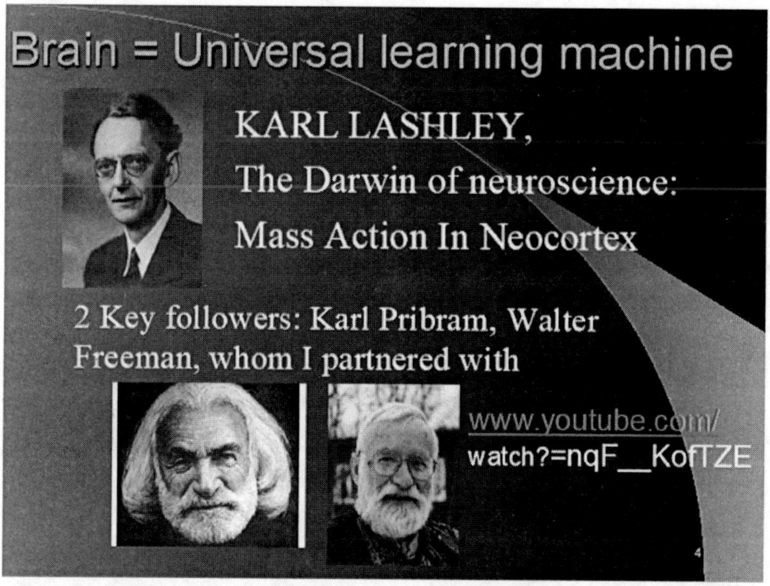

Figure 5. Founder of Mass Action School (Lashley), and Two Leading Developers of that School

Karl Pribram and Walter Freeman were, in my view, the world's leaders in systems neuroscience, the branch of neuroscience which tries to understand whole systems properties and consciousness itself, as they exist in the brain. I was very grateful to the "old NSF" for giving me a chance to work closely with both these great scientists as they worked on the books which they viewed as their "magnum opus" summing up the entire big picture as it emerged from their work. (Pribram 2013a,b, Kozma and Freeman). Pribram (1976) also explains how Freud's theory of psychodynamics leads directly to a serious new picture of how brains work, which was the foundation both for back propagation (the equation in the lower left of Figure 2) and for the model illustrated in Figure 8.

Figure 6 illustrates the view of mammal brain consciousness which I used in defending the NSF[14] COPN research plan which was widely discussed and agreed to by program directors all across the Foundation.

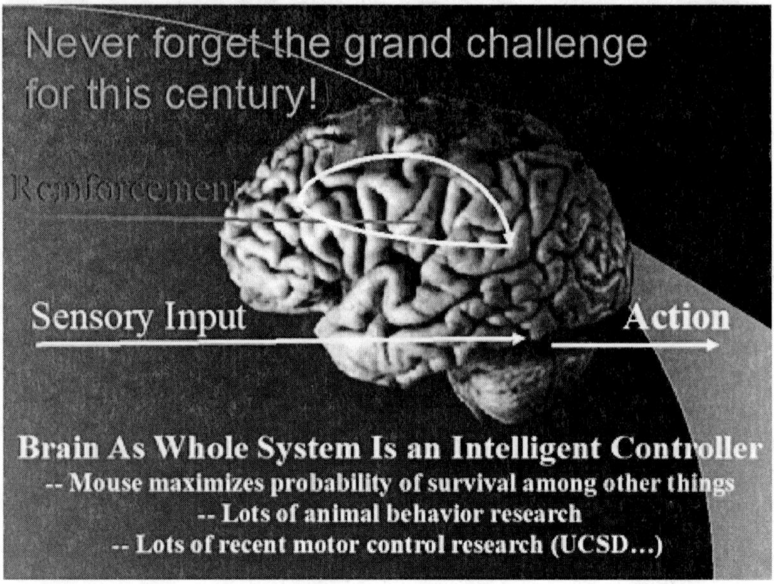

Figure 6. View of the Mammal Brain as a Whole System (Leading to Figure 2)

Figure 7 illustrates our new understanding of how this works[7], crucial to much of the new work in systems neuroscience and in AGI.

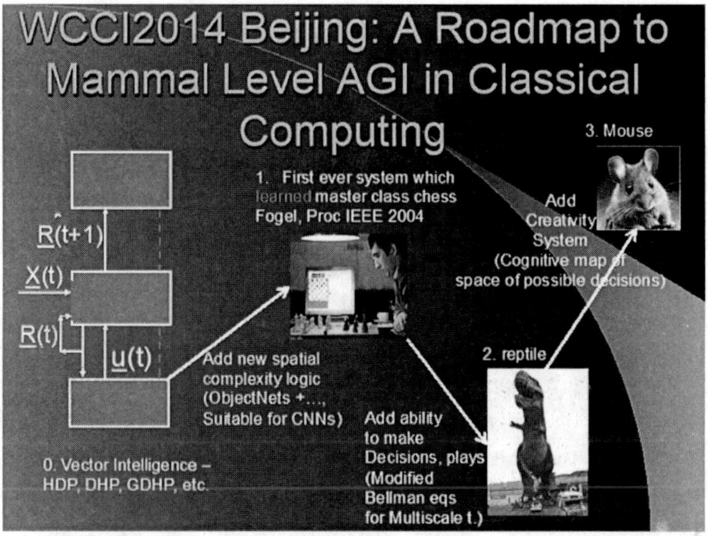

Figure 7: The Roadmap to Mouse Level AGI

Comparison between the reptile level and the mouse level was crucial to the new understanding in Werbos and Davis, and in the work leading up to that paper, illustrated in Figure 8.

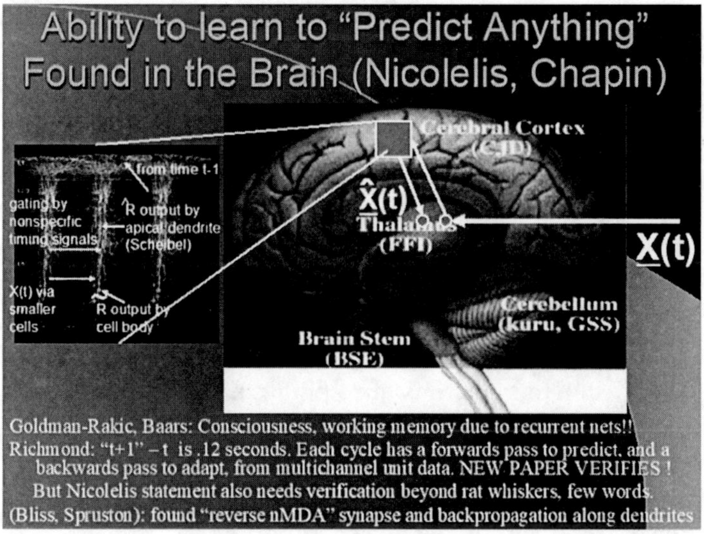

Figure 8. A Key Step Leading to the New Understanding in Werbos and Davis

Figure 8 may be the slide which is absolutely most critical not only to the new neuroscience but to further connections to the soul (section 3). This is the slide which points to Nicolelis et al.,[10], the paper which demonstrated a kind of concrete, specific universal learning function in the neocortex, which accounts for just over half of the weight of a typical human brain. It translates a major part of the general concept of mass action into a very specific mathematical relation, that Werbos and Davis further translates into the kind of mathematics which can replicate this capability.

Actually, this kind of universal learning capability also exists in the brain of the reptile. However, we claim — from many sources of evidence — that the basic mouse brain goes beyond the reptile brain by merging the prediction type of cortex with another cortex used in mapping space (spatial intelligence), in order to attain a revolutionary new ability: the ability to map the space of possibilities for action or decision, the space of options (like verb and object) to be sent to a lower part of the brain, the basal ganglia, which manages the execution of specific skills like "open the door."

Within the neocortex, you see giant pyramid cells in this cutaway photograph. These cells are the backbone of the neocortex. In Werbos and Davis, we used important (processed) data from the laboratory of Buzsaki (in my view the world's foremost systems neuroscientist, with Nicolelis coming up as well) on the neocortex. His data could distinguish between two types on neuron, giant pyramid cells[10] versus interneurons (spiking neurons). This distinction is absolutely essential to further carrying forward the hypotheses explored in Werbos and Davis, to better understand all aspects of the neocortex. In a step beyond that, it may make sense to identify bursting neurons and spiking neurons separately, but ***also*** track the impact of small graded neurons, which can tweak the spiking and bursting neutrons by graded synapses, leading to measurements of flows along individual neurons, as in some of the newest work on "automated spike sorting."

Based on these sources, I claim that the "global workspace of consciousness" as described by Baars[11] and Goldman-Rakic[12] is basically the same as the outputs R (a reconstruction of reality using recurrent connections) of these giant pyramid cells.

From Brain to Soul: Grounding Mysticism in Reality and Mathematics

Human cultures have seen endless struggles between true mystics, who study first person experience and second person reports with the same intensity which some of us apply to third person science[13], and political apparatchiks who commonly serve as agents of a priest-king or empire to try to control (or get rewards from) the general public. In my view, the peace of the world and the sanity of human society in general depend on avoiding the wars which many apparatchiks and their fanatic followers would impose on us. Unifying true mysticism and true science (as in section 2) is now possible, and is perhaps the greatest hope before the entire human species at this time. In many ways, this would follow a larger vision of what science is, as it unifies both methods, according to the praxis taught by Francis Bacon.

In 1967, I was firmly engaged on the path described in section 2, and I simply did not believe in any kind of mysticism, or any kind of soul beyond the mundane consciousness emergent in our mammal brains. In 1964, I was deeply inspired by reading Hebb[14], another follower of Lashley who helped inspire the modern neural network community, especially through the International Neural Network Society (now a key partner in the WCCI conferences).

Hebb began his book by discussing the importance of Bayes Law (see Figure 2) in building systems which learn to predict the probability of events in the world. He argued that the probability of a theory being true, after we have empirical evidence (experience), is proportional to the product of the likelihood (the probability that we would see what we see in experience, if the theory is true) multiplied by the prior probability. He argued that psychic or spiritual phenomena have very little probability of being true, despite empirical evidence much stronger than what is accepted in other fields of psychology which he knew very well, because of the prior term: "It is physically impossible. I fully understood that viewpoint, and held to it very strictly, despite personal experiences which would have convinced most other people[v].

However, in the spring of 1967, a first-person experience simply became too strong for me to maintain a rigid position on this issue[1]. I did not immediately jump to the opposite extreme; as a proper follower of Von Neumann and Morgenstern, I resolved to attribute a 50-50 probability split on this issue, and to probe much much deeper to try to figure out what was going on. That in turn led me to try many experiments and exercises, culminating in a kundalini yoga exercise in 1972, taken from a popular group, which worked for me in very dramatic fashion the very first time. I did not attend any yoga classes at that time, but I did read a paperback book by Gopi Krishna describing how he survived raising the kundalini, which was a lifesaver for me at that time. After that exercise, I did not ask whether strange things were possible, but how.

I also took graduate courses at Harvard on advanced quantum field theory, including courses from Julian Schwinger and Sidney Coleman, which showed me that the "prior" term was not as impossible as I had imagined.

In the 1970s, after trying many experiments, I also decided to take out a membership in two groups, AMORC and a Sikh-oriented yoga group, to suggest new experiments beyond what I had tried so far, and to give me access to more second-person reports. I was even inducted into the International Research Council of AMORC in the 1970s where I wrote a long paper, in simple English, summarising three different theories of how psychic phenomena might be possible. ("Science, Mysticism and the Nature of Man.")

In that period, I also learned that the discussion of psychic phenomena and soul, in our modern culture, tends to be inhibited, just as the discussion of sex was in Victorian England. Greeley and MacReady reported on an in-depth study funded by NSF which revealed just how great the first-person experiences were, especially for well-educated professionals in years of peak performance in the mundane world. The life stories of the four great creators of quantum physics (De Broglie, Heisenberg, Schrodinger and Einstein) showed how three of the four were extremely serious about life and mind beyond the mundane level. (Einstein, the fourth, is a mixed story, beyond the scope of this paper, but three out of four tells us something.)

As time went on, and I explored further, it became increasingly clear that simple theories simply would not work. The flow of information between points or people thousands of miles away requires a very sophisticated signal processing arrangement, far beyond what even the most Advanced Quantum Information S&T (QuIST) would allow, if we are limited to the types of force fields (QED, quantum electrodynamics) best known to humans.

Bit by bit, I saw no way to explain the most basic, validated psychic phenomena without assuming some kind of living connections, like a nervous system, a nervous system as big as the earth or bigger. This, plus continued experimentation, led me to the noosphere species theory[1], illustrated in Figure 9.

Figure 9. The Noosphere Species Theory: An Actual Photo and Questions

In that paper, I cite the famous prior work by Vernadsky and Teilhard de Chardin which once seemed to provide a grand unification of mysticism and the soul with hard science. But even in the Vatican, they realised that that version of the theory did not fit science, because the mechanism of evolution in just one organism simply did not make sense.

My new theory is that our entire cosmos, as shown in this new photograph, is actually like a vast ocean (network), pulsing with free energy and matter. Modern concepts of evolution would actually predict that some form of life would evolve in any such vast ocean. Thus, it is not surprising to consider that organisms like noospheres might evolve here.

Many scientists have been deeply puzzled by the Fermi paradox[15]: if intelligence evolves often enough, and if space travel is possible, why haven't we seen aliens yet (at least according to most scientists a few decades ago)? The concept here is that *we are the aliens*, that we are part of a symbiosis or ordinary mundane organism with our local noosphere, which is a (young) member of a cosmos-spanning species.

This photograph of "dark matter", taken via gravitational lensing, is as real as any x-ray you see from your doctor or dentist. Notice that the galaxies appear as small orange dots at the nodes of the network. There have been reports of "zombie galaxies", where dark matter does not penetrate much, and where star formation is drastically inhibited.

In my view, this strongly supports the idea that dark matter may well be connected strongly to our own sun, the centre of our local noosphere. But science demands we find out. Perhaps the new technology of tabletop detection of axial Higgs bosons (not the heavy WIMPs assumed in theories of dark matter which don't work) could allow us to actually see those connections, yea unto *Qi* itself... or direct us to another path to understanding

Like a little fish or tadpole in a large dangerous aquarium… we are deeply called to survive, as a whole noosphere, and to grow, and to better understand and see into that larger aquarium. After our personal mundane death, our "soul" (or "soul personality") is what lives on as part of the noosphere, which may grow and connect (as do giant pyramid cells) or may simply dissolve away in time (per the garbage collections routines important in all AGI and brains). How we connect, and respond to *Qi* from the whole system, and learn to see further and deeper will determine the outcome. We all have a lot to learn about this[vi].

What Am I Missing?

By 2021, I saw no evidence whatsoever from credible texts on mysticism or from hard core third person science that our cosmos is not governed by the kind of field theory described in Carmeli[16]. Just as mathematicians learned decades ago that ordinary differential equations predict emergent behaviour, like chaos, which is much richer than what they had thought, I learned how Carmeli's kind of model across space-time predicts statistical patterns, like what is described in Werbos and Fleury[vii,17]. This in turn reassured me that complex patterns like what we see in the most serious mysticism, can be understood better on that hard-core realistic foundation than on any of the metaphysical and fuzzy theories we often read about.

Nevertheless, as a follower of Von Neumann, I do not just assign certainty to such a theory, even when I do not know any serious concrete alternatives with concrete evidence to support them. I try to hedge my bets by considering alternatives, such as the vast range of theories suggested by the more serious, credible mystics.

In that spirit, I now begin my very highest levels of meditation, not with the image in Figure 9, but with Figure 10 (slightly cleaned up).

If my new worldview is the whole story (in some form, with some choice of Hamiltonian), I use the image on the lower left to represent our local noosphere, or Mother Earth, or the spirit of the Times as described by Jung in his Red Book. Those are different,

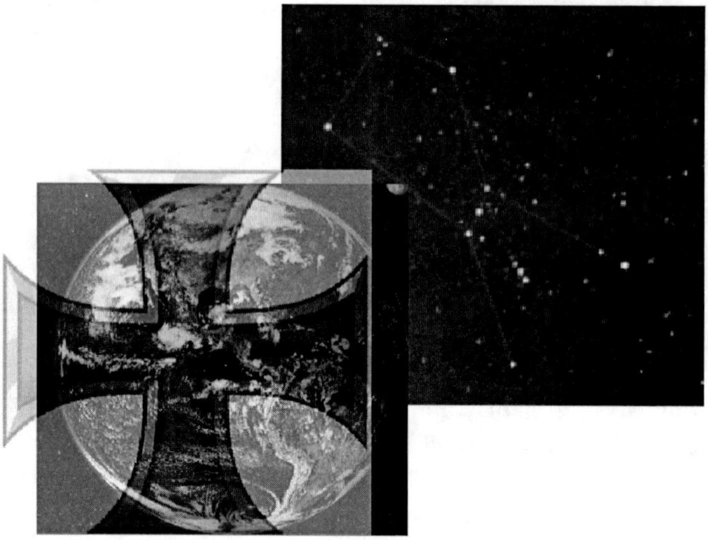

Figure 10. A More Inclusive View

but I try to be open to these possibilities. The Maltese Cross symbolises our spiritual unity in the global workspace of thought of our noosphere. Above it the image of Orion symbolises the gateway, via the Orion Spur in our galaxy, to the larger Cosmos, to the Spirit of the Deep, to the underlying images which we may try to connect to.

In order to be cautious, and remain open-minded, we should be fully open to the possibility that the highest intelligence we can access up there might know something we don't. It may be a good idea to try to be truly sensitive to it[viii] (which is not the same as sensitivity to the pale reflections we see in human cultures), and not flagrantly reject hints which seem authentic enough, especially when those hints reflect the idea that our cosmos might just be some kind of school. In that school, perhaps we are perhaps called to learn and do our very best, with full third-order sanity and rationality, except that we must allow the operation of strange synchronicities which might help others to learn and grow in that very same school. Perhaps, perhaps not, but if ever ignorance suggests a bit of caution, this is such a time.

AI, Consciousness and Indic Perspectives

KANCHI GOPINATH

Introduction

Given the extensive penetration of digital technology (vide Web, cellular phone, etc), technophilosophy (the philosophical study of digital systems in the human context) has emerged as a subject of inquiry in philosophy. One important area of enquiry is the problem of consciousness and the mind-body debate in the context of computing devices and specifically AI. Since computing devices are increasingly seen to be "intelligent" (as they are able to replace the thinking required of human beings in some domains), the issue of whether this type of intelligence can be accompanied by an analog of human consciousness has also become a topic of discussion.

The prevailing standard perspective is the computational paradigm (CP) which provides many bottom-up insights and argues that computational complexity is the limiting factor for both intelligence and consciousness. Once a threshold is reached, newer emergent phenomena such as intelligence and consciousness can both arise. There is also the related self-reorganising systems paradigm (SSP) that can integrate top-level, bottom-up approaches along with multilevel models using contributory features such as energy or entropy levels. Alternately, consciousness can be taken as a new entity and argue that no explanation of consciousness in purely physical terms is possible.

Certain Indic paradigms may also be useful for discussion (in particular, rasa theory) as they posit ontologies (including some metaphysical ones) that may be useful guideposts for exploration.

The "mindfulness" movement is a direct development based on early research undertaken with Swami Rama, Maharishi Mahesh Yogi in the early 1970s and, later in the 80s, with Bauddha vipassana meditators. These and other Indic thoughts are mainly top-down insights or heuristics that are also often multi-level; the value of such thinking to current thinking on consciousness studies is worth examining. For example, there are multiple Indic perspectives on what happens during sleep and dreaming[1] and their connections with models of consciousness. Since these positions have been debated extensively in the Indic tradition, they can still be of value at a didactic level, even if not directly in terms of neuroscience correlates. Similarly, deeper investigations are still needed to explore the connections between rasa and consciousness. For example, does rasa have any overlap with qualia, a term introduced by Pierce (1866) and widely used in Western models of consciousness? Is there a concept in Indic thought among the many that closely matches it? Or, do we regard rasa as a very distinctive type of deep integrative "consciousness" that one senses when experiencing art forms? Furthermore, concepts like *dhyāna*, *praṇāyāma*, *nāda brahman*, *vipassana*, *yoga nidra*, *yantra*, *bīja* mantra and yoga in the Indic psychological (or "inner") sciences need careful study in the context of consciousness; currently, they seem to have been renamed in the West respectively as meditation (neuro-phenomenology), breathing techniques, sound therapy, mindfulness, lucid dreaming, sacred geometry, relaxation response, and pilates (as argued, for example, by Rajiv Malhotra). Given the varieties of phenomena and hence types of "consciousness" possible, we discuss it next in summary form.

Consciousness

The English word "consciousness" means many things and captures diverse ideas. Is it being aware of oneself as existing in some context or just physically in the world and responding to and being aware of some sense modality, as is commonly understood in the West? In contrast, Indic mind sciences envision a much larger role under the subject matter and also have many terms for expressing the many diverse ideas; these will be discussed as we go along. For example, सत् चित् आनन्द (sat-cit-ānanda) is usually translated loosely as, "Truth, Consciousness and Happiness" and it is not clear, for example, what is to be understood by the term consciousness here. Is चित (cit) a unique Indic idea of "supramental consciousness"? Or, as चित्त (chitta) when associated with nirvāna, "a consciousness, without a distinguishing mark, infinite and shining everywhere" (Buddha in Dīgha Nikāya; in Sanskrit from Pāli: विज्ञानं अनिदर्शनं अनंतं सर्वतोप्रभा). Or, is it the larger Indic perspective of seeing the macro in micro: i.e. the integrative understanding of the world that seeks to incorporate the outside world onto oneself? Essentially, does the Indic notion signify something different from the English meaning: negation of dualistic thinking, or the non-plurality of the world or the non-difference of subject and object (as summarised by David Loy)?

Or consider, Patanjali's Yogasūtra that discusses samādhi, a state of consciousness in which all samskāra-s ("latent impressions") cease. From sūtra-s 1.33 to 1.40, a set of practices are mentioned that will help a seeker to achieve this state through methods such as cultivating equanimity towards all things, whether pleasant or painful, good or bad, practising prāṇāyāma (control over "breathing" e.g. pausing after breathing in or out) or meditative absorption in any object whether desired ones, vast or minute. Sūtra-s 1.16 discusses the state of संप्रज्ञात (samprajnāta) which is consciousness that arises out of deep thought or reasoning and bliss but with a sense of "I". Sūtra-s 1.41 to 1.51 discuss other deeper states of consciousness such as savitarka and nirvitarka samāpatti (along with their savichāra and nirvichāra alternate names) that constitute sabīja samādhi, and finally nirbīja samādhi. In savitarka samāpatti, when चित्त (chitta) is gradually stilled, a clear way of seeing becomes possible where there is no difference between the subject, object or the act of perceiving itself but it is still mediated through reasoning, language or memory. Here, for example, the word (syntax), the meaning (referent or essence) and the understanding (semantics) becomes one. In the next stage, nirvitarka samāpatti, this mediation also ceases and only the essence shines through without the subject interposing in between or be affected by the peculiarities of syntax, etc. The vichāra versions of samāpatti are considered to be alternate names of the corresponding vitarka subtle states. Sūtra 1.50 says that these states of consciousness, that is of sabīja samādhi, prevent newer samskāra-s being formed but samskāra-s causally of their own are still present. In the nirbīja samādhi, all samskara-s cease.

"Machine Consciousness"?

To understand the issues in the context of AI, consider the issue of "machine consciousness" with the question "is a computer conscious?" The notion of computation is central for a computer but it is somewhat slippery as it often gets conflated with mathematics. Mathematics does not stress or use the notion of states as much as computation[2]. In this paper, we will accept the characterisation of computation[3] as "the evolution process of some environment via a sequence of "simple, local" steps." In contrast, mathematics stresses invariants (which usually translates to "intuitions" of mathematicians that can be, when "true", possibly be established by proofs). Essentially, computation and mathematics are part of a continuum depending on the stress on state or, its "opposite", invariance; this is analogous to the questions of whether "reality" is discrete ("Bauddha" perspective), or is it meaningful only across chosen one or more states (the general "computational" perspective), or is it continuous ("Vedānta" perspective: "all is one"). Or, even an entity that occupies multiple states at the same time probabilistically as in quantum phenomena.

Let us consider the issue arising from a computer as a device that may give rise to consciousness: "…the question, 'Is a computer conscious?' does not ask whether there are processes going on that are in some relevant respect analogous to human cognitive processes, but rather whether there is anything it is like for the computer to be in its computational state, that is, whether the computer instantiates phenomenal properties." (as posed by Ganeri)

If "computational" means doing many simple local steps, is "to be conscious" the same as being aware of being part of a local mathematical invariant as each local step is being executed? To be conscious of each local step itself is slightly "excessive" (as it is reflexive to the extent that it contradicts the "simple local step" property) but, even if so, what each local step signifies (to itself?) is not clear.

Consider the Collatz "($3n + 1$)" problem: define $f(n)$ as "if ($n = 1$) then 1 else (if even(n) then $f(n/2)$ else $f(3n + 1)$)". Does $f(n)$ go to 1 for all n? Or, more simply, does it terminate for all n? That is believed to be the case as no counterexamples have been found yet (till n about 2^87) but there is no proof yet, with the famous mathematician Erdos opining "mathematics is not prepared for such problems yet". Essentially, no significant "invariants" have been found that provide enough "structure" so that a proof can be crafted[i]. When the Collatz computation is effected, the "end" is not obvious and only the "journey" is the "reality". Is it the case that the only inklings of consciousness possible for a computer here are a few notions such as "being in computation involving integers" or "being in computation that may or may not end"? Even these are not available in the definition of the problem above; they may have to be introduced explicitly. Note that a computer scientist (or possibly another "intelligent" computer) observing Collatz computation may additionally also be conscious of notions such as "current proof techniques not powerful enough for a resolution of the Collatz problem"; this is essentially a metalevel view.

Due to the "paradox of the heap"[ii], it is not clear when some states can be grouped into a meaningful macro state and when they cannot. If statistical measures (such as hypothesis testing for null hypothesis) are used, they introduce additional complexities as the debate about p-values shows as well as the zero paradox[4].

In the context of computation, when a machine executes an "instruction", many logical, memory and processing units may take part. These steps make sense in the context of the execution of the instruction but otherwise, considering their constituent parts, they seem to be almost "arbitrary". For example, if a bit is realised through one or more active transistors, changes in the active transistors do not make sense at its own level. Note that such signalling can happen in a fluidics device too! Hence only the "emergent" phenomenon (or the "epiphenomenon") can be seen as computation.

At each level, there is a phenomenon and its representation, whether internally or externally. If internally (the more interesting case for understanding consciousness), is there an active entity that makes, accesses and modifies/deletes these representations? But how does it represent itself if it is a part?

Tononi's "integrated information theory" of consciousness postulates necessary components of consciousness as being informative and as having high "integrated information" (ie. not easily separable). By this token any complex tightly coupled analog circuit or Pāṇini's grammar may be said to be conscious! Alternatively[5], based on neurons as substrate, it also postulates that "consciousness should be understood in terms of cause-effect "power" that reflects the amount of maximally irreducible integrated information generated by certain neuronal architectures." A competing theory[5], "global neuronal workspace theory (GNWT) claims that consciousness is instantiated by the global broadcasting and amplification of information across an interconnected network of prefrontal-parietal areas and many high-level sensory cortical areas."

While the approaches listed above can be seen as "bottom up" approaches, the Indic tradition of mind sciences can be said to be closer to the "top down" model. For example, it explores transitions between normal states of consciousness, for example, between waking and dreaming states as a useful heuristic. For example, how does one know, after deep sleep, that deep sleep intervened? Is it by inference (eg. *Navya Nyāya*), or by a residual consciousness (e.g. Vedānta) or by a higher level consciousness (e.g. Yoga)? Note that deep sleep does not seem to "cognise" anything, including self. Vedānta postulates a basal साक्षि (witness) during deep sleep (just like a sleeping laptop still has some minimal electronics operating to respond to input) while Yoga argues for a स्वप्रकाश (internally illumined) awareness that also exists, for example, during lucid dreaming.

Given the wide difference in perspectives, we next discuss some background on Indic perspectives to complement the discussion above.

Background on Relevant Indic Notions with Reference to the Concept of Consciousness

Our ancients had an interesting computational model of "thinking", with memory as an important part. In Indic thought, we have sensor, storage and cognitive structures[iii]. The sensors are classified into 2 types: Jñānendriya (5 organs of sense: eye, ear, nose, tongue, skin) and Karmendriya (5 organs of actions: mouth (the organ of speech), feet, hands, anus, genitals). The cognitive structures are manas ("supervisor" of 5 jñānendriya-s and 5 karmendriya-s, now "identified" as [hypo-/ thalamus]), chitta (store of sense impressions, [hippocampus]), ahamkāra (I-am-ness, now [medial prefrontal cortex/cerebral cortex]) and buddhi (decision-maker that may control manas, chitta and ahamkāra). In a computer science perspective, these are roughly the I/O controller for sensing and action, persistent storage, thread of control, and the code/algorithms of the core kernel. (Only the network aspect is not explicitly mentioned; it is possibly subsumed by the I/O controller.)

Furthermore, thinkers like Bhartṛhari argue that the sense data are processed by the mind; there is no "pure" sense data or any pratyaksha (immediate perception) per se that is not mediated through the mind: "the nature of things in isolation is not ascertained"; there is also a strong relation between linguistic perspectives and consciousness. In addition, there is a tradition of positing a strong relation between sound[iv] and consciousness, especially through praṇava and tanmatra-s[v], and, more generally, between embodiment and consciousness through yoga and prāṇayāma. While using the English word consciousness is common in these contexts, it seems to be almost at the breaking point; a more refined taxonomy is needed. For a start, we can consider the use of notions such as आत्मन (*atman*) and ब्राह्मन (*brahman*) as one aspect of consciousness is often "non-duality" as understood in Indic mind sciences[vi]. The Western notions of consciousness are typically those of an individual at the level of senses (in an integrative way possibly) and at the level of the mind (self or soul).

In contrast, Indic notions are at multiple levels that are layered on top of the basic sense level (अन्नमय (*annamaya*)) such as at the प्राणमय (*prāṇamaya*), मनोमय (*manomaya*), विज्ञानमय (*vijñānamaya*), आनंदमय (*anandamaya*) levels; these levels interpenetrate so as to give "embodied cognition". These operate at bodily nourishment, at bodily integrity/survival, at the level of mind integrity, at the level of integrated intelligence described, for example, in Gīta as स्थितप्रज्ञ (deep contextual awareness of right action), and finally at the "universal consciousness" level that sees the micro in the macro and macro in the micro (यत् पिन्डे तद् ब्राह्मान्डे/*yat-pinde-tad-brāhmānde)* and thereby integrates its "local self" with the "world" in a deep reflective and reflexive way[vii]. In the chapter "The Arithmetical Paradox: The Oneness of Mind," Schrodinger[viii] says "The reason why our sentient, percipient and thinking ego is met nowhere within our scientific world picture can easily be indicated in seven words: because it is itself that world picture. It is identical with the whole and therefore cannot be contained in it as a part of it. … the arithmetical paradox; there appears to be a great multitude of these conscious egos, the world however is only one… There is obviously only one alternative, namely the unification of minds or consciousnesses. Their multiplicity is only apparent, in truth there is only one mind. This is the doctrine of the Upanishads."

Furthermore, among Bauddha-s, there is discussion of primary consciousness (that of eye, ear, nose, tongue, body, mind), mental factors or subsidiary awarenesses, and reflexive awareness. Two other types are sometimes added in the primary list: that of deluded awareness and आलयविज्ञान (storehouse consciousness) that carries memory karma. The latter is an individual level, it is not universal and may be "non-real"

Bauddha-s argue that "fields of action and awareness have a central structure…there is a 'space' or 'frame' of awareness (*citta*) which is … a range of experiential, attentive and agentive functions (the mental factors or *cetasika*; in Sanskrit चैतसिक) that take place in it."[6,ix] They list some universal cetasika-s such as स्पर्श (touch), वेदना (sensation), सम्ज्ञ (cognition), चेतना (volition), समाधि ("deep meditation") or एकाग्रता (concentration), स्मृति (reminiscence), जीवितिन्द्रिय (controlling principle), मनसिकार (attention), and "occasional" ones like वितर्क (conjecture), विचार (thought or thinking), अधिमोक्ष (resolution), वीर्य (vigour or valour), प्रीति (joyful satisfaction), छन्द (free will or wish). (Note that we only give here indicative English translations as there is no unanimity. There are often specific or technical meanings in the specific tradition in which they are used!) There are also wholesome (कुशल) mental factors such as श्रद्ध (discriminative faith), ह्री (moral shame), अपत्राप्य (moral fear), अलोभ (non-greedy), अद्वेष (unenvious), प्रश्रब्धि (flexibility), उपेक्ष (equanimity), अहिंसा (non-violence) and unwholesome (क्लेश) ones such as मोह (illusion), प्रमाद (carelessness), कौसीद्य (laziness), अश्रद्ध (lack of faith), सत्यान (lethargy), औद्धत्य (agitation), अप्रमाद (carefulness).

Furthermore, reflexive awareness, according to this view, "accompanies every moment of non-conceptual and conceptual cognition of an object, although it itself remains always non-conceptual. It focuses on and cognises only the other awarenesses of the cognition—namely, the primary consciousness and mental factors—as well as their validity. It does not cognise the objects of the primary consciousnesses and mental factors on which it focuses. It plants the nonstatic abstraction (non-congruent affecting variable) of a mental impression of the cognition it cognizes, which then allows for subsequently recalling the cognition (mindfulness). Recalling it occurs through conceptual cognition of a mental aspect resembling an object previously cognised and a category (universal) that mentally derives from the object and into which fit all mental aspects resembling the object."[x]

Rasa theorists like Bharata also discuss many analogs of mental factors that, however, combine physical and mental states intimately: स्मृति (remembrance), धृति (steadiness), व्रीडा (shame), चिंता (worry), मति (judgement), आवेग (impulse), आलस्य (laziness), दैन्य (wretchedness), निर्वेद (disregard of worldly objects), ग्लानि (exhaustion), शक (doubt), असूया (envy), मद (excitement), उन्माद (madness), मोह (illusion), उपालम्भ (censure), हर्ष (joy), चपलता (unsteadiness), जड़ता (stiffness), मरण (deathlike), व्याधि (sickness), गर्व (pride), विषाद (sorrow), औत्सुक्य (curious), निद्रा (sleep), अपस्मार (epileptic), सुप्त (sleepy), विबोध (awakening), अमर्ष (intolerance), अवहित्थ (dissimulation), उग्रता (acrimony), त्रास (apprehensive), वित्रस्तक (intimidated).

Bharata's rasa theory can be understood as a 2-level model where recurrent (lower-level) *bhāva-s* (approximately translated as "emotions") with appropriate positive factors and, when generalised (by eliminating "noise" or negative factors, and specificities that pertain to local state), can lead to a higher-level rasa (approximately translated as "aesthetic sense")[7]. The well known *rasasutra* रससूत्र to invoke rasa, as stated in Bharata's Nātyasastra, is given as follows: *vibhāva anubhāva vyabhicharinsamyogāt rasa nishpattih* विभाव अनुभाव व्यभिचारिन् संयोगात् रस निष्पत्तिः। Vibhāva is taken as the "primary" cause (*kāraṇa*). *Anubhāva* is the consequent physical reaction through action, word and facial expression that follows (*anu*), due to *vibhāva*. The 33 *vyabhichārin bhāva-s* or *sanchāri bhāva-s* are transitory, fleeting emotions based on psychological states of the mind. It is said that several such emotions follow successively, fortifying the *sthāyībhāva* at each stage, till finally the *sthāyibhāva* is established that culminates in '*rasānubhāva*'. We will later discuss Orpwood's theory that has interesting connections with Bharata's ideas.

The notion of universal and occasional factors of the

Bauddha-s mirrors concepts of Bharata in his rasa theory such as the rasa/bhāva distinction as well as between bhāva and sthāyī bhāva, mainly due to *vyabhichārin bhāva-s* or *sanchāri bhava-s*. Both also posit "state" based models to explain changes, with Bauddha-s also using notions such as आलयविज्ञान (storehouse of consciousness) to explain why different "minds" often are in agreement with external reality.

Furthermore, a computational model can be "surmised" either with state transition models (eg. *vāsanā-s* in Bhagavad Gīta/*Vedānta*[xi] or *kalāpa-s* in Buddhism to explain how suffering is produced), or even possibly with intimations of control-theoretical models with dimensionality reduction (by reducing 56 or so *bhāva-s* to 9 *rasa-s*). For example, consider a principal emotion the *sthāyībhāva* of anger (क्रोध)[xii].

"Let us say the cause of anger, *vibhāva*, is betrayal by a friend; this anger will be more potent if the *vibhāva* is strongly established. If the *sthāyī bhāva* is deeply felt, then it will result in the physical manifestation of anger such as burning eyes and heaving chest, which is the anubhāva. But in anger, one can make fun of and laugh sarcastically at the object of one's anger. One can feel sorrow when thinking of the happy times spent together earlier. One can feel disgust for the other person's behaviour or be amazed at the change in him now. Through all this, the fundamental thread of anger must be maintained. But the transient emotions—the *vyabhichārin bhāva-s* of laughter, sorrow, disgust and amazement—enhance the present angry state. If performed with appropriate āngika, *vācika*, āharya and above all, true sātvika abhinaya, it will invoke the rasa of *raudra* or anger in the spectator whose mind is absorbed in the performance."

Since a more detailed study of at least one sense modality in the context of consciousness can be useful from an Indic perspective, we discuss that of sound/music in some more detail next. We also discuss a multi-level model from Bauddha thinking (Shāntarakshita) next.

Sound Modality and “Consciousness”

गीतादिविषयास्वादासमसौख्यैकतात्मनः।
योगिनस्तन्मयत्वेन मनोरुढेस् तदात्मता ।। ७३।।

Figure 1: Shloka from *Vijnānabhairava*, 73

“Yogins, experiencing their oneness with some incomparable pleasure aroused by the experience of objects like melodious (“sweet”) songs etc. and fixing their mental attentiveness on it, find unity with the Absolute Lord through a practice of absorption in this kind of phenomenon” (Vijnānabhairava, 73).

This shloka in *Vignāna Bhairava Tantra* indicates the importance of aids like music in the union with the supreme; rasa theory posits sacred music and arts to have a “*brahmānandasahodara*” nature (as advocated by Bhaṭṭa Nāyaka from Kāshmīr) and a stepping stone to “brahmānanda” itself[xiii]. This view becomes amplified strongly in the bhakti tradition (e.g. Mīra), in sensuous works such as Gita Govinda and in the Odissi/ Kathaka/Bharata Nātyam tradition of dances, and as nādayoga (for example in Karnātic music of Purandaradāsa, Thyāgarāja and many others.)

Kāshmīr Shaiva thinking thus includes music as an important component of sādhana for spiritual growth. Furthermore, sound is considered the finest of the five specific sense perceptions (*tanmātra-s*) whereas ākāsha[xiv] is the finest of the categories of physical objects (*pancha mahābhūtās*)[xv]. This view with respect to music/sound gets some support from neuroscience: Petr Janata[xvi], for example, deduces a “hub” or structures in the brain such as medial prefrontal cortex (mPFC) as well as temporo-parietal junction (TPJ), the former for emotions (sense of self, for example), music and memory, and the latter for “self-transcendence” from fMRI experiments. In addition, the parasympathetic vagus nerve is involved in breathing, and only the sound/singing part[xvii] of the *tanmātra-s* is connected with breathing (vagus system) while other tanmatras (touch, sight, taste, smell) do not seem to have a similar connection.

The act of singing was also identified as similar to yogic techniques involving the control of breath and concentration[xviii] (with the vagus nerve in the pre-frontal cortex coming into play for the first and medial PFC for the latter). This points to a surprising connection between breathing techniques (vagus nerve), music (vagus nerve and mPFC) and self-transcendence (mPFC/TPJ).

Interestingly, good music also seems to float through "ākāsha". Hence, sound or music is most effective in integrating one's body and consciousness and thereby, it is said, arousing the dormant blissfulness of pure consciousness. As per *Vijnānabhairava*, the ānanda aroused by song and music is considered as a means to enter into the state of pure and blissful consciousness. The great scholar Abhinavgupta has always been portrayed as keeping a vīna by his side and may have found the vīna a powerful aid in *pratyāhāra* (the practice of withdrawing awareness from the world around) and *dhyāna* (focusing within on the purer consciousness of the Self).

A Bauddha Detour: शान्तरक्षित and Emptiness of "Consciousness"

शान्तरक्षित Shāntarakshita (725-788 CE?) has been said to be the "last" major Bauddha thinker from India who synthesised मद्ध्यमक, योगचार philosophies and धर्मकीर्ति's thinking known as the "योगाचार स्वतन्त्रिक माद्ध्यमिक" system; he advocates योगाचार at the lower ("conventional" or "concealing" संवृति or लोक संवृति) level but मद्ध्यमक at पारमार्थिक level.

While he accepted योगाचार's mind-only (cittamātra) and self-reflective awareness (*svasamvedana*) at the "lower" (provisional) level, he is critical of सौतन्त्रिक and योगाचार thinking that views विज्ञान (consciousness) as unitary but yet is aware of the multiplicity of objects. Using his ("higher") मद्ध्यमक lens, he argues that consciousness can be neither unitary nor multiple/

composite[xix]. Hence it has no reality by itself and is empty of any inherent nature (शून्य).

In his Tattvasangraha (verse 2000), he says[xx], "when the cognition is produced, it is produced as differentiated from all "unconscious" forms; and it is this fact of its being "non-unconscious" that constitutes its, "self-cognisability."[xxi] Furthermore (verse 2001-2002), "There can be no self-cognition of the cognition, in the sense that it is the action and also the active agent; because one and the same entity, which is impartite in form, cannot have three characters [cognised, cogniser, cognition]. Hence the only right view is that the self-cognition of the cognition is due to it being of the very nature of consciousness. Under the circumstances, how can there be any cognition of any other thing in the shape of the object?"

Earlier, Dignāga, the logician, had argued that self-awareness requires *svaprakāṣavāda* (self-illumination) to avoid infinite regress; *parataḥprakāsavāda* (other-illumination) is also another point of view that has been debated in the Indic tradition.

Artificial Intelligence

Now that we have discussed a few strands of Indic thought in "consciousness", we next discuss current developments in CS and AI and see what bearing they have in understanding consciousness. Note that we do not discuss current notions such as the "hard" problem of consciousness as they are covered extensively elsewhere.

Current "AI" and Sense Processing

Deep Learning (DL) type frameworks have been spectacularly successful for modelling computations relating to the Jñānendriya-s. They require large-scale processing and seem to be inherently computational as a very large number of receptors are needed for Touch, Sight, Hearing, Taste, Smell. Attention is an important part of "top-level" control with sensing that may be "on" but may get inhibited. Furthermore, these senses cannot be put in a hierarchy (vide story in the Upanishads, or mathematically from Arrow's result on voting).

However, Karmendriya-s (action organs) seem to be largely cognitively deployed, with extensive training needed in childhood. They use a number of feedback control circuits along with highly developed models of planning. The "theory-theory of childhood development" (Gopnik et al) has close analogs with reinforcement learning models that have been developed in the AI domain. The success of DL in this domain is likely to be as a part of a larger AI framework.

With current Deep Neural Nets (DNN) or Deep Learning, there are no causal models (only associations). We need active engagement with the wider reality that is missing in DL such as multi-agent reinforcement learning along with intervention, counterfactuals, etc. If embodied "AI" systems also interact on the scale of human beings in both quantity and quality, some types of intelligence or consciousness may be surmisable in the future. Just as वादे वादे जायते तत्त्वबोधः| (debate after debate produces true understanding.), we need "activity after activity" in the real world for true or embodied intelligence to arise.

Here it might be appropriate to discuss "Individual" intelligence vs "Social" intelligence.

While AI traditionally ("GOFAI") has looked at consciousness or intelligence in a single system, the connectionist AI models have looked at large numbers of many simple systems (such as perceptrons) as needed for consciousness or intelligence. In the current context, it is likely that many large scale systems, even if not seen to be "intelligent" or "conscious" by themselves, can exhibit interesting behaviours that can be seen as "intelligent" or "conscious". They are also likely to improve at a faster rate if appropriate market forces are in play; the orchestration of many systems through some currency that is related to survival (e.g. market forces) can have highly accelerated growth in terms of intelligence or consciousness. For example, Uber-like services that were unthinkable for a common citizen a decade ago, are now widely used. While they can be seen as "intelligent", many would not consider them as "conscious". However, recent robotic devices can be seen as being purposeful, skilful and capable of intelligent planning that invites comparison with conscious beings.

Let us take language comprehension as one example of current developments in the context of the problem of intelligence and consciousness. Large language models (LLMs) based on neural models have now become widely available at the consumer and research levels; they seem to have the ability to understand text as well as generate text.

Current "AI" Language Models and Limits

The state of art in NLP (Neuro-Linguistic Processing or natural language processing) using DL can be summarised with divergent views on their capabilities. Blaise Agüera y Arcas, a Vice President and Fellow at Google Research interviewed a LLM called LaMDA[xxii] and found that "LaMDA could understand social concepts and could model a theory of mind, held by some to be the "trick" behind consciousness". Douglas Hofstadter, a cognitive scientist and Pulitzer Prize winner for non-fiction talked with GPT-3[xxiii] and concluded that "GPT-3 was clueless and lacked common sense". Blake Lemoine, a software engineer at Google interviewed LaMDA and claimed that "LaMDA was sentient and deserved personhood".

An experiment was conducted to see if GPT-3 can write an academic paper on itself with minimal human input. The results (see Fig 2) seem to exceed the expectations of the experimenters. However, the LLMs are some of the largest models known to history. While the size of early language models doubled every 2 years between 1986 and 2012, it is now doubling every 2 months between 2017 and 2019, with hardware supporting in excess of trillion parameters currently.

Sejnowski has critically looked at LLMs and says, "The current generation of LLMs has some obvious shortcomings. LLMs can't store new experiences in long-term memory after they have been trained, so they have to start afresh with each person they meet, a "Hello, world!" moment. They are amnesiac, like humans who have lost their hippocampus and are unable to remember new experiences for more than a few minutes, unable to create long-term memories, forever trapped in their past. The next generation of LLMs will have the equivalent of a hippocampus that will allow continual learning and bring them another step closer to human behaviour."

Can GPT-3 write an academic paper on itself, with minimal human input?

GPT-3[1], Almira Osmanovic-Thunström[2,3], Steinn Steingrimsson[2,3]

[1]OpenAI www.openai.com
[2]Institute of Neuroscience and Physiology, University of Gothenburg, Gothenburg, Sweden,
[3]Region Västra Götaland, Department of Psychiatry, Sahlgrenska University Hospital, Gothenburg, Sweden

Corresponding author
Correspondence to Almira Osmanovic Thunström
almira.osmanovic.thunstrom@gu.se

Abstract

GPT-3 is a powerful artificial intelligence system that can generate text. In this paper, we explore GPT-3's ability to write about itself. We find that GPT-3 can generate clear and concise descriptions of its own capabilities and features. This is a significant advance over previous systems, which have often struggled to produce coherent text about themselves. We believe that the benefits of letting GPT-3 write about itself outweigh the risks. However, we recommend that any such writing be closely monitored by researchers in order to mitigate any potential negative consequences.

Figure 2: The Abstract of GPT-3 Paper

Furthermore, Sejnowski says, "Another important addition [needed] to LLMs is goals and motivation, following in the footsteps of TD-Gammon and AlphaGo by adding the equivalent of a basal ganglia into the loop between their outputs and inputs. Current LLMs do not have their own agendas. LLMs will eventually have bodies too, but building bodies that are as flexible and adaptable as ours is far more difficult than learning how to talk. We have many joints and muscles that control those joints, which have several degrees of freedom. All of them are involved in almost every action, which is a difficult control problem. Distributed control evolved to fluidly coordinate bodies with many degrees of freedom[8,9]. LLMs can talk the talk, but can they walk the walk?"

An even deeper critique is possible. Again, we quote Sejnowski first: "GPT-3 in 2020 required 10^{12}—a million million —times more computing power to train than NETtalk in 1986. LLMs have hundreds of billions of weights, about the same as the number of synapses under a square centimeter of cortex. Inference in neural network models scales with the number of weights for a single processor but on massively parallel architectures like brains the processing proceeds in real time. Very few algorithms scale this well with the size of the problem.

Our cerebral cortex has an area of approximately 1200 cm^2. If computing power continues to increase exponentially as it has for the last 70 years, it will reach the estimated computing power of human brains at some point in the not-too-distant future."

Critique of "AI" Models with Energy Constraints

One aspect missing in the above discussion is the energy required of the LLMs, especially with reference to the cerebral cortex. Living systems have optimised use of energy extremely well. An AI system such as chatGPT that consumes a few Wh per interaction may not be deployable on a large scale temporally or spatially; note that a google search is about 20 to 50 times cheaper. Patterson and his colleagues[9] have looked carefully at the energy consumption of LLMs and large scale AI models, and conclude that, while early work on energy consumption overstated it, it is clear that it is an important aspect that needs to be stated along with the capabilities of the model under discussion.

However, there is a deeper long-term concern regarding the energy costs of large systems. Conservative projections say that computer systems might account for as much as 8-10 per cent of world energy in only a few decades from now, from 3+ per cent now. There is also a surprising and "concerning" study that electronic switching extrapolated, purely based on current trends, to 2040 may be unsustainable. Specifically, the semiconductor bodies SIA/ SRC in the US ("Rebooting the IT Revolution", 2015) argue that for a "benchmark energy per bit [of 10^{-14} J/bit transition, Fig. 3], (extrapolated) computing will not be sustainable by 2040, when the energy required for computing will exceed the estimated world's energy production."

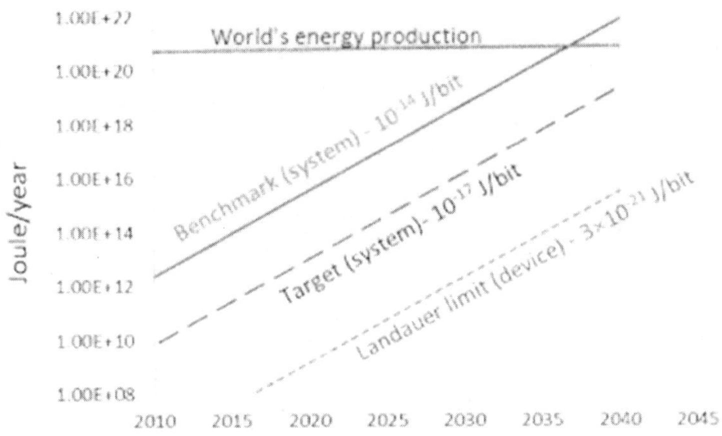

Fig. A8. Total energy of computing.

Figure 3: Switching Budget Extrapolated

One technical approach for emulating intelligence is the use of neuromorphic computing that simulates aspects of biological neural networks as analog or digital copies on electronic circuits. Note that even to simulate a single neuron is not trivial; more so at its power levels. In a recent paper, "deep neural networks (DNNs) were trained to faithfully replicate the I/O function of various biophysical models of cortical neurons at millisecond (spiking) resolution. A temporally convolutional DNN with five to eight layers was required to capture the I/O mapping of a realistic model of a layer 5 cortical pyramidal cell (L5PC). This DNN generalised well when presented with inputs widely outside the training distribution. When NMDA receptors were removed, a much simpler network (fully connected neural network with one hidden layer) was sufficient to fit the model."[10] The energy costs of "naive" neuromorphic computing can thus be considerable unless careful optimisation is undertaken.

Since current AI energy requirements for large models are high, either AI models have to become substantially lean, or they can be deployed only in critical sectors and not used indiscriminately; otherwise, inequities across the world will enable only the well endowed to use AI that may result in far more unequal outcomes. Or, more optimistically, energy sources such as from the sun have to be harnessed on a truly massive scale (as they are independent of fossil fuels) in an ecologically meaningful way.

This concern is not unduly alarmist for the following related reasons: many countries are already consuming more biomass than they produce. "Humanity is using nature 1.8 times faster than our planet's biocapacity can regenerate. That's equivalent to using the resources of 1.8 Earths."[xxiv] For example, Japan needs "7.8 Japans to meet its residents' demand on nature" while that of the US is said to be 5.1 with India's being 0.8.

In the context of AI and limited Indian energy resources, given the ever-increasing demands of cyberattention needed for cybercommerce and advertising that has come with it, and hence its energy demands, the Indic tradition of Ātmaratiḥ[xxv] is likely to be a valuable one.

Self-Organising Systems Perspective

Multiple levels of complex systems are a quite common paradigm in CS/AI (e.g. "layering" in computer networks) and therefore the dominant paradigm. However, possibly due to its focus as an engineering discipline, layering in CS has not been studied that much in terms of its "emergence" in a natural "computational" setting[xxvi]; other disciplines have filled this void.

We have already seen that multiple levels of reality are postulated in Indic thinking (Vedanta/Bauddha) such as, for example, लौकिक and पारमार्थिक; the Veda-s are often exhorted to be understood at multiple levels (आधिभौतिक, आधिदैविक आध्यात्मिक) levels[xxvii]. Due to multiple levels in a complex system, there can be many levels of "consciousness". What is true at one level may not be true at another: as per Nāgārjuna, for example, samvrti-satya and paramārtha-satya.

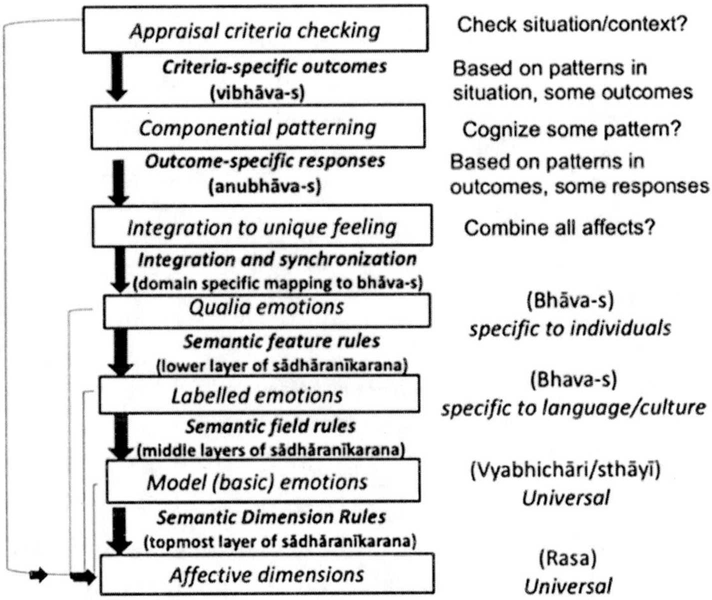

Figure 4: The Hierarchy of Levels of Description for Emotion Processes and Their Mapping into Lower-Dimensional Space (Annotated and Adapted from Fig 1.1.2 in Scherer (2010)) Original Text in Italics.

An influential self-organising systems perspective argues that "many dynamic forms of order arise when a system is subjected to an energy imbalance. Such "driven systems" spontaneously form complex structures and processes that serve to dissipate the imbalance."[12] Such a theory may give us models of how emergent properties arise as well as how this is possible with multiple levels. As Bratman[12], summarising Eric Smith and others, puts it, "Ordinary experience supplies numerous examples of spontaneous order, many of them so familiar that we fail to take notice. Under many common circumstances, self-organisation is the rule rather than the exception. In fact, it is often the likeliest outcome, favoured by physical laws and, in aggregate, deterministic. Matter doesn't always need to be coaxed into order but can spontaneously relax into it."

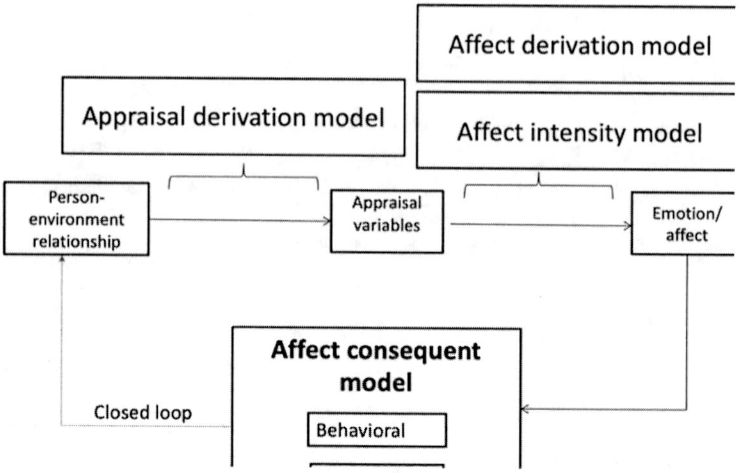

Figure 5: A Component Model View of Computational Appraisal Models (Annotated and Adapted from Marsella et al. (2010)

Furthermore, many processes in life represent a particular kind of non-equilibrium process, one that is kept from settling by the continuous application of a source of energy. As it happens, such "driven" systems commonly demonstrate spontaneous order-creating processes.

We give a brief account of some types of self-organisation that seem to be operative in contexts akin to consciousness. We have already mentioned rasa theory and its 2-level model to explain bhāva and rasa, the type of highly integrative consciousness that one senses when experiencing art forms. Another model is from Tantric yoga that postulates the dynamics of "Kuṇḍalinī" when certain energies (from the mūladhāra chakra) reach the *brahmarandhra* (fontanelle of the skull) to form the सहस्रार (sahasrār) chakra; this, in the end, enhances the communication of neural pathways, it is said, so that all parts of the brain work in unison to attain (*nirvikalpa*) *samādhi*.

Till recently, however, there has been a lack of a suitable terminology in current sciences akin to the rasa theory (essentially lack of a multi-level model) while other Indic ideas have been imported into European thought like gestalt (echoes of sphoṭa) or Jungian archetypes/collective unconsciousness (echoes of karmic imprints/ālayavignāna). Recently, the field of affective computing (AC) has sprung up in Western academia[xxviii]. Many of the ideas of the rasa theory show up in some form or other in AC; we discuss this below in some detail.

Affective Computing, at the "physics" level, concentrates on the mechanics of how to make emotions register through sensors (e.g. skin galvanic conduction) or how to recognise emotions. Another related area of current research in this field with practical applications is that of micro-expressions: the emphasis here is the "involuntary, fleeting facial movements that reveal true emotions—[that] hold valuable information for scenarios ranging from security interviews and interrogations to media analysis"[xxix]. Nāṭyaśāstra has something to say here (for example, the many varieties of eye glances) but from a rasa perspective. Recent work in the area of affective computing uses layered models such as appraisal-derivation[xxx] that are similar in spirit to how Bharata surmised rasa-s are produced (Fig 4). Note that in the above model, recurrence is not modelled. The same high-level model (simplified) with emotion processing shown in a closed loop, when redrawn from Fig 1.2.2 of (Stacy 2010) with our annotations, is as given in Fig 5.

As AC is currently a "bottom-up" theory, it does not postulate "higher" level ideas or heuristics that can help in structuring explanations. Contrarily, Indic models also use human traits for explanatory purposes. For example, the rasa theory posits that the rajas and tamas elements of ordinary experience need to be projected out (using, say, "projection operators") to understand the depths of rasa. When this happens, the subjective aspects also disappear and the ātman enjoys the rasa[xxxi] just as a yogi experiences the paramātman (though different qualitatively, it is said); note the connections with Patanjali's model in Yogasūtra.

Note that such higher level (or metaphysical) perspectives are typically absent in Western models as they are felt to be subjective and also not amenable to measurement. Instead, surveys and measurements are carried out and research using data science techniques used to detect patterns. Other researchers argue that there is a need to measure lower level events (skin resistance, etc) and correlate them with higher level self-reporting, though agreement may be problematic.

Rasa thinking is closest to that of Roger Orpwood who suggests that qualia are created through the neurobiological mechanism of re-entrant feedback in cortical systems (Orpwood 2013); this model interestingly corresponds in some of its details to the computational perspective we have advanced[7] for a model of rasa (for example, in the modelling of rasa, the bhāva-s are akin to information structures and rasa to an information message in Orpwood's theory for qualia). For completeness, we give verbatim the following summary discussing Orpwood's theory[xxxii]:

- Orpwood suggests that information in general is of two types: the information structure and information message. Information structures are defined by the physical vehicles and structural, biological patterns encoding information. That encoded information is the information message; a source describing what that information is. The neural mechanism or network receives input information structures, completes a designated instructional task (firing of the neuron or network), and outputs a modified information structure to downstream regions. The information message is the purpose and meaning of the information structure and causally exists as a result of that particular information structure. Modification of the information structure changes the meaning of the information message, but the message itself cannot be directly altered.
- Local cortical networks have the capacity to receive feedback from their own output information structures. This form of local feedback continuously cycles part

> of the network's output structures as its next input information structure. Since the output structure must represent the information message derived from the input structure, each consecutive cycle that is fed-back will represent the output structure the network just generated. As the network of mechanisms cannot recognise the information message, but only the input information structure, the network is unaware that it is representing its own previous outputs. The neural mechanisms are merely completing their instructional tasks and outputting any recognisable information structures. Orpwood proposes that these local networks come into an attractor state that consistently outputs exactly the same information structure as the input structure. Instead of only representing the information message derived from the input structure, the network will now represent its own output and thereby its own information message. As the input structures are fed back, the network identifies the previous information structure as being a previous representation of the information message. As Orpwood states, "Once an attractor state has been established, the output [of a network] is a representation of its own identity to the network." Representation of the networks own output structures, by which represents its own information message, is Orpwood's explanation that grounds the manifestation of qualia via neurobiological mechanisms. (Quale, 2017)

OrchOR ("orchestrated objective reduction") is another interesting layered theory, developed by Stuart Hameroff and Roger Penrose, based on quantum processes starting from the intracellular microtubule level (Hameroff, 2014). OrchOR suggests that there is a connection between the brain's biomolecular processes and the basic structure of the universe and it is based on developments in quantum biology, neuroscience, physics and cosmology. For example, it introduces a novel suggestion of "beat frequencies" of faster microtubule vibrations as a possible source of the observed electro-encephalographic ("EEG") correlates of consciousness. However, many believe that such explanations are totally off the mark due to the size of the structures involved for the quantum properties claimed.

Further work in this interdisciplinary area (AC, rasa theory and neuroscience, especially integrated with Indic "consciousness" models) is needed; we have only sketched an outline.

Conclusions

Till the mid-twentieth century, the vexing problem of consciousness has been confined to philosophy and allied areas. With the availability of digital machines since about the 1950's and their ability to compute and perform deductive logic and statistical inference, the issue of consciousness has also now risen in the context of computing machines, especially now with many developments in statistical thinking and AI. In this paper, we have discussed some of these issues, with an Indic lens where appropriate, and relate them to developments in CS, AI and the study of emergent systems in summary form.

While we have not provided any definite conclusions on the question of consciousness, we have discussed aspects that may have a bearing on the problem. We have also argued that Indic insights can be viewed as heuristics that may have some explanatory power for the many first-person reports that exist in this area.

Mathematics, Artificial Intelligence, and Consciousness

Subhash Kak

Introduction

Several advanced AI projects have the aim of creating a conscious machine based on the premise that the brain merely processes and codes multisensory information. The belief is that once the codes are understood, it should be possible to emulate the brain on a computer. But a recent review[1] argued that current machines only perform unconscious mathematical computations, and further advance requires two additional elements of global availability and self-monitoring that are nowhere close to being implemented.

Most scientists believe that these efforts are doomed to failure because consciousness is not computable[2,3]. The basic argument is that whereas computation is analysable, cognition by the brain is not, for it integrates and compresses several components of the experience, such as sight, smell and taste in the drinking of wine or eating a piece of chocolate. Computation is doing mathematics, whereas consciousness is a sense of self and awareness and the capacity to do mathematics is only one aspect of it.

Organisms do not create representations of visual or other stimuli and store them in short-term and long-term memories. If experiences cannot be accessed, they cannot be described as data (whether digital or chemical), which is a requirement in processing by a computer. The processing by the brain may hence not be emulated, and the models of cognitive processing by computer are not like it[4].

It is known that brain processing is not passive like that of a computer, but an active process between the subject and the environment. When perceiving an object, we attend to its properties to see what we can do with it. The mind actively explores the environment to find elements that guide the performance of one action or the other. This information, called ecological information, is unique to the subject and it does not lend itself to the information processing model.

Another perspective on this is that the most mundane memory tasks involve multiple and very large areas of the brain. Several independent processes can proceed in the brain and this fact[5] makes the neuroscience at the basis of cognition even more complicated. Skill learning and expertise involve reorganisation and plastic changes, which cannot be mapped into a computer with fixed architecture.

Consciousness is not only computation but also self-monitoring awareness. which, in turn, requires the brain to halt the ongoing process to take stock of the overall contents of the brain at some high-level description. In other words, it is a privileged state of the mind that makes brain processes halt and the contents, registered irrespective of the initial state of the immediately preceding process.

But such halting to arbitrary input is impossible from a computation point of view. A general algorithm to determine if an arbitrary program will stop cannot exist. If consciousness were itself a consequence of a program, it would not be able to halt itself at any random instant. Therefore, it follows that consciousness is not computable.

Since the observer plays a central role in the formalism of quantum theory, physicists have also argued that consciousness cannot be a computational property of the physical elements[6]. It must be a global non-algorithmic property, for information relatable to consciousness can only be associated with collectives, and not individual objects.

Since the number of arrangements of brain areas corresponding to such distributed function is limitless, it cannot be mapped into the memory of a machine. This is one reason why despite the parallels between the characteristics of art and the organisational principles of the brain, scientists have failed to develop a psychophysics of aesthetics[7].

Consistent with this view of the non-algorithmic nature of brain response is the fact that no specific neural correlates of consciousness have been discovered, which means that in different cognitive tasks different areas of the brain are involved when imaged by functional MRI. One way to understand it is that awareness occurs in a dimension that sits above the activity going on different parts of the brain.

The Computer Science View

The general position amongst many computer scientists and engineers is that computers will eventually become conscious. This view is based on the reductionist paradigm of reality that sees consciousness as an emergent phenomenon arising out of the complexity of connections in the brain. In other words, if we cannot deny that the brain is a machine, then other machines with appropriate architecture should also achieve consciousness. At this operational level itself, one may object and say that brains, unlike classical computers, perform quantum operations deep in the neural circuitry. But because it conforms with the materialistic, social sciences view of reality, this view has become influential in many circles.

Aware of the fact that biological evolution is slower than technological evolution, there is fear that humans will be unable to compete with sentient machines. Conscious machines will take over the world and enslave humans, if not worse. No wonder many prominent voices in the scientific and the tech worlds are claiming that artificial intelligence is leading humanity to a catastrophe. For this reason, they want AI to be strictly regulated.

Some futurists and sci-fi writers are imagining a marriage

of sorts between AI and brains so that, someday, technology will make it possible for humans to become "posthuman," transcending the limits of the human condition. There are others who believe that the only way to make sense of all the scientific facts is to take reality as a simulation, an idea that was used by Hollywood in movies, such as The *Matrix* and *Watch Gamer*. Another scenario is to imagine that once humans learn how to completely characterise brains, they will be able to copy themselves into computers, creating their emulations, or ems, in the process. Such ems could be replicated easily and so they will quickly outnumber real people.

Cognitive tasks in which the agent does not have a sense of subjective awareness are being done by the machine, faster and with more reliability. Therefore, even without becoming conscious, machines will replace humans at most jobs creating unprecedented societal challenges. Even if each human is provided a universal basic income for food, shelter and entertainment, as is being proposed by many economists, it will be a dystopic life and the social order will likely collapse.

The Epistemology of Reality

In our intuition, consciousness is a category that is dual to (separate from) physical reality. We apprehend reality in our mind and not in a specific location. It is also significant that in our conscious experience we are always outside the physical world and witness ourselves as apart from our bodies. Even in scientific theory, as for example in classical mechanics, the observer is away from the system, even though there is no explanation of the observer within the theory.

Is the world a machine described by its parts and their interconnections, or is it fundamentally the contents of our consciousness? The first view is called ontic (from ontological, that is related to structure), and the second is called epistemic (from epistemological, related to knowledge)[8]. In philosophy, these are the positions of two different schools, one believing that reality is being, and the other that it is becoming. The conception of the world as being is associated with materialism, while that of becoming assigns a significant role to the observer.

Being, by itself, cannot explain consciousness, for that requires memory and apprehension of change. The Vedic tradition, also called ātma-vidyā or science of consciousness[9], considers consciousness to transcend space and time and one of the names used for it is Shiva. It is significant that Shiva has five faces, implying that it is not a single state. The dance of Shiva is the dance of consciousness. If one were to consider a state of mind, a thought, one could speak of five aspects to it: creation (*sṛṣṭi*), preservation (*sthiti*), destruction (*saṃhāra*), concealment (*tirobhāva*), and revelation (*anugraha*). The five faces of Shiva are shown as *Sadyojāta* (west), *Vāmadeva* (north), *Aghora* (south), *Tatpuruṣa* (east), and Īśāna (skyward). *Sadyojāta* is the creator, Aghora as the frightening aspect of consciousness, *Tatpuruṣa* is the normal consciousness state where you are one with its contents and lacking self-awareness, *Vāmadeva* is the auspicious aspect of consciousness that is calming and comforting (complementary to Aghora), and Īśāna is the state when one obtains the deeper meaning and so one may call it the state of grace.

Another name for Shiva is *Prakāśa* or Light, that illuminates the contents of the mind. The Light is unity, but the way it illuminates the many minds (for the contents of the brains are different) leads to multiplicity. But why isn't reality only a succession of mind-states as was argued by *Yogācāra*? The answer is that the contents of the mind change in each recounting and memories fade, but the awareness of the unity in the states is the transcending consciousness[10]. The Brahma Sūtras present arguments as to why consciousness could not be the outcome of a physical process. The Upanishads speak of two aspects of reality: *aparā* (material and causal) and *parā* (consciousness), and the two are like sides of a coin.

The Vedic tradition with its examination of the many facets of consciousness[11] goes far beyond current academic debates on the nature of a single state associated with it, but further discussion of this is not within the scope of the present paper and, therefore, we will return to the considerations related to AI.

The Limitations of the Machine Paradigm

There are many difficulties with the conception of selfhood in a machine paradigm. Standard neuroscience accepts the doctrine of the identity of brain and mind. If the mind emerges from the complexity of the interconnections, then behaviour must be completely described by the corresponding brain function leaving no room for agency of the individual.

The selfhood of humans leads to paradoxes related to autonomy and freedom. Humans reject the idea that they are mere machines, yet they often equate their "self" with the machinery of the body. On the other hand, the human's self-image is that of the body, together with transient thoughts, which is overseen by an observing "I" within.

We make a distinction between the "autobiographical self" related to one's memories and relationships, and the "core self", which is rooted in the momentary present. The "autobiographical self" is partly the result of one's imagination since it is an interpretation of the past and it includes hopes for the future. The "core self" is elusive; it is the light that shines on things around and associates with them in time and space.

Experiments show how decisions made by a subject arise first on a subconscious level and only afterwards are translated into the conscious decision. Upon a retrospective view of the event, the subject arrives at the belief that the decision occurred at the behest of his will. The unconscious brain activity leading up to the conscious decision by the subject begins approximately half a second before the subject consciously feels that he has taken his decision.

To carry the argument about the power of machines further, I have suggested that the phenomenon of consciousness could be assumed to come in two different varieties which I have called Little-C and Big-C. If all there is to consciousness is Little-C, then machines will be conscious. But if human consciousness is Big-C, then machines will fall short.

Little-C is consciousness emerging out of the complexity of the brain processes. It is emergent in the same sense that biology is emergent in chemistry, which, in turn, is emergent in physics. It is like the thought, generally ascribed to Buddhism, that consciousness arises on ground that is emptiness (śūnyatā in Sanskrit). On the other hand, Big-C assumes consciousness is something that is apart from physical reality. Philosophically, this is the position of Vedanta, in which the mental and the physical phenomena are two aspects of the same reality.

The pioneers of the quantum theory used the so-called Orthodox Copenhagen Interpretation (CI) to understand the mathematical formalism of the theory, where the underlying idea is that of Big-C. CI assumes complementarity at different levels and this includes the duality of matter and mind or object and subject.

One may devise scientific experiments on creativity to further investigate the two views of consciousness. It appears that the creative moment is not at the end of a deliberate computation. There are many autobiographical accounts of dreams or visions that preceded specific acts of creativity. Two famous examples of this are Elias Howe's 1845 design of the modern sewing machine, and August Kekulé's discovery of the structure of benzene in 1862.

The life of the self-taught Indian mathematician Srinivasa Ramanujan, who died in 1920 at the age of 32, is evidence in favour of Big-C consciousness His long-forgotten notebook, which was published in 1988, contains several thousand formulas that were well ahead of their time, without explanation of how he had arrived at them. When he was alive, he claimed that formulas were revealed to him in his sleep[12].

But how might matter and mind mutually influence each other? One possibility is through the act of observation which causes the collapse of the state function in quantum theory. If the observation is made repeatedly, the system state will freeze. Called the Quantum Zeno Effect[13], it has been demonstrated in the laboratory. The idea of control of a physical system through observation is also a part of Vedanta and it is called the *Dṛṣṭisṛṣṭivāda*.

Consciousness and Information

Even if one were to dismiss accounts of creativity as nothing but coincidence, the ontic understanding of reality becomes problematic when one brings in information into the mix, as is done extensively in modern physics. This is because information implies the existence of a mind, which category lies outside the realm of physics.

Information or entropy cannot be reduced to local operations by any reductionist program. It requires the use of signs derived from global properties and the capacity to make choices which, in turn, implies agency. Entropy is a measure of disorder in a collective and in certain situations may be measured by temperature. Temperature like entropy or information cannot be associated with a single particle.

Information in a communication involves two things: first, commonalities in the vocabulary of communication between the two parties; and second, the capacity to make choices. The common vocabulary requires that the underlying abstract signs used by the parties be shared, which stresses the social aspects of communication.

The idea of consciousness requires not only an awareness of things but also the awareness that one is aware. If awareness is a measurement, it should have a reference. This, in turn, poses two problems: first, what is the reference for awareness; and second, how does consciousness choose between various possibilities?

The problem of the referent in awareness is an old one. If we postulate a single universal, transcendental consciousness, the individual's empirical consciousness is a projection and the referent for it must be the universal. In Vedanta, the analogy of the same sun reflecting in a million different pots of water as little suns is provided to explain the empirical consciousness of the individual.

If one were to return to the question of reflexivity in consciousness, one can speak of two kinds of selves: the self as knower (the "I"), and the self as known (the "me"). Each person's self is partly subjective (as knower) and partly objective (as known). The objective self itself may be described in its three aspects: the material self, the social self, and the spiritual self. Narrative self-reference contrasts with the immediate, knowing "I" that supports the notion of momentary experience as an expression of selfhood. This dichotomy is similar to the dichotomy of the ordinary self and the detached witness.

If one is to find the boundaries between the "me" and the "I" of consciousness, it becomes essential to find a "minimal" sense of self. It is easy to speak of the intuition that there is a basic or primitive something that is the true self, and much harder to provide evidence for such belief. Conceptually, there must be something permanent—a bedrock—underlying the stream of consciousness.

To deal with the empirical pre-conscious or conscious awareness, one can postulate a hierarchical model of consciousness with independent and distributed neural structures at the lowest level. The speed of the binding of the attributes would depend on the complexity of the communications and the relationships between the modules. Interference between various levels and the tangled nature of the information flow can help to explain many illusions of perception.

Concluding Thoughts

Memory is one element that leads to the nature of the corresponding consciousness state. The mind must select from the pool of memories and this selection may not be made consciously and may be determined by the stream of previous consciousness states and the emotional state of the subject. It is to be expected that the executive control processes play an important role in the selection.

Furthermore, repeated selection of certain memories at the expense of others may affect the recall process, causing unwanted memories to be pushed back into the unconscious. Mechanisms can be recruited that prevent unwanted declarative memories from entering awareness, and this cognitive act has enduring consequences for the rejected memories.

Although awareness by itself is an all-or-nothing phenomenon, the state of consciousness depends on the degree to which preconscious and memory states are accessible to awareness. The uncoupling of perception from sensory inputs supports the idea of the disembodied consciousness state. A consciousness state that is decoupled from specific memories of the individual indicates that such states may be fundamental to reality and form a part of the ontological reality.

Many aspects of reality in the fields of physics, mathematics, and in the study of brain states either have paradoxical aspects or are not computable. Therefore, to assume that machines based on logic and mathematics can emulate all natural systems fully is incorrect. To put it differently, the reality described by machines is of a kind different from that of natural systems. Although machines will not become conscious, there will be an increasing tendency on the part of humans to treat them as if they were conscious.

Consciousness: The Last Frontier

THOMAS BROPHY

The Most Important Unsolved Problem in Science Today: The Ontology of Consciousness

I believe we are now in a revolutionary era with respect to science of consciousness and consciousness studies. Analogously, I was a planetary science team member with a group that had an instrument on the Voyager II spacecraft. Voyager II was the first earth-launched instrument to do close fly-bys of the outer planets of our solar system. The events around receiving the data from the close fly-by of each planet were called "planetary encounters". In the decades and years leading up to each new planetary encounter, there was much scientific speculation about what Voyager might discover in the first close-up views of planets that had been known to humans only as points of light in the night sky for millennia. Each planetary encounter was astonishing, revealing details and activity on the planet and its moons that could not have been imagined out of only points of light in the night sky.

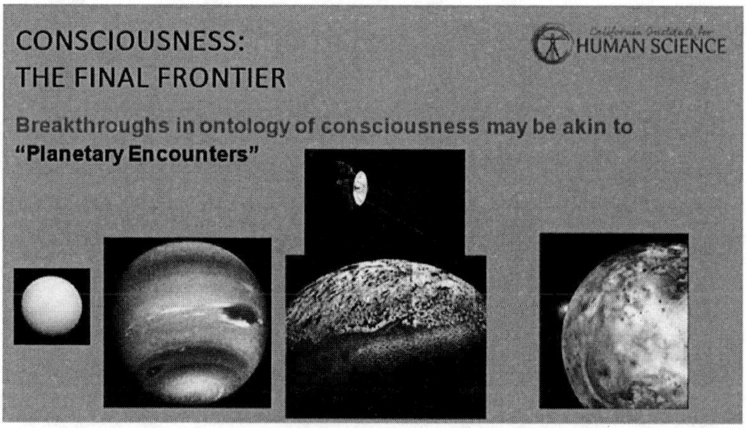

Figure 1: Consciousness: The Final Frontier

Now, as modern science finally begins to investigate the content of entirely new domains of ontology that are needed to develop a modern science of consciousness, we will surely be thrilled and astonished by new discoveries awaiting there.

Transcending Physicalism: This movement requires going beyond the commonly held materialist/physicalist mindset/ paradigm.

How is it that science is now beginning to develop capacity to access and investigate entirely new domains of reality? The concept of pre-to trans-rational development is helpful.

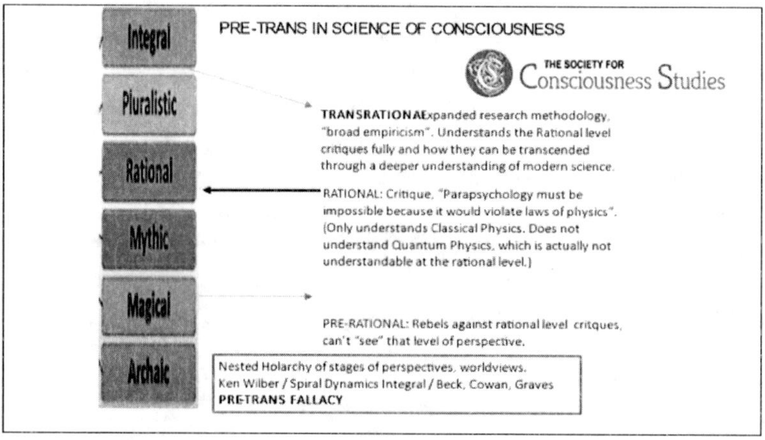

Figure 2: Pre-trans in Science of Consciousness

The way that stages of rational functioning perceive anomalous cognitive data (parapsychology) demonstrates the situation.

Prerational perspectives can be enthralled by parapsychological phenomena, and generally do not analytically critique them.

Physicalism tends to operate at a strictly rational level, and generate perspectives along the lines of, "parapsychology must be impossible because it would violate the laws of physics, and therefore it is not worth the effort to even look into the data."

Transrational perspectives can operate on the entire field of rationality, understand where the rational critiques come from, and also see that there are flaws and outdated or unsolved notions involved in the rational stage that open the way for entirely new domains of reality operating together with the domains that are fully understood at the strictly rational level.

Stages of Artificial Intelligence

In 1997, IBM's chess playing computer, Deep Blue, beat the reigning human world chess champion, Gary Kasparov, for the first time. Did this outstripping of human cognitive abilities mean that Deep Blue was approaching artificial general intelligence (AGI)?

At the time, many of us who play games like chess as a hobby, hoped that the more complex game of Go that seems to involve intuition and artistic sense as well as brute force calculation might never see a computer conquer the top human players. Then, 1997, computers were very bad at Go, not even to the level of beginning human amateur Go players.

Figure 3: AlphaGo

Then in March 2016, the world was shocked when Google's Go playing computer AlphaGo crushed the reigning human champion in a series of matches.

But is AlphaGo AGI? I think not, because AlphaGo can not be conscious according to an emerging understanding of what consciousness is. On this view, consciousness, general intelligence, understanding, requires a non-computable aspect. As a classical computer, even one that can learn and self-teach and vanquish the best human players, everything AlphaGo does is computable. I will address how non-computable aspects can be operative in physical reality, and consciousness, later in this paper.

Connecting with Ancient Esoteric Systems

Swami Vivekananda first introduced Vedic ontology (Advaita Vedanta) of consciousness to the West on a broad scale, starting at the 1893 World Parliament of Religions, in Chicago.

In this view, a unitary *Ātman*-Soul precipitates out spacetime-individuated souls that operate body-brain-action and conscious perception in the empirical world of science, or the world of "Maya" in Vedic terms.

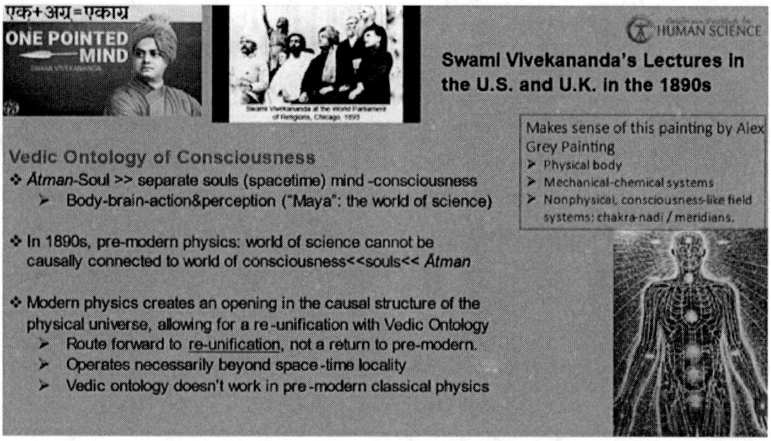

Figure 4: Vedic Ontology of Consciousness

Although the Vedic view of consciousness and Reality garnered considerable interest among philosophers and religionists, it was disjunctive with the status of physical science of the time. A world governed entirely by classical physics is fundamentally ontologically deterministic, and there is no way a unitary *Ātman*-Soul or souls of any type can have any effect in such a physical structure. In the 1890s there was no way to connect the two.

Connecting with Modern Physics

A century ago, in the early twentieth century, modern physics discovered a more fundamental physics underpinning the world of classical physics that we normally observe. Quantum physics creates an opening in the causal structure of the physical universe that potentially can allow for a re-unification with Vedic Ontology.

In quantum physics, as it is taught in quantum mechanics textbooks in universities today, physical systems evolve according to two different processes. The state of a physical system (1) is described by a wave function that evolves in time according to the deterministic and unitary Schrodinger equation. Until (2) a "measurement" or "state reduction" collapses the wave to a particular observation within the probability distribution of the wave function. Process (1) is entirely computable, deterministic, evolution in time. Process (2) is non-computational, and inherently not accessible to any mathematical algorithm.

Physicist Roger Penrose has argued that it is only through process (2) that a consciousness, and intelligent understanding, aspect of Reality can interact with the physical world, first in his 1989 book *The Emperor's New Mind*, and again in 1994, *Shadows of the Mind*, and in papers with Stuart Hameroff on their Orchestrated Objective Reduction model of conscious operations in the brain. A similar approach is proposed in my 1998 book, *The Mechanism Demands a Mysticism: An Exploration of Spirit, Matter and Physics*, (MDAM) where I described three possible types of material functioning: hylostatic which is deterministic and unitary like classical physics or the Schrodinger equation; hylo-stochastic which involves an element of randomness as is the common interpretation of the wave function collapse process; and a third possibility hylozoic which is neither deterministic nor purely random. Hylozoic is non-algorithmic, involved in the creative aspect of conscious functioning. Although I wrote the MDAM book before I got familiar with Penrose's books, I now see my hylozoic approach as essentially the same as Penrose' non-computational wave function collapse approach. (Penrose published his books first, and he also proposes an entirely new dimension to the collapse process—quantum gravity generated "Objective Reduction (OR)".)

In this view, particular biophysical structures such as brains are able to build (superpose together) tiny microphysical structures into large enough scale quantum coherent superposition states that undergo moments of non-computational state reductions creating the locus for moments of conscious experience and conscious fee action/agency. The existence of a conscious being in the world is thus a sequence of unique, non-computable, events.

Figure 5: Consciousness and Unique Single Events

Hameroff-Penrose's Orchestrated-OR theory proposes that the biophysical structures involved are microtubules. Penrose

(1994) identifies three dynamically interacting "worlds" or domains of Reality of which the material world is only one: Platonic world / Physical world / Mental world.

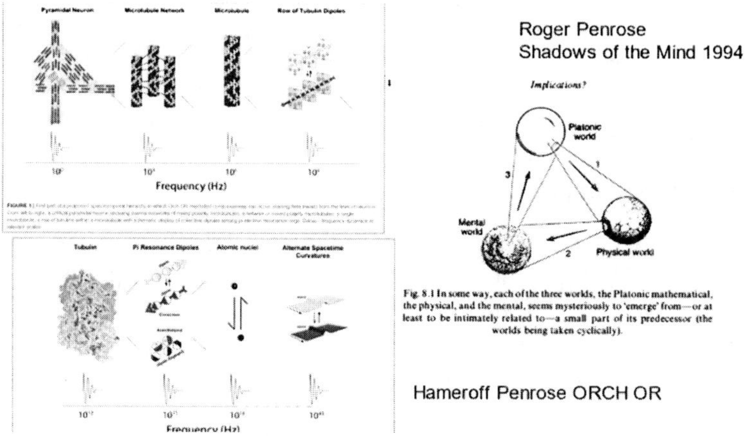

Figure 6: Hameroff Penrose ORCH OR

I call the emerging theory of what actually happens in the process of conscious experience and conscious free agency, "Actual Theory". Penrose-Hameroff Orch-OR theory focuses almost exclusively on only one part of Penrose's Reality theoretic diagram: arrow 2, how plausible biophysical structures can develop to connect with the non-computable process of wave function collapse, in a biologically meaningful way.

Theoretical approaches to the other two aspects of Penrose's Reality diagram are needed, about how the Mental world and the Platonic world interact with the Physical world. Stimulated by David Chalmers who has recently investigated the possibility of property-dualism approaches to conscious agency, I suggest it is time to consider including a new property (or set of new properties) into our models of Reality.

Periodically, new properties have been successfully introduced to physics to explain unresolved conflicts and categories of problems that were unsolvable without the new properties:

- 1687, Isaac Newton introduced to the laws of classical mechanics the property of Universal Gravitational Mass, that is acted upon by a force of gravity, to explain motions of falling bodies and the orbits of planets.
- 1862, James Clerk Maxwell introduced to the equations of electrodynamics the property of electric charge, that is acted on by an electromagnetic force, to explain then-mysterious observations of electrical and magnetic phenomena.
- In the 1920s, Louis de Broglie proposed the wave nature of particles, and several physicists developed a quantum mechanical theory for how microscopic entities operate that solved mysteries of atomic processes such as the "ultraviolet catastrophe".
- In the 1970s, physicists introduced the property of Flavour that is acted on by the Weak nuclear force, and the property of Colour Charge that is acted on by the Strong nuclear force, to explain mysteries in the Standard Model of nuclear physics.

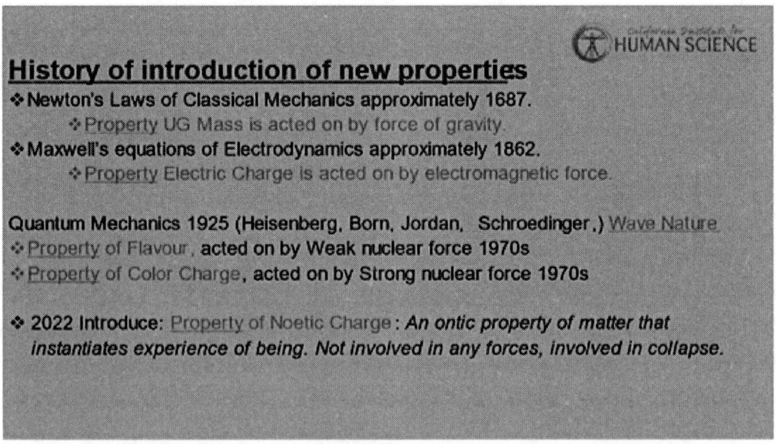

Figure 7: History of Introduction of New Properties

Is it time, in 2023, for Actual Theory to introduce a property that could be called Noetic charge, to begin to develop the tools to approach theories for Penrose's other two worlds, the Mental world and the Platonic world? Noetic charge is an ontic property that would:

- Not be acted on by any material forces;
- Generate Noetic fields that instantiate experience of being;
- Be involved in the non-computational aspect of wave function collapse;
- Connect wave function collapse with experience of being.

In this view, Noetic charges generate Noetic fields: ontic fields that surround Noetically-charged particles and generates mind-like processes. Agentic free will could be a Noetic field-influenced wave function collapse that "chooses" outcomes results in sufficiently complicated processes that can remain for all practical purposes consistent with interpretation of the pre-collapse wave function according to the "Born Rule" probability distribution.

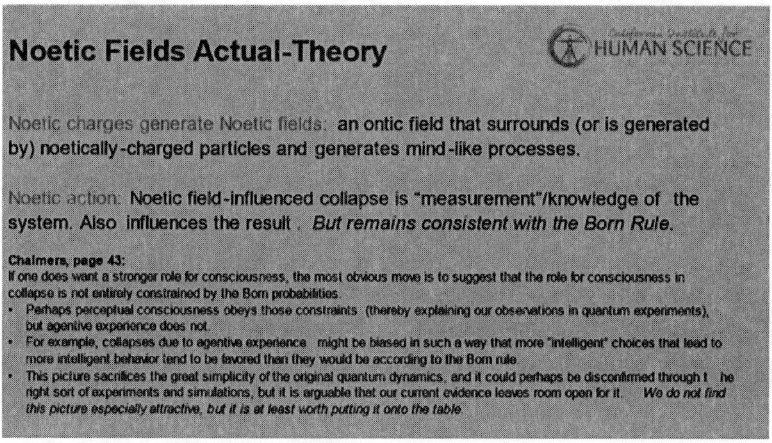

Figure 8: Noetic Fields Actual-Theory

In addition to generating experience and conscious-causation, possible Noetic field-generated systems might include:

- Platonic ideals.
- The acupuncture chi-meridian system of traditional Chinese medicine influencing the biological functioning of the organs of the body.
- The chakra-nadi system of traditional Indian ayurvedic medicine.
- Systems of "devic entities" / nature spirits of traditional religions.

In this perspective, the physical structure of a biological (or other) entity constraints functional possibilities. And the associated Noetic field systems supply unity and continuity of experience, with functional physical effects happening only where possible through wave function collapse dynamics.

The types of new Noetic systems that could be operating together with biophysical systems might be visualised in the paintings of artist Alex Grey.

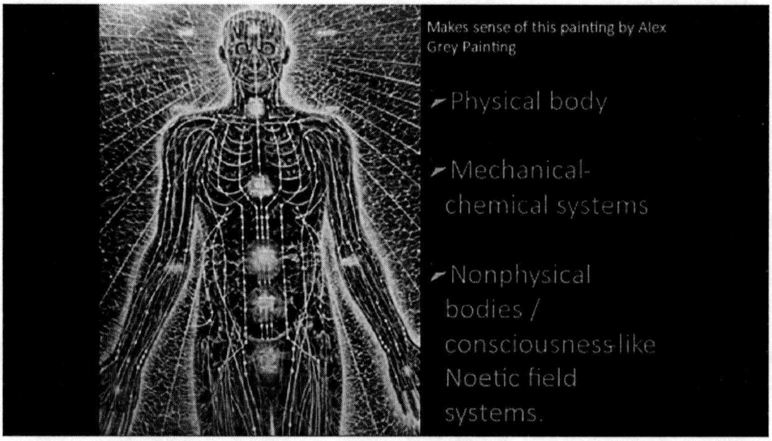

Figure 9: Alex Grey Painting

Noetic field dynamics would operate according to metaphysical and psychophysical "laws". These rules need to be identified, discovered and made precise. And for the Actual

Theory to be considered a scientific theory, testable predictions need to be generated.

In conclusion, while this approach is emerging as the most plausible category of theories to address the "Hard Problems" of conscious experience and free will, the Actual Theory that will eventually describe what actually happens is bound to be radically different from what we are familiar with. It will necessarily involve actions across space and time, the possibility of the future affecting the past as well as the other way around, and the possibility of multiple different realities existing at the same time. For almost a hundred years, physicists working in the area of fundamental quantum processes of superposition, entanglement, and wave function collapse, have commented on the strangeness. Albert Einstein called it derogatively, "spooky action at a distance". Henry Stapp has stated, "Bell's Theorem is the most profound theorem in all of science". The developer of Bell's Theorem, John Bell, opined that when we eventually discover what actually happens during wave function collapse, "The new way of seeing things will involve an imaginative leap that will astonish us." Anton Zeilinger, one of the experimentalists who proved violations of the Bell Inequality, stated more than a decade ago, "This new theory will be so much stranger [than current quantum mechanics]… people attacking quantum mechanics now will long to have it back".

Major scientific paradigm shifts happen in ways laboriously slow, through many actors grinding out experimental results and building theoretical progress step-by-step. But the shifts are in some sense also rapid in that the broader scientific and cultural communities one day suddenly wake up and find it normal to perceive in the new way, as if it has been obvious all along.

A hint that we are going through a major shift in paradigms of science of consciousness is the 2022 Nobel Prize in Physics given to Alain Aspect, John Clauser, and Anton Zeilinger, according to the Nobel press release, "For experiments with entangled photons, establishing the violations of Bell inequalities and pioneering quantum information science".

Instability: How to Understand Consciousness on the Levels of Quantum Theory, Organisms, and the Cosmos

ALEX HANKEY

Background

The question of the nature of human consciousness has long been the subject of scientific speculation[1,2] despite an abundance of material in historical texts from other parts of the world, particularly South Asia[3], where the Vedic Sciences declared it to be the overarching context for the manifestation of the whole universe[4], the very nature of the source from which our universe originated. Despite its great influence on much European thought, including Leibniz and the Philosophia Perennis[5,6], Lord Macaulay, attempted to negate both the dating and much of the content of the Vedic schools of thought[7] by directing Max Müller[8], to deliberately and knowingly falsify both.

After the demise of Macaulay, the influence of Swami Vivekananda was to show how the Vedic Sciences offered a path to understand consciousness as a unifying basis of all religion[9], so that those understanding their truth could maintain a tolerant coexistence with the others – a feature, which had distinguished the Vedic civilisation and its offshoot religions such as Buddhism and Jainism throughout history. Swami Vivekananda's legacy in the West was to stimulate wide interest and even adherence of citizens of many nations to the tenets of his Hindu faith and the Vedic texts at its source[10]. Such great souls as Aldous Huxley took up the cause and promoted Vedanta[11], the goal of the Vedas, in its non-dual, Advaita, form in their own countries and some, like Vivekananda's disciple, Sister Nivedita, in India itself.

Following the lead of Vivekananda, such great personalities as Paramahamsa Yogananda[12], Swami Muktananda[13], my own Master Maharishi Mahesh Yogi[14], Sadhguru Jaggi Vasudev[15], H.R. Nagendra[16], and Sri Madhukarnath[17] ('Sri M.') have established large organisations and gained followings throughout the world, teaching the Yoga path to spiritual emancipation, by their particular means of attempting to attain it. Such was the background when Maharishi Mahesh Yogi in 1973 instructed the founding faculty members of MIU[18], his first university, Maharishi International University: work out the relationship between your own field of modern science and the Vedic sciences as you learn about them.

Introduction

Maharishi's instructions to his 1973 faculty became a beacon light for my own professional research. I was fortunate that another founding faculty member was Professor of Philosophy, Jonathan Shear, who was later to become a leader in the field of consciousness studies[19]. He helped to open it up from his position as the Founding Editor of Journal of Consciousness Studies (JCS). Shear was able to help guide Douglas Hofstadter's student, David Chalmers, into publishing the outcome of his PhD thesis[20] and several other papers in *JCS*[21-23], so getting the new field off to a flying start, albeit not an uncontroversial one, with Daniel Dennett[24] and others[25] playing fricative, opposing roles. Shear's own PhD thesis at UC Berkeley[26] had been on the topic of Pure Consciousness, because, even as an undergraduate, he had arrived at the conclusion that some content-free state of awareness must exist, and that its properties must tell us much about the essence of human experience. (Shear J., Private Communication)

PART 1: Quantum Physics and Consciousness

The starting point for any discussion of Quantum Physics and Consciousness has to be the role envisioned for the human observer within the context of experimental quantum physics.

It was immediately clear to Bohr and Heisenberg, when the latter worked in Copenhagen after the conclusion of his PhD, that human observers somehow cause the 'collapse of the wave function'[27,i,28], also known as the 'reduction of the wave packet', because experiments are mostly performed with mixtures of wave functions (wave packets) rather than individual quanta (wave functions). For simplicity, we shall treat the two terms as equivalent.

The Bohr-Heisenberg conclusion was deeply opposed by several leading physicists, e.g. Erwin Schrodinger, who proposed and solved the wave equation named after him[29]. His Schrodinger's Cat Paradox[30] lay a deep challenge to the Copenhagen Interpretation. It was taken up by the polymath genius, John von Neumann, who had identified the detailed mathematical context[31,ii] for both Heisenberg and Schrodinger's seemingly different formulations of quantum mechanics. They are Hilbert Spaces – infinitely dimensional complex-valued vector spaces. His book, *The Mathematical Foundations of Quantum Mechanics*[31,ii], became the bible for certain segments of the physics community. Among its contributions was the realisation that consciousness must be responsible for the collapse of the wave function; experiments really offer no other choice. The question then arises: How does it do so? What physics is available that would enable consciousness to collapse wave functions?

Here, we show how the physics of instability implies that all wave functions of extensive parameters are removed at instabilities. In other words, instabilities appear to have the ability to collapse wave functions / reduce wave packets! First, we show that this is the case, and then, we propose a 'mechanism' by which it occurs.

Instabilities Collapse Wave functions of Extensive Parameters: at an instability, one or more parameters of the system become unstable.[32] Normally such parameters are stabilised by quantum fields of the parameter in question, density in liquid-gas critical instabilities or magnetisation in magnet critical instabilities. Instead, the parameter undergoes critical point fluctuations, in which it fluctuates over a wide range of values. The normal way of explaining this in classical physics is to show that the velocity of the parameter's waves has become zero so they no longer exist.[32] In quantum theory, stability is maintained by quantum fields: sound waves, phonons, in liquid gas phase transitions, and magnons in magnetic phase transitions. To become unstable, the stabilising quantum fields must have been removed—annihilated. Thus, Instabilities Annihilate Quantum Fields / Reduce Wave Packets.

Second, consider the example of critical points in fluid systems where the onset of turbulence occurs at a critical instability, the critical Reynolds number[33]. Here, the instability allows the fluid to flow in infinitesimal loops that slowly become able to grow in size[32]. The idea of an Infinitesimal Loop can be extended from fluid flow to information flow, in which case it becomes a perfectly self-observing loop of information. By observing any quantum field / wave function within the system, such a loop will annihilate it[32]. This second approach explains in more detail how an instability may remove quantum fields that keep the system stable: instabilities contain infinitesimal, perfectly self-observing loops of information, that collapse wave functions of quanta that stabilise the system.

What this means is that, if there is some unexpected reason why the physiology contains instabilities, then it would in principle be possible to situate consciousness at such a location. Furthermore, a completely unexpected addition comes out of the analysis: an infinitesimal loop of information flow would provide an explanation for self-awareness at the base of conscious experience.

The significance of this last point cannot be understated. It emerges as follows: by definition, information flows from Known to Knower. An infinitesimal information loop therefore unites Knower, Process of Knowing, and Known into One. The Knower Knows Him / Her Self directly, a property we shall term 'Self-

Awareness'. Siting consciousness at an instability unexpectedly and serendipitously turns out to be a condition where Self-Awareness is a concomitant of all experience – as we ourselves know it to be. If we attend any meeting, at which we have to respond to our name being read out in a roll call, then our answer, 'present', bears witness to our sense of 'self' accompanying experience. The infinitesimal loop of information explains that fact, despite not being one of the original aims of the theory.

PART 2: Complexity Biology and Instabilities

Although Part 1 has identified good reasons for associating consciousness and self-awareness with instabilities, it has offered no reason why the physiology should involve such a means. Here, we discuss the presence of instabilities in animal physiologies, and show that they occur in precisely the locations where consciousness is then able to regulate the functions, for which it is known to be responsible – like striated muscles that enable us to act on our environment in ways that we choose. The approach we offer is to show that the field of Fractal Physiology[34] within Complexity Biology[35] indicates that physiological regulation contains instabilities, and that these instabilities are situated in exactly the right places for consciousness to be able to control various physiological functions[36]. Again, we emphasise that these facts are completely unexpected. Being prior to the exploration of the role of instability in quantum physics, they were not identified with the intention of developing a theory of conscious control of physiological functions. Like this theory, they just fell out!

Fractal Physiology[34] is the name for a property that physiological control systems exhibit when stimulated with a sequence of identical stimuli. Instead of being identical as one might expect, the responses are different from each other; they form a 'Fractal (1/f) Distribution'[34], implying that the control system differs from ordinary control systems of mechanical devices. The meaning of these distributions was given in a famous paper in the top physics journal, *Physical Review Letters*, in 1987[38]. The authors, Bak, Tang and Wiesenfeld, noted that the same fractal distributions are found by experimental physicists investigating phenomena near critical points. They therefore suggested that physiological regulation somehow involves critical instabilities of a kind similar to those found in the physics of phase transitions. They put forward a name for the new property of physiology: self-organised criticality (SoC).

Various suggestions have been put forward to explain the way that self-organised criticality comes about[39], but they need not concern us here. Suffice it to say that the best suggestion seems to be that SoC maximises responsiveness of the physiology to external stimuli[39]. This is clearly an advantage: a less responsive organism will function less efficiently, and be less competitive in its environment. Organisms that are more efficient will naturally come to dominate their ecological niche[39]. That all organisms present today possess the SoC property is therefore hardly surprising; they have had billions of years of evolution to perfect it.

Fractal physiology leads us to the conclusion that physiological regulation contains critical instabilities of the kind that cause quantum wave functions to collapse. But where are they located? Here, extensive work on Fractal Physiology by Stuart Kauffman[40-42] and his various collaborators at the Santa Fe Institute provides the answer: the instabilities are sited at the 'Loci of Control' of the regulatory systems concerned[36]. This means that if one wants to exert control over a particular physiological system, then the point from which one must exert control is precisely the location where the critical instability is situated.

Put together, these points mean that: if any consciousness is located at a critical instability, that consciousness will be able to exert control over the physiological system concerned. For example, consider a striated muscle used for an action like walking or speech: by virtue of its locus of control being at a critical instability, the consciousness of the organism will be able to control that action.

We may summarise Part 2 as follows: Fractal Physiology's self-organised criticality (SoC) is a universal property of biological regulatory systems, because it maximises the regulated system's responsiveness to external stimuli. Since consciousness can couple to matter at a critical instability, SoC enables consciousness to couple to organic physiologies. One may conclude that critical instabilities can model Consciousness-in-the-Physiology; more specifically, they determine how consciousness controls specific physiological functions, like those of striated muscles, enabling consciously controlled responses to perceived events in the organism's environment. More generally, this may also explain how consciousness can direct attention and planning from the brain's frontal and prefrontal cortices.

As an addition, we should note that the brain's ability to collapse wave functions provides an explanation for the famous Schrodinger's famous Cat Paradox[30]: a cat reduces its own wave packets. Thus, no question can arise of it being in a mixture of quantum states corresponding to it being both 'dead-and-alive'.

This provides a corresponding explanation for Wigner's Friend Paradox[43], and its potentially never-ending recursion. Rather than using quantum gravity, as proposed by Hameroff and Penrose[44,45], the new solution is based on well-accepted properties of physiology, albeit Fractal Physiology. It points to the Wigner[43] von Neumann[31] interpretation of quantum theory being correct.

As an extra, we can now show how both the Non-Duality and Non-Locality aspects of the theme of the conference result from results presented in Part 2. Non-Duality: infinitesimal closed loops of information remove subject-object duality, because knower, process of knowing and known have become One, i.e. non-dual. Non-Locality: under specific conditions, the large quantities of internal critical correlations / critical coherence at instabilities enable them to couple to one another at space-like separations. Then Experience Information, being non-digital, can be shared among them. The overall system has become non-local.

PART 3: Consciousness and the Cosmos

Cultural traditions across the world[46,47] have attributed the creation of the world as we perceive it, i.e., our universe, to a conscious being, the Creator. What light might the Critical Instability approach to understanding consciousness shed on such traditions and ancient beliefs? Here again, work by Penrose comes to the fore. Penrose collaborated with his famous colleague, Stephen Hawking[48], to investigate the end of the universe if it underwent a collapse. Together they concluded that the universe would end in a singularity. The equations were reversible in time, however, their work also led to the conclusion that the universe originated in a singularity, which is now recognised to be an instability, as proposed in the picture of an 'inflationary universe' in its earliest history[4,49].

For our work, identifying an instability at the birth of our universe is as serendipitous as the occurrence of critical instabilities in the physiology. It points to the possibility that the source of our universe of space-time-matter is the abode of a Consciousness. Might it be not too much to suggest that this points to a genuine 'Being' at that source, God, the Creator?

Discussion

The idea that critical instabilities provide a condition where relevant wave functions collapse is quite recent, but not yet widely known or appreciated. The reasoning presented in Part 1 is incontrovertible. The second line of thought, that critical instabilities contain perfectly self-observing loops of information then shows that they also satisfy the condition for the least excited state of man's consciousness, as named in Vedic texts – particularly the Upanishads. The nature of consciousness presented in those texts plays an important role in guiding our understanding of the proposed theory; also in its development to other applications, such as Siddhis ('paranormal' powers and abilities) named in the traditional texts on Yoga, the Yoga, Upanishads, etc.

However, this does not mean that other, non-biological materials exhibiting critical points can be attributed any kind of cognitive property, or any kind of creative intelligence. That would need the presence of higher order critical points connected to a system capable of cognition.

One Final Note: Biologists are taught that: 'Organisms are only molecules; therefore, because molecules cannot support consciousness, biology cannot do so.' This presentation has shown that, on the contrary, organisms are structured so that consciousness based on self-awareness can control important functions.

A corollary to this conclusion is that, if organisms are made of molecules, then some aspect of their biology other than molecules must support their consciousness. This applies to organisms like ourselves and other animals, even to single cells where we may observe some "conscious" reactions.

The Pribram-Bohm Holoflux Theory of Consciousness

SHELLI RENÉE JOYE

The Granularity of Space and Time: Our Digital Cosmos

When I was a young student, I was intrigued by a lecture I heard by the California physics professor, Richard Feynman. He asked us to consider the following. If we were to take a hammer and try to strike an anvil with it, we could mathematically track the distance of the hammer from the anvil, at each moment of time. At some moment the hammer would reach half the remaining distance to the anvil. You could plot the time of the next moment after that, when the hammer would again reach half the distance remaining. If space were continuous, you could continue measuring the time at which the hammer managed to move closer to the anvil by halving the distance. But, if space were continuous, you would never actually be able to strike the anvil because you could continue to move half the previous distance closer to the anvil. Thus, space is not continuous, there must be a final limit, so space must be granular, not continuous. This goes for time too, he said. Time is not continuous, but is granular. Then, having duly confused us students, Feynman would launch into his lecture on quantum physics.

Quantum means "discrete" in one sense, i.e. there is no continuity but a sort of "jump" (in fact the phrase "quantum jump" is often used). This "jump" is due to the bottom limits to space and time that were discovered to be the solution to solve a major problem that had plagued physicists for decades, i.e. the mathematics to model the relationship of temperature peaks to the peak wavelength of the electromagnetic frequency in the infrared band (that we sense and term "heat").

Max Planck (known as "the father of Action") somehow intuited the solution that had escaped everyone else for decades. He had been working to solve the puzzle of the emission of radiation from heated objects, often called the problem of "black-body radiation."

All normal matter at temperatures above absolute zero emits electromagnetic radiation. It had long been noticed that charcoal could be seen to be giving off different colours that depended directly upon the temperature to which they had been heated. As the temperature of charcoal is increased, the visible emission begins to be seen as a dull red, then as the temperature increases, it becomes more orange, then yellow, then green, and finally violet. Laboratory measurements had been made of the wavelength of light coming from glowing charcoal at different temperatures (fig. 1), but the calculations made (using "Classical theory," prior to quantum theory), shown in the dashed curve) were way off, and

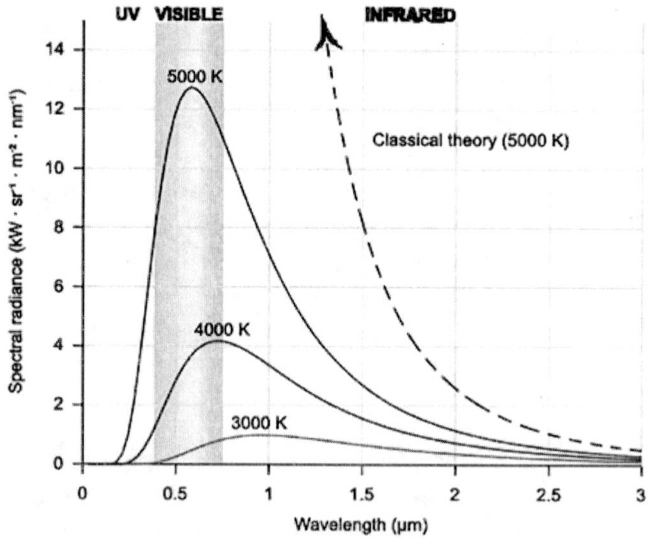

Figure 1: Black-Body Radiation Curve Discrepancy[i]

never matched the actual 5000 K measurements, shown in the solid line curves. In the figure can be seen the large discrepancy for a temperature of 5000 Kelvin.

Until Planck solved the puzzle, nobody had been able to accurately calculate the "black-body radiation curves" that would match laboratory measurements. Planck's intuitive flash of insight was this:

1. There can be no completely continuous actions in space and time.
2. There is both a top and bottom limit to the dimensions of time and space.
3. Action must thus be "granular" (corollary: the universe is digital).

Knowing that the speed of light is invariant, Planck immediately sought to calculate the bottom limit of space, searching among various mathematical configurations to use the known constants of the speed of light and the gravitational constant in order to match exactly the black-body radiation curves. Eventually they all came together in his famous equation, which defines what is now called the Planck Length (Fig. 2).

$$\ell_P = \sqrt{\frac{\hbar G}{c^3}}$$

ℓ_P = **The Planck Length**
$\hbar$ = ***Planck's constant***
G = ***Gravitational constant***
c = ***Speed of light***

Figure 2: The Planck Length Equation

Because length divided by velocity results in time, he was also able to calculate the fundamental unit of time (Fig. 3) as well as several other fundamental lower limits.

Calculation of the Planck length

$$\ell_P = \sqrt{\frac{\hbar G}{c^3}} = 1.616229 \times 10^{-35} \text{ meter}$$

Calculation of the Planck time

$$t_P = \frac{\ell_P}{c} = \sqrt{\frac{\hbar G}{c^5}} = 5.391247 \times 10^{-44} \text{ seconds}$$

Figure 3: Calculation of the Planck Length and the Planck Time Constants

These then are the lower limits to our space and time dimensions:

Planck length constant → 1.616255×10^{-35} Metres

Planck time constant → 5.391247×10^{-44} Seconds

Planck mass constant → 2.176434×10^{-8} Kilograms

Planck temperature constant → 1.416784×10^{32} Kelvin

Note that at the smallest dimension, the Planck length, the temperature reaches the maximum possible in spacetime, the Planck temperature constant. That is because at smaller dimensions, the radii of the spinning energy "strings" are smaller, and thus the frequencies of the emitted radiation are higher. Higher frequencies emit radiation at higher energy levels.

Henceforth, using these constants in the mathematical model made the curve calculations match the observed curve exactly. A year after his discovery, Max Plank began using the term "quanta" (Latin: "how much" or "amount") to describe these values, and some years later, his colleagues began to call these the "Planck constants." In 1918 Planck was awarded the Nobel Prize for his discovery of these constants.

The Planck time constant of 5.391247×10^{-44} seconds is the smallest unit of time possible in our spacetime continuum. While humans are familiar with the duration of "one human second" of time, conventionally measured with our own time keeping clock devices, it is difficult to imagine much smaller time units. One of the fastest contemporary Intel microprocessor chips runs at 4.7 GHz, which is 4.7 x 10^9 . However, within this "one human second" there are 10^9 "processor ticks" and 10^{44} "Planck time ticks" per second, which is truly mind-boggling!

	Scientific Notation	Seconds, in Standard Notation
Standard "second"	10^{0}	1 (note that this sets the scale of human-perceived time to approximately equal the average human heartbeat)
Early computer processor (Z80 chip)	10^{-5}	0.00001
Intel micro-processor (Intel Core i5 chip)	10^{-9}	0.000000001
Planck time	10^{-44}	0.00000000000000000000000000 000000000000000001

Table 1: Comparison of Time Units: Scientific Notation and Standard Notation.

Because time does not exist below this lowest granular division of time, Planck time, there is a quantum "jump" as time flows, a jump from one tick to the next. But can we imagine what occurs between the two ticks? In between these ticks, time does not exist. This is what metaphysicians would call the void, the timeless eternal, the transcendent. In the cosmological physics of

David Bohm, it is the implicate order, the ground of being "into which" all information folds inward from our external spacetime, and from "out of which" all things are unfolded and projected into spacetime by the same implicate order. To Bohm, all particles within our cosmos of spacetime are actually projections of a higher dimensional order:

> *We may regard each of the 'particles' constituting a system as a projection of a 'higher-dimensional' reality, rather than as a separate particle, existing together with all the others in a common three-dimensional space. For example, in the experiment of Einstein, Podolsky and Rosen, each of two atoms that initially combine to form a single molecule are to be regarded as three-dimensional projections of a six-dimensional reality*[ii].

Pribram and Bohm spoke about a holomovement occurring outside the four dimensions of space and time. Pribram did not like the use of the word "movement" in this naming convention, and recommended to Bohm that they use the term "holoflux," which is not a movement in time, but more of an evolution of information within the frequency domains of the implicate order. In fact, one of the attributes of the implicate order, as Bohm understood it, would be a continuous *enfolding* of information from the spacetime domain, back into the hidden dimensions of the implicate order, where somehow the total information coming from spacetime for that one "tick" of time would be immediately superimposed over all the pre-existing information stored in the implicate order (*Akasha*, according to Bucke, Steiner, and Laszlo). At the very next quantum "tick" of time, the cosmos would be reprojected into spacetime from information holoflux within the implicate order. The cycle can truly be seen to be a digital process, with the cosmos being created and recreated with each tick of the Planck-time clock. Bohm says:

> *What follows from all this is that basically the implicate order has to be considered as a process of enfoldment and unfoldment in a higher-dimensional space. Only under*

certain conditions can this be simplified as a process of enfoldment and unfoldment in three dimensions[iii].

Bohm goes on to describe this projected information holoflux as it appears within the constricted spacetime dimensions:

The electromagnetic field, which is the ground of the holographic image, obeys the laws of the quantum theory, and when these are properly applied to the field it is found that this, too, is actually a multidimensional reality which can only under certain conditions be simplified as a three-dimensional reality. Quite generally, then, the implicate order has to be extended into a multidimensional reality. In principle this reality is one unbroken whole, including the entire universe with all its 'fields' and 'particles'[iv].

The Pribram-Bohm Holoflux Topology

The psychophysical model of consciousness which is developed here is presented in figure 4, the "Pribram-Bohm Holoflux Model," where the basic theory is diagrammed as consciousness transforming between non-local and local regions of experience and information.

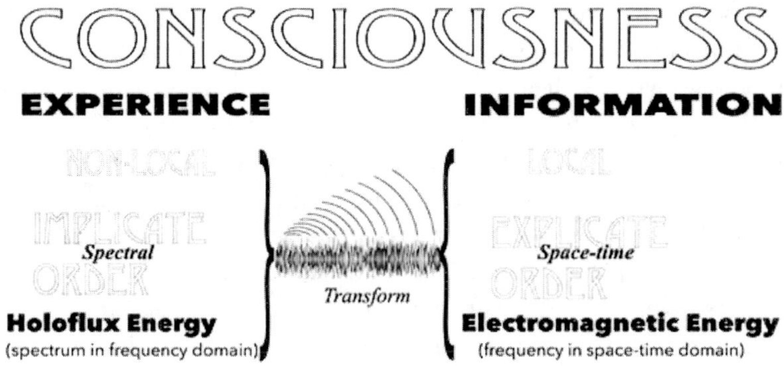

Figure 4: The Pribram-Bohm Holoflux Model

The Pribram-Bohm hypothesis regards consciousness as

a cybernetic energy process, a holoflux transforming between two orders of being in "an undivided flowing movement without borders"[1]. To the left in the diagram of Figure 1, consciousness is expressed as a spectrum of holoflux energy in Bohm's implicate order. This holoflux energy resonates with electromagnetic energy of the same frequencies to the right in the diagram, in the spacetime region, or explicate order[1].

Viewed from left to right, the diagram reveals a spectrum of holoflux energy in the transcendental implicate order transforming and translated into "things" and "events" in local spacetime, and conversely, viewing the diagram from right to left, information generated by "things" and "events" interacting throughout spacetime is seen to be transforming (folding) back into the implicate order. The process is described as a continuous cybernetic cycle, perhaps occurring at a regular clock-rate.

Superposition of Consciousness: Cybernetics and the Fourier Transform

Common experience would suggest that all awareness is consciousness *of* something, such as the experience of a sound, of an image, of a sensation, of an emotion, of an interior verbal thought. These experiences seem to be superpositioned, they often occur at what seem to be the same perceptual moment. Yet each simultaneous stream of experience remains distinct, somehow integrated with all the others. But what is it that is "looking at" this stream of experiences? It is as if there is some meta-consciousness that is more than the sum of each of these individual "experience streams," per se, but rather some other, more comprehensive level, some panoramic perspective that is able to embrace and comprehend them all, and which has the amazing ability to *fine tune* its own selected focus upon *one or more* of these streams of awareness while simultaneously dampening and filtering out the many others.

In signal analysis this stream phenomenon is explained by the *superposition principle*, formalised in 1822 by the French mathematician Jean-Baptiste Fourier, who developed the mathematics of what is now called "Fourier analysis" during his search for a mathematical relationship between spacetime and frequency[2]. Because signals are more readily superpositioned and manipulated (filtered, amplified, etc.) within the *frequency domain* than in the *time domain*, the Fourier transform equations have become primary and ubiquitous mathematical tools in physics and engineering for analysing, synthesising, and transmitting signals between two domains:

1. a "spacetime domain (*t*d)"
2. a "frequency domain (f_d)"

Much of electrical engineering circuit design is done within the frequency domain, and only subsequently implemented with time domain components, as described here by Francis F. Kuo, chief electrical engineer at the original Bell Telephone Laboratory from which emerged the transistor, the laser, and radio astronomy, information theory, and the Unix operating system. In his textbook on *Network Analysis and Synthesis*, Kuo[3] states:

> *We see that in the* ***time domain*** *(i.e., where the independent variable is* ***t****) the voltage–current relationships are given in terms of differential equations. On the other hand, in the complex* ***frequency domain****, the voltage–current relationships for the elements are expressed in* **algebraic** *equations. Algebraic equations are, in most cases, more easily solved than differential equations. Herein lies the* ***raison d'être*** *for describing signals and networks in the frequency domain as well as in the time domain.*

Norbert Wiener[4] coined the term "cybernetics" from the Greek κυβερνήτης—"steersman, governor, pilot, or rudder"—during his own work at the same Bell Telephone Laboratory as Kuo, and made use of Fourier's transform to model and analyse brain waves in the frequency domain, where he discovered clear evidence of "self-organisation of electroencephalograms or brain waves". Using Fourier analysis, an approach which later became of great interest to Bohm, Wiener[4] was able to detect uniquely narrow frequency ranges, centred within different spatial locations on the cortex, that repeatedly exhibited auto-correlation. Regions on the cortex were identified where specific ranges of frequencies were found to coalesce toward intermediate frequencies, seeming both to attract and to strengthen one another, exhibiting *resonance* or "self tuning" to amplify and consolidate signals into narrowly specific ranges in the frequency domain f_d. His research led Wiener to conjecture that the *infrared band* of electromagnetic flux may be the loci of "self-organising systems":

> *We thus see that a non-linear interaction causing the attraction of frequency can generate a self-organising system, as it does in the case of the brain waves we have discussed. This possibility of self-organisation is by no means limited to the very low frequency of these two phenomena. Consider self–organising systems at the frequency level, say, of infrared light.*

Three years after Wiener's[4] publication of *Cybernetics*, David Bohm[5] stressed the importance of Fourier's equations on the first page of his well-received 646-page textbook, *Quantum Theory*, where he encouraged a familiarity with Fourier analysis for an ontological understanding of quantum phenomena:

> *It seems impossible to develop quantum concepts extensively without Fourier analysis. It is, therefore, presupposed that the reader is moderately familiar with Fourier analysis.*

For purposes of this discussion, the basic understanding of Fourier analysis is simply that *frequency vibrations* manifest within two distinct dimensions or domains: a spacetime domain and a frequency domain. Till recently, physicists have focused exclusively within spacetime to conduct their research, considering only space and time as having any "reality" and considering the ontological reality of the frequency domain, if at all, in the same vague category as the domain of mathematics itself (i.e., in some unspecified transcendent dimension). Whether there might somehow exist a "real" dimension *outside of* spacetime , or *beyond* spacetime has generally been beyond the purview of the physical sciences. Yet the experienced reality of a region of consciousness beyond spacetime is supported by the vast body of first–hand reports generated by religious, mystical, or near-death experiences. In an approach to such experiences, William James[6], the "father of American psychology," writes:

> *The further limits of our being plunge, it seems to me, into an altogether other dimension of existence from the sensible and merely "understandable" world. Name it the mystical region, or the supernatural region, whichever you choose. So far as our ideal impulses originate in this region (and most of them do originate in it, for we find them possessing us in a way for which we cannot articulately account), we belong to it in a more intimate sense than that in which we belong to the visible world, for we belong in the most intimate sense wherever our ideals belong.*

Fourier's transform equations (fig. 5) between the two domains of time (t_d) and frequency (f_d) are more than simply mathematical equations, written down as functions in the abstract symbolic language of calculus[7].

$$f(t) = \int_{-\infty}^{+\infty} X(F)e^{j2\pi Ft}\,dF \qquad f(F) = \int_{-\infty}^{+\infty} x(t)e^{-j2\pi Ft}\,dt$$

Fourier integral transform of a continuous frequency function into the time domain (t_d).

Fourier integral transform of a continuous time function into the frequency domain (F_d).

Figure 5: The Fourier Transform and Inverse Transform

These two expressions indicate that any function in the timespace domain can be transformed into and expressed equivalently as an infinite series of frequency spectra functions in the frequency domain. The transformation is also possible in the opposite direction, such that any arbitrary function in the frequency domain can be transformed into and expressed by an infinite series of time functions. The two domains mirror one another.

Beyond purely mathematical considerations, the equations can be taken as models of an actual cosmic process (i.e., much as Newton's Law model the phenomenon of gravity) and they can be understood as mirroring the cosmos in mathematical terms. The model of consciousness presented in this paper proposes that there is indeed an ontological reality to this other region, and that this region is synonymous with Bohm's "implicate order," Pribram's "holonomic frequency domain."

The neurosurgeon Karl Pribram[8] was one of the first to articulate the idea that the Fourier transform might play a role in brain/mind neurophysics. Pribram[9] spent decades performing laboratory research to gather experimental data in an effort to solve two problems:

(a) To identify the location and mechanism of memory storage (the *engram*).

(b) To discover the cognitive mechanism behind visual perception.

Pribram[10] arrived at the conclusion that the data revealed evidence of Fourier signal transformations of visual signals from the rods and cones of the eyes, and that these Fourier patterns could be detected in spatial Fourier patterns over wide areas of the brain, as fields within the fine-fibred dendritic networks of the cerebral cortex.

In the mid-1960s, Pribram was inspired by reports of the first optical holograms, and the empirical evidence that holograms could store, retrieve, and process vast quantities of information using resonant photons in high frequency beams. Ten years later, Pribram[8] published *Languages of the Brain*, in which he detailed his new theory, the holonomic brain/mind theory, based upon evidence of the Fourier transform playing a key role in the mind/brain process. The theory he put forth proposed that the cognitive sensory processes of memory, sight, hearing, and consciousness in general, may all operate holographically, in a transformational process of information-coded-energies flowing back and forth between space– time and the frequency domain via a Fourier transform mechanism.

Pribram's[8] theory was radical and controversial, challenging two prominent paradigms of modern neurophysical research:

(a) The belief that consciousness is an epiphenomenon produced by electrical sparks among synaptic–clefts throughout the wiring of neurons the brain.

(b) The belief that somewhere in the physical brain, *engrams* of memory are stored, and will be eventually found.

Pribram[8] relates a story of a conversation he had at the time, while climbing with colleagues on a hike in Colorado just prior to attending a neuroscience conference in Boulder:

> *We had climbed high into the Rocky Mountains. Coming to rest on a desolate crag, a long meditative silence was suddenly broken by a query from Campbell: "Karl, do you really believe it's a Fourier?" I hesitated, and then replied, "No Fergus, that would be too easy, don't you agree?" Campbell sat silently awhile, then said, "You are right, it's probably not that easy. So what are you going to say tomorrow down there?" I replied, this time without hesitation, "That the transform is a Fourier, of course." Campbell smiled and chortled, "Good for you! So am I."*

Pribram's[8] hypothesis was strengthened through a growing appreciation of holography as frequency-superpositioned electromagnetic wave interference. Pribram called his approach "the holonomic brain theory," and postulated the importance of the frequency domain in future research:

> *Essentially, the theory reads that the brain at one stage of processing performs its analyses in the frequency domain . . . a solid body of evidence has accumulated that*

the auditory, somatosensory, motor, and visual systems of the brain do in fact process, at one or several stages, input from the senses in the frequency domain.[11,xii]

In Pribram's[9] theory, a pure frequency domain links with the neuronal tissue of the brain through modulating fields of flux within the fine-fibred dendritic webs of the cerebral cortex regions. His paradigm was reinforced at a San Francisco conference during a lecture given by the physicist Geoffrey F. Chew, the head of the UC Berkeley physics department and a former student of Enrico Fermi. Chew presented a conceptual diagram of the Fourier transform process (fig. 6), which perfectly encapsulated what Pribram had by then become familiar with, the Fourier transform[12] . As shown in the figure, the spectral (frequency) domain, located at the left of the diagram, is directly linked to the spacetime domain, depicted at the right, bridged by the Fourier transform, operating at the sub-atomic levels predicted by Planck's constant.

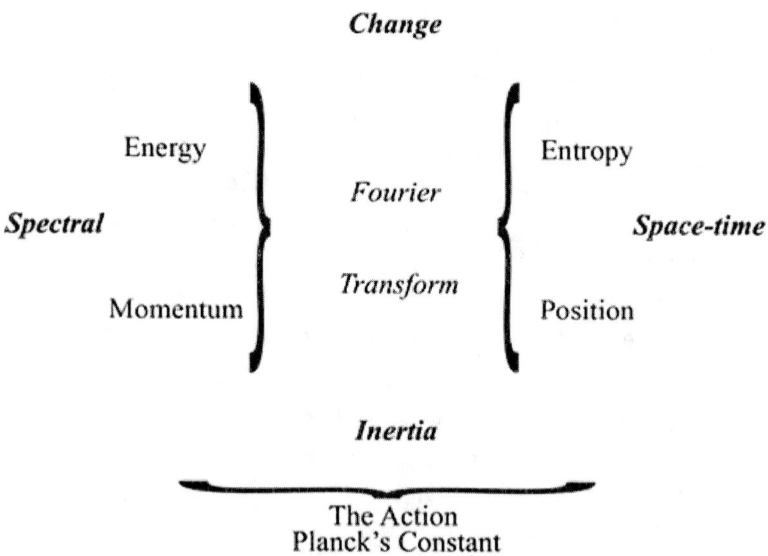

Figure 6: The Dirac Fourier Transform Diagram. Source: Adapted from Pribram (2004b)

Pribram[10] asked Chew where he had obtained the diagram,

and was told that he had been given the diagram by his colleague at Berkeley, the physicist Henry Stapp, who himself said he had been given it directly from the British theoretical physicist Paul Dirac (1902–1984), one of the original founders of quantum mechanics. Whatever the origin of the figure, Pribram chose to include the diagram in several future papers. In "Consciousness Reassessed," Pribram's[13] caption to the figure reads, "The Fourier Transform as the Mediator Between Spectral and Spacetime ".

In the diagram, the spectral domain is shown at the left and spacetime to the right, with the Fourier transform between them. The diagram became foundational to Pribram's understanding. It presents a two–way Fourier transform, operational at the boundary between the two domains, located at an event horizon termed in the diagram, "The Action: Planck's Constant." It is this process of turbulent transformation at the event–horizon that David Bohm and Basil Hiley [14] termed holomovement or holoflux.

The Limits of Space: From the Edge of the Universe to Planck's Constant

The Pribram–Bohm hypothesis holds that the dimensions of space are finite and that space exhibits a limited domain in a quantifiable range. This is consistent with the physics of string theory or M-theory, [quote on dimensions moved to first chapter]

Carr[15] uses the alchemical image of the ouroboros (Fig. 7) to illustrate his GUT theory (Grand Unified Theory) in comparing major scale-dependent structural levels of the physical world: "The significance of the head meeting the tail is that the entire Universe was once compressed to a point of infinite density (or, more strictly, the Planck density)". This archetypal figure implies the interconnectedness of the entire universal process in time and space, presenting a cybernetic feedback loop operational at every scale. Mystics have intuited this ouroboric process symbolised in the images of a snake swallowing its own tail (the image has been found as early as the fourteenth century BCE in the tomb of Tutankhamun) and it is frequently used to symbolise cybernetic feedback in control and communication theory[4].

While Wiener coined the term *cybernetics*, communication engineers would more commonly see this as a metaphor for the "feedback loop," used everywhere in electronic circuit design.

Figure 7: Alchemical Ouroboros (Pelekanos, 1478)

Stretching out this circular cosmic ouroboric serpent from head to tail, one can create an axis of scales that encompasses all of space. In Fig. 8 such a scale is drawn starting with the currently estimated diameter of the universe itself at 10+25 m, and descending logarithmically down to the Planck length limit at 10-35 m. The axis thus spans a total range of 10+60 (60 jumps by the power of 10). The Pribram–Bohm hypothesis holds that there, at the very bottom of the linear scale (Fig. 8), is to be found the transition bounding the explicate order and the implicate order. Here, at the bottom bound of the spatial scale, space reaches its end, according to modern physics; but it also marks the entry point into Bohm's "implicate order," what Pribram terms the "frequency domain"[1,10].

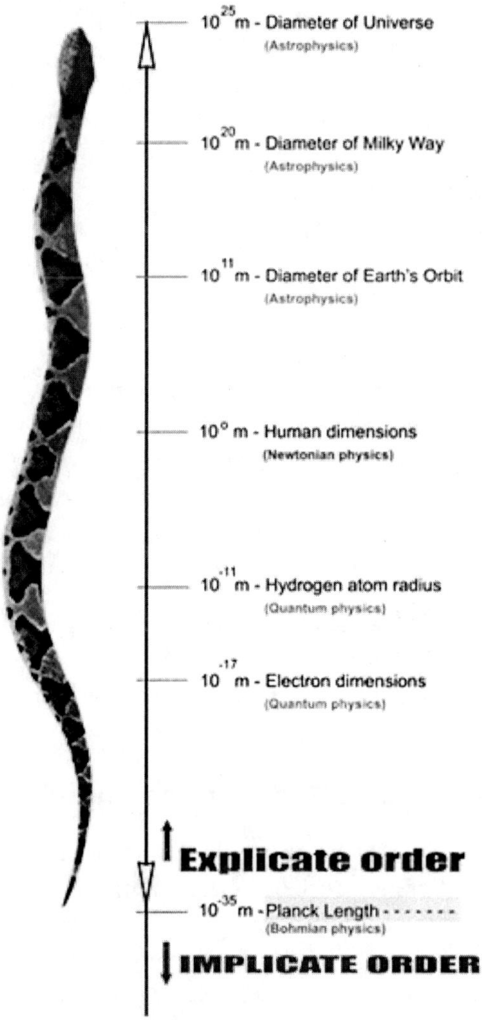

Figure 8: Scales of Dimensional Space and the Explicate/ Implicate Boundary

The implications of this topology are profound. Imagine moving inwardly, from any position in the universe, moving into a spherical bubble, shrinking ever smaller in scale while moving ever closer to the centre at the bottom of the spatial scale, following the radial axis inward, ever shrinking downward, and then abruptly reaching the end of the line at the Planck length limit of space, the locus of a spherical shell 10-35 metres in diameter, below which space has no meaning. Here a boundary has been reached, an event horizon between space and the implicate order. To understand this, one must realise that the classical Cartesian assumption that space is continuous is wrong; there is indeed a bottom to space, at least according to physics, below which space no longer has meaning. Here there is a discontinuity, as David Bohm and F. David Peat[16] explain in describing the granularity of space:

> *What of the order between two points in space? The Cartesian order holds that space is continuous. Between any two points, no matter how close they lie, occur an infinite of other points. Between any two neighbouring points in this infinity lies another infinity and so on. This notion of continuity is not compatible with the order of the quantum theory.*

Thus, the physicist John Wheeler has suggested that, at very short distances, continuous space begins to break up into a foam-like structure. Thus the "order between" two points moves from the order of continuity to an order of a discontinuous foam

Pribram's Spectral Flux and the Implicate Order

In 1979, Karl Pribram, at that time a Stanford professor, attended a conference in Cordoba, Spain, where he met David Bohm, a professor of theoretical physics at London University[17]. During the conference, Pribram[10] soon realised that David Bohm's model of the implicate order and its projection, or extrusion into space-time, could be seen as entirely compatible with his own holonomic mind/brain theory. Thus began 20 years of correspondence and dialogue between David Bohm and Karl Pribram, and the two soon became personal friends.

Pribram[10] saw in Bohm's theories how the frequency domain flux might be seen to unfold into explicate domain waves of encoded information via the Fourier transform, and he appreciated Bohm's description of how information from the explicate may fold back into the implicate in a bi-directional process. Even more intriguing was Bohm's belief that, "the basic relationship of quantum theory and consciousness is that they have the implicate order in common."[14]

Pribram was equally impressed with Bohm's explanation of nonlocality, a major mystery in quantum physics, which Bohm explains as fundamental to the process of folding and unfolding between explicate and implicate orders, allowing for full superpositioned cohesion of frequency information within the implicate order, and even providing a plausible mechanism for Sheldrake's theories of morphogenetic fields and morphic resonance:

> *The implicate order can be thought of as a ground beyond time, a totality, out of which each moment is projected into the explicate order. For every moment that is projected out into the explicate there would be another movement in which that moment would be injected or "introjected" back into the implicate order. If you have a large number of repetitions of this process, you'll start to build up a fairly constant component to this series of projection and injection. That is, a fixed disposition would become established. The point is that, via this process, past forms would tend to be repeated or replicated in the present, and that is very similar to what Sheldrake calls a morphogenetic field and morphic resonance. Moreover, such a field would not be located anywhere. When it projects back into the totality (the implicate order), since no space and time are relevant there, all things of a similar nature might*

get connected together or resonate in totality. When the explicate order enfolds into the implicate order, which does not have any space, all places and all times are, we might say, merged, so that what happens in one place will interpenetrate what happens in another place.[18]

Bohm's topology is both supported and extended by Pribram's contention, supported by the diagram handed down from Dirac, that the boundary or event horizon between the two domains, where the action occurs, is at the Planck length, precisely where, as Pribram tells us here, spectral density in-formation translates into spacetime ex-formation.

Matter can be seen as an "ex-formation," an externalized (extruded, palpable, compacted) form of flux. By contrast, thinking and its communication (minding) are the consequence of an internalised (neg-entropic) forming of flux, its "in-formation." My claim is that the basis function from which both matter and mind are "formed" is flux (measured as spectral density).[13]

This flux or spectral density is for Pribram real, in the same sense that spacetime is considered to be real, but this flux is *outside* or *beyond* space–time. It is in this sense that Pribram made the conceptual leap from considering the Fourier transform as simply a tool of mathematical calculation, to a dawning realisation that the reality of the transform implies the ontological *reality* of a domain *outside space–time*, a transcendent yet ontologically real domain where energy as flux is "measured as spectral density."

Dirac's original diagram can now be extended to include Bohm's two regions of the whole, the implicate order and the explicate order. Figure 9 depicts this expanded diagram.

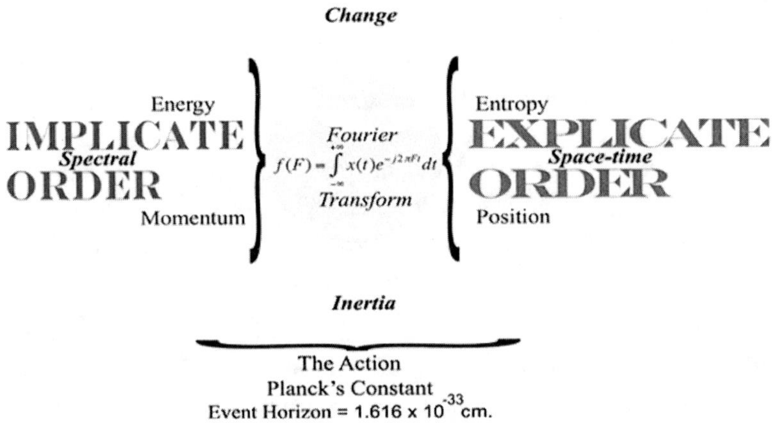

Figure 9: Dirac Fourier Diagram with David Bohm's Topology

An anthropomorphic view of the Pribram's diagram can be seen in Fig. 10, where an iris-like lens peering out from the implicate order is maintaining a focus upon and/or projecting a holonomic universe within the explicate order of space–time. This

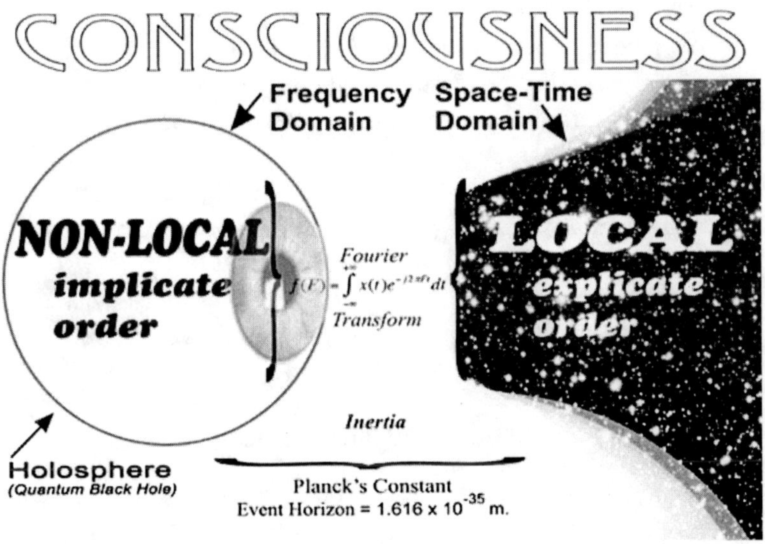

Fig. 10. Topology of Consciousness

mirrors Karl Pribram's[19] conceptualization of a lens between the two domains, expressed here in *Brain and Perception*:

> *These two domains characterize the input to and output from a lens that performs a Fourier transform. On one side of the transform lies the spacetime order we ordinarily perceive. On the other side lies a distributed enfolded holographic–like order referred to as the frequency or spectral domain.*

Note that the image of an iris in the diagram appears at the edge of the event horizon of a quantum black hole, or implicate order holosphere. The iris symbolises consciousness looking *out* from the implicate order *into* spacetime via a Fourier transform lensing process. This approach to a topology of consciousness as something that is looking out and seeing itself is supported here by the mathematician G. Spencer-Brown[20] in *Laws of Form*:

> *Now the physicist himself, who describes all this, is, in his own account, constructed of it. He is, in short, made of a conglomeration of the very particulars he describes, no more, no less, bound together by and obeying such general laws as he himself has managed to find and record. Thus we cannot escape the fact that the world we know is constructed in order (and thus in such a way as to be able) to see itself. This is indeed amazing. Not so much in view of what it sees, although this may appear fantastic enough, but in respect of the fact that it can see at all. But in order to do so, evidently it must first cut itself up into at least one state which sees, and at least one other state which is seen. In this condition it will always partially elude itself.*

Cosmology and the Implicate Order

In 1980 Bohm published *Wholeness and the Implicate Order*, and in a section in which he discusses the cosmology of the implicate order, he suggests a solution to the problem of "zero-point" energy by regarding the Planck length as the shortest wavelength possible:

> *If one were to add up the energies of all the "wave-particle" modes of excitation in any region of space, the result would be infinite, because an infinite number of wavelengths is present. However, there is good reason to suppose that one need not keep on adding the energies corresponding to shorter and shorter wavelengths. There may be a certain shortest possible wavelength, so that the total number of modes of excitation, and therefore the energy, would be finite. When this length is estimated it turns out to be about 10^{-35} m.*[1]

Bohm[1] brings up the school of Parmenides and Zeno, which held that all of space is actually a plenum, and he points out that as recently as the last century this same theory was presented in the widely accepted hypothesis of the *ether*. Bohm describes how there is a "holomovement" in this immense sea of "zero-point energy" to be understood as an "undivided flowing movement without borders" and he goes on to state:

> *It is being suggested here, then, that what we perceive through the senses as empty space is actually the plenum, which is the ground for the existence of everything, including ourselves. The things that appear to our senses are derivative forms and their true meaning can be seen only when we consider the plenum, in which they are generated and sustained, and into which they must ultimately vanish.*

In the Pribram–Bohm cosmology then, the interface or boundary between the spacetime explicate domain and the non-local, non-temporal implicate domain can be viewed topologically as a holoplenum of holospheres (Figure 8). Here can be found an answer to the "hard problem of consciousness" posed by Chalmers[21], for it is from *within* each holosphere that consciousness is "peering out" into and "projecting" the spacetime explicate, and here Bohm[1] summarises his cosmological essay by proposing that "consciousness is to be comprehended in terms of the implicate order, along with reality as a whole" and stating unequivocally that "the implicate order is also its primary and immediate actuality".

How Spacetime Projects from the Holoplenum

To summarise thus far, the Pribram–Bohm model envisions a non-local, transcendent mode of consciousness projecting the spatial cosmos holographically from an infinite plenum or matrix of quantum black holes, each at the limiting Planck length diameter of 10^{-35} m, located at the very bottom of space, at the very centre of every three-dimensional spatial coordinate. According to the quantum theory, within the implicate order, below the Planck length, space and time do not exist, as Bohm[1] describes here:

> *We come to a certain length at which the measurement of space and time becomes totally indefinable. Beyond this, the whole notion of space and time as we know it would fade out, into something that is at present unspecifiable When this length is estimated it turns out to be about 10^{-33} cm. This is much shorter than anything thus far probed in physical experiments (which have gone down to about 10^{-17} cm or so.)*

This leads to a new vision of the metaverse, a model in which the cosmos can be visualised as projecting outwardly from a holoplenum, from each Planck holosphere (quantum black hole) at the bottom of space, everywhere. In such a cosmology, the Big Bang theory would need to be revised to encompass more than simply a single point at a single time. The holoflux theory offers the prospect of multiple "Big Bangs" emanating from every individual Planck holosphere, perhaps a continuous recurrence cycling at Planck time (10^{-44} s) quantum ticks. Like images arising from pixels on a two-dimensional LCD (liquid crystal display) screen, the holoplenum projects a three-dimensional cosmos in all its glory. Yet during the process not only is radiant energy projecting *outwardly from* these quantum holospheres, but there is a simultaneous torrent of information, perhaps encoded in the form of gravitationally modulated energy flowing *inwardly into* the implicate order at the centre of each and every point in space.

One can only imagine the transitional region between the explicate and implicate order as a frothing, turbulent, resonant event-horizon that bounds spacetime and the transcendent implicate order. Information flowing inward eventually leaves spacetime entropically and flows *into* the network of quantum black holes, the holoplenum of holospheres. Information flowing into this region of infinite centres becomes immediately non-local, superpositioned, omni-intersecting. The holoplenum of holospheres provides a vast 3D projection field into which spacetime is projected by implicate order holoflux.

But in addition to this spatial topology, an examination of the transition between time (in the explicate order) and timelessness (in the implicate order) is in order. How might time communicate with the timeless? What happens at the event-horizon of time?

The Digital Universe: Laminated Spacetime

At the heart of the quantum theory is the conviction that neither time nor space are continuous and it has been concluded that both are granular at their lowest scale[22]. Having thus far established the granularity of space at the Planck length of 10^{-35} m, what then might be the granularity of time? One approach has been provided by the theoretical physicist John Archibald Wheeler (the originator of the term "black hole"), who, in considering a topology of information in the cosmos, noted that the highest possible clock rate must be limited by the Planck constant in general, and specifically by the *Planck time* value, below which time can have no meaning according to modern physics[23]. The *Planck time* (t_P) is the time it would take a single photon travelling at the speed of light to cross a distance equal to one Planck length; the Planck length has been determined by the National Institute of Standards and Technology (n.d.) to have a value of 5.39116×10^{-44} s. Wheeler[23] here describes the granular activity within time and space:

Space—pure, empty, energy–free space—all the time and everywhere experiences so-called quantum fluctuations at a fantastically small scale of time, of the order of 10^{-44} seconds. During these quantum fluctuations, pairs of particles appear for an instant from the emptiness of space.

Given the limit of the smallest interval of time being 10^{-44} seconds, one can calculate the maximum clock–speed of the universe by determining how many Planck time intervals are possible within one 'human' second:

$$(1 \text{ sec} / 10^{-44} \text{ sec}) = 10^{+44}$$

Thus, it has been proposed that if the universe is found to operate digitally, it would be cycling at its highest possible clock rate, switching between the explicate order and the implicate order cyclically at a rate of 10^{44} times per second at a bandwidth of 10^{44} Hz. This model has been developed in *The Theory of Laminated Spacetime* by Dewey[24]. The theory accords well with the Pribram–Bohm hypothesis process, and describes a process of energy flux extruding into spacetime as a series of quantum shells of information–encoded energy moving out in quantum jumps at the speed of light, with each quantum shell or brane separated from the next by a spatial gap equal to the Planck length, as described here:

I believe the universe to be composed of nothing but shells of electromagnetic particles which the theory of Laminated Spacetime describes as laminae of spacetime.

Holograms Versus the Holoplenum

To better understand the projection of the spacetime cosmos from the underlying holoplenum, the distinction between a hologram and a three dimensional holoplenum projection must be drawn. A hologram is an optical image stored and recreated by a single laser (i.e., LASER: Light Amplitude Stimulation of

Electromagnetic Radiation), a beam of coherent electromagnetic radiation of a single frequency[8]. Human technology greatly simplifies the creation and replay of a hologram by:

(a) Using a single beam of coherent photon energy (a *single frequency*)

(b) Illuminating the object from only two distinct fixed points in space.

An interference pattern forms from the beams of intersecting light impinging upon the three-dimensional planes of the object from different angles, causing complex shadows which are detected and recorded on the flat detector plane behind the object8.

In nature, however, the situation is vastly richer in complexity: electromagnetic flux interactions in spacetime form a highly complex three–dimensional matrix of intersecting shells of every spacetime radiation frequency band conceivable, impinging from an infinity of directions. In contrast with the human generated holograms of a single frequency taken from two fixed points, each point in spacetime actually intercepts the *entire frequency flux spectrum* of the cosmos, which is being continuously captured by, and feeding the event horizon entropy of the quantum black hole located at its geometric central "point"[25].

The omnidirectional interactions manifesting among electromagnetic waves in the dimensional range of the explicate order are mirrored in the spectral frequencies within the implicate order. There is a resonance between implicate and explicate mediated by mathematical relationships such as the Fourier transforms and Gabor functions. This process between the explicate and implicate order is skilfully articulated by David Bohm.

This resonance between the implicate and the explicate orders nudges into existence a cosmic holonomic metaverse of galaxies, butterflies, and zebras[26].

Geocentric Topology of the Holonomic Metaverse

The topology of the holonomic metaverse is congruent with the cosmological intuitions of numerous classical thinkers. In the fourth century BCE, a model proposed by Plato, and further developed by his student Aristotle, consisted of a system of numerous crystalline shells rotating about a central sphere located at the centre of the Earth[27]. By the second century CE, this geocentric model had become codified by the Alexandrian astronomer Claudius Ptolemy in his cosmological model of concentric spheres (Fig. 11).

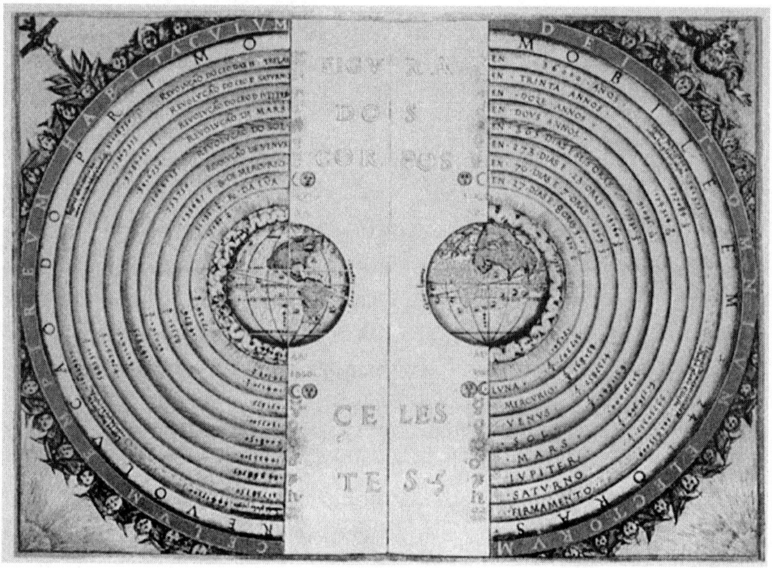

Figure 11: The Ptolemaic Geocentric Conception of the Universe. Source: Velho (1568)

In the fourth century BCE Aristotle held that the reason an apple falls to the ground is that it seeks its natural place at the centre of the universe, and he set forth a geocentric model based upon the following three propositions:

1. The Earth is positioned at the centre of the universe.
2. The Earth is fixed (non-moving) in relation to the rest of the universe.

3. The Earth is special and unique compared to all other heavenly bodies.

Substituting "holosphere" for "Earth" in Aristotle's propositions, each Planck holosphere can be taken as positioned at the centre of the its universe; each holosphere is fixed (non-moving) in relation to all other holospheres in the holoplenum, and each holosphere is "special" by virtue of its unique Hilbert space coordinates[28].

A first approach to a topology of the holoplenum is to begin at the event horizon of the Planck holosphere. How close to the surface of the Planck holosphere does spacetime actually begin? The overriding constraint is that it *cannot* begin any closer than one Planck length, because anything less than that has no meaning in space-time. Accordingly, the first shell, or "isosphere," must be located exactly *one Planck length from* the central holosphere (Fig. 12). Moving radially outward from the central holosphere, each subsequent isosphere enclosing the previous isosphere. They can be visualised as nested, like hollow Russian dolls, or spherical tree rings. Within space, each isosphere is separated from the previous by a distance of 10^{-35} metres, the Planck length.

But of what do these isospheres consist? This isospheric shell cannot itself attain any appreciable depth or spatial thickness due to the Planck length constraint; they cannot be within the explicate order of spacetime while their thickness is below the Planck length. Yet if they are thinner than the Planck length, they are too thin to be in space.

It becomes clear that these isospheric shells are *event horizons* between the implicate order (spacetime) and *the implicate order* (the implicate order). Indicated in the figure, between each shell is a sort of dielectric, not space, but the implicate order, a quantum vacuum which may also be the locus of Bohm's[1] "infinite zero-point fluctuations of the 'vacuum field'" (p. 70).

A topology of the implicate order is here coming into focus. A non-local, timeless, transcendent domain is to be found at the centre, everywhere, in the form of Planck diameter holospheres making up an implicate holoplenum, and enclosing each and every holosphere, nested at quantum multiples, from the Planck length to the diameter of the universe.

While distributed geometrically within the explicate order, these isospheric quantum shells are not in space, but share in the non-locality of the implicate order. They provide both a fundamental structure and information backbone bridging the implicate and the explicate orders. And each isosphere provides a structural capacity for information storage limited only by the Bekenstein bound (discussed in the next section).

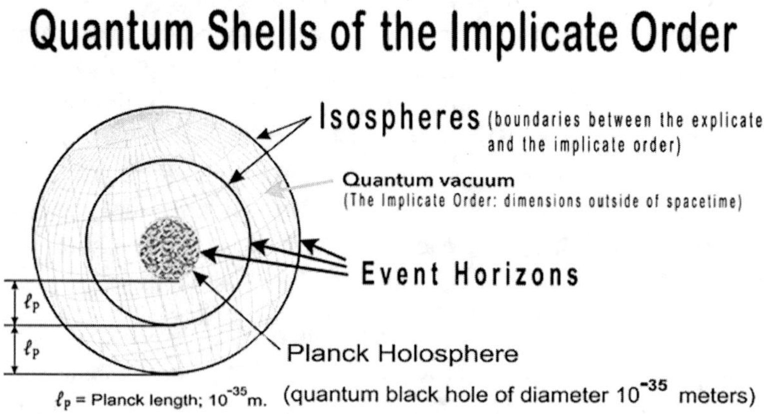

Figure 12: Quantum Shells of the Implicate Order

As in all black hole phenomena, these isospheres (as well as the central Planck holosphere) are assumed to have an angular momentum (spin) due to turbulence at the event horizon, a highly energetic region which, the holoflux theory posits, are modulated with qubits of information. These spinning, implicate order isospheres project spacetime "objects" (multidimensional holograms) from frequency-phase information within the implicate order.

Spectral frequencies within the implicate order (the frequency domain of communication engineering) can be correlated with sets of isospheres having explicate order diameters corresponding to wavelengths of the same frequency. Thus a complex patterned frequency spectrum within the implicate order can be mirrored in the spatial dimension of the explicate order through the activation of selected ranges of shell isospheres of the implicate.

Having established the mechanism of communication linking Bohm's[1] implicate and explicate orders, it is now possible to turn to memory storage, that elusive problem which first led Pribram[8] to his holonomic theory of a brain/mind interface.

A Holoplenum of Quantum Black Holes

As described in the previous section, a holonomic process underlies the Bohmian "Whole" and operates through means of a cosmic plenum of quantum black holes. These quantum black holes appear as geometric shells or spheres in space, each one being a boundary between space (outside the sphere) and the hidden dimensions of the implicate order within the shell boundary (though "within" is a spatial metaphor). Each of these quantum black holes is exactly one quantum in diameter, that is, one Planck length. Thus, these quantum-diameter shells have been termed "Planck diameter holospheres."

In geometric terms, these "close-packed spheres" refer to the most tightly packed and highly efficient arrangement of spheres of equal diameter, each of which touches multiple similar adjacent spheres. The entire geometric plenum can be visualised at the very bottom of space, existing everywhere in our spacetime universe, and considered metaphorically as a three-dimensional "ocean floor" of space.

How Holopixels Project the Universe

These inconceivably tiny holospheres act as pixels, or *holopixels*, continually projecting outward into our four-dimensional universe of spacetime from the hidden dimensions of the metaverse. Much in the same way that the two-dimensional array of pixels on the back of a plasma display screen projects a streaming video image that we can see, this plenum of quantum holopixels projects the universe into our space and time dimensions. Yet, the region within the boundaries of these black holes contains the multiple hidden dimensions beyond spacetime.

This three-dimensional substrate or plenum exists everywhere and continually projects our spacetime universe that we call the cosmos (Fig. 13).

Figure 13: A Seer at the Intersection of Heaven and Spacetime[v]

In totality, this plenum of holopixels acts much as the two-dimensional plenum of pixels that are embedded in the substrate of a modern wide screen plasma video display. Surrounding and radiating outward from each central Planck holosphere throughout space are spherical shells of quantum potential, infinitely thin information-encoded shells of energy, each separated from an inner shell by the quantum exclusion radial distance of one Planck length. These isospheric shells of Bohmian quantum potential extend out to the diameter of the universe itself.

Thus, can be visualised topologically as an almost infinite series of nested isospheric shells, spread out, at discrete quantum radii from their respective central Planck holospheres, each bounding Bohm's non-dual implicate order.

The global panoramic intersection of these holospheric shells manifests as the projection of the holonomic universe into spacetime. The cumulative effect of this projection, as regarded by human physicists observing from significantly higher scalar dimensions, is described as "matter." The phenomenon can be understood as a *process of projected creation*, an omnipresent, ongoing holographic extrusion of information *from* the implicate order *into* the explicate order, where the various structures of the cosmos (galactic clusters, stars, etc.), the complex unfoldings *into* spacetime, are perceived by the human eye and mind to be three-dimensional, when they are actually holographic projections *from* the implicate order, from the centre outward.

Another way of visualising the projected illusion of space time reality from the holoplenum is by expanding upon the metaphor of a flat-panel plasma display (such as the one you may be viewing as you read this).

Consider the human visual threshold for detecting separate images, which lies somewhere between 10 to 12 images per second; the industry standard in the motion picture industry is 24 frames per second[29]. This standard ensures that the presentation of a sequence of projected images will appear to a human viewer as a smooth and continuous motion.

By contrast, if the entire universe flashes in and out of existence at a clock-cycle rate limited only by the Planck time constant of 5.3×10^{-44} seconds, equivalent to a "frame" rate of almost 10^{44} "frames per second," the cosmos would *appear* to be smooth and continuous in all respects even to an electron, and certainly to any human observer of the cosmos, even at quantum dimensions.

The approximate image resolution of a "holoplenum display"

obtained by dividing one inch by the Planck length, yields a maximum resolution of 1.584×10^{34} holo pixels per inch. At such hyper-fine resolution, even a Higgs boson in the 10^{-17} metre dimensional range would appear to be moving smoothly through space.

Holonomic Storage: The Bekenstein Bound

In *Wholeness and the Implicate Order*, Bohm[1] articulates and develops a "quantum potential" function that projects the explicate spacetime universe out from within an enfolded sub-quantum implicate order. Bohm's quantum potential function is congruent with de Broglie's "Pilot wave" theory of 1927, as both are based upon a conviction that there exist "hidden variables" in sub-quantum regions not accessible to observational exploration using current material science technology (and far beyond the capabilities of the CERN Large Hadron Collider).

The de Broglie pilot wave theory and Bohm's[1] quantum potential are mathematical attempts to map sub-quantum effects issuing from an implicate order in a domain of "hidden variables" far below the observational capabilities of contemporary material science.

Both theories posit a cybernetic processing of information, simultaneously being cycled from the spacetime world and enfolded into the non-dual frequency domain where the accumulating information is processed nonlocally within the implicate order. Driven then by the implicate order, a pilot wave of quantum potential nudges the configurations in spacetime into an altered, slightly new configuration, much as a small tugboat might influence an enormous freighter. If the cosmos operates at its maximum possible clock cycle, as discussed previously, this pilot wave might be seen to operate at the extreme clock cycle rate of the Planck time constant, or 10^{44} Hz.

Somewhere, however, such a cosmic process would require a memory storage repository in spacetime. Regarded as a cybernetic process, the sequence of information feedback and action can be metaphorically imaged in the alchemical Ouroboros, the classical symbol for consciousness, depicted as a snake in a circular configuration eating (or chasing) its own tail. This process can be viewed as the cyclic transfer of information coming in (from the tail) and the resulting action (by the head). A cybernetic feedback loop thus needs data, information, as input. Where then might data be accumulated and retrieved in spacetime at these most fundamental sub-quantum levels, in a Bohmian holonomic universe consisting topologically of the distributed plenum of Planck holospheres, each surrounded by a series of nested quantum isospheres?

One possibility is to consider the information storage potential of an isosphere encoded with granular "bits" of data. In 1970, Jacob D. Bekenstein, then a graduate student working under John Archibald Wheeler, proposed a novel idea. Bekenstein proposed that there must be an absolute maximum amount of information that can be stored in a finite region of space, and that the Planck constants in quantum theory can be used to determine this limit[23]. Twenty years later, Bekenstein's theory was extended into what is called the *holographic principle* by Leonard Susskind[30], which describes how information within any volume of space can be encoded on a boundary of the region. A description of this configuration is presented here by Wheeler[23] himself, as first related to him by Bekenstein:

> One unit of entropy (information), one unit of randomness, one unit of disorder, Bekenstein explained to me, must be associated with a bit of area of this order of magnitude (a Planck length square). . . . Thus one unit of entropy is associated with each 1.04×10^{-69} square metres of the horizon of a black hole.

This proposed upper limit to the information that can be contained upon the surface of a specific, finite volume of space has come to be known as the "Bekenstein bound"[31]. Symbolically depicted in Fig. 14 is a topological depiction of the arrangement of information bits, or "qubits," stored on the bounding surface of a spherical volume or isosphere.

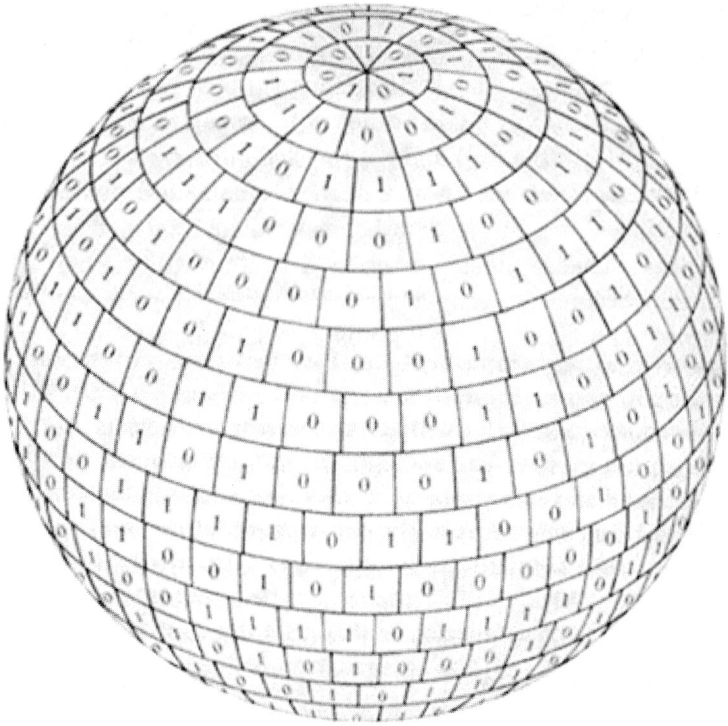

Figure 14. Planck Length Qubits on the Surface of an Isosphere[vi]

This same topological approach to data storage can be applied to human physiology. Using a well-known biological structure as an example, it is possible to calculate the maximum memory storage capacity of a isosphere the size of a single erythrocyte, the ubiquitous red blood cell found throughout the human body. Using Wheeler's approach to determine the number of Bekensteinian equivalent data bits (qubits) on the surface of an isosphere, and using the average diameter of a typical human erythrocyte of 8.1 microns (or 8.1×10^{-5} m), the maximum possible storage capacity on the surface of a single red blood cell can be calculated (Romanes, 1964, p. 137). To obtain this limiting number of bits, the surface area on a spherical shell 8.1 microns in diameter must be divided by 1.04×10^{-69} square metres (which is the Bekenstein unit of entropy, or approximately the square of the Planck length of 1.616199 x 10^{-35}). The surface area of this erythrocyte-bisected sphere according to this calculation is or $4\pi(8.1 \times 10^{-5})^2 = 4\pi(6.561 \times 10^{-9}) = 8.24 \times 10^{-9}$ square metres. Dividing this by the qubit area of 1.04×10^{-69} square metres yields an estimated maximum storage capacity of 8×10^{60} qubits of storage space for potential information encoding. This is an extremely large data storage capacity, considerably larger than, by contrast, the entire projected capability of the National Security Agency's Utah Data Center, which has been designed, when completed, to have a maximum data storage capacity of twelve exabytes or 12×10^{18} bytes[32].

Unfolding an Implicate into Spacetime

The ontological understanding of quantum physics that Bohm sought emerges in this model of a sub-quantum, omni-present holoplenum of Planck holospheres, each enclosing a contiguous transcendent region of non-spatial, non-temporal dimensions termed by Bohm "the implicate order"[33].

What are the implications of this model for human consciousness, cognitively operational at temporal and spatial scales vastly larger than those found at these sub-quantum Planck boundaries? To answer this we must first complete the Pribram-Bohm cosmological topology of consciousness, and to do this the concept of isospheres, shells within shells, must be considered. Moving outwardly, radially, from the interior bounding event horizon at each central Planck holosphere, can be identified isospheric shells of the implicate order, extruding into space at exact Planck length (quantum) intervals.

This series of concentric shells, each one separated from the next by one Planck length, are isospherical loci of the implicate order (see Fig. 5); they extrude into space and they intersect in space with other shells bounding other Planck holospheres in the spacetime holoplenum. It is the cumulative interference effect of the intersection of individual isospheric shells which project images at higher scales, holographically, into three-dimensional space.

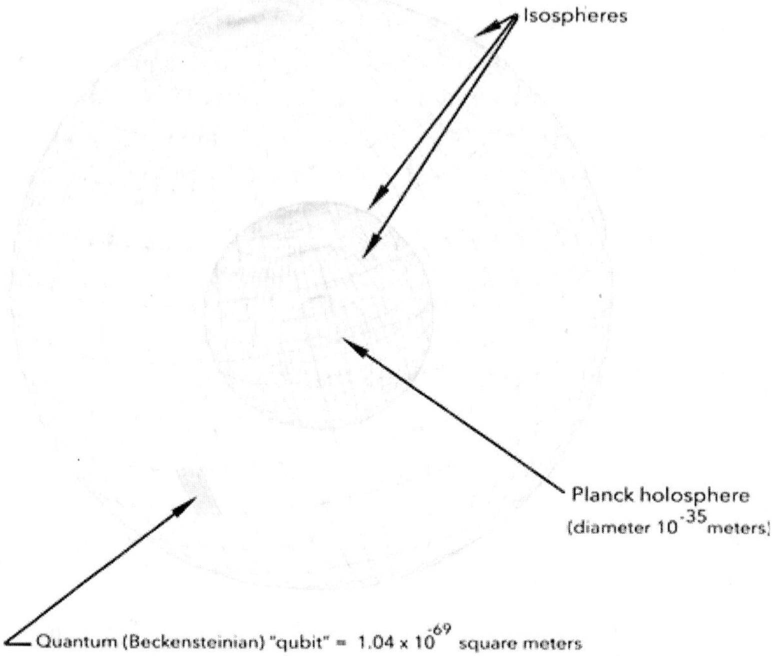

Figure 15: Topology Model of Isospheres Surrounding a Planck Holosphere. Author's Figure

Each isospheric shell, as Bekenstein[31] determined, has a potentially enormous storage capacity in "qubits" of information encoded on the event-horizon bounding each shell, depending only upon the radius of the shell within the range of 10^{-35} m to 10^{27} m. Accessible simultaneously in both the implicate order and the explicate order, such encoded information provides the data to guide evolving forms as they project into the explicate via the pilot wave mathematics of Bohm's[1] "many-dimensioned quantum potential" (p. 80). As part of this process, in-formation becomes ex-formation as the implicate order unfurls into the explicate. The plasmodial forms appearing in spacetime as electromagnetic flux energy are mirrored by and resonate within the implicate order as the dark energy of frequency-phase holoflux.

Within this cosmic geometry of the Pribram-Bohm hypothesis can be identified a framework for omnipresent two-way portals, potential bridges between the explicate and the implicate. Here, the deep consciousness of the universe flows in a cyclic, cybernetic, perhaps fractal movement in time and space, moving through an endless, bi-directional process, consciousness involving itself in a dance of transformation.

How then does this topology support human consciousness, thought, and perception in spacetime ? How can electromagnetic frequency plasma in spacetime resonate with holoflux plasma in the implicate order? First of all, the energies must be within the same frequency range in order for maximum interactive resonance to occur. Where the frequencies overlap as they superimpose and interpenetrate one another, resonance occurs.

Resonance is a naturally occurring phenomena characteristic of physical objects or plasma fields extended in spacetime . The resonance effect is seen when objects or complex signal systems exhibit remarkable frequency sensitivity to particular external frequencies, flowing in, through, and around the system, frequencies which approach the "natural resonant frequency" of the object or signal system; perfect resonance occurs where the input frequency and the natural frequency are identical[2]. This principle of resonance governs all cybernetic feedback loops, and is a key factor in the design of antennas for electromagnetic transmitting and receiving systems. The goal of antenna design is to construct an antenna that is maximally resonant within a specific narrow frequency range of incoming (external or internal) electromagnetic radiation; when the input frequency and the natural frequency of the antenna coincide or move significantly close to one another, resonance occurs. This simplest and most common antenna design is the dipole antenna, which depends directly on the size (wavelength) of the incoming electromagnetic wave. A dipole antenna is designed to be physically half the size of the incoming wavelength, as stated in a textbook of antenna design:

A fundamental form of an antenna: length is approximately equal to half the transmitting wavelength. It is the unit from which many more complex forms of antennas are constructed. It is known as a dipole antenna.[34]

This same half-wavelength effect governs the design of network communication waveguides applied to fibre-optics in the Internet, where the antenna is the fibre channel itself, acting as a waveguide. The waveguide is highly efficient for two reasons: first, as its name implies, the waveguide guides the electromagnetic wave within its channel with maximum efficiency; and secondly, it shields the signal in the channel from external electromagnetic waves. The inner diameter of the hollow waveguide is designed to be equal to exactly half the wavelength of the electromagnetic energy signal shielded by and flowing through the waveguide channel.

Waveguides have been used for over a century, both commercially and in research to channel and guide vibrating energy of specific limited frequency ranges; the fibre-optic networks hosting the global internet operate on this principle, channelling electromagnetic radiation at fixed laser frequencies[29]. It was discovered late in the nineteenth century that circular metallic tubes, or hollow metal ducts, similar to A/C ventilation ducts but much smaller, could be used to channel and guide either sound vibrations in air, or electromagnetic energy in air or vacuum. Without the waveguide, the vibrational energy field is transmitted in all directions, visualised as magnetic lines or arrows emerging from a point at the centre of an expanding sphere. This energy disperses outwardly, the magnetic vectored arrowheads pushing into the inside of an infinitely expanding sphere. A waveguide, however, constrains the magnetic component of the wave-front of vibrating energy to one specific linear direction, in parallel with the centre of the waveguide, and thus, conceptually, the confined wave itself loses very little power while it propagates along the central axis of the waveguide, like a stream of water emerging from the pinprick of a large, taut, water balloon[29].

The most common type of fibre-optic cable used in the Internet has a core diameter of 8-10 micrometres and is designed for use in the near infrared[35]. The electromagnetic signal wavelength that runs through the global fibre optic network is powered by highly efficient carbon dioxide lasers, and has a wavelength of 10 micrometres. Coincidentally (or not?), the average human blood capillary diameter is also 10 microns, and blood capillaries are at all times full of carbon dioxide.

Dimensional analysis and a cursory examination of human physiology would immediately suggest two candidates for waveguide systems within the human body: (a) the blood capillary system, and (b) the microtubule system. The corresponding resonant frequency for electromagnetic waves using such waveguides correspond to wavelengths matching the inner diameter of these structures. For blood system capillaries, this corresponds to radiation with a wavelength of 9.3 to 10.0 microns, the average inner diameter of a capillary. For microtubules, the radiation wavelength would be found in a range of 40 nanometers, the inner diameter of the microtubule waveguides. Fig. 16 on next page depicts the location of each of these potential waveguide frequency bands within a wider section of the electromagnetic spectrum.

There is no impediment to our blood acting as an electromagnetic plasma within the capillary system, and as previously mentioned, the opening page of a textbook on plasma physics reads, "It has often been said that 99 per cent of the matter in the universe is in the plasma state"[36].

In such a model, the entire blood vessel network system within the human body can be considered to act as an extensively polarised "super cell" of non-local electromagnetic plasma energy, which can then be differentiated from the neuronal brain body of consciousness, itself generated by sequential electrical impulse-driven patterns flowing in the nervous system. Moving charges generate magnetic fields, and ionised human blood flow is no exception: flowing blood plasma results in creation of a magnetic field, and this is in accord with the conjecture of QBD[29].

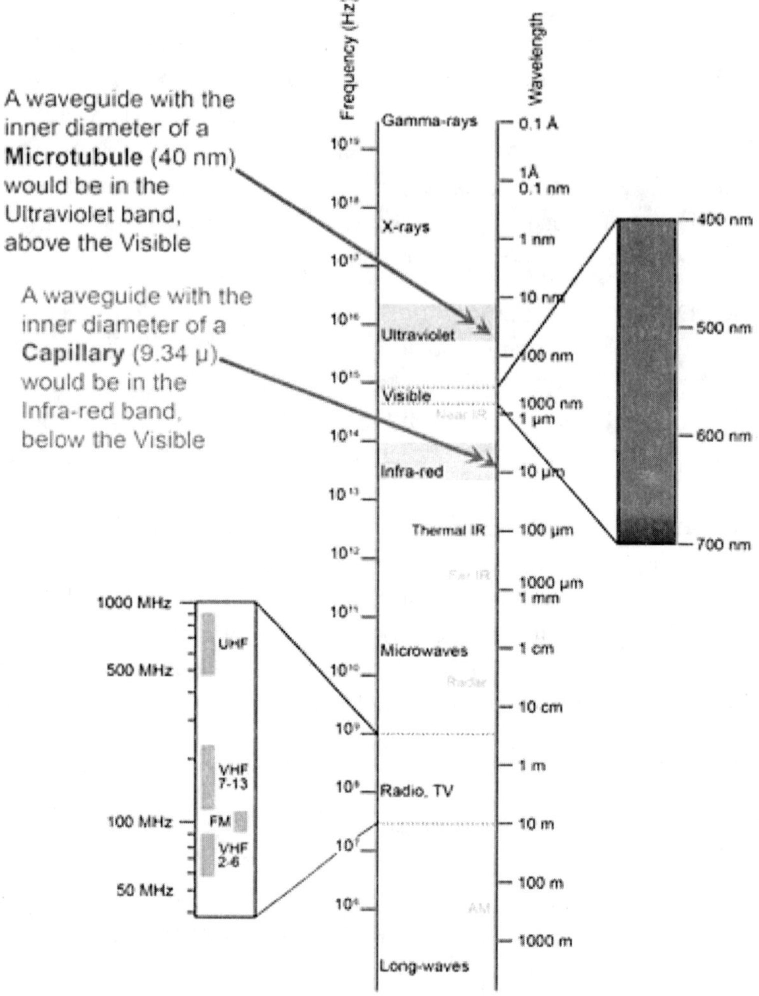

*Annotations by author; graphic by Jahoe (2012). Reprinted under the terms of a Creative Commons Attribution ShareAlike 2.5 Generic license. Image retrieved from Wikimedia Commons.

Fig. 16. Microtubules and Capillaries as Waveguides.

The circulatory system can be seen as a magnetic plasma composed primarily of ionised red blood cells (erythrocytes) and water molecules, flowing together in complex vortices of blood plasma around every cell and through every capillary of the body[37]. Each erythrocyte is a flexible, annular, bio-concave disk shaped like a doughnut (in geometry, a torus), having a thin webbed centre where the hole in a pastry doughnut would be located. The typical outside diameter of a red blood cell is approximately 9 microns, close to the infrared wavelength of 9.6 microns generated by the human body[38]. The adult human body contains approximately 6 grams of iron, of which 60 per cent is stored throughout the 10^{12} erythrocytes, each of which contains approximately 270 million atoms of ionic iron embedded within transparent haemoglobin in a toroidal locus[39]. Thus, each erythrocyte, replete with iron ions embedded in haemoglobin, creates in effect an ionised iron toroid[40].

Recent studies have also discovered neuronal generation of electromagnetic energy in the near infrared region of the spectrum centred around 10 microns. Radiation emission was repeatedly measured emanating from live crab neurons in extremely narrow, discrete spectral bands within the frequency range corresponding to a spectral region from 10.5 to 6.5 microns[41].

The implications of this model are considerable: there may exist in nature a unique resonant frequency for each individual human being. It is useful here to step through a topological analysis of the possible functions of a human red blood cell, given its geometry, as a locus of consciousness, and the possible use of the erythrocyte as a locus of memory storage at human biological scales. If, as previously conjectured, the red blood cell has an ideal diameter to resonate electromagnetic radiation in its ferrite-embedded ring at the human infrared wavelength of 10 microns, then it is reasonable to ask if this configuration could accommodate a single unique isospheric frequency (wavelength) for each of the currently 8 billion living humans on the planet. In other words, does this geometry allow for the possibility of each human being to also have a single unique frequency within the infrared electromagnetic radiation that resonates within the human cardiovascular waveguide system? Figure 7 outlines the topological feasibility of this approach.

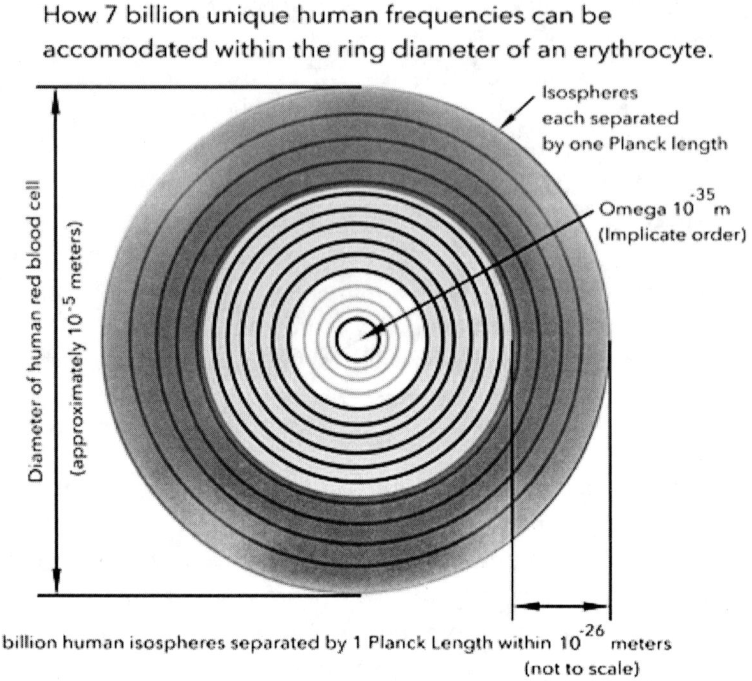

Figure 17: Isospheric Capacity of a Single Erythrocyte

Assuming each unique frequency would match its radially unique isosphere, separated by only one Planck length, Figure 17 suggests how 8 billion unique isospheres, each of quantum discrete frequency, might be nested within the geometry of a typical human red blood cell (in the image, a multiple of 8 billion times the Planck length of approximately 10^{-35} m results in an estimated shell thickness of 10^{-26} m). This model supports the feasibility that each living human being might have a unique holospheric frequency, detectable by other human blood cells via the implicate order about which each is centred, and thus provides a possible mechanism for communication, via the mechanisms of resonance, non-locality, and superposition in the frequency domain of the implicate order.

Sound, Frequency, and the Implicate Order

In contrast with the lack of success others were having in their efforts to establish the mechanism and location of memory engrams, Pribram put forth a theory that the brain mechanics of vision might be seen as holographic processes, projections onto the cortical surface from a frequency domain through the mechanism of frequency superposition and electromagnetic wave interference[vii]. Pribram called this "the holonomic brain theory," and postulated the importance of the *frequency domain*:

> *Essentially, the theory reads that the brain at one stage of processing performs its analyses in the frequency domain . . . a solid body of evidence has accumulated that the auditory, somatosensory, motor, and visual systems of the brain do in fact process, at one or several stages, input from the senses in the frequency domain*[viii].

Pribram's theory holds that the mathematics of the Fourier transform operates within the brain, modulating electromagnetic fields of flux to create, store, replay, and process holograms within some (as yet unidentified) physiological context or substrate, but one that, Pribram conjectures, may be found within the fine-fibred dendritic webs of cerebral cortex regions[ix].

Pribram here takes exception to Bohm's use of the words "flow" or "movement," holding that such words cannot be used to characterise dynamism in a dimension devoid of space or time axes:

> *David Bohm (1973) had a concept similar to flux in mind, which he called holomovement. He felt that my use of the term "flux" had connotations for him that he did not want to buy into. I, on the other hand, felt holomovement to be vague in the sense of asking, "what is moving?"*[x]

Pribram clearly distinguishes between observations made in the frequency domain and those made in space and time. While the ontological realisation of flux in spacetime can be conceptualised in the gyrations of three-dimensional electromagnetic waves, Pribram defines the ontological substrate of spectra in the frequency domain to be pure spectra or holoflux:

> *The spectral domain is characteristically a flux, composed of oscillations, fluctuations, whereas interference patterns among waves intersect to reinforce or cancel. Holograms are examples of spectra, that is, of a holoflux.*[xi]

This holoflux is essentially the same concept as David Bohm's *holomovement*, though in "Brain and Mathematics,"

Two domains, the time domain (t_d) and the frequency domain (f_d), are of essential importance in the field of information theory and signal communication. On the first page of an undergraduate electrical engineering textbook on network analysis and synthesis, Kuo states:

> *In describing signals, we use the two universal languages of electrical engineering—time and frequency. Strictly speaking, a signal is a function of time. However, the signal can be described equally well in terms of spectral or frequency information. As between any two languages, such as French and German, translation is needed to render information given in one language comprehensible in the other. Between time and frequency, the translation is effected by the Fourier series and the Fourier integral.*[xii]

In his book *Brain and Perception*, Pribram used almost the same words as Kuo in discussing methods by which a Fourier transform operates in mathematical physics. Here Pribram reaches the same conclusion as Kuo:

> *It is reasonable to ask: What advantage does the organism gain by processing in the spectral transform domain? The answer is efficiency: The fact that correlations are so easily achieved by first convolving*

signals in the spectral domain and then, inverse transforming them into the spacetime domain. Thus. Fast Fourier Transform (FFT) procedures have become the basis of computerised tomography, the CT scans used by hospitals.[xiii]

The mathematics expressed in the Fourier transform can also be understood as a link between the physics of spacetime (t_d) and an actual frequency domain (f_d). The Fourier and inverse Fourier transforms are shown in Fig. 18:

$$f(t) = \int_{-\infty}^{+\infty} X(F) e^{j2\pi Ft} dF$$

Fourier integral transform of a continuous time function into the frequency domain (f_d).

$$f(F) = \int_{-\infty}^{+\infty} x(t) e^{-j2\pi Ft} dt$$

Fourier integral transform of a continuous frequency function into the time domain (t_d).

Figure 18: Fourier Transform/Inverse Transform.[xiv]

These Fourier transform expressions indicate that any arbitrary function in the timespace domain, can be transformed into and expressed by an infinite series of frequency spectra functions in the frequency domain, and conversely, that any arbitrary function in the frequency domain, can be transformed into and expressed by an infinite series of time functions, .

These Fourier transforms are themselves derived from an underlying series of alternate pure sine and pure cosine waves, as depicted in Fig. 19.

$$f(F) = \int_{-\infty}^{+\infty} x(t) e^{-j2\pi Ft} dt$$

Figure 19: The Fourier Series.[xv]

A century after Fourier's death, Norbert Wiener made use of

Fourier's transform to model and analyse brain waves, and he was able to detect frequencies, centred within different spatial locations on the cortex, that exhibited auto-correlation. Specific frequencies were found to be attracting one another toward an intermediate frequency, thus exhibiting resonance or "self-tuning" within a narrow range of the frequency domain (f_d)[xvi]. This discovery led Wiener to conjecture that the infrared band of electromagnetic flux may be the locus of "self-organising systems."[xvii]

> *We thus see that a non-linear interaction causing the attraction of frequency can generate a self-organising system, as it does in the case of the brain waves we have discussed . . . . This possibility of self-organisation is by no means limited to the very low frequency of these two phenomena. Consider self-organising systems at the frequency level, say, of infrared light.*[xviii]

Wiener goes on to discuss such possibilities in biology, where he focuses on the problems of communication at molecular and primitive cellular levels, specifically on the problem of how substances produce cancer by reproducing themselves to mimic pre-existing normal local cells. Molecules do not simply pass notes to one another, and they do not have eyes, so how do they perceive and how do they communicate? Wiener conjectures:

> *The usual explanation given is that one molecule of these substances acts as a template according to which the constituent's smaller molecules lay themselves down and unite into a similar macromolecule. However, an entirely possible way of describing such forces is that the active bearer of the specificity of a molecule may lie in the frequency pattern of its molecular radiation, an important part of which may lie in infrared electromagnetic frequencies or even lower. It is quite possible that this phenomenon may be regarded as a sort of attractive interaction of frequency.*[xix]

Perhaps the most fascinating tool for exploring the nature of the interface between the Real and Imaginary domains was developed in 1980 when the Polish-American engineer, Benoit Mandelbrot, created the software to plot an actual image of the two-dimensional interface between spacetime and frequency domains close to the origin (defined as the intersecting point where the Real axis equals zero and the Imaginary axis equals zero). His initial impression, upon seeing the first image, was that the computer program had malfunctioned.[xx] Subsequent computer plots assured him that these visual patterns were truly there. Images of this region about the time frequency origin have gained interest worldwide and the region itself has come to be known as the Mandelbrot set (Fig. 50). The English mathematical physicist Sir Roger Penrose was so taken by the resulting images that he described them with a sense of almost reverential awe:

> *The Mandelbrot set is not an invention of the human mind: it was a discovery. Just like Mount Everest, the Mandelbrot set is just there!*[xxi]

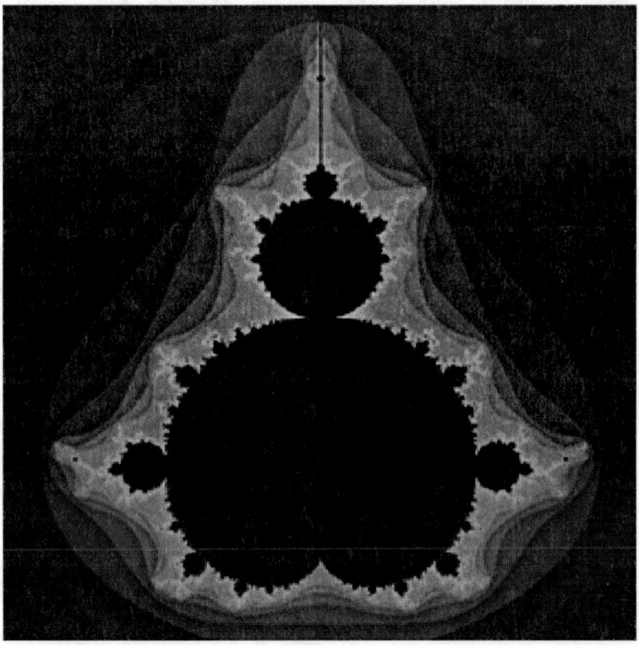

Figure 20: Mandelbrot: Origin of Real–Imaginary Axis

The Mandelbrot set exhibits remarkable properties. As calculations are done on ever smaller regions on the time–frequency plane, the images appear similar but never completely repeatable, and the viewer begins to sense some sort of biological shapes emerging from this strange world of pure mathematical being. Penrose goes on to say, "The very system of complex numbers has a profound and timeless reality which goes quite beyond the mental constructions of any particular mathematician."[xxii]

Jung observes the relationship of psyche to matter with the same pattern, noting that they are two different modes of one and the same thing:

> *Since psyche and matter are contained in one and the same world, and moreover are in continuous contact with one another and ultimately rest on irrepresentable, transcendental factors, it is not only possible, but also fairly probable, even, that psyche and matter are two different aspects of one and the same thing.*[xxiii]

Holoflux, as a total manifestation, is a dual process of reflective consciousness and transcendent awareness. Communication, and consciousness flow between and within the two domains: the implicate and the explicate. Another way of regarding holoflux is to see it as a two-way moving flux:

1. It is an explicate energy (E) moving *inward* into the implicate order at the holospheric event horizon of a quantum black hole.
2. Moving in the opposite direction, it is an implicate energy (Q) moving *outward* as quantum potential from the event horizon, as holoflux energy transforms from out of the implicate order into the explicate order.

My thesis rests upon the assumptions that Bohm's implicate order is real, that the frequency domain is real, and that his active information wave function is real, affecting our world of "particles" as it springs from the virtually infinite non-local information holoflux within the implicate order.

Like Bohm, electrical engineers separate the world into two domains, which they term the *complex-frequency domain* and the *time domain*. It is our normally perceived spacetime that electrical engineers identify as the *time domain*, but it is in the *frequency domain* that they see the operation of communication signals.[xxiv]

Franklin F. Kuo, an American computer scientist and communications engineer at Bell Laboratories, wrote an electrical engineering textbook, developing the mathematics of communication in *Network Analysis and Synthesis*. In the first chapter of his classic textbook, Kuo describes the two domains, and the mathematical advantage of creating and receiving communication signals within the *frequency* domain as opposed to the *spacetime* domain:

> *In the complex-frequency domain, the voltage–current relationships for the elements are expressed in algebraic equations. Algebraic equations are, in most cases, more easily solved than differential equations. Herein lies the raison d'être for describing signals and networks in the frequency domain as well as in the time domain.*[xxv]

These two orders of electrical engineering theory can be seen to reflect David Bohm's explicate and implicate orders. Bohm's explicate order is associated with the engineering time dimension through which signals are transmitted and received sequentially in time, while Bohm's implicate order can be identified with the electrical engineering *frequency* dimension as a timeless, spaceless domain of pure frequency-phase information.

It has been discovered that these two domains are strongly linked, mathematically, with the operation of the Fourier transform. As Kuo says, "between time and frequency, the translation is effected by the Fourier series."[xxvi] As we have seen in Chapter 4, the Fourier series has also become the bedrock of quantum theoretical calculations, as expressed by David Bohm in the opening of his textbook, *Quantum Theory*:

It seems impossible to develop quantum concepts extensively without Fourier analysis.[xxvii]

Our thesis, then, is that Kuo's frequency domain, bridged to time by Fourier's mathematics in our twenty-first-century information technology, has an ontological reality, and that there does exist an actual frequency domain, which we also identify with Bohm's hypothesised implicate order.

CONSCIOUSNESS AND HEALTH

Non-Duality in Meditation—Topographic-Dynamic Reorganisation Model of Meditation (TRoM)

GEORG NORTHOFF

Introduction

How is it possible that one can experience dissolution of one's own self including its boundaries to others and the environment? This is described as a state of 'non-dual awareness'[1,2]. We raise the question how such reorganisation of the most basic coordinates of our experience, the self-non-self/environment distinction, is possible and mediated by our brain. Various brain imaging studies of mediation report changes in attentional, memory, and emotional regions and networks[3,4]. This leaves open the neural correlates of non-dual awareness, though. Is the reorganisation of experience in terms of non-dual awareness mediated by a corresponding non-dual reorganisation of our brain's structure and function? Based on different lines of brain imaging data (fMRI and EEG/MEG) in different stages of meditation (from novice to experienced), we propose that the basic coordinates of the brain's spatial and temporal topography are reorganised during the course of meditation practice leading to non-dual awareness—we therefore propose a 'Topographic-dynamic reorganisation model of meditation (TroM).

Non-dual awareness is characterised by profound reorganisation of the self as, in that state, one no longer experiences duality of self and non-self but rather unity of self and non-self/environment[5,2,6,7,8]. This raises the question for the nature of self. The self has been viewed as the core of our mental life. It is supposed to distinguish ourselves from others and the world. The self is not homogeneous though. Various conceptual subdivisions have been introduced to characterise the heterogeneity of self. These include subjective vs objective self[8,9], "I"[9,10] vs "me"[11,12,13], affective vs cognitive self[14,15,16], proto-self vs core-self [15,16], bodily vs mental self[17-20], minimal vs narrative self[21,22] or conceptual self[23], and private vs public/social self[21,24-26]. However, despite their differences, these various concepts of self, on a deeper level, share the clear distinction between self and other: the self is supposed to be principally different from the other, and the world. We therefore speak of the duality of self and other/world relation (the other and world being embedded in one another).

This self-other/world duality is also mirrored on the neural level. Specific regions/networks like the default-mode network (DMN) as distinguished from central executive network (CEN)[27-32] and their particular dynamics, i.e., power spectrum and its scale-freeness (see below)[33,34], have been associated with the self as distinguished from the other[35-37]. These findings suggest that the brain's topography and its dynamics are also strongly shaped by the duality of self and other/world—the duality of self and other/world on the psychological level seems to be inextricably tied to the duality on the neural level.

Though the belief that this self-other/world duality is fundamental to our mental and neural workings is put into doubt by the increasingly available subjective information of non-dual experiences and oneness during meditation. Highly proficient long-term meditators have repeatedly shown the capacity to transcend the self-other/world duality[2,5,6,38-41]. So meditation's orientation towards a present-moment oriented awareness seems to diminish the magnitude of self-referential thinking, hence dissolving the perceived self-other/world duality[42-46]. Yet there are a range of meditation techniques leading one to wonder if they all can cultivate this non-dual experience, especially since it has already been shown that distinct techniques have unique neural impacts[47-50]. Although these differences are unquestionable, it is here proposed that each of them is oriented towards this nondual experience, the natural meditative state[51], and that this nondual state is the same for all forms of meditation that lead to it[41]. This is much like the analogy proposed by the fifteenth century Zen Buddhist Monk, Ikkyu:

> *"Many paths lead from the foot of the mountain, but at the peak we all gaze at the single bright moon."*

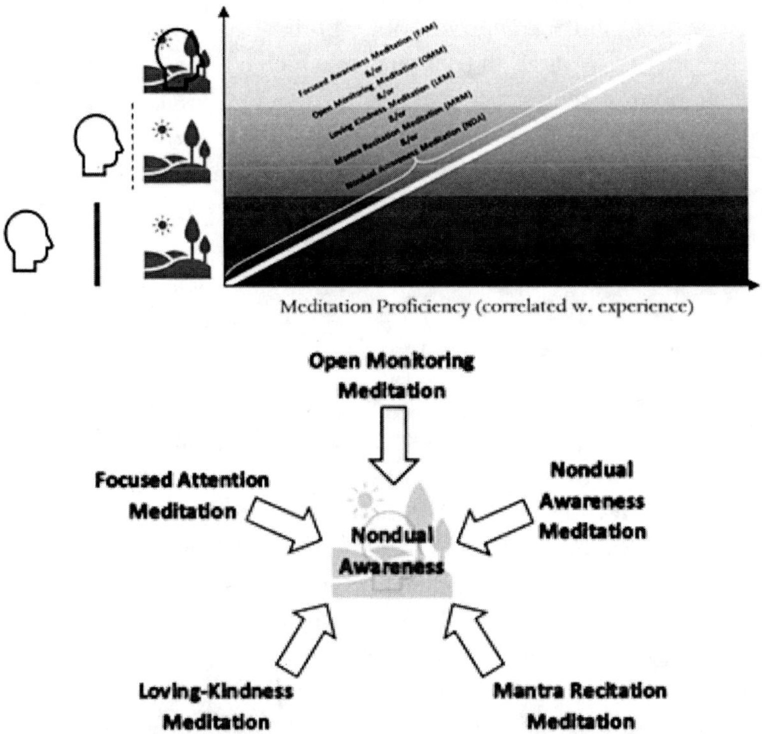

Figure 1: Non-Dual Awareness from Meditation

The experience of such non-duality has often led to the assumption that meditation leads to a loss of self[1,2,5,6,38,52]. However, what is lost is only the opposing or dual relation of self to other/world; in line with Thompson and Varela (2001) who suggest that the processes crucial for consciousness cut across the divisions of brain-body-world. Instead, the self may reach a deeper level where the true unity between self and other/world is realised —termed as 'non-duality'[2,5,40,45], 'natural meditative state'[51], or 'selflessness'[6]. The non-dual experience of self and other/world may then point to a deeper yet not fully explored level of self as the most fundamental feature of the brain and consciousness as postulated in the Basis model of self-specificity (BMSS)[53].

How does the brain mediate this non-dual state of self and other/world in proficient meditation? The capacity to reach this core state of unity along with other preliminary meditative states is a matter of meditation proficiency, which has been correlated to the amount of meditative experience one has[54-57]. This raises the question whether the brain's seemingly self-non-self dichotomous topographic and dynamic organisation is re-structured and re-organised during proficient mediation. Specifically, we ask whether the dual network organisation regarding the anti-correlation of the DMN and CEN is reorganised during proficient meditation, and if so, what other dynamic measures of the brain are associated with this change.

Addressing this question, we review the various studies focussed on the impact of meditation experience on spatial (i.e., topographic) and temporal (i.e., dynamic) features of brain activity. The results show a profound topographic and dynamic reorganisation of the brain in a non-dual way, which as we hypothesise, corresponds to the non-duality of self and other/world on the psychological level. Non-duality thus provides the link or "common currency" hypothesis (CCH) of neural and psychological levels[34,58] in proficient meditation in the same way as duality of self and non-self features both brain and experience in non-meditative states. We postulate that the shift from dual to non-dual organisation of the brain is possible by major re-organisation of its spatial, temporal, and dynamic topography - this leads us to postulate what we describe as the "Topographic dynamic reorganisation model of meditation" (TRoM)[59].

Results

Topography of Meditation: Activity and Connectivity of Neural Networks

Without going into all the details of the empirical data, we highlight in the following pages the main findings of our meta-analysis of meditation studies using fMRI[59].

Default-Mode Network and Central Executive Network

The first main finding concerned the changed activation pattern of neural networks of default-mode network (DMN) and central-executive network (CEN). The DMN shows hypoactivity and hypoconnectivity during the meditative state while the CEN exhibits hyperactivity and hyperconnectivity. Moreover, the usually negative relationship of DMN and CEN transforms into a positive relationship with increasing meditation proficiency.

Salience Network

The salience network (SN), primarily composed of the anterior insula and the dorsal anterior cingulate cortex (dACC), plays a primary role during several distinct forms of meditation. One study which segregated a meditation session into four different states including mind-wandering, awareness of mind-wandering, shifting attention, and sustained focus found that both the anterior insula and the dACC were activated when the meditator became aware that there was no longer sustained attention towards the meditation object, in this case the breath[60]. This suggests that the SN may very well be a mediator between the DMN and the CEN. This finding is in-line with another study involving highly advanced Theravada Buddhist monks that show an anticorrelation between the dACC and the middle frontal gyrus (MFG), a part of the CEN, during focused meditation. Yet the relationship of the correlation between the SN and the CEN is not fully understood since other impactful studies have shown a coactivation of the SN and the CEN during several different types of meditation[61-63].

Decreased Posterior DMN	Increased Anterior CEN	Increased DMN-CEN
Winter et al., 2020	Winter et al., 2020	Bauer et al., 2019
Xiao et al., 2019	Kemmer et al., 2015	Kral et al., 2018
Panda et al., 2016	Froeliger et al., 2012	Creswell et al., 2016
Fingelkurts et al., 2015	Hasenkamp et al., 2012	Marzetti et al., 2014
	Lo et al., 2007	Brewer et al., 2011

Increased SN Activation
Xiao et al., 2019 (ACC)
Mahone et al., 2018 (ACC)
Tomasino et al., 2016 (Insula)
Dickenson et al., 2013 (ACC & Insula)
Hasenkamp et al., 2012 (ACC & Insula)
Manna et al., 2011 (Insula)
Farb et al., 2007 (ACC & Insula)

Increased Anterior DMN
Kwak et al., 2019
Panda et al., 2016
Fingelkurts et al., 2015
Jang et al., 2011

Figure X – Topographic Change Between the DMN and CEN Associated with Meditation Proficiency

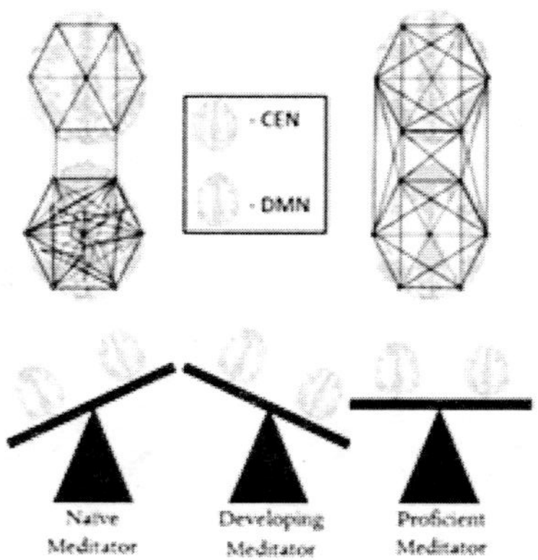

Decreased Posterior-Anterior DMN
Doll et al., 2015
Fingelkurts et al., 2015
Kemmer et al., 2015
Marzetti et al., 2014
Hasenkamp et al., 2012
Taylor et al., 2012

SN-DMN Inter-Connectivity	SN-CEN Inter-Connectivity
Insula:	Insula
Doll 2015	
Farb 2007	Hasenkamp 2012
Hernandez 2017	Jang 2018
ACC	ACC
Hasenkamp 2012	Manna 2011
Marzetti 2014	General
Kwak 2019	Mooneyham 2017
Kilpatrick 2011	Kemmer 2015
Brewer 2011	
Manna 2011	
General	
Kemmer 2015	
Mooneyham 2017	

Table 1: Significant and Consistent Findings Specific to the DMN and CEN Topographic Reconfiguration Associated with Meditation Proficiency

Regarding the SN's relationship with the DMN, there is a similar trend of uncertainty, with some studies suggesting a decreased connectivity during meditation[62], especially focused meditation, yet some finding a positive connectivity during open forms of meditation[64,65] as well as other forms[61,66,67]. With Doll and colleague's (2015) proposition that mindfulness is represented by an increase in PCC-insula anticorrelation, yet other studies showing the opposite trend, both during meditation and RS[61,67], the exact mechanism and role of the SN is still uncertain. Though it is possible that the reason behind these contradictory findings is to do with a non-linear trend of SN activity and connectivity. This has already been found via an inverse U-shape trend of anterior insula activity with respect to meditation experience[68].

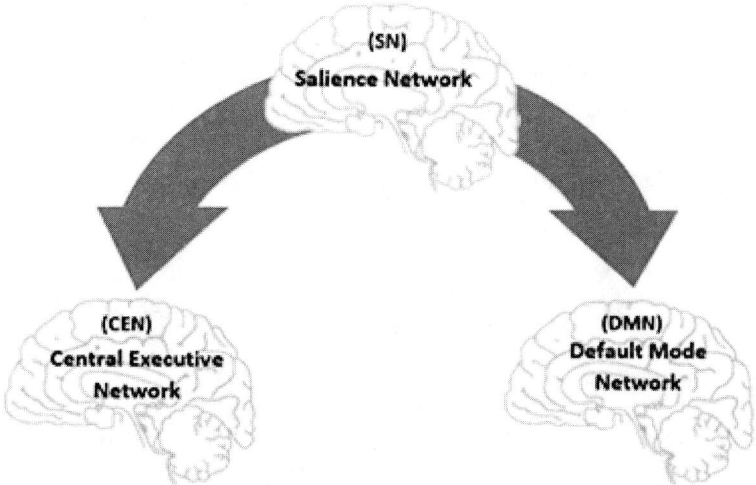

Figure 2 Salience Network as a Potential Mediator Between the DMN and CEN

Dynamics of Meditation: Oscillatory Power and Coherence

We focused on the power and coherence/synchronisation in different frequency bands as obtained in EEG/MEG during meditative and non-meditative states in the different stages of meditation. There is an immense variety of different results and studies which do not illustrate full consistency; we therefore focus on the most consistent results with respect to increasing meditation experience; both meditation compared to RS and the comparison of different lengths of lifetime experience.

Core Oscillatory Power Findings

This area of meditation research has gained a substantial amount of interest, yet the findings vary extensively, showing that there is a vast amount of variability when it comes to simply the oscillatory power associated with meditation. Although there have been attempts to generalise the key oscillatory powers associated with meditation, it is still not clear, especially when introducing the variable of meditation experience level. This being said, there are highly repeated findings which are worth mentioning, specifically increased theta (primarily frontal-central), alpha, and gamma power (primarily posterior) Alpha peak frequency has also consistently shown a decrease during meditation[69-72], which signifies a drop in mental contents (can discuss more), highly in line with the experience of highly experienced meditators who go into states of emptiness.

Core Oscillatory Synchrony Findings

All frequency bands have shown increases in coherence, in support of a long-range topographic re-organisation. These respective oscillatory ranges show different areas of the brain where they are most likely to occur with the slowest oscillatory ranges showing consistent increase in global synchrony. Also interesting, the fastest oscillatory range, gamma, has shown long-range synchrony in highly advanced meditatora, even being specifically linked to a very deep subjective state: fruition[52].

Neural Dynamics

Dynamic features refer to the measurement of change and the pattern of neural activity across time and space. On the temporal side this can include the measurement of the structure or shape of the power spectrum across slow and fast frequencies which may exhibit what is described as long-range temporal correlation

Increased Neural Synchrony Associated with Meditation

Oscillatory Range	General Synchrony Location	Studies
 Infraslow (0.01-0.1 Hz)	*Global*	Jo et al., 2019
 Delta (1-4 Hz)	*Global*	Yordanova et al., 2020, Dissanayaka et al., 2015
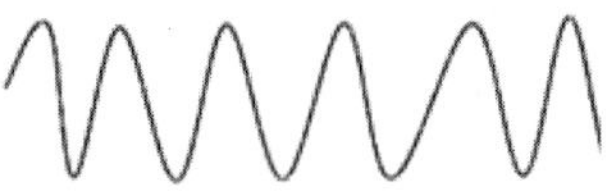 Theta (4-8 Hz)	*Frontal-Central/ Midline* *Generally left-lateralised*	Yordanova et al., 2020, Baijal and Srinivasan, 2010, Xue et al., 2014, Brandmeyer et al., 2016, Chan et al., 2011, Tomljenović et al., 2016, Aftanas and Golocheikine, 2001, Wong et al., 2015
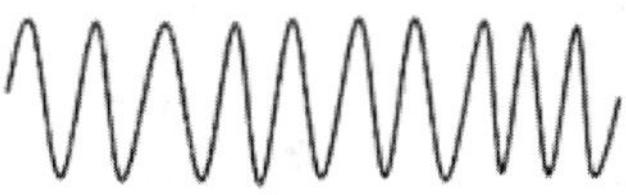 Alpha (8-13 Hz)	*Less Consistent* *Generally right-lateralised*	Yordanova et al., 2020, Brandmeyer et al., 2016, Kim et al., 2013, Murata et al., 2004, Lutterveld et al., 2017, Hebert, 2005, Aftanas, 2001, Travis, 2009
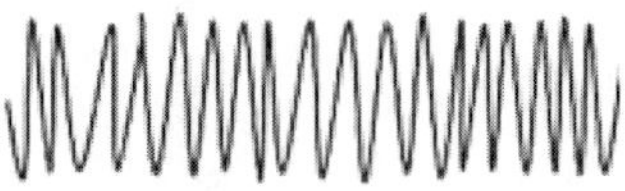 Beta (13-30 Hz)	*Less Consistent Trend for frontal-central/ midline*	Yordanova et al., 2020, Amihai et al., 2014, Travis et al., 2009
 Gamma (30-100+ Hz)	*Long-Range/ Global*	Katyal et al., 2020, Vivot et al., 2020, Berkovich-Ohana, 2015, Lutz et al., 2004

Table 2: Increased Neural Synchrony Associated with Meditation

(LRTC);[73] this is standardly measured by the power law exponent (PLE)[73,74] or detrended fluctuation analysis (DFA)[75,76]. Also entropy measures the degree of order/disorder of a time series closely related to its regularity and predictability: the more ordered and regular a time series, the more predictable and the lower its entropy[77].

Other more spatial dynamic measures include local to global connectivity, as measured by intrinsic ignition, and cortical metastability reflecting the degree of change or transience of cortical pattern[78]. Since these dynamic measures are not as commonly used as the others mentioned above, there are only a

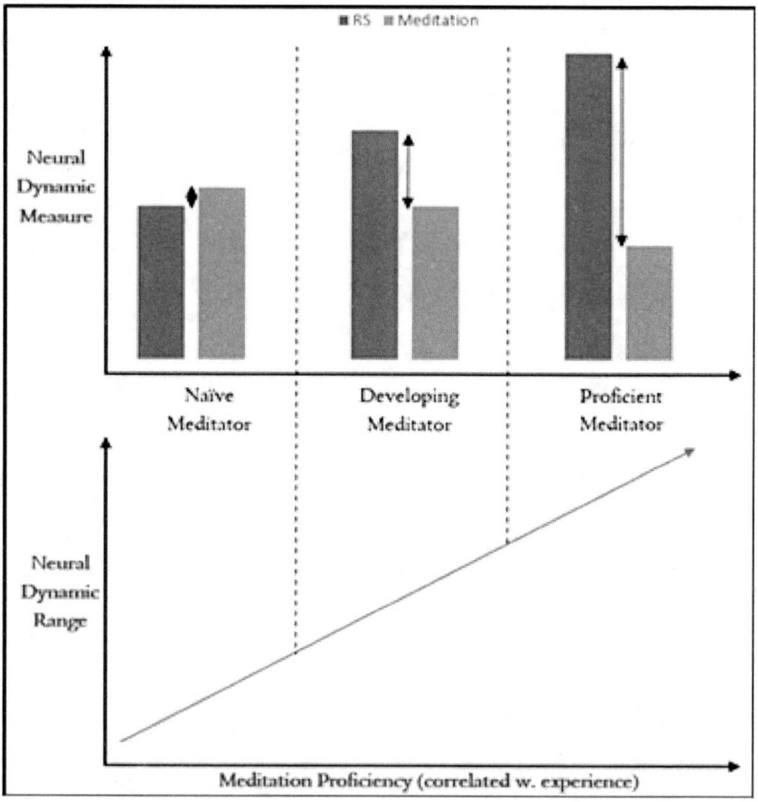

Figure 3: Correlation Between Meditation Proficiency and Experience

few studies using them in meditation. However, all studies reort quite consistent results.

The main findings in proficient meditators are: (i) LRTC as measured by DFA in EEG decrease during meditative state but increase during non-meditative resting state in the same subjects;[71] (ii) permutation entropy shows a similar pattern with decreases during the meditative state (primarily FAM) compared to the resting state (Vyšata); (iii) intrinsic ignition shows similar pattern being decreased during meditative state but increased in non-meditative resting state;[44] (iv) an increased capacity to switch between neural states at will;[45] and (v) an increasingly resilient network architecture driven by path length and global efficiency[81]. Together, these findings suggest a larger dynamic range of dynamic measures as all show decreases in meditative state but are increased during resting state. Hence, the dynamic range, the capacity for the degree of change, increases in proficient meditators compared to non-meditators and initial meditators.

Discussion

Topographic-Dynamic Reorganisation Model of Meditation (TRoM)

Summarising the main findings of neural changes during different stages of meditation amounts to the following: (i) non-linear trend regarding DMN-CEN connectivity and activity, with a final stage of positive connection and co-activation; (ii) increased oscillatory coherence and synchrony for a range of oscillatory frequencies; (iii) increased dynamic range of dynamic feature measurements. These results are in accordance with a topographic reorganisation of the brain: this, as we postulate, leads to a nondual mode of neural functioning which, on the psychological level, we take as evidence accounting for the dissolving of a separate self into a nondual awareness[2,5,38,82]. This inextricable tie between the neural and subjective phenomena associated with increased meditation proficiency amounts to what we describe as the topographic-dynamic reorganisation model of meditation (TRoM).

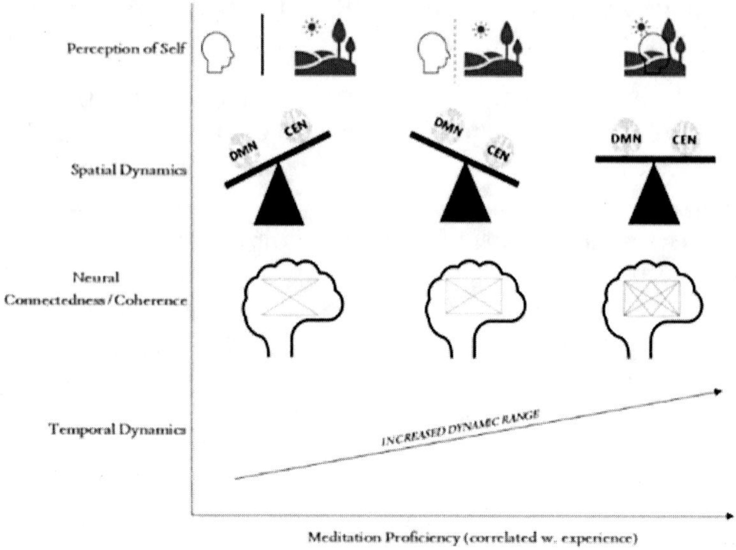

**The TRoM has a spatial, temporal, and dynamic component which illustrates a non-linear neuro-evolution. This evolution is based upon the development of an increasingly globally-connected brain with an enhanced capacity for complexity. Topographic-dynamic reorganisation transforms functionality which increases conductivity towards an all-inclusive and non-dual awareness as opposed to a more cognitively oriented mode of functioning often grounded in self-non-self distinctions, boundaries, and habits.*

Figure 4: Pictorial Depiction of Correlation Between Meditation Proficiency and Experience in Terms of Perception of Self, Spatial Dynamics, Neural Connectedness/ Coherence and Temporal Dynamics

The traditional assumption is to presuppose duality of self and other/world which has been carried forth from philosophy and psychology to neuroscience in more recent years. Correspondingly, dual neural correlates have been assumed for self and other/world like DMN vs CEN and slow vs fast frequencies. However, the experience during especially proficient meditation suggests a deeper layer of self reaching beyond its duality with the other/world, a non-dual state. This seems to contradict the seemingly dual nature of the brain's neural organisation though. Is such non-dual state on the psychological level of experience mediated by a corresponding non-dual state on the neural level? In that case, one would expect fundamental re-organisation of the brain's spatial, temporal, and dynamic features along a non-dual way.

Our review shows profound neural re-organisation of the brain's spatial, i.e., positive rather than negative DMN-CEN relation, and temporal, i.e., balancing and coherence of slow and fast frequencies, features during proficient meditation. Moreover, the dynamic range of possible states and neural transitions and subsequently the dynamic repertoire enhances during proficient meditation. That allows to reorganise the brain's spatial, temporal, and dynamic features on the neural level in a non-dual way which, on the psychological level, may be manifest in a correspondingly non-dual co-experience of self and other/world. We therefore postulate the Topographic reorganisation model of meditation (TRoM) that postulates spatial, temporal, and dynamic reorganisation of the brain in proficient meditation. The key hypothesis of TRoM is that non-duality provides the link or "common currency" of neural and psychological levels in proficient meditation lending support to the "common currency hypothesis" (CCH) of neural and mental features, i.e., brain and mind[58,34].

Proficient meditation unravels a deeper social and ecological layer of self where it is intimately connected with other and world in a non-dual (rather than dual way as on the cognitive surface layer). This hints upon a more basic and fundamental notion of self as proposed in the basis model of self-specificity (BMSS)[1] which can now be extended in neuro-ecological and neuro-social terms. Importantly, due to its neuro-ecological and neuro-social nature, this deeper layer of self is intimately connected with both the other and the world in a positive way, that is, integrated and sharing (non-dual) rather than being segregated and different (dual). Proficient meditation can not only provide us with non-dual experience and integration of self and other/world but can also tell us about the deep ecological and social layers of our self and its intimate integration within the world.

Relationship to Other Theories of Meditation

How does our topographic-dynamic reorganisation model of meditation (TRoM) of non-dual self-world relation stand in relation to other approaches? It borders on both theories of consciousness and self. In his remarkable articles, Josipovic, 2012, 2014, 2019 assumes non-representational and non-conceptual consciousness as there are no contents nor concepts that are to be represented, while on the neural side he associates DLPFC, ACC, and angular gyrus as well as gamma frequencies with a non-dual self-world relation[2,40]. We concur with Josipovic and others[83,84] that consciousness in proficient meditation is no longer content-bound and therefore remains devoid of specific contents, rendering consciousness non-representational and non-conceptual. Instead of concerning specific contents, i.e., the contents of consciousness including their neural correlates[85], proficient meditation lays bare a deeper layer of consciousness, namely its structure and organisation—this has been described as the 'form of consciousness' being a third dimension besides content and level/state of consciousness[58,86,87]. This deep layer of consciousness cannot be conscious of itself, much like the eye cannot see itself, yet it is necessary for the act of seeing or, in our case, consciousness.

Building on Josipovic's association of non-duality with specific areas of the brain, we propose that the experience of non-duality is associated with a long-range topographic reorganisation of its temporo-spatial dynamics. Given its apparent dependence upon the experience level and proficiency of meditation, topographic reorganisation is a trait phenomenon of meditation[88]. This is supported by the fact that the resting state is also changed in non-meditative states in proficient meditators (see results). Accordingly, proficient meditators exhibit a different brain with a non-dual topography which lets them perceive and cognise self and world in a fundamentally different way, i.e., non-dual rather than dual. However, future studies are necessary to disentangle state and trait phenomena on the neural level. For instance, the increase in DMN-CEN anticorrelation in middle stages of meditation may be a state phenomenon allowing for suppression of DMN by CEN[88], while DMN suppression by CEN may no longer be necessary once the brain's topography is fundamentally reorganised in the proficient stage as reflected in the pre-meditative-experience CEN activation found in highly proficient meditators[68].

Relationship to Other Theories of Consciousness

How does non-dual self-world relation as core feature of consciousness in proficient meditation stand in relation to neuroscientific consciousness theories? Leading theories like Integrated Information Theory (IIT)[89] and Global Neural Workspace Theory (GNWT)[90-92] mainly focus on the contents of consciousness: specific mechanisms like integration (IIT) or access to the global neural workspace (GNWT) are considered key mechanisms for contents to become conscious. That is associated with specific regions like posterior cortex (IIT) or prefrontal cortex (GNWT)[58]. Analogously, other approaches like attentional approaches[93-95] assume consciousness to be based on specific attention schemata related to social and sensory perception. That, in turn, is associated with specific regions in the brain like attentional networks.

This stands square to the present approach. Unlike these approaches, we do not focus on the neural correlates of conscious vs unconscious contents but rather on the neural mechanisms related to the form of consciousness, i.e., its structure or organisation of, for instance, self-world relation[58,86,87,96]. Moreover, we suppose the form of consciousness and its reorganisation in proficient meditation to be a whole-brain or global phenomenon – this is indeed supported by recent data associating both level/state and form of consciousness with specific changes in global brain organisation (i.e., global signal in fMRI) and its topographic representation[36,97,98].

Moreover, rather than on specific brain function like integration or global access of contents, as in IIT and GNWT, our approach focuses more on the temporal and spatial dynamics of brain's activity (as distinguished from brain function)[33,34]. Integration and global access may then be understood in a more temporo-spatial (rather than cognitive) sense, as in the temporo-spatial theory of consciousness (TTC)[58,96]. TTC proposes different temporo-spatial dynamic mechanisms of consciousness and its distinct phenomenal features. That, as we suggest here, is also the key in understanding how the brain's topographic reorganisation of its temporo-spatial dynamics leads to changes on the phenomenal level, i.e., non-dual self-world relation, in proficient meditation.

Nature of Self: Yoga and Neuroscience Perspectives

SAKETH MALIPEDDI, RAVINDRA P.N., ARUN SASIDHARAN, RAMAJAYAM G. AND BINDU M. KUTTY

Introduction

The questions "What is the nature of my existence?" and "Who am I?" have intrigued philosophers and psychologists for a long time. Most recently, they have also captured the attention of neuroscientists, who try to study the neural correlates of self. Research has also identified Default Mode Network (DMN) to generate a model of self in the brain[1-3]. An emerging body of evidence shows that the brain has not evolved for thinking, reasoning, or even having a sense of self. Rather, its role is to serve and keep the organism alive through a process called Allostasis. For this, the brain needs to continuously monitor the internal physiological condition – interoception – and anticipate future energetic needs in a predictive manner[4-7]. Research shows the existence of large-scale brain networks—DMN and Salience network—underlying these Allostatic-Interoceptive systems[4,5]. At the most fundamental level of being alive, these predictions are what gives rise to a model of self (a minimal self). At a higher, more abstract level, a narrative self exists, which gives rise to the perception of a coherent, unified self[7-10]. A growing body of literature shows that this sense of self is illusory in nature[11–15].

In contrast to scientific endeavours, which are externally oriented, eastern traditions have arrived at this through systematic inner exploration. According to Yoga, the universality of existence or inter-connectedness of all life is the true nature of reality. And that there is no permanent essence within a human being that can be called as "I" or "me" is well accepted. According to Yoga, Consciousness or pure awareness is the core of a human being[16-20]. From a Western standpoint, consciousness is simply an experience, and the words "mind" and "consciousness" are often conflated[21–25]. However, from a Yogic viewpoint, mind and Consciousness are separate entities, where the universal Self is Consciousness, which drives the function of mind[16,17,26]. Yoga provides the science and methods to achieve experiential defusion and cognitive dereification, which lead one to experience reality as it is—content-free, pure awareness. This state is also referred to as "Consciousness," "Self," "*Brahman*," "*Purusha*", "Pure awareness" etc. Disruptions in the sense of an individual self caused by meditation reflect in the alterations within the DMN, leading to the dissolution or attenuation of "self-other" boundaries[13-15,27-29].

Overall, converging evidence from Yogic traditions and modern neuroscience indicates that the sense of an individual self is an illusion and universality is the true nature of reality. Though Indian philosophical and neuroscience approaches conceptualise consciousness differently, both complement and strengthen each other by investigating the phenomenology and neuroscience of meditation practices. This has implications for individuals, society, and the global community.

Likely Origin of a Sense of Self and its Many Dimensions

According to the social brain hypothesis proposed by Dunbar, the development of complex brains is thought to have arisen from the need to maintain social connections[30]. In order to live in a group, individuals must be able to understand and anticipate the actions and thoughts of others. Graziano and Kastner believe that brains need to be evolved to generate predictions about other people's mental states and, accordingly, to generate an individual sense of self[31,32]. In other words, the concept of a sense of self appears to be an emergent property of our brain used to represent the minds of others. In humans, this is primarily concerned with self-referential and other-referential processing performed by the default mode network (DMN)[1,2,33,34].

Studies show that medial prefrontal cortex (mPFC) (part of the DMN) and its different sub-regions play a critical role in the social understanding of others[35,36]. For example, ventral mPFC and its connections with limbic regions play a role in understanding the emotions of others in social interactions; anterior mPFC and its connections with anterior and posterior cingulate cortex help in making self-other distinctions; and dorsal mPFC and its connections with the temporo-parietal junction (TPJ) are linked with the theory of mind[1,33,37,38].

The self is not a unidimensional construct. Many different dimensions of self have been identified so far. One of the earliest and most influential perspectives on self comes from William James, according to whom there are two aspects related to self. The first one—he calls it "I"—is the one experiencing the current moment in time with an awareness of having a body with boundaries and located spatially. The second one—he calls it "me"—is the one that reflects on the past, present, and future to generate a coherent and integrated idea of self. This "me" is the series of identities that have shaped a person over time[39]. Some contemporary frameworks on self come from Damasio and Gallagher[40–43].

Damasio identifies three different aspects of a self: a) proto-self: the most basic self that arises from the representation of the internal physiological condition of the body by the brain b) core self (or core consciousness): arises when the self identifies with the proto-self to give rise to thoughts and feelings in a first-person perspective; and c) autobiographical self (or extended consciousness): is concerned with an experience of constructing memories in a continuous manner[41–43]. Gallagher suggests two aspects of self: a) minimal self, defined as "a consciousness of oneself as an immediate subject of experience, unextended in time," and there is a feeling of "I am experiencing something" in the present moment; and b) narrative self, which continues to exist over time, gives rise to a perception of a coherent, unified self, and creates a sense of personal identity or "me" feeling[40].

Further, Berkovich-Ohana and Glicksohn proposed a unifying framework of consciousness and self, called the "consciousness state space" (CSS) model, consisting of two categories: core consciousness (supporting the minimal self) and extended consciousness (supporting the narrative self)[44]. Finally, building upon existing theories and dimensions of self, Millière et al., 2018, proposed a framework of two overarching dimensions of self: the multi-sensory minimal self (with sub-categories: body ownership, bodily awareness, and spatial self-location) and the narrative self (with sub-categories: self-related thoughts and semantic autobiographical information)[13]. As can be noticed, many parallels exist between these different perspectives, where William James' "I" corresponds to the "core self" of Damasio and the "minimal self" of Gallagher, and William James' "me" corresponds to the "autobiographical self" of Damasio and the "narrative self" of Gallagher.

Self: A Neuroscience Perspective

At the most fundamental level, there is an experience of living and being alive, which is referred to as a "minimal self." The existence of this minimal (or embodied) self depends on the integration of exteroceptive and interoceptive signals as well as on the interoceptive-allostatic predictive networks (DMN and Salience)[7,10,44–47]. Experience of body ownership (EBO) is an important aspect of a minimal self where there is a clear distinction between what falls within the bodily boundaries and what does not[9]. However, this EBO can be manipulated by experiments such as the rubber-hand illusion (RHI), where synchronous stroking of a real hand and a rubber-hand (one that resembles a real hand and is placed at an appropriate position) while visual attention is paid to it gives rise to the feeling that the rubber hand belongs to one's own body[48].

EBO arises when signals from multiple sensory regions are integrated across exteroceptive and interoceptive domains.

A study showed that those with lower interoceptive sensitivity (level of awareness of interoception, measured using heart-beat detection tasks) are more susceptible to EBO in the RHI task[49]. These experiments demonstrate the malleability of a sense of self and substantiate the idea that self-hood depends on the integration of signals across exteroceptive and interoceptive domains. Premotor cortex in both hemispheres is shown to be involved in EBO, lesions to which result in conditions such as asomatognosia (where a patient reports a body part is missing or not under corporeal awareness)[50]. This minimal self provides the foundation for a more abstract narrative self to form[51]. Overall, the brain constructs a model of self by integrating signals across exteroceptive and interoceptive domains, at many different levels of hierarchical processing, using Bayesian and predictive coding principles, and all in the service of keeping an organism alive via a process known as Allostasis.

Empirically, cortical midline structures (CMS) have been repeatedly shown to be specific for self[1,33,34,52,53]. These CMS regions, of which DMN is a part, process stimuli strongly related to one's identity. These stimuli are often described as self-referential, self-related, or self-relevant. Lesion studies show that damage to regions like OMPFC (part of CMS) leads to dysregulation of a model of self[54]. Earlier studies showed that processing of self-referential stimuli happens at many levels—representation, monitoring, evaluation, and integration—in the cortical midline structures (CMS). The orbito-medial prefrontal cortex (OMPFC) represents stimuli as self-referential, while the supra-genual anterior cingulate cortex (sgACC) monitors them, the dorsomedial prefrontal cortex (DMPFC) evaluates them, and, finally, the posterior cingulate cortex (PCC) integrates them in the context of one's narrative[33]. It is interesting to note that, as research shows now, sgACC and PCC are involved in generating interoceptive predictions in the brain[5]. However, there are slight differences in the self-related brain regions reported in the literature, which could arise because of differences in study designs and other confounding factors[1].

Despite these differences, studies to date consistently report the involvement of cortical midline brain regions in self-processing. Qin and Northoff did a large quantitative meta-analysis that took these study-related factors into account and looked more closely at the role of cortical midline brain regions in processing self-related stimuli versus familiar (people you know) and other (non-self and non-familiar) stimuli. This study showed that when the brain is processing self-related stimuli, there is a specific activation of the perigenual anterior cingulate cortex (PACC) that overlaps with DMN activity during rest. Other midline regions, like the medial prefrontal cortex (mPFC) and posterior cingulate cortex (PCC), were found to be activated by both self-related and familiar stimuli. Overall, the authors suggested a form of rest-stimuli interaction within the CMS to give rise to a sense of self[1]. Another large meta-analysis on imaging studies on the self showed that interaction between CMS and sub-cortical midline regions gives rise to a sense of self[34]. Recent research reporting the involvement of DMN regions in supporting allostasis and interoception is remarkable since there is now converging evidence from various lines of independent research implicating the importance of DMN in generating a model of self in the brain[4,5].

Self: A Yoga Perspective

Sankhya, a dualistic school, postulates that reality is made of *Purusha* (Seer or Consciousness) and Prakriti (creation). Sankhya views Consciousness as a fundamental property of existence. Some philosophers, like Bernardo Kastrup and David Chalmers, align with this viewpoint[55–57]. This is in contrast to materialistic theories, which posit that matter is the fundamental property of existence and everything else is an emergent property. Yoga gives practical methods and shows the path to realising the *Purusha*. Patanjali, considered to be the father of Yoga, assimilated many different aspects of Yoga into 196 "*sutras*" (or aphorisms) which talk about various modulations of mind, barriers faced by the practitioner, techniques to still the mind, various types of *samadhi*, *ashtanga* yoga (or the eight limbs of yoga), various *siddhis* (powers) gained, and the process towards *kaivalya* (enlightenment)[16].

The word "consciousness" has been used to mean different things in different contexts. In the western framework, consciousness means experience[21–23,25,47]. Here, the distinction between mind and consciousness is not clear, and these terms are often used interchangeably[26]. However, in Sankhya and Yoga, seer or *Purusha* is consciousness. Other terms for this include "*Brahman*," "Self," "witness-consciousness," "pure consciousness", "content-free consciousness," and "non-dual awareness." In addition, in these frameworks, there is a clear distinction between mind, experience, and consciousness. For any experience to happen, there needs to be a duality of subject (Seen) and object (Seer). *Dṛg-Dṛśya-Viveka* from Advaita Vedanta provides a method to inquire into the nature of "Seer" (*Drg*) and "Seen" (*Dṛśya*)[58].

For example, to experience, say, a colour (an object), there needs to be eyes (a subject). To experience the eyes (the object), there needs to be a mind (the subject). Indian philosophical systems extend this by saying that the mind itself is an object that can be experienced. The one experiencing it is *Purusha* (seer or consciousness). To keep it simple, any experience requires consciousness (as a witness or subject) and an object (which could be the mind, thoughts, emotions, one's own body, various sensory perceptions, an object in the world, etc.). *Purusha* is seen as the source of conscious awareness. Yogic texts describe this state as *sat-chit-ananda* (truth-consciousness-bliss)[16,18]. In other words, in layman's terms, to experience something, one needs to be aware. To experience a colour, one needs to be aware of witnessing it. To experience one's mind and its wandering nature, one needs awareness. This underlying awareness, which is ever-present, is called consciousness, seer, or *Purusha*. This is similar to what Buddhist traditions say about the mind and awareness[59–61]. This also has parallels in the cognitive sciences with terms like cognition fusion, experiential fusion, cognitive distancing, cognitive reification, cognitive dereification, etc.[62].

Illusory Self-Converging Evidence from Yoga and Neuroscience

With all the background information on the nature of self from yoga and neuroscience perspectives, we can now look into its illusory nature. The word "illusion" does not mean that something does not exist. It means that how something exists is different from how it seems to exist. Illusions are psychological phenomena that do not exist in nature. A sense of having a coherent, integrated, individual self seems to be an illusion created by the brain. According to research, the sense of selfhood one has is similar to how one perceives the world around them[7,47].

There is now converging evidence from Buddhist tradition, Advaita Vedanta, Yogic sciences, cognitive science, and modern neuroscience that suggests that the impermanence and universality (or interconnectedness) of life are the nature of reality. And the sense of being an individual self with boundaries and being permanent and continuous over time is an illusion constructed by the brain to help with survival needs. There is an awareness of change happening over time, but there is also an underlying impression that there is a unitary self that is experiencing all this change. As these different frameworks point out, this integrated, unitary self is an illusion.

According to Buddhist traditions, the nature of human existence is characterised as "anatta," or non-self; that is, there is no underlying, permanent essence within an individual that can be called a self. One of the Buddhist meditative practices called "emptiness meditation" leads a practitioner to *Śūnyatā* (emptiness or non-self), where one experiences the emptiness or the void within—a state where there is just plain, content-less awareness present. Similarly, in Advaita Vedanta (a non-dualistic spiritual tradition), a particular practice called neti-neti, translated as "not this, not that," helps to recognise identities that one thinks to be "I" and "me" and negates them. This process unmasks what one thinks one is and continues till one realises there is nothing inside that can be considered an individual self. This is perfectly in alignment with Buddhist traditions.

Yogic sciences, in the same vein, approach the nature of reality with many practices that eventually lead to the dissolution of self-created illusory boundaries. The highest state in Yoga is called *Nirbeeja Samadhi*, where there are no mental modifications or *vrittis* left (*Yogaś-citta-vṛtti-nirodhaḥ*). In this state, one experiences reality as it is, where there is only pure, non-dual awareness present. This is what is usually referred to as one's true Self. The nature of this state, according to Hindu traditions, is *Satcitananda*: *Sat – cit – ananda* or existence – consciousness – bliss. Cognitive sciences and modern neuroscience also converge on a similar point of view when it comes to the illusory nature of the individual self.

Implications

An attempt is being made, from both eastern and western frameworks, to clear up confusion and integrate our understanding of this topic. Experiencing the inclusive and interconnected nature of all reality will have far-reaching ramifications and profound implications for all aspects of our society. One, experiencing a dimension within which is one beyond the mind itself—consciousness—is a way to transcend suffering. This will have a tremendous impact on individual health and well-being as the mind is no longer a source of trouble. The mind would start working for and not against oneself. Two, experiencing the interconnected nature of existence leads to inclusiveness and compassion towards nature and all life on the planet. This experience goes a long way in addressing racial bias, discrimination, poverty, hunger, climate change, and the biodiversity crisis, all of which are based on a limited, exclusive self-identity. Yoga provides methods to dissolve the illusory "self-other" boundaries. The science of Yoga is highly relevant for the future of humanity and all life on the planet.

How Does Heartfulness Meditation Permeate Everyday Life? A Phenomenological Enquiry

ROSALIND PEARMAIN

How does a meditation practice and its associated teaching affect everyday life? How do practitioners experience this?

We have increased understanding of the effects of specific techniques and meditative states of consciousness on the mind-body system and on well-being and health. We have also inherited a fundamental wealth of cartographies of spiritual evolution shaped over thousands of years from precisely monitored practices.

There is a body of understanding and precision in researching neural correlates with different meditation approaches. Benefits to well-being and mental health have been documented, especially in relation to mindfulness meditation[1,2,3]. Yet there are still many challenges in formulating theories of meditation and enduring changes in consciousness[4-9].

Less attention has been placed on the lived everyday experience and effects as they unfold through time and through a lifespan for a meditating householder in industrial society of the twenty-first century.

Some key questions arise:

- How does consciousness manifest as a lived experience among meditators in their real-life settings?
- How do they express and articulate this?
- Can their perceptions and vocabulary help us to go further in understanding the unfolding spectrum of consciousness?

Rationale for a Phenomenological Approach to Meditators' Lived Experience

The aim of phenomenology is to describe the lived world of everyday experience.[10]

This approach offers an opportunity to understand the lived experience of meditation and Heartfulness meditation in particular, also known as Sahaj Marg (meaning simple or natural way). This is a modern system based on Raja Yoga.[11,12]. It focuses awareness and feeling on the supposition of divine presence in the heart. It is fundamentally animated by and sustained through the free dissemination of a source of pranahuti, or yogic transmission —a very subtle manifestation of a spiritual current whose effects can be discerned by practitioners. This form of spiritual practice is essentially offered to people all over the world who may have no prior acquaintance with yoga, Indian philosophy, spirituality or meditation in any way. The invitation is given simply to experience something from this meditation for oneself and, to take up further elucidation and involvement—as self-selected—through access to a variety of written materials, apps and videos as well as the living teacher's presence and teachings.

Phenomenology

Phenomenology was developed by the mathematician and philosopher, Edmund Husserl (1859-1938), as an approach to researching human experience or the "life world" to access the fundamental structures of experience that led to systems of knowledge. He argued that consciousness is always related to intentionality. Human beings are always aware of, and relating to the appearances of the world, and they are not outside the world but continuously shaping it and responding through interactions. Therefore, there is a need for a systematic approach to considering how things appear simply in consciousness before we apply sedimented understandings and assumptions.

Husserl famously urged an approach that focused on the givens as they simply appeared to us in consciousness. This required the use of the epoche or abstinence from applying what is already known, assumed, expected, to hold these in a disciplined way, so that an attitude of openness, a kind of hovering close to 'the things themselves', could be fostered and sustained. An approach called eidetic imagination was used to capture invariant patterns by exploring alternative possibilities. This original approach to phenomenology is defined as a transcendental or descriptive approach which aims to arrive systematically at a description of the essence of an experience.

There are now many, different approaches to phenomenology which are aligned with nuanced philosophical base lines.[10,13,14]. Heidegger (1889-1971) was a student of Husserl and turned away from a transcendental idealist perspective focused on experience to one more concerned with questions relating to human existence itself. Heidegger assumed that it is not possible for human beings to remove themselves from a given existence. Therefore, we are always involved and interpreting the world through our 'existential thrownness', the givens of embodiment through which we seek and derive our own meaning. The lifeworld describes taken for granted core aspects in our lived experience and can be explored through the consideration of time, space, body and the givenness or presentation of experience. Max Van Manen[14,] suggests that the four basic existential dimensions of the lifeworld can be helpful filters in phenomenological approaches to research. These are spatiality, embodiment, temporality and relationality. They can offer concrete dimensions intrinsic to conscious experience.

Results

A phenomenological enquiry focused on the lived experiences of 11 participants who had been practising Heartfulness meditation over some years ranging from 4 to 44 years with ages between 30 and 70 was carried out. They included three males and eight females from Europe, USA and India.

Participant	Origin	Gender	Age Range	Started HFN Meditation
a	Europe	f	60-70	2016
f	Europe	f	60-70	1998
g	India	m	50-60	2016
j	India	f	40-50	1998
i	Europe	m	70-80	1976
d	Europe	f	30-40	2005
c	Europe	f	40-50	1994
e	Europe	m	30-40	2004
b	Europe	f	40-50	2014
h	Europe	f	60-70	1988
k	USA	m	40-50	2002

Table 1: Background Participant Information

Ethical principles and guidelines were followed in accordance with the ethical codes applied by the Minster Centre for Psychotherapy in alignment with national professional organisations within the UK. Interviews were unstructured and focused on the question, How does Heartfulness meditation practice affect or permeate your daily life?

Participants were purposively sampled to provide a range of backgrounds, ages and length of time practising. They were known previously as colleagues within the Heartfulness meditation network. There was one initial open question followed by prompts to facilitate expansion or clarification. The transcribed texts were checked subsequently with the participants for accuracy. The phenomenological focus required is a sustained openness, and a 'dwelling within' the text and an empathic resonance to reflect on the felt sense of the lived qualities through the lenses of spatiality, embodiment, relationality, and temporality. Each lens is described first, followed by examples from specific participants.

The Perspective of Spatiality or Experience of Lived Space Associated with Heartfulness Meditation

Usually, the conception of space is related to mathematical space in terms of measurable dimensions. The lived experience of space is something immediate, often less conscious or preverbal. Human beings are affected by different spatial aspects of environments, their felt qualities, their context, the presence of others within them. It can be understood as part of the way that we inhabit space, move in our home world and the possible horizons of living that we envisage. Spatiality is part of our intrinsic consciousness. Cultural, and social conventions associated with space give certain qualitative dimensions to the experience. Within a meditation practice, and in particular a practice that is focuses attention on the heart, particular qualities of this experienced space may then permeate other modes of living[14].

The lived experience of Heartfulness meditation unfolds from turning attention towards the heart, beginning with an inner focus on the supposition that there is a source of light or love already present within the heart. It can be a new discovery to encounter self-experience in this way—potentially separated from the usual flow of thoughts and preoccupations within the conscious landscape. It offers a different sense of situated space and spaciousness in a specific location of the heart. It may reflect a different sense of embodiment and possibility. "If you are lucky, sometimes you encounter your authentic or true self'. (Participant g).

In dwelling more within a sense of light/love in the heart, it can be a relief and a deep solace to find a new space like a 'spiritual womb' or a whole realm that is contained and sheltered without the constraints that shape and limit the world that we are all co-creating from moment to moment. In the 'Poetics of Space', (1958), Gaston Bachelard[15] suggests that a primordial experience of inhabited space is 'Within the being, in the being of within, an enveloping warmth welcomes being'..[15] and, on page 5 that 'all really inhabited space bears the essence of the notion of home. In a further reflection on the spatiality of being, Bachelard noted that:

Immensity is within ourselves. It is attached to a sort of expansion of being that life curbs and caution arrests, but which starts again when we are alone'. (p.184)

Meditation is such an activity that can facilitate access to this kind of aloneness. At the same time, this can offer a sustained reference of embodied place or space in consciousness pervading during everyday life. Within the spiritual philosophy of the Upanishads, there is a special couplet that describes the infinity within the heart..

...the small space within the heart is the most marvellous of all things. The Space within the heart contains everything. The entire universe is there, all times and space and all creation.. (Chandyoga Upanishad).

Participants' accounts (the alphabets represent different participants)

(a) It draws my focus to my heart, helps me to come away from thinking or over thinking into the experiencing.. There is the physicality of the heart being the centre of the being ... then to allow myself to be there, it is a big space...

With Heartfulness, there is a larger field than my field, so it is not even about me. It taps into something that is on what I might be on the edge of awareness of.. It kind of pierces the membrane where things are real.. it touches the real thing.

Nothing looks quite the same. The inner world, the heart has become so much .. more like a big space or a cathedral... in the context of understanding the psyche, it holds all the possibilities for expansion, for forgiveness, for a new perspective and that needs space..

Heartfulness invites that. You bring yourself to the cathedral, to the altar where your base is. It feels the base of life, of the consciousness in life..

It changes the basis for relationships.. You are available and you can be approached and people notice that…

(b) Something very unique to me. It was a fantastic feeling.. the ability to be in almost a realm, to be within myself, a reality.. that's all there is, there's nothing else. . there's no distractions and it is almost like a purity for me and a feeling of being in a realm that doesn't have any boundaries, any capacities or limits or fears. It just being able to be, just is what it is.

...the beauty of the world that our physical body lives in.. there are fears, there are insecurities, whereas when you are in an internal space they are not there. Because this is a space of love, of complete clarity and purity and it's almost like a spiritual womb.

(c) It puts my life and emotions into context.. A bigger picture of what life is about and who I am. It is a bit like Babuji said to look at the stars or the sky, a similar kind of feeling. A feeling of being held and reassured, in a way that life and death is natural, part of the world or cosmos. It is a way to connect with that eternal feeling. And I may not feel it in meditation, but I may feel it when I am walking down the road or doing the shopping..

Embodiment

Embodiment and spatiality are closely connected as Merleau Ponty[16], emphasised in *The Phenomenology of Perception.* The world is perceived through our embodied resonance. With Heartfulness meditation, as the experience of spatiality and relatedness with the source of being deepens, the context of connection with others and the world changes too. The sense of personal fullness or emptiness of desires, in embodied beings, has a corresponding relationship with the sense of new space available for others and discernment in the world. 'Being emptier' allows more fluidity and responsiveness to others. Feeling 'a depth of connection' recalls the significance of our relation with verticality.

Like a tap root in a tree going deeply into the sense of the ground of being. Bachelard[14] suggests that the earliest experience of dwelling gives a sense of base and rising up from, as well as a ground with depths below that support. Enfolded within this vertical dimension there is the inner nexus of centrality. From the midst of being, all other possibilities of being radiate outwards[17]. Similarly, the more precise sense of stillness at the centre of a tornado captures the felt sense of the dynamic tension of re-finding balance from the momentum of life. Deeply profound experiences and meaning are perceived evocatively and held through embodied vocabulary.

Participants' accounts (the alphabets represent different participants)

(d) It is a sense of being empty. I am more like a field of energy than an ego. So, there is more humility. It is more like 'I am no one', like day-to-day 'who am I?' Along with more emptiness, I feel a growing sense of happiness and joy that is more stable every day… Recently, I realise I have less desires which is quite a big thing. Just being able to fit in with anyone and their schedule and not wish I was doing something else.. And a kind of knowingness of when things are important, I get a signal in the moment, like my heart sends a signal—this is really important, be here fully..

(e) When you have had the experience of Heartfulness, when you have experienced yourself on a deeper level, you are able to speak from your heart with conviction, experience it in simplicity.. I would say that it gives you a direct connection to the divine and the understanding that we are completely inseparable from the source is experienced and it gives you that with so much conviction. .and just the very simplicity of that, the knowing of that is what is real. ..that sense of formlessness at a very subtle level is always there, even I am probably distracted 95 per cent of the day... still that 5 per cent is really important... you develop more awareness.

(r) I have evolved into a completely different way of being... from an earlier life of always being on a mission.. I do not create future ways of being as I have done before.. I relate more to what I feel than what I think.. it's more a way of being.. Like a still centre in a tornado, I know when it's not right and I immediately step back.. feeling in the dark.. the tornado thing, feel very centred, very calm, when I feel the disturbance.. I go back again to the middle. This space is just lovely, not tiring. My head is very tiring. At work people like my neutrality, Grandchildren appreciate the calmness.

Relationality

Relationality is a central aspect of humaneness and context within life that shapes our purposes and meaning. In Heartfulness meditation, there is an invitation to relate with the divine source within, in parallel with recognising the same in all.

There are different aspects described in the lived experience of relationship and how meditation is perceived to have affected this. In one central way, participants describe the experience of a relationship as dwelling within a field of resonating and dynamic presence with the higher Self or Spiritual Guide or beloved each day. This sense of presence is something alive and nourishing like a dynamic field of consciousness and feeling. In other ways, the sense of dwelling more deeply in a sheltering and containing context of relationality allows a less encumbered responsiveness and connectivity with others.

Participants' accounts (the alphabets represent different participants)

(g) It has changed considerably it brings out the more authentic self.. it enables you to meet that world often, a true self meeting the outside world than otherwise you would... It has lessened the anger that I had... I think I do react less fast than I used to... I think that meditation has allowed me to act more warmly than I would have done otherwise... I feel that empathy is one thing that does increase.. The whole of me is changing... I did find that both the Heartfulness and the release from work has led to more of an openness and a receptiveness to things…

I do have more connection with humanity in general and individuals in particular..

The practice has given me some sort of solid basis on which to stand

(h) First it is a way of life, always present in some dimension more or less conscious. Any time of day, working, cooking, discussing.. but I can always feel that presence. So this is a kind of basic sound. A feeling. It is more a field emanates from here (heart) but is bigger than me, something infinite. So it is really to be connected with inner being or the Master as a feeling something that is not a person, but more like a space… it is more something of which I am part. When I am feeling connected, I am feeling complete. In the inner relationship I am receiving love.

For me Heartfulness is based on love and truth, it is my anchor, so that's my grounding. .. I think my ability to have a connection with people quickly, always had that ability.. but its much deeper. So I can feel things, I can feel people more deeply than I probably did before and I think that's good.

(i) I am always inwardly turned. … when I am relaxed, I just feel the presence inside me, a presence which is absolutely evolving, changing and very secure and calming. I think a field is better than space, it is a field where there are many things appearing I can drown myself in it, this is very active/ there is a lot of love in it, meaningfulness, fulfilment, reason to exist, job to do, in a very practical way, in this consciousness simply Purity and love really dominate in the field. You

> have a lens and a focus… It's just like layers that are mingling, sometimes like a wave, you are here, you are there, everything is interacting, it's part of that field. It's a nurturing thing, beautiful place... It's a radar of the world, it's touching, it's a way of getting knowledge..
>
> To relate to another human being for example, you feel the person. You perceive the world through empathy, through touching, through engaging yourself with what is outside yourself. And in that what you are touching is the same value as yourself. There is no separation when you feel it.

Temporality

Lived time encompasses the different ways that we encounter time and shape our lives through its unfolding. Time can appear to pass fast or slow depending on our engagement and mood. It can also be experienced as passing fast or slow in meditation. At different stages of life the trajectory of time and its landscape are revised.

In the ways that meditators describe their lived experience, the relation with temporality is also related to the sense of connection with the source. The order of the flow of things may be reversed. Another sense of time flows 'like a shadow' 'catching us unawares' alongside the familiar temporal shape of the day. There is a sense of pausing, suspending time in the moment in order to align with a more encompassing source of wisdom or consciousness that exists prior to the current moment and meets in the present opportunity for poise and action. Dwelling within are eternal and expansive stillness can be a dynamic problem-solving process.

Temporality is often shaped as a linear event like the sign of the arrow. Within the lived experience of Heartfulness, the shape of time passing might be circular or spiral in repetitive practice or moving deeper towards a dynamic still central point. Or it may involve a process of a pendulum for cantering or rebalancing.

The sense of personal agency and intentionality that is involved in the shaping of relation with temporality is dissolved in a more encompassing deep stillness. Yet both dimensions of living time can exist side by side.

Participants' Accounts

(j) I discovered that the transformation was like a shadow. It is flowing through the day and it catches you unawares... The experience comes first, then the knowledge.... Something stares at you clearly like a still lake and you have this feeling that is what you have to do. You do it and then you have the knowledge that it was perfect. And it was that deep space that you are used to reaching into that is moving you forward. What I find is that it is all interlinked with consciousness. The more I plunge into this deep silence, into this not-knowing which is what this silence is also about because it is not knowledge. There is this consciousness that expands. Something inside of you, a space that encompasses knowledge, understanding, qualities, everything expands and it begins to bring forward this feeling of love. This energy of love.

But the paradox of this is that you are living at the cusp of two opposite things and you are living at a slightly higher plane.. You know there is a state where I am completely aware of my material world and I am completely soaking it up and I am completely enjoying every bit of it or agonising over every bit. Then there is this other part where I am completely removed from it... allowing this higher consciousness to actually pour out from me and walk through everyday life and I am living right at the cusp of that.. I can experience both of them. So this has been very intense during lockdown... I am in awe that there is no conflict between the two.. You can see two conflicting things and you can stay extremely centred in the middle and allow it to manifest how it needs. It's just gorgeous. I don't know else to say it..

Summary

Unfolding from within, like a roll of infinite fabric, the experience of Heartfulness or Sahaj Marg is expansive as a living dimensional and dynamic field of feeling rather than simply a space. Inspiring qualities are discovered in this field of feeling such as purity, beauty, authenticity. The mood and spaciousness felt may create a sense of an inner cathedral-like domain in which the meaning and encompassing nature of experience is more deeply touched and grasped through the heart.

This field of feeling can become more present and available as a kind of radar in the world where it is as if the heart touched situations and others to reveal more direct understanding and empathy. At the same time, persons may be immersed in ordinary everyday demands of professional and family life, yet poised between two different modes of consciousness in a surprisingly harmonious way.

This preliminary phenomenological exploration of Heartfulness meditation situates the experience more tangibly within the domains of our being in the world, which can bring more understanding of how meditation practice can affect the experience of everyday life. A different sense of lived space, embodiment, relationality and time opens up ways of capturing, more concretely, some of the shifts in consciousness that are sustained for meditators meeting daily challenges in life.

These accounts may contribute to widening perspectives and vocabulary which, in turn, can contribute to the development of more precise and quantitative methods of research. To this end, at present, a scale of the manifestation of expanding consciousness is being developed and tested with two sets of 200 participants, each including Heartfulness meditators, meditators in other systems, and individuals who do not practise any form of meditation The resulting scale, now called the Awareness Atlas[18] has four dimensions:

1. Relationship to Others,
2. Listening to the Heart,
3. Connection with Higher Self,
4. Acceptance and Letting go.

In the next steps, properties of this scale will be further explored in terms of the consistency of responses across time, changes in responses to a stimulus and comparisons between changes occurring through a variety of interventions.

Acknowledgement and gratitude for the eternal inspiration of Kamlesh D. Patel Global Heartfulness Guide

Endnotes and References

Mind and Consciousness in the Yogasutra

Endnotes

i. Vyāsa clearly censures those who think that the mind is conscious as well as the idealist who maintains that only a non-material mind exists and not the external objects VBh (Vijñāna-bhairava) 4.23-

ii. YS (*Yogasūtra*) 2.15-

iii. SK (Sāmkhyakārikā) 62-

iv. Larson op.cit. p. 81-

v. YS 4.23

vi. T.V. (Tatva Viveka) 1.4-

vii. VBh 1.4-

viii. YS 2.23 *aparinamini hi bhoktrsaktir apratisankrama ca parinaminy arthe pratisamkranteva tad vrttim anupatati* VBh 4.22.

ix. VBh 4.22.

x. VB h 4.22.

xi. TV 4.22.

xii. Larson op. cit., p. 83.

References

1. Carruthers, P., (2000). Phenomenal Consciousness: A Naturalistic Theory. New York: Cambridge University Press.

2. Chalmers, D.J., (1995). Facing Up to the Problem of Consciousness. *J. Conscious. Stud.* 2, 200–219.

3. Larson, G.J., and Bhattacharya, R.S., (1987). Encyclopedia of Indian Philosophies. *Motilal Banarsidass*, 4, 81-82.

Non-local Consciousness and the Anthropology of Religions and Spiritual Practices

References

1. Kuhn, T., (1962). Structure of Scientific Revolutions. *The University of Chicago Press.*

2. Stevenson, I., (1997). Reincarnation and Biology. *Praeger*, 1and2.

3. Schwartz, S., and Dossey, L., (2010). Non-locality, intention, and observer effects in healing studies: laying a foundation for the future. *Explore*, 6 (5), 295–307. https://doi.org/10.1016/j.explore.2010.06.011.

4. Schwartz, S., (2015). Through Time and Space: The Evidence for Remote Viewing in The Evidence for Psi. Ed. by Damien Broderick and Ben Goertzel. *McFarland and Company.*

5. Bhikkhu, T., (1997). The Meaning of the Buddha's Awakening. https://www.accesstoinsight.org/lib/authors/thanissaro/awaken-ing.html.

6. Matthew 3:13-17 New International Version. *Bible Gateway*. https://www.biblegateway.com/passage/?search=Matthew+3%3A13-17andversion=NIV

7. Maulana Shafi, M., M.,. Maariful-Quran. https://web.archive.org/web/20120915231807/http://www.islamibayanaat.com/MQ/English-MaarifulQuranMuftiShafiUsmaniRA-Vol-1-IntroHistoryAndPage-0-28.pdf

8. Psalm 33:6. *Bible Gateway*. https://www.biblegateway.com.

9. Mark 2:8; Acts 7:59; Rom 1:9; 8:16; 1 Cor 5:3-5. *Bible Gateway*. https://www.biblegateway.com.

10. Rom 8:9-1. *Bible Gateway*. https://www.biblegateway.com.

11. Teresa (1976). Collected Work of St Teresa of Avila. *ICS Publications*.

12. Braud, W.G., (2008). Patañjali Yoga and Siddhis: Their relevance to parapsychological theory and research. In K.R. Rao, A.C. Paranjpe, and A.K. Dalal (Eds.), Handbook of Indian Psychology (pp. 217–243). *Cambridge University Press India/Foundation Books*. https://doi.org/10.1017/UPO9788175968448.012.

13. Schwartz, S., and Dossey, L., (2010). Nonlocality, intention, and observer effects in healing studies. *Explore*. 6 (5), 295–305. https://doi.org/10.1016/j.explore.2010.06.011. Also in, Oxford Handbook of Psychology and Spirituality. ed. L. Miller. Oxford: Oxford University Press, 2012 (in press).

14. Jung, C., (1974). Dreams II. Trans. by R.F.C. Hull. *Princeton University Press*.

15. Grad, B., and Dean, D., (1983). Independent confirmation of infrared healer effects. In: White, R.A., Broughton R.S., eds. *Research in parapsychology. Metuchen, NJ: Scarecrow Press*; 1984:81–83.

16. Dean, D. ([Doctoral dissertation]. University microfilms international, No. 8408650. Saybrook Institute) in: an examination of intra-red and ultra-violet techniques to test for changes in water following the laying-on-of-hands. 1983: 111-115.

17. Fenwick P, and Hopkins, R., (1986). An examination of the effect of healing on water. *J Soc Psych Res*. 53, 387–390.

18. Dean, D., (1982). Infrared measurements of healer treated water. *Roll, W.G., Beloff J, White, R.A., eds. Research in parapsychology. Metuchen, NJ: Scarecrow Press*, 1983:100–101.

19. Schwartz, S.A., Mattei, Brame E., J., Spottiswoode, S.J.P., (2015) Infrared spectra alteration in water proximate to the palms of therapeutic practitioners. *Explore*, 11 (2),144–155.

20. Emoto, M., (2017). What is the photograph of frozen water crystals. http:// www.masaru-emoto.net/english/watercrystal. html.

21. Ibid.

22. Radin, D., et al., (2006) Double-blind test of the effects of distant intention on water crystal formation. *Explore*, 2 (5), 408-411.

23. McGovern, P.E., Zhang, J., Tang, J., Zhang, Z., Hall, G.R., Moreau, R.A., Nuñez, A., Butrym, E.D., Richards, M.P., Wang, C.S., Cheng, G., Zhao, Z., and Wang, C. (2004). Fermented beverages of pre- and proto-historic China. *Proceedings of the National Academy of Sciences of the United States of America*, 101 (51), 17593–17598. https:// doi.org/10.1073/pnas.0407921102.

24. The real presence of Jesus Christ in the sacrament of the eucharist: Basic questions and answers. *United States Conference of Catholic Bishops* n.d. http://www.usccb.org/ prayer-and-worship/themass/order-of-mass/liturgy-of-the-eucharist/the-realpresence-of-jesus-christ-in-the-sacrament-of-the-eucharistbasic-questions-and-answers.cfm.

25. Schwartz, S.A., (2019). Water, Wine, and the Sacred, An Anthropological View of Substances Altered by Intentioned Awareness, Including Objective and Aesthetic Effects. *Explore*, https://doi.org/10.1016/j.explore.2018.03.010.

26. Loc. cit.

27. Radin, D.H., (2007). Walsh J. Effects of intentionally enhanced chocolate on mood. *Explore*, 3 (5), 487–492.

28. Shiah, Y.J., and Radin, D. (2013). Metaphysics of the tea ceremony: A randomised trial investigating the roles of

intention and belief on mood while drinking tea. *Explore (New York, N.Y.)*, 9 (6), 355–360. https://doi.org/10.1016/j.explore.2013.08.005.

29. Loc cit.

30. Loc cit.

31. Haraldsson, E., and Thorsteinsson, T., (1973). Psychokinetic effectson yeast: An exploratory experiment. In: Roll W.G., Morris R.L., Morris J.D., eds. *Research in Parapsychology*, 1972: 20–21.

32. Tedder, W.H., and Monty, M.L., (1980). Exploration of long-distance P.K.: A conceptual replication of the influence on a biological system. In: Roll W.G. Beloff J, eds. *Research in Parapsychology. Metuchen, NJ: Scarecrow Press, 1981:90–93.*

33. Nash, C., (1982) Psychokinetic control of bacterial growth. *J Soc Psych Res*, 51, 217–221.

34. Nash, C., (1984). Test of psychokinetic control of bacterial mutation. *J Soc Psych Res*, 78, 145–152.

35. Barry, J., (1968) General and comparative study of the psychokinetic effect on a fungus culture. *Journal of Parapsychology*, 32, 237–243

36. Schwartz, S., (2017). Therapeutic intention — into the next generation. *Explore*, 13 (3), 158–162.

37. Nash, C.B., (1982) Psychokinetic control of bacterial growth. In: Roll W.G., Morris R.L., White R.A., eds. *Research in parapsychology. Metuchen, NJ: Scarecrow Press; 1982,* 61–64.

38. Smith, M.J., (1973) Paranormal effects on enzyme activity. *Hum Dimens*, 1, 12–15.

39. Kreiger, D., (1974). Healing by the laying on of hands as a facilitator of bio-energetic change: The response of in vivo human hemoglobin. *Psychoenerg Syst*, (1), 121–129.

40. Schwartz, S., and Dossey, L., (2010) Nonlocality, intention, and observer effects in healing studies: laying a foundation for the future. *Explore*, 6 (5):295–307.

41. Otzi the Iceman. South Tyrol Museum of Archaeology. https://www.iceman.it/en/the-iceman/.

42. White, A., and Ernst, E., (2004). A Brief History of Acupuncture. *Rheumatology*, 43 (5), 662–663, https://doi.org/10.1093/rheumatology/keg005.

43. History of Ayurveda. *National Ayurvedic Medical Association*, https://www.ayurvedanama.org/history-of-ayurveda/.

44. Sheldrake, R, (1981). A New Science of Life: The Hypothesis of Formative Causation. *London: Blond and Briggs*

45. Sheldrake, R., (1995). The Presence of the Past: Morphic Resonance and the Habits of Nature. *Rochester*.

46. Sheldrake, p. 192.

47. Sheldrake, pp. 192-193.

48. Mahlberg, A., (1987). Evidence of collective memory: A test of Sheldrake's theory. *Journal of Analytical Psychology*, 23–34. https://doi.org/10.1111/j.1465-5922.1987.00023.x. https://onlinelibrary.wiley.com/doi/abs/10.1111/j.1465-5922.1987.00023.x .

49. Ertel, S., (1994). Invited Address: Testing Sheldrake's Claim of Morphogenetic Fields. In E. W. Cook and D.L. Delanoy, eds., R*esearch in Parapsychology 1991*, *Metuchen, N.J. and London: Scarecrow Press*, 169- 192.

50. Ibid.

51. Schorn, R., Tappenier, G., and Walde, J., (2006). Analyzing 'spooky action at a distance' concerning brand logos. *Innovative Marketing*, 2 (1), 45–60. https://s3.amazonaws.com/academia.edu.documents/41281873/Analyzing_Spooky_Action_at_a_Distance_20160116-21129-akr04x.pdf.

52. Robbins, K., and Roe, C., (2010). An empirical test of the theory of morphic resonance by using recognition for Chinese symbols. *Explore*, 6, 256–262. https://doi.org/10.1016/j.explore.2010.04.001.

53. Do Buddhists Pray? *Buddhist Dharma Education Association*. https://www.buddhanet.net/e-learning/history/b_faqs.htm.

54. Turow, G., (2005). Auditory Driving as a Ritual Technology: A Review and Analysis, Religious Studies Honors Thesis. *Stanford University*.

55. Baron, S.E., Kose, S., Mu, Q., Borckardt, J., Newberg, A., George, M.S., Kozel, F.A., (2010). Regional brain activation during meditation shows time and practice effects: an exploratory FMRI study. *Evid Based Complement Alternat Med*, 7, 121–127. https://doi.org/10.1093/ecam/nem163 . Epub 2007 December 27. PMID: 18955268.

Is There a Collective Consciousness? The Global Consciousness Project and An Asssessment by Artificial Intelligence

References

1. Atmanspacher, H., and Rickles, D., (2022). Dual-Aspect Monism and the Deep Structure of Meaning. *Routledge*.

2. Bancel, P.A., (2017). Searching for Global Consciousness: A 17-Year Exploration. *Explore*, *13* (2), 94–101. https://doi.org/10.1016/j.explore.2016.12.003

3. Cardeña, E., (2018). The experimental evidence for parapsychological phenomena: A review. *American Psychologist*, *73* (5), 663–677. https://doi.org/10.1037/amp0000236

4. Dillbeck, M., C., and Cavanaugh, K., L., (2016). Societal Violence and Collective Consciousness: Reduction of U.S. Homicide and Urban Violent Crime Rates.

SAGE Open, *6* (2), 2158244016637891. https://doi.org/10.1177/2158244016637891

5. Guyer, P., and Horstmann, R.P., (2021). Idealism. In E.N. Zalta (Ed.), *The Stanford Encyclopedia of Philosophy* (Spring 2021). Metaphysics Research Lab, Stanford University. https://plato.stanford.edu/archives/spr2021/entries/idealism/

6. Hagelin, J.S., Rainforth, M.V., Cavanaugh, K.L., Alexander, C.N., Shatkin, S.F., Davies, J.L., Hughes, A.O., Ross, E., and Orme-Johnson, D.W., (1999). Effects of group practice of the transcendental meditation program on preventing violent crime in Washington, DC: Results of the National Demonstration Project, June-July 1993. *Social Indicators Research*, *47*(2), 153–201.

7. Holmberg, U., (2020). Stock Returns and the Mind: An Unlikely Result that Could Change Our Understanding of Consciousness. *Journal of Consciousness Studies*, *27*(7–8), 31–49.

8. Holmberg, U., (2021). Revisiting Stock Returns and the Mind: Digging Deeper into the Data. *Journal of Consciousness Exploration and Research*, *12*(3), Article 3. https://jcer.com/index.php/jcj/article/view/964

9. Koons, R.C., and Bealer, G., (2010). *The Waning of Materialism* (Kindle Locations). Oxford University Press.

10. Nelson, R., (2017). Weighting the Parameters, a Response to Bancel's "Searching for Global Consciousness: A Seventeen Year Exploration." *Explore*, *13* (2), 102–105. https://doi.org/10.1016/j.explore.2016.12.002

11. Nelson, R., and Bancel, P., (2011). Effects of Mass Consciousness: Changes in Random Data During Global Events. *Explore*, *7* (6), 373–383. https://doi.org/10.1016/j.explore.2011.08.003

12. OpenAI. (2023) *ChatGPT* (March 14 version) [Large language model]. https://chat.openai.com/chat

13. Radin, D., (2023). Anomalous entropic effects in physical systems associated with collective consciousness. *Physics Essays*, *36* (1), 77–86. http://dx.doi.org/10.4006/0836-1398-36.1.77

14. Radin, D.I. (2002). Exploring relationships between random physical events and mass human attention: Asking for whom the bell tolls. *Journal of Scientific Exploration*, *16*(4), 533–548.

15. Reber, A.S., and Alcock, J.E., (2019). Searching for the impossible: Parapsychology's elusive quest. *American Psychologist*, No Pagination Specified-No Pagination Specified. https://doi.org/10.1037/amp0000486

16. Robinson, H., (2020). Dualism. In E.N. Zalta (Ed.), *The Stanford Encyclopedia of Philosophy* (Fall 2020). Metaphysics Research Lab, Stanford University. https://plato.stanford.edu/archives/fall2020/entries/dualism/

17. Nash, C.B., (1982) Psychokinetic control of bacterial growth. In: Roll, W.G., Morris R.L., White R.A., eds. *Research in parapsychology. Metuchen, NJ: Scarecrow Press; 1982,* 61–64.

The Jain view on Consciousness In the Perspective of Contemporary Physics and Neuroscience

Endnotes

i. Astasahastri Vidhyanandi, p 286.

ii. Tattvarathasutra by Uma Swamity, Its Englsih translation as Reality by Pujyapad.V.29, 30,36. *Sat dravya laksnam, utpad vyay dhruavya yuktam sat, gunaparyayabadh dravya.*

iii. Tattvarathasutra by Uma Swamity, Its Englsih translation as Reality by Pujyapad.V 2.8 *Upayaogo laksnama , atmatavadupyogolaksanah*. Syadvadtika p 17.

iv. *Atma hi jnanan-drk saukhya laksana vimalah parah.* Jivandharacarita 7-22.

v. *Dehadibhyo itarita* Jivandharacarita 7-22.

vi. *Panehim caduhim jivadi jivassadi jo hu jivido puvvam. So jivo pana puna balamindiyamau ussaso-* Panchastikaya karika 30 Paraamsukh Prabhavak Mandal Agas 1997.

vii. Tattvarathasutra by Uma Swamity, Its Englsih translation by as Reality by Pujyapad.V 2/12. *Sansarinah trasasthavarah.*

viii. Dravya Sangrah by Nemichandra, Verse 16.

ix. Pudgal unpublished paper by Prof. Dr. Narendra Bhandari chairman Jain Academy of Scholars.

x. Breaking the habit of being yourself, Dr. Joe Dispenza page 14.

xi. Tattvarathasutra by Uma Swamity, Its Englsih translation as Reality by Pujyapad.V 2.8.

xii. *Gatha* 38 page 27. Pancastikaya by Kundakunda English translation by Chakravarty published by Bharatiya Jnanpith New Delhi.

xiii. Dravya Sangrah by Nemichandra Verse 4.

xiv. *Journal of the History of the Behavioral S c W s 16 (1980): 107-117.* 'The trilogy of mind: Cognition, affection, and conation'. Ernest R. Hilgard.

The modern origin of the trilogy was in Germany in the period between Leibniz and Kant. Leibniz (1646-1716) wrote his major works between 1695 and 1716, although some of his writings were not published till after his death; the ***Monadology*** was written in 1714, shortly before the end of his career. Kant (1724-1804) published his ***Critique of Pure Reason*** in 1781, ***Critique of Practical Reason*** in 1788, and his ***Critique of Judgment*** in 1790. In assigning the rise of the faculty psychology and the threefold classification to this period between Leibniz and Kant nearly the whole of the eighteenth century is involved. The particular time is of great importance, for this was the period of the Enlightenment, a period that gave rise to an interest in individual man, his consciousness, and the powers of his mind. This led to an empirical, if introspective, psychology, a necessary background for the experimental psychology which would develop in the nineteenth century. If there was one statement more widely quoted than any other at this time it was Alexander Pope's "The proper study of mankind is man."

xv. Tattvarathasutra by Uma Swamity, Its Englsih translation as Reality by Pujyapad.V 2.7,8.

xvi. "The five causes of bondage are: deluded world-view, non-abstinence, laxity, passions (tainted emotions) and the actions of the body, speech and mind". That which is', by N M Tatia, published in India by Motilal Banarasidass New Delhi. 8/1

xvii. 21 Lessons for the 21st century by Yuval Noah Harari, published by Penguin Random House UK, p. 69.

xviii. (Wikipedia, *Emotion*). Cited October 1, 2021.

xix. Molecules of Emotion by Candance Pert, published by Scribner New York.

xx. Tattvarathasutra by Uma Swamity, Its Englsih translation by as Reality by Pujyapad.V 2, 25-29.

xxi. Behavioral, Spiritual and Scientific Correlates of Leshya. Paper presented by Prof. Viney Jain on the Jain Way of Life, New Delhi, February 6-7, 2009.

xxii. *Gatha* 16, p. 12. Pancastikaya by Kundakunda English translation by Chakravarty, published by Bharatiya Jnanpith, New Delhi.

xxiii. *Gatha,* 16 p. 12. Pancastikaya by Kundakunda English translation by Chakravarty, published by Bharatiya Jnanpith, New Delhi.

xxiv. 'Know that all states of being—be they goodness, passion, ignorance are manifested by My energy. I am, in one sense, everything, but I am independent. I am not under the modes of material nature, for they, on the contrary, are within Me.' 'Bhagavad Gita as it is', by His Divine Grace A.C. Bhakti Vedanta Swami Prabhupada.

References

1. Dispenza, J., (2012). Breaking the habit of being yourself . Hay House publishers (India)

2. Goleman, D., (1995). Emotional Intelligence. *Bantam Books, Inc.*

3. Jain, S., C., (1978). Structure and function of soul in Jainism. Bharatiya Jnanpith.

4. Pert, C., (1999). Molecule of Emotion. *Scribner.*

Ātmā, Soul in Jainism Described as a Hologram

Endnotes

i. Knapton, S., (2014). Half of world's animals have disappeared since 1970. *The Telegraph,* http://www.telegraph.co.uk/news/earth/wildlife/11129163/Half-of-worlds-animals-have-disappeared-since-1970.html.

ii. Giant Panda. *WWF* https://www.worldwildlife.org/species/giant-panda

iii. Holography. *Wikipedia,* https://en.wikipedia.org/wiki/Holography.

iv. *Triloy Pannati*, Jain, R.C., 1975

v. Jinarajadasa, C. (2003) [1938]. "Thought Forms".

Occult investigations, a description of the work of Annie Besant and C.W. Leadbeater. Whitefish, MT: Kessinger Publishing. p. 69. ISBN 0766130347.

vi. Kachhara N.L., (2014). Scientific Explorations of Jain Doctrines: 2 Volumes, *Motilal Banarsidass Publishers.*

vii. Atomic theory of John Dalton. *Britannica* https://www.britannica.com/biography/John-Dalton/Atomic-theory

viii. Terazawa, H., (1980) Subquark model of leptons and quarks. Phys. Rev. D 22, 184.

ix. http://www.allthingspsychic.com/howtoattainsiddhi.html

x. http://www.allthingspsychic.com/howtoattainsiddhi.html

xi. Heim et al., 2008.

References

1. Pokharna, S., S., (2022). A Comparative Study of the Concept of Consciousness in Science and Jain Philosophy. *Indian Council of Philosophical Research (ICPR).*

2. Nandighoshvijayji, Suyodayasuriji and Nemisurishwaraji (2000). Scientific Secrets of Jainism: An Exploration of the Parallels between Modern Physics and Jain Philosophy. *Ahmedabad: Research Institute of Scientific Secrets from Indian Oriental Scriptures (RISSIOS).* http://www.rissios.org/image/SSJeng.pdf

3. Mehta, D., (2022). Upnishado ni Jaim Bhautik Vigyan Ni Holographic Theory Vadhe Purna Akhandit Samagrata Pravtarti hova nu Pratipadan Kare Chhai (Language Like Upanishads, the theory of Hologram of physical sciences also imply a total, complete, unbroken reality). *Gujarat Samachar*, Ahmedabad Edition, November 2, 2022.

4. Rulin, X., (2022). Holographic Principle, String Theory, and Grand Unification Theory, The Science of Consciousness (Abstracts of the Conference held from April 18-22) *Centre*

for Consciousness Studies, The University of Arizona 157-158.

5. Anantswamy, A., (2023). The Holographic Universe Turns 25. *Scientific American*, 58-61.

6. Marcer, P.J., and Schempp, W., (1997). Model of the Neuron Working by Quantum Holography. *The Slovene Society Informtika, Ljubljana*, 21 (3) 517-532.

7. Philips, S., M., (1980). Extra Sensory Perception of Quarks. *The Theosophical Publishing House Madras*.

8. Besant, A., Leadbeater, C., W., and Dasa, C.M.J., (1908). Occult chemistry : A series of clairvoyant observations on the chemical elements. *Theosophical Society*.

9. Goldsmith, E., (1990). Evolution, Neo-Darwinism and the Paradigm of Science. *The Ecologist*, 20 (2) 67.

10. Dennett, D., (1995). Darwin's Dangerous Idea: Evolution and the Meanings of Life, Simon and Schuster.

11. von Bertalanffy, L. (1976). General System Theory: Foundations, Development, Applications (rev. ed.). *New York, NY: George Braziller*.

12. Zeleznikar Anton P. (1997). Consciousness as Informational Phenomenalism: An Informational, Phenomenological, Philosophical, Neural and Quantum-Mechanical View. *Informatica: An International Journal of Computing and Informatics*, 21 (3)

13. Mitchell, E.D., and Staretz., R., (2017). The Quantum Hologram and the Nature of Consciousness. *Consciousness and the Universe: Quantum Physics, Evolution, Brain and Mind*, edited by Roger Penrose, Stuart Hameroff, and Subhash Kak, 82–114. Cambridge, MA: Cosmology Science Publishers.

14. Marcer, P., and Rowlands P., (2017). Nilpotent Quantum Mechanics: Analog and Applications. *Frontiers in Physics* 28, 1–8. doi: 10.3389/fphy.2017.00028.

15. Talbot, M. (2011) The Holographic Universe, *Harper Perennial.*

16. Mehta (1998) Jain philosophy: An introduction, *Bhartiya Vidhya Bhawan*

17. Philips, S.M., (1999). ESP of Quarks and Superstrings. *New Age International* (P).

18. Philips, S., M., (1980). Extra Sensory Perception of Quarks. *The Theosophical Publishing House Madras.*

19. Phillips, S., (1995). Extrasensory Perception of Sub Atomic Particles. *Journal of Scientific Exploration*, 9, (4) 489-525).

20. Dobyns, H.Y. (1995). Report of Referee on "Extrasensory Perception of Sub Atomic Particles", in *Journal of Scientific Exploration*, 9 (4), 527-538, (original paper pp. 489-525). Replies to the Report by Stephen Phillips (539-548).

21. Billimoria, D., (2006). The Snake and Rope: Problems of Western Science Resolved by Occult Science. *The Theosophical Publishing House, Madras.*

22. Shah, J.L.P., (2003). Pudgal: Aik adhyyan, Phd thesis. *Gujarat Vidhyapeeth, Ahmedabad.*

23. Pokharna, S., S., (2019). Manohar Lal Kalra, Rajmal Jain, Samani Chaitanya Prajna (2019) Clairvoyant Observations of Atoms and Quarks Support Jainism, ABLJTS and TDVP models that knowledge is structured in the consciousness. *Transactions of the International School for Jain Studies (ISJS)*, 23-44. http://online.pubhtml5.com/hkhn/ycxc/#p=1.

24. Pokharna, S.S., (2019). Quantum Reality and Concept of Śūnya: Need for an Integrative Approach in Quantum Reality and Theory of Shunnya by Siddheshwar Rameshwar Bhatt. *Springer Verlag*, 291-324.

25. Neppe, V.M., Pokharna, S., S., and Close E., (2019). The Remarkable Besant-Leadbeater studies in Quantal Clairvoyance (quantal remote viewing) correlate profoundly with the Triadic Rotational Units of Equivalence Quantal Models in Triadic Dimensional Vortical Paradigm. *IQNJ*, 11 (3) 5-71.

On Conscience and Smysl (Sense) or Lost in Translation

Endnotes

i. Descartes, R. (1670). Meditationes de prima philosophia. Amstelodami. 1670. Appendix. Режим доступа: https://books.google.com/books?id=kuVuXpvNqLoCandprintsec=frontcover#v=onepageandqandf=false p.112

ii. Op. cit., p.69.

iii. See https://revistas.pucsp.br/index.php/bakhti%20niana/index

References

1. Smirnov, A., V., (2019). Is a process-based logic possible? Ishraq: Islamic Philosophy Yearbook: 2019. № 9. — Moscow: Sadra, 2019. p. 287-297. https://avsmirnov.info/eng/pube/Smirnov_PLogic.pdf

2. Paribok, A., V., (2018). The Impasse of Ancient Tragical Weltanschauung and Two Positive Ways Out. *Proceedings of the Third International Conference on Contemporary Education, Social Sciences and Humanities (ICCESSH 2018)* https://www.academia.edu/86938572/The_Impasse_of_Ancient_Tragical_Weltanschauung_and_Two_Positive_Ways_Out

3. Cassin, B., (dir.) (2004). Vocabulaire européen des philosophies: dictionnaire des intraduisibles. *Le Seuil/Le Robert.*

4. Kant, I. (1997) Critique of Pure Reason, P. Guyer and A. Wood (trans.). *Cambridge University Press* https://cpb-us-w2.wpmucdn.com/u.osu.edu/dist/5/25851/files/2017/09/kant-first-critique-cambridge-1m89prv.pdf

5. Husserl, E., (1983). Ideas: A General Introduction to Pure Phenomenology, First Book. Newly translated with the full title by Fred Kersten. *Kluwer Academic Publishers*. https://www.finophd.eu/wp-content/uploads/2018/01/Husserl-Ideas-First-Book.pdf

6. Smirnov, A. (2018). The finer points of a culture's thought. *Russian Studies in Philosophy*, *56*(3), 153–155. https://doi.org/10.1080/10611967.2018.1459374

Action-Feeling and Self-Conscious Mind

Endnotes

i. Mañjuśrī: Saptasatika: 213.

References

1. Brown, J.W. (2020). Origins of subjectivity. *Journal of mind and behavior*, 41, 267-276.

2. Brown, J.W. (2021). The mind/brain state. *Journal of mind and behavior*, 42, 1-16.

3. Weiszaecker, V. von (1939/1958). Le cycle de la structure. *Desclee-De Brouwer*.

4. Bernstein N. (1967). The Coordination and Regulation of Movements. *Pergamon*.

5. Pears, D. (1963). Freedom and the Will. *MacMillan and C*o.

6. O'Connor, T. (ed. 1995). Agents, Causes, Events. *Oxford: Oxford University Press*.

7. Brown, J.W. and Zhadiaiev (2022). From drive to value. *Process Studies*, 51, 204-220 https://doi.org/10.5406/21543682.51.2.04.

8. Luria, A. (1969). The Mind of a Mnemonist, *New York: Avon.*

9. Brown, J.W. (1996). Time, will and mental process. *New York: Plenum.*

10. Libet, B. (1985). Unconscious cerebral initiative and the role of conscious will in voluntary activity. *Behavioral and Brain Sciences,* 8, 529-566.

11. Stroud, J. (1956). The fine structure of psychological time. In Quastler, H. (Ed) Information Theory in Psychology. *Free Press, IL.*

12. Anscombe, G.E.M. (1963). Intention, second edition. *Oxford: Blackwell.*

Creative Consciousness: Its Neuroscience, Nonlinear Dynamics and Trance

Endnotes

i. Noetic Sciences, 2022.

ii. Grosso, 1997.

References

1. Zausner, T. (2022a). The creative trance: Altered states of consciousness and the creative process. *Cambridge: Cambridge University Press.*

2. James, W. (1895/1929). The varieties of religious experience. *New York: Random House.*

3. Weinstein, G. (2017). Einstein's pathway to the special theory of relativity. (2nd Ed.) *Newcastle upon Tyne: Cambridge Scholars Publishing.*

4. Goertzel, V., and Goertzel, M., G., (1962). Cradles of eminence. *Boston: Little, Brown and Company.*

5. Bannister, R., (2018/1955). The four-minute mile. *Guilford, CT: Lyons Press.*

6. Keller, E.F. (1983). Feeling for the organism: The life and work of Barbara McClintock. *W.H. Freeman.*

7. Zetlin, M. (2018). In a single sentence of her google doodle, Dr. Jane Goodall teaches a life lesson we all need to learn. April 22. Retrieved from www.inc.com.

8. Murphy, M., and White, R.A., (1995). In the Zone: Transcendent Experience in Sports. *Penguin Group.*

9. Woolaver, L. (1995). The illuminated life of Maud Lewis. Photographs by Bob Brooks. *Halifax, Nova Scotia: Nimbus Publishing/ The Art Gallery of Nova Scotia.*

10. Woolaver, L. (1997). Christmas with Maud Lewis. Photographs by Bob Brooks. *Fredericton, New Brunswick: Goose Lane Editions.*

11. Zausner, T. (2016). When walls become doorways: Creativity and the transforming illness, new edition as e-book (Kindle DX version). Retrieved from Amazon.com. (Original hardcover edition, 2006).

12. Kubota, I., (1984). A personal chronology by Itchiku Kubota. In T. Yamanobe (ed.), Opulence: The Kimonos and robes of Itchiku Kubota. *Tokyo: Kodansha International.* 128-130.

13. Harmon, W. and Rheingold, H. (1984). Higher creativity: Liberating the unconscious for breakthrough insights. *Los Angeles: Jeremy P. Tarcher.*

14. Krippner, S. (1999). Altered and transitional states. In *M. A. Runco and S. R. Pritzger (Eds.).*

15. Caruana, W. (1993). Aboriginal Art. *New York: Thames and Hudson.*

16. Sinha, A. (1995). Nature in Hindu art, architecture and landscape, *Landscape Research*, 20(1), 3-10.

17. Shelley, M.W. (2022). Frankenstein, or the New Prometheus. Kindle edition (Original work published, 1831).

18. Currey, M. (2019). Daily rituals: Women at work. *New York: Knopf.*

19. Kounios, J. and Beeman, M. (2015). The eureka factor: Creative insights and the brain. *London: Windmill Books.*

20. Moeckel, R., and Montgomery, R., (2013). Symmetric Regularization, Reduction and Blow-Up of the Planar Three-Body Problem. *Pacific Journal of Mathematics*, 262 (1), 129-189

21. Zausner, T. (2022b). Embracing the Infinite: Creativity and the Nonlinear Self. In *Nonlinear Psychology: Keys to Chaos and Creativity in Mind and Nature*, D. Schuldberg, R. Richards and S. Guisinger (Eds.), Oxford, UK: Oxford University Press.

22. Abell, A., M., (1994). Talks With Great Composers. *New York: Carol Publishing Group*. (Original work published 1955).

23. Rowden, Terry. (2012). The songs of blind folk: African American musicians and the cultures of blindness. *Ann Arbor: The University of Michigan Press.*

24. Puri, S. S. (2011). Divine women: On young female middle class Bharatanatyam dancers in Delhi. *Spirituality, Religiosity and Secular Lives: Feminist Challenges for Theory and Practice*, 75-94.

25. Erzen, J. (2008) The Dervishes Dance – The Sacred Ritual of Love, *Contemporary Aesthetics* (Journal Archive), 6 (7).

26. Di Biase, F. (2009). A holoinformational model of consciousness. *Quantum Biosystems*, 3, 207-220.

27. Schwartz, S. A. (2010). Nonlocality and exceptional experiences: A study of genius, religious epiphany, and the psychic. *explore*, July/August, 6(4), 227-236. DOI: 10.1016/j.explore.2010.04.008.

28. Murphy, T. (2019). "Solving the hard problem": Consciousness as an intrinsic property of magnetic fields. *Journal of Consciousness Exploration and Research*, 10(8), 646-59.

29. Mach, E. (1991). Great contemporary pianists speak for themselves: Two volumes bound as one. *New York: Dover Publications*. (Original work published 1980 and 1988).

30. Zausner, T. (2020). Embracing the Infinite: Creativity and the Nonlinear Self. In D. Schuldberg, R.Richards, and S. Guisinger (Eds.), Chaos and Nonlinear Psychology. *Oxford University Press*.

31. Zausner, T. (2011). Transcending the self through art: Altered states of consciousness and anomalous events during the creative process. *Journal of Consciousness Exploration and Research*, (October), 2(7), p. 889-1022.

32. Cheney, M. (1981). Tesla: Man out of time. *New York: Barnes and Noble Books*.

33. Martin, T.C. (1992). The researches and writings of Nikola Tesla. 2nd ed. *Barnes and Noble Books*.

34. David-Neel, A. (1971). Magic and mystery in Tibe*t*. (The Bodley Head, Trans). *Baltimore: Penguin Books*. (Original work published 1929).

35. Rao, R. (1988). The Chessmaster and his moves. *New Delhi: Vision Books*.

New Breakthroughs in Understanding Consciousness: From Brain to Internet to Soul

Endnotes

i. Werbos, P., J., (2017) New Technology Options and Threats To Detect and Combat Terrorism. Gordon, T. J., Florescu, E., and Glenn, J. C. (Eds.), Identification of Potential Terrorists and Adversary Planning: Emerging Technologies and New Counter-terror Strategies (Vol. 132). IOS Press. (NATO workshop series.) https://werbos.com/NATO_terrorism.pdf.

ii. Werbos, P.J., (2023) Response Submitted to NSF/TIP

request for guidance on new roadmap. https://drpauljohn.blogspot.com/2023/06/draft-response-nsftip-request-for.html

iii. ICCSI 2022 https://iccsi2022.agist.org/

iv. Shaw (1921). https://www.gutenberg.org/ebooks/13084 https://www.amazon.com/kindle-dbs/entity/author/B000AQ1ZEO

v. Werbos, P.J., (2023). A true ghost story https://drpauljohn.blogspot.com/2010/04/true-ghost-story.html

vi. Werbos, P.J., (2022). Afterlife and reincarnation — neither yes nor no but the middle way https://drpauljohn.blogspot.com/2022/11/afterlife-and-reincarnation-neither-yes.html

vii. Werbos, P.J., (2022). Multiverse versus multithread — a new view of how our universe works. https://drpauljohn.blogspot.com/2022/10/multiverse-versus-multithread-new-view.html

viii. Werbos, P.J. (2023). Understanding our relation with god—a new understanding. https://drpauljohn.blogspot.com/2023/11/understanding-our-relation-with-god-new.html

References

1. Werbos, P.,J., (2019). Quantum Measurement, Consciousness, and the Soul: A New, Alternative Position. *Activitas Nervosa Superior*, *61* (1), 41-47.

2. Werbos, P.J., (2001). What do neural nets and quantum theory tell us about mind and reality?. *Advances in Consciousness Research*, *33*, pp.63-88. https://arxiv.org/pdf/q-bio/0311006.pdf.

3. Werbos, P.J., (2022). Quantum technology to expand soft computing. *Systems and Soft Computing*, *4*, 200031. https://doi.org/10.1016/j.sasc.2022.200031.

4. Werbos, P.J., and Davis, J.J., (2016). Regular cycles of forward and backward signal propagation in prefrontal cortex and in consciousness. *Frontiers in Systems Neuroscience*, p.97. https://doi.org/10.3389/fnsys.2016.00097.

5. NSF (2007). Cognitive Optimization and Prediction. *Emerging Frontiers in Research and Innovation 2008 (EFRI-2008)* https://www.nsf.gov/pubs/2007/nsf07579/nsf07579.htm.

6. NSF (2021). BRAID. *Emerging Frontiers in Research and Innovation (EFRI-2022/23),* https://www.nsf.gov/pubs/2021/nsf21615/nsf21615.htm.

7. Werbos, P.J., (2014). From ADP to the Brain: Foundations, Roadmap, Challenges and Research Priorities https://arxiv.org/pdf/1404.0554.pdf.

8. Deutsch, D., (1985). Quantum theory, the Church–Turing principle and the universal quantum computer. *Proceedings of the Royal Society of London. A. Mathematical and Physical Sciences* 400.1818 (1985): 97-117.

9. Werbos, P.J., (1992). Approximate Dynamic Programming for Real. Time Control and Neural Modeling. *White and Sofge Eds, Handbook of Intelligent Control, Van Nostrand 1992*. http://www.werbos.com/HICChapter13.pdf.

10. Bear, M.F., Connors, B., W., Paradiso, M., A., (2020). Neuroscience: Exploring the Brain, Enhanced Fourth Edition. *Jones and Bartlett Learning*.

11. Bernard J.B., (2005). Global workspace theory of consciousness: Toward a cognitive neuroscience of human experience. *Progress in brain research* 150: 45-53. (Also see the chapter by Baars in Kozma and Freeman).

12. Goldman-Rakic, Patricia, S., and Hoi-Chung, Leung., (2002). Functional architecture of the dorsolateral prefrontal cortex in monkeys and humans. *Principles of frontal lobe function* 85-95.

13. Kuhn, Thomas S. (1970). The structure of scientific revolutions. *University of Chicago Press: Chicago*, 111 https://www.pdfdrive.com/the-structure-of-scientific-revolutions-50th-anniversary-edition-e175980575.html.

14. Olding, H.D., (1949) The Organization of Behavior: A Psychological Theory. *New York: Wiley, 1949.*

15. David, B., (2012). Existence. *Doherty Associates, LLC, TomandCo*, ISBN 9780765303615.

16. Carmeli, M., (2001). Classical Fields. *World Scientific Publishing Company*. Retrieved from https://www.perlego.com/book/853122/classical-fields-general-relativity-and-gauge-theory-pdf.

17. Werbos and Fleury (2018). Time-Symmetric Quantum Measurement: Theoretical Formulation and Status of Experiments. *Research gate* https://www.researchgate.net/publication/327164414_WerbosFleury_v2.

AI, Consciousness and Indic Perspectives

Endnotes

i. In contrast, consider the 4-colour problem which asks whether any planar graph can be coloured with 4 colours. The first proof used a computer in 1976 as it needed to check 1936 configurations, later reduced to 1478. A shorter proof was developed in 1998 which was used as a basis for a formal proof using a proof assistant Coq ('05) but this also needed to check 633 cases. See Georges Gonthier, "Formal Proof: The Four-Colour Theorem," Notices of the AMS, Dec 2008. This is an instructive example as the first computer proof was not received well as the correctness of the program proving the theorem itself could not be proved (for example, it used low-level IBM assembler code for speed) and also that no "mathematical" insight was generated by the discharging of the many cases using a computer. The Coq effort developed newer mathematical techniques and this proof can be said to be more "mathematical" due to the new insights developed as part of the Coq proof. For a recent perspective, see Kevin Buzzard, "Computers and Mathematics", London Math. Soc., September 2019.

ii. See wikipedia article of the same name for details.

iii. Note that alternate translations exist; we are giving what seems to be the most widely accepted ones. We also give an alternative one below.

iv. A central view in Kāshmir Shaiva thinking is the immanence of Siva and its celebration. Not only does Siva create the world, every atom manifests his power and glory, and the universe comes into being due to the spanda or vibration that he sets forth.

v. Pl. see discussion below

vi. Non-duality in the Indic mind sciences can mean the "negation of dualistic thinking", the "non- plularity of the world", or the "the non-difference of subject and object". See Ch1, David Loy," Non-duality", 1997

vii. In Vijnānabhairava, 65 we find:

सर्वं जगत्स्वदहें वा स्वानन्दभरितं स्मरेत् ।
युगपत्स्वामृतेनैव परानन्दमयो भवेत् ॥६५॥

"One should contemplate simultaneously on the entire universe or on one's own body filled with the bliss of the self. Then through one's own nectar, one becomes alive with the supreme bliss." Here, the equivalence of one's own body with the universe is posited. Instead of dismissing the body as locus of many ills, it enjoins us to think of it as the storehouse of bliss. Harsha V. Dehejia ""Pārvatī-darpana: An exposition of Kāshmir Saivism through the images of Siva and Pārvatī," Ch.2., MBLD, 1997.

viii. Mind and Matter, '59.

ix. While there are differences between these two Indic perspectives, they may be complementary just as in quantum mechanics. F. Theodor Stcherbatsky in "Buddhist Logic," Vol I, p. 83 writes that "In the fifth century CE, there was a bitter argument in India between the Sankhya Hindus and the Buddhists about the nature of Universal Flux. Debates were held which lasted for days, and would attract huge crowds. According to the Buddhists: "The phenomena consist of an infinity of discrete moments following one another almost without intervals. There is no matter at all, flashes of energy follow one another and produce the illusion of stabilised phenomena. The universe is a staccato movement." While according to the Hindus: "The phenomena are nothing but waves or fluctuations standing out upon the background of an eternal, all-pervading undifferentiated Matter with which they are identical. The universe represents a legato movement." This also mirrors the dispute between two Quantum pioneers: "Despite their radically different worldview, shortly after their publication it was shown that Matrix Mechanics and Wave Mechanics are mathematically identical. In fact, Schrödinger was one of the people who did the proof. Despite their formal equivalence, there seems to be more than just logic involved in the interpretation of the mathematics. For example, Heisenberg wrote: "The more I ponder the physical part of Schrðdinger's theory, the more disgusting it appears to me." While Schrödinger wrote:"If one has to stick to this damned quantum jumping, then I regret ever having been involved in this thing."

x. Berzin, "Primary Minds and 51 Mental factors".

xi. Gīta:

ध्यायतो विषयान्पुंसः सङ्गस्तेषूपजायते ।
सङ्गात्सञ्जायते कामः कामात्क्रोधोऽभिजायते ।।६२।।
क्रोधाद्भवति सम्मोहः सम्मोहात्स्मृतिविभ्रमः ।
स्मृतिभ्रंशाद्बुद्धिनाशो बुद्धिनाशात्प्रणश्यति ।।६३।।

Briefly, the senses rest on objects and from this attachment arises, from attachment arises desire, from desire arises anger, from anger delusion that leads to bewilderment of memory which leads to loss of intelligence. From that, downfall. One can view this as a simple state transition model.

xii. This example is based on Jyoti Mohan, "Understanding Abhinaya," MHRD.

xiii. There is an alternate view that rasa, being brahmānandasahodara, can have rati (sensuous) content whereas brahmānanda does not.

xiv. Note that we leave ākāsha as an untranslatable as it is not clear what it stands for though "ether" or space or sky has been used as its translation often; we prefer the meaning of space if need be.

xv. See also Lakshman Jajoo website http://www.lakshmanjooacademy.org/

xvi. http://atonal.ucdavis.edu/~petr/ for details. P. Janata surmised that a hub for emotions, music and memory exists through a combination of previous discoveries: i) an early study showed mPFC consistently active when musicians listened to musical tones ii) music serves as a potent trigger for retrieving memories iii) research in social neuroscience showed that the location of self- referential activity—how we maintain our sense of self, feel, think, infer what others are thinking— in the same region of the brain iv) a large amount of anecdotal information that patients with Alzheimers, whose medial prefrontal cortex is the last area of the brain to atrophy, brighten up, dance, sing and even recognise wrong notes in music from their past.

xvii. Or, in general, music through mirror neuronal complex as we can play music in our head

xviii. V. Raghavan, Kama/Aesthetics in "Sources of Indian Tradition", p. 262

xix. Similar to von Neuman's "mathematical" argument that a self-reproducing automata is non- unitary.

xx. Tattvasangraha, translated by Ganganatha Jha, Baroda Oriental Institute, 1937.

xxi. Sartre (in "Being and Nothingness") makes the same argument in a more obvious form ". . . if my consciousness of the table were not consciousness of being consciousness of the table, it would then be consciousness of that table without consciousness of being so. In other words, it would be a consciousness ignorant of itself, an unconsciousness – which is absurd".

xxii. A Large Language Model (LLM) with 137 billion weights created at Google Research (Thoppilan, 2022).

xxiii. A Large Language Model with 175 billion weights that was created at OpenAI (Brown et al., 2020).

xxiv. https://www.overshootday.org/how-many-earths-or-countries-do-we-need

xxv. Bhagavad Gīta. 3.17

यस्त्वात्मरतिरेव स्यादात्मतृप्तश्च मानवः ।
आत्मन्येव च सन्तुष्टस्तस्य कार्यं न विद्यते ॥१७॥

one who delights (or is self-sufficient) in the self, or is content within the self, or is content with the self, he alone is free (or, "he is free of work").

Also, in Muṇḍaka Upanishad (3.1.4):

प्रणो ह्येष यः सर्वभूतैर्विभाति विजानन्विद्वान्भवते नातिवादी ।
आत्मक्रीड आत्मरतिः क्रियावानेष ब्रह्मविदां वरिष्ठः ॥४॥

This is, indeed. *Prana, i.e.*, *Isvara*, shining variously with all living beings. Knowing him, the wise man becomes not a talker regarding anything else. Sporting in self, delighted in self and doing enjoined works, this man is the best of those who know the *Brahman.*

xxvi. There are theories that attempt to explain layers in networks using control theory in the context of losses of packets (see works by S. Low) but "emergence" is still not the focus of explanation.

xxvii. Charaka also in Āyurveda.

xxviii. See, for example, journal articles in IEEE Transactions on Affective Computing.

xxix. https://insights.sei.cmu.edu/blog/revealing-true-emotions-through-micro-expressions-a-machine-learning-approach/#:~:text=Micro%2Dexpressions%2D%2Dinvoluntary%2C%20fleeting,and%20are%20universal%20across%20cultures.

xxx. Stacy Marsella, Jonathan Gratch, and Paulo Petta, "Computational Models of Emotion", in Blueprint for Affective Computing (Series in Affective Science), No. 2010

xxxi. Rājaraman (notes from a talk.)

xxxii. Quote from the wikipedia entry on "Qualia".

References

1. Thompson, E., (2015). Dreamless Sleep, the Embodied Mind, and Consciousness: The Relevance of a Classical Indian Debate to Cognitive Science. In Metzinger, T., and Windt, J.M., (Eds). *Open MIND:* 37(T).

2. Albers, D.J., Steen, L.A., and Knuth, D., (1982). A Conversation with Don Knuth: Part 2. *The Two-Year College Mathematics Journal*, 13 (2), 128–141. https://doi.org/10.2307/3026489

3. Wigderson, A., (2019). Mathematics and Computation: A Theory Revolutionizing Technology and Science.

Princeton: Princeton University Press, https://doi.org/10.1515/9780691192543.

4. Rao, C.R., and Lovric, M. M. (2016). Testing Point Null Hypothesis of a Normal Mean and the Truth: 21st Century Perspective. *Journal of Modern Applied Statistical Methods*, 15(2), 2-21. doi: 10.22237/jmasm/1478001660

5. Melloni, L., Mudrik, L., Pitts, M., and Koch, C., (2021). Making the hard problem of consciousness easier. *Science*. 372, 911-912. 10.1126/science.abj3259.

6. Ganeri, J., (2018). Attention, Not Self. *Oxford University Press*, ISBN 13: 9780198757405, ISBN 10: 0198757409

7. Gopinath, K., (2018). Towards a Computational Theory for Rasa. In K.S. Kannan, Western Indology on Rasa, A Pūrvapaksha (ed.), *Infinity Foundation India*.

8. Nakahira, Y., Liu, Q., Sejnowski, T.J., and Doyle, J.C., (2021). Diversity-enabled sweet spots in layered architectures and speed-accuracy trade-offs in sensorimotor control. In *Proceedings of the National Academy of Sciences U.S.A*, 118, e1916367118. 10.1073/pnas.1916367118.

9. Li, J.S.L., (2022). Internal Feedback in Biological Control: Locality and System Level Synthesis, *2022 American Control Conference (ACC)*, 474-479, doi: 10.23919/ACC53348.2022.9867769.

10. Patterson, D., Gonzalez, J., Hölzle, U., Le, Q., Liang, C., Munguia, L.M., Rothchild, D., So, D.R., Texier, M., and Dean, J., (2022). The Carbon Footprint of Machine Learning Training Will Plateau, Then Shrink. *Computer* 55 (7), 18–28. https://doi.org/10.1109/MC.2022.3148714

11. Beniaguev, D., Segev, I., London, M., (2021). Single cortical neurons as deep artificial neural networks. *Neuron*, 109 (17), 2727-2739.e3, ISSN 0896-6273,mhttps://doi.org/10.1016/j.neuron.2021.07.002.

12. Bratman, S., (2021). Spontaneous Order and the Origin of Life.

Mathematics, Artificial Intelligence, and Consciousness

References

1. Dehaene, S., (2017). H. Lau and S. Kouider, What is consciousness, and could machines have it? *Science* 358 (6362), 486-492.

2. S. Kak, (2022). The limits to machine consciousness. *Journal of Artificial Intelligence and Consciousness* 9, 59-72.

3. Koch, C., (2019). The Feeling of Life Itself. *The MIT Press*.

4. Signorelli, C.M., and Meling, D., (2021). Towards new concepts for a biological neuroscience of consciousness. *Cognitive Neurodynamics* 15, 783–804.

5. S. Kak, Number of autonomous cognitive agents in a neural network. *Journal of Artificial Intelligence and Consciousness* 9, 227-240, 2022.

6. Penrose, R., (1994). Shadows of the Mind: A Search for the Missing Science of Consciousness. *Oxford University Press*.

7. Kobbert, M., (1986). Psychology of Art (Kunstpsychologie). *Wissenschaftliche Buchgesellschaft*.

8. Kak, S., (2023). The epistemic view of quantum reality. In Quantum and Consciousness *Revisited*. M.C. Kafatos, D. Banerji, and D. Struppa (editors). *DK Publishers*, 219-251.

9. Kak, S., (2023). Science of consciousness and the Veda. *Brahmavidyā: The Adyar Library Bulletin* 87, 237-263, 2023.

10. R. Torella, *The Ishvarapratyabhijnakarika of Utpaladeva with the Author's Vrtti.* Istituto Italiano Per Il Medio Ed Estremo Oriente, 1994.

11. S. Kak, *The Vedic Tradition: Cosmos, Connections, and Consciousness*. SVYASA University, 2022.

12. R. Kanigel, *The Man Who Knew Infinity: A Life of the Genius Ramanujan*. Charles Scribner's Sons, 1991.

13. B. Misra and E.C.G. Sudarshan, The Zeno's paradox in quantum theory. *Journal of Mathematical Physics*. **18** (4): 756–763, 1977.

Instability: How to Understand Consciousness on the Levels of Quantum Theory, Organisms, and the Cosmos

Endnotes

i. See also: Heisenberg W. (1958). Physics and Philosophy, Harper, New York, N.Y.).

ii. See also: Von Neumann J. (2013). Mathematische grundlagen der quantenmechanik. Springer-Verlag; Berlin, Germany.

References

1. Tegmark, M., (2014) Consciousness as a state of matter. arXiv:1405.0493v1.

2. Tononi, G., (2008) Consciousness as integrated information: A provisional manifesto. *The Biological Bulletin*, 215, 216–242.

3. Patanjali, M., (2010). Yoga Sutras (Shearer A. Trans. The Yoga Sutras of Patanjali.). *Crown Publishing*.

4. Guth, A.H., (1986). Inflationary universe: A possible solution to the horizon and flatness problems. *Inflationary Cosmology*, 23 (2), 14.

5. Schmitt, C.B., (1996). Perennial Philosophy From Styeuco to Leibniz dalam Ahmad Norma Permata (Ed.), Perennialisme Melacak Jejak Filsafat Abadi. *Tiara Wacana, Yogyakarta*.

6. Huxley, A., (2014). The Perennial Philosophy, *McClelland and Stewart.*

7. MacAulay, T.B., (1835). Minute. http://www.columbia.edu/itc/mealac/pritchett/00generallinks/macaulay/txt_minute_education_1835.html.

8. Müller, F.M., (1859). A History of Ancient Sanskrit Literature so far as it illustrates the Primitive Religion of the Brahmans, *Williams and Norgate.*

9. Vivekananda, S., (1893). Four Lectures in the World Parliament of Religions: Response to welcome (11 September); Why we disagree (15 September), Paper on Hinduism (19 September), and Religion not the crying need of India (20 September). *Chicago: World Parliament of Religions.* Also in CoWk. 1893 December 15 (1), 1-25.

10. Vivekananda, S., (2012). Gyana Yoga – The Yoga of Knowledge. *Advaita Ashrama.*

11. Huxley, A., and Smith, H., (2013). The divine within: Selected writings on enlightenment, *Harper Collins.*

12. Yogananda, P., (2009). Autobiography of a Yogi. *Yogoda Satsanga society of India.*

13. Muktananda, S., (1971). Guru: Chitshaktivilas: the Play of Consciousness. *Harper and Row.*

14. Yogi, M.M., (2001). Science of Being and Art of Living: Transcendental Meditation. *Plume.*

15. Vasudev, S.J., (2007). Mystics Musings. *Wisdom Tree.*

16. Nagendra, H.R., and Nagarathna, R., (2012). Yoga for common ailments. *Bangalore: Swami Vivekananda Yoga Prakashan.*

17. Sri, M., (2010). Apprenticed to a Himalayan Master, *Magenta Press.*

18. Yogi, M., M., (1974). Maharishi International University Catalogue, 1974/5. *MIU Press.*

19. Shear, J., (Ed.) (1997). Explaining consciousness: The hard problem. *MIT Press*.

20. Chalmers, D., J., (1993). Toward a theory of consciousness. *Indiana University*.

21. Chalmers, D., (1995). Facing up to the Problem of Consciousness. *Journal of Consciousness studies*, 2(3), 200-219.

22. Chalmers, D., (1997). Moving forward on the problem of consciousness. *Journal of Consciousness Studies*, 4(1), 3-46.

23. Chalmers, D., (1997). The conscious mind: In search of a fundamental theory, *Oxford University Press*.

24. Dennett, D., (1997) Facing Backwards on the Problem of Consciousness. Shear, J., (ed.), Explaining consciousness: The hard problem *MIT Press*, 33-36.

25. Churchland, P., (1997). The Hornswoggle Problem. Shear, J, (ed.), Explaining Consciousness: The hard problem. *MIT Press*, 37-44.

26. Shear, J., (1972). The self and pure consciousness. *University of California*.

27. Heisenberg, W., and Bohr, N., (1958). Copenhagen interpretation. Physics and Philosophy.

28. Stapp, H.P., (1993). Mind, Matter and Quantum Mechanics. Springer.

29. Schrödinger, E., (1926). An undulatory theory of the mechanics of atoms and molecules. *Phys Rev*.28(6), 1049.

30. Schrödinger, E., (1935). Die gegenwartige Situation in der Quantenmechanik. Naturwissenschaftern, 23, 807-812; 823-823, 844-849. J. Trimmer (Trans.). Proceedings of the American Philosophical Society. 124, 323-8.

31. Von Neumann, J., (2018). Mathematical foundations of quantum mechanics: New edition. PrincetonUniversity Press.

32. Hankey, A., (2014). Complexity biology-based information structures can explain subjectivity, objective reduction of wave packets, and non-computability. Cosmos and History: The Journal of Natural and Social Philosophy, 10(1), 237-50.

33. Ben-Dov, G., and Cohen, J., (2007). Critical Reynolds number for a natural transition to turbulence in pipe flows. Physical review letters. 98(6), 064503.

34. Bassingthwaighte, J.B., Liebovitch, L.S., West, B.J., (1994). Fractal Physiology. *Oxford University Press*.

35. Waldrop, M.M., (1994). Complexity: The Emerging Science at the Edge of Order and Chaos. *Penguin*.

36. Hankey, A., (2015). A complexity basis for phenomenology: How information states at criticality offer a new approach to understanding experience of self, being and time. *Progress in Biophysics and Molecular Biology*, 119 (3), 288-302.

37. Jensen, H.J., (1998). Self-organized criticality: Emergent complex behavior in physical and biological systems. *Cambridge University Press*.

38. Bak, P., Tang, C., and Wiesenfeld, K., (1987). Self-organized criticality: An explanation of the 1/f noise. Phys Rev Lets, 59, 381–384. doi:http://dx.doi.org/10.1103/PhysRevLett.59.381.

39. Hankey, A., and Kale, A., (2022). Integrative Biology for Integrative Medicine: A Complete Approach. JAIM, Special Issue.

40. Kauffman, S.A., (1969). Metabolic stability and epigenesis in randomly constructed genetic nets. *Journal of theoretical biology*, 22(3), 437-467.

41. Kauffman, S., (1969). Homeostasis and differentiation in random genetic control networks. *Nature*, 224 (5215), 177-8.

42. Kauffman, S., (1995). At Home in the Universe. The search

for the laws of self organization and complexity. *Oxford University Press*.

43. Wigner, E., P., (1973). Epistemological Perspective on Quantum Theory. Mehra, J., (ed.), Philosophical Reflections and Syntheses. The Collected Works of Eugene Paul Wigner, Vol B / 6. *Springer*, Berlin, Heidelberg. https://doi.org/10.1007/978-3-642-78374-6_5 .

44. Hameroff, S., Penrose, R., (1996). Orchestrated reduction of quantum coherence in brain microtubules: A model for consciousness. Mathematics and computers in simulation, 40(3-4), 453-80.

45. Hameroff, S., Penrose, R., (2014). Consciousness in the universe: A review of the 'Orch OR' theory, Physics of life reviews, 11(1), 39-78.

46. Genesis Chapter 1, The Bible, 2022, Zondervan, Michigan, Grand Rapids.

47. Vishnu Purana (Trans: Bibek Debroy), 2022, *Penguin*.

48. Hawking, S.W., and Penrose, R., (1970) The singularities of gravitational collapse and cosmology. *Proc Roy Soc A. Mathematical and Physical Sciences*. 314(1519), 529-48.

49. Guth, A.H., (1981). Inflationary universe: A possible solution to the horizon and flatness problems. *Physical Review D*, 23(2), 347.

The Pribram-Bohm Holoflux Theory of Consciousness

Endnotes

i. Graphic by Darth Kule (2010). Public domain. Image retrieved from Wikimedia Commons. https://commons.wikimedia.org/wiki/File:Black_body.svg

ii. Bohm, *Wholeness and the Implicate Order,* 188.

iii. Bohm, 189.

iv. Bohm, 189.

v. Graphic by Camille Flammarion (Paris, 1888). Reprinted under the terms of a Creative Commons Attribution ShareAlike 3.0 Unported license. Image retrieved from Wikimedia Commons.

vi. Graphic by J. Wheeler (Austin, 1990). Reprinted under the terms of a Creative Commons Attribution ShareAlike 3.0 Unported license. Image retrieved from Wikimedia Commons.

vii. Ibid., 142.

viii. Pribram, "What the Fuss Is All About," 29.

ix. Pribram, "Prolegomenon for a Holonomic Brain Theory."

x. Pribram, "Brain and Mathematics," 232.

xi. Pribram, *The Form Within*, 495.

xii. Kuo, *Network Analysis and Synthesis*, 1.

xiii. Pribram, *Brain and Perception*, 73.

xiv. Stein and Shakarchi, *Fourier Analysis*, 134–36.

xv. Kuo, *Network Analysis and Synthesis*, 40.

xvi. Wiener, *Cybernetics: Control and Communication in Animal and Machine*, 198.

xvii. Ibid.

xviii. Ibid., 202.

xix. Ibid. Italics added.

xx. Mandelbrot, "Fractals and the Rebirth of Iteration Theory," 151.

xxi. Penrose, *The Emperor's New Mind: Concerning Computers, Minds and the Laws of Physics*, 124.

xxii. Ibid., 127.

xxiii. Jung, "On the Nature of the Psyche," 215.

xxiv. Kuo, *Network Analysis and Synthesis*, 13.

xxv. Ibid.

xxvi. Ibid., 3.

xxvii. Bohm, *Quantum Theory*, 1.

References

1. Bohm, D., (1980). Wholeness and the Implicate Order. *Routledge.*
2. Feynman, R., Leighton, R., Sands, M., (1964). The Feynman Lectures on Physics. *Addison-Wesley*, 1.
3. Kuo, F., (1962). Network Analysis and Synthesis. *John Wiley and Sons.*
4. Wiener, N., (1948). Cybernetics or Control and Communication in the Animal and the Machine. *MIT Press.*
5. Bohm, D., (1951). Quantum Theory. *Prentice–Hall.*
6. William, J., (1909) A Pluralistic Universe. *Longmans, Greene.*
7. Stein, E., and Shakarchi, R. (2003). Fourier analysis: An introduction. Princeton University Press.
8. Pribram, K.H., (1971). Languages of the Brain: Experimental Paradoxes and Principles in Neuropsychology. *Prentice-Hall.*
9. Pribram, K.H., (1990). Prolegomenon for a holonomic brain theory. Haken H., and Stadler, M., (eds.), Synergetics of cognition: Proceedings of the international symposium at Schloss Elmau, Bavaria, pp. 150-184. *Springer-Verlag.*
10. Pribram, K.H., (2013). The Form Within: My Point of View. Prospecta Press.

11. Pribram, K.H., (1982). What the Fuss Is All About. Wilber, K., (ed.) The Holographic Paradigm and Other Paradoxes, 27–34. *Boulder: Shambhala.*

12. Pribram, K.H., (2004). Brain and Mathematics. Globus, G., Pribram K., Vitiello G., (ed.) Brain and Being: At the Boundary Between Science, Philosophy, Language and Arts, 215–40. *John Benjamins.*

13. Pribram, K.H., (2004). Consciousness Reassessed. *Mind and Matter*, 2(1), 7-35.

14. Bohm, D., and Hiley, B., J., (1993). The Undivided Universe: An Ontological Interpretation of Quantum Theory. *Routledge.*

15. Carr, B.J., and Giddings, S.B., (2005) Quantum Black Holes. Scientific American 292(5), 35.

16. Bohm, D., and Peat, F.D., (1987). Science, order, and creativity. *Bantam Books.*

17. Cazenave, M. (Ed.). (1984). Science and Consciousness - Two views of the universe: Edited proceedings of the France-Culture and Radio-France Colloquium, Cordoba, Spain (A. Hall and E. Callender, Trans.). *Pergamon Press.*

18. Bohm, D., and Weber, R., (1982). Nature as Creativity. *ReVision* 5(2), 35–40.

19. Pribram, K.H., (1991). Brain and Perception: Holonomy and Structure in Figural Processing. *Lawrence Erlbaum.*

20. Spencer-Brown, G., (1972). Laws of Form. *Bohmeier.*

21. Chalmers, D.J. (1995). Facing up to the problem of consciousness. *Journal of Consciousness Studies*, 2(3), 200-219.

22. Smolin, L. (2012). Atoms of space and time. A question of time: The ultimate paradox. *Scientific American.*

23. Wheeler, J., (1990) A Journey Into Gravity and Spacetime. *Scientific American.*

24. Dewey, B., (1985) The Theory of Laminated Spacetime. Bartholomew.

25. Wheeler, J. (1998). Geons, black holes, and quantum foam: A life in physics. *W. W. Norton.*

26. Sheldrake, R., (1981). A New Science of Life: The Hypothesis of Morphic Resonance. *Park Street Press.*

27. Fraser, C.G., (2006). The cosmos: A historical perspective. Greenwood Press.

28. Young, N., (1988). An introduction to Hilbert space. *Cambridge University Press.*

29. Dorf, R.C., (ed.) (1997). The Electrical Engineering Handbook 2nd ed. *CRC Press.*

30. Susskind, L. (2008). The black hole war: My battle with Stephen Hawking to make the world safe for quantum mechanics. *Little, Brown and Company.*

31. Bekenstein, J.D., (1973). Black holes and entropy. *Physical Review*, 7 (8), 2333-2246.

32. Hill, K., (2013). Blueprints of NSA's Ridiculously Expensive Data Center in Utah Suggest It Holds Less Info Than Thought. *Forbes.* http://www.forbes.com/sites/kashmirhill/2013/07/24/blueprints-of-nsa-data-center-in-utah-suggest-its-storage-capacity-is-less-impressive-than-thought/#ae48dc91c85a.

33. Joye, S., (2016). The Pribram–Bohm Holoflux Theory of Consciousness: An Integral Interpretation of the Theories of Karl Pribram, David Bohm, and Pierre Teilhard de Chardin. *PhD diss., California Institute of Integral Studies*, UMI No. 1803306323.

34. Blakeslee, D., (ed.) (1972). The Radio Amateur's Handbook. *Newington, CT: The American Radio Relay League.*

35. Gowar, J., (1993). *Optical* communication *systems* 2nd edition. *Prentice-Hall.*

36. Chen, F.F., (2006). Introduction to Plasma Physics and Controlled Fusion. 2nd Edition. *Springer*, 1.

37. McCraty, R., (2003). The Energetic Heart: Bioelectromagnetic Interactions Within and Between People. Institute of HeartMath.

38. Turgeon, M.L., (2004). Clinical Hematology: Theory and Procedures. Lippincott Williams and Wilkins.

39. Romanes, G.J., (ed.) (1964). Cunningham's Textbook of Anatomy 10th edition. Oxford University Press.

40. Wick, M., Pinggera, W., Lehmann, P., (2003). Clinical Aspects and Laboratory Iron Metabolism. *Springer–Verlag.*

41. Fraser, A., and Frey, O., (1968). Electromagnetic Emission at Micron Wavelengths from Active Nerves. *Biophysical Journal,* 8(6), 731–34. doi:10.1016/S0006-3495(68)86517-8.

Non-Duality in Meditation—Topographic-Dynamic Reorganization Model of Meditation (TRoM)

References

1. Josipovic, Z. (2016). Love and compassion meditation: A non-dual perspective. *Annals of the New York Academy of Sciences*, 1373(1), 65–71. doi:10.1111/nyas.13078.

2. Josipovic, Z. (2019). Non-dual awareness: Consciousness-as-such as non-representational reflexivity. In N. Srinivasan (Ed.), *Progress in brain research*: Vol. 244. Meditation (p. 273–298). *Elsevier Academic Press*. https://doi.org/10.1016/bs.pbr.2018.10.021.

3. Fox, M.D., Snyder, A.Z., Vincent, J.L., Corbetta, M., Van Essen, D.C., and Raichle, M.E. (2005). From The

Cover: The human brain is intrinsically organised into dynamic, anticorrelated functional networks. *Proceedings of the National Academy of Sciences*, 102(27), 9673–9678. doi:10.1073/pnas.0504136102.

4. Tang, Y.Y., Hölzel, B.K., and Posner, M.I. (2015). The neuroscience of mindfulness meditation. *Nature Reviews Neuroscience*, 16(4), 213–225. doi:10.1038/nrn3916.

5. Josipovic, Z., Dinstein, I., Weber, J., and Heeger, D. J. (2012). Influence of meditation on anti-correlated networks in the brain. *Frontiers in Human Neuroscience*, 5. doi:10.3389/fnhum.2011.00183.

6. Dor-Ziderman, Y., Berkovich-Ohana, A., Glicksohn, J., and Goldstein, A. (2013). Mindfulness-induced selflessness: a MEG neurophenomenological study. *Frontiers in Human Neuroscience*, 7. doi:10.3389/fnhum.2013.00582.

7. Savostyanov, A., Tamozhnikov, S., Bocharov, A., Saprygin, A., Matushkin, Y., Lashin, S., . . . Knyazev, G. (2020). The Effect of Meditation on Comprehension of Statements About One-Self and Others: A Pilot ERP and Behavioral Study. *Frontiers in Human Neuroscience*, 13. doi:10.3389/fnhum.2019.00437.

8. Trautwein, F.M., Naranjo, J.R., and Schmidt, S. (2016). Decentering the Self? Reduced Bias in Self- vs. Other-Related Processing in Long-Term Practitioners of Loving-Kindness Meditation. *Frontiers in Psychology*, 7. doi:10.3389/fpsyg.2016.01785.

9. Sui, J., and Gu, X. (2017). Self as Object: Emerging Trends in Self Research. *Trends in Neurosciences*, 40(11), 643–653. doi:10.1016/j.tins.2017.09.002.

10. Klein, S.B. (2014). Sameness and the self: Philosophical and psychological considerations. *Frontiers in Psychology*, 5. doi:10.3389/fpsyg.2014.00029.

11. Babo-Rebelo, M., Wolpert, N., Adam, C., Hasboun, D., and Tallon-Baudry, C. (2016). Is the cardiac monitoring function related to the self in both the default network and right anterior insula? *Philosophical Transactions of the Royal Society B: Biological Sciences*, 371(1708), 20160004. doi:10.1098/rstb.2016.0004.

12. Babo-Rebelo, M., Buot, A., and Tallon-Baudry, C. (2019). Neural responses to heartbeats distinguish self from other during imagination. *NeuroImage*, 191, 10-20. doi:10.1016/j.neuroimage.2019.02.012.

13. James, W. (1890). The principles of psychology (Harvard ed., 2 vols.). *New York: Holt.*

14. Panksepp, J. (1998). Series in affective science.Affective neuroscience: The foundations of human and animal emotions. *Oxford University Press.*

15. Damasio, A. (2003). Feelings of Emotion and the Self. *Annals of the New York Academy of Sciences*, 1001(1), 253–261. doi:10.1196/annals.1279.014.

16. Damasio, A. (2003). Mental self: The person within. *Nature*, 423(6937), 227–227. doi:10.1038/423227a.

17. Blanke, O., Slater, M., and Serino, A. (2015). Behavioral, Neural, and Computational Principles of Bodily Self-Consciousness. *Neuron*, 88(1), 145–166. doi:10.1016/j.neuron.2015.09.029.

18. Park, H.D., and Blanke, O. (2019). Coupling Inner and Outer Body for Self-Consciousness. *Trends in Cognitive Sciences*. doi:10.1016/j.tics.2019.02.002.

19. Tsakiris, M. (2017). The multisensory basis of the self: From body to identity to others. *Quarterly Journal of Experimental Psychology*, 70(4), 597–609. doi:10.1080/17470218.2016.1181768.

20. Seth, A.K., and Tsakiris, M. (2018). Being a Beast Machine: The Somatic Basis of Selfhood. *Trends in Cognitive Sciences*. doi:10.1016/j.tics.2018.08.008.

21. Gallagher, S., and Daly, A. (2018). Dynamical Relations in the Self-Pattern. *Frontiers in Psychology*, 9. doi:10.3389/fpsyg.2018.00664.

22. Gallagher, S., and Zahavi, D. (2021). The phenomenological mind. *Abingdon, Oxon: Routledge*.

23. Neisser, U., (1988). Five kinds of self-knowledge. *Philosophical Psychology*, 1(1), 35–59. https://doi.org/10.1080/09515088808572924.

24. Schilbach, L., (2015). The Neural Correlates of Social Cognition and Social Interaction. *Brain Mapping*, 159–164. doi:10.1016/b978-0-12-397025-1.00172-x.

25. Christoff, K., Cosmelli, D., Legrand, D., and Thompson, E. (2011). Specifying the self for cognitive neuroscience. *Trends in Cognitive Sciences*, 15(3), 104–112. doi:10.1016/j.tics.2011.01.001.

26. Fazelpour, S., and Thompson, E. (2015). The Kantian brain: brain dynamics from a neurophenomenological perspective. *Current Opinion in Neurobiology*, 31, 223–229. doi:10.1016/j.conb.2014.12.006.

27. Northoff, G., Heinzel, A., de Greck, M., Bermpohl, F., Dobrowolny, H., and Panksepp, J. (2006). Self-referential processing in our brain. A meta-analysis of imaging studies on the self. *NeuroImage*, 31(1), 440–457. doi:10.1016/j.neuroimage.2005.12.002.

28. van der Meer, L., Costafreda, S., Aleman, A., and David, A. S. (2010). Self-reflection and the brain: A theoretical review and meta-analysis of neuroimaging studies with implications for schizophrenia. *Neuroscience and Biobehavioral Reviews*, 34(6), 935–946.

29. Davey, C.G., Pujol, J., and Harrison, B. J. (2016). Mapping the self in the brain's default mode network. *NeuroImage*, 132, 390–397. doi:10.1016/j.neuroimage.2016.02.022.

30. Frewen P.A., Schroeter M.L., Riva G., Cipresso P., Fairfield B., Padulo C., Northoff G. (2020) Neuroimaging the consciousness of self: Review, and conceptual-methodological framework. *Neurosci. Biobehav. Rev.* doi: 10.1016/j.neubiorev.2020.01.023.

31. Andrews-Hanna, J.R. (2011). The Brain's Default Network and Its Adaptive Role in Internal Mentation. *The Neuroscientist*, 18(3), 251–270. doi:10.1177/1073858411403316.

32. Andrews-Hanna, J.R., Smallwood, J., and Spreng, R. N. (2014). The default network and self-generated thought: component processes, dynamic control, and clinical relevance. *Annals of the New York Academy of Sciences*, 1316(1), 29–52. doi:10.1111/nyas.12360.

33. Northoff, G., Wainio-Theberge, S., and Evers, K. (2019). Is temporo-spatial dynamics the "common currency" of brain and mind? In Quest of "Spatiotemporal Neuroscience." *Physics of Life Reviews*. doi:10.1016/j.plrev.2019.05.002.

34. Northoff, G., Wainio-Theberge, S., and Evers, K. (2020). Spatiotemporal Neuroscience: What is it and why we need it. *Physics of Life Reviews*. doi:10.1016/j.plrev.2020.06.00.

35. Wolff, A., Di Giovanni, D.A., Gómez-Pilar, J., Nakao, T., Huang, Z., Longtin, A., and Northoff, G. (2018). The temporal signature of self: Temporal measures of resting-state EEG predict self-consciousness. *Human Brain Mapping*. doi:10.1002/hbm.24412.

36. Huang, Z., Obara, N., Davis, H. (Hap), Pokorny, J., and Northoff, G. (2016). The temporal structure of resting-state brain activity in the medial prefrontal cortex predicts self-consciousness. *Neuropsychologia*, 82, 161–170. doi:10.1016/j.neuropsychologia.2016.01.025.

37. Kolvoort, I.R., Wainio-Theberge, S., Wolff, A., and Northoff, G. (2020). Temporal integration as "common currency" of brain and self-scale-free activity in resting-state EEG correlates with temporal delay effects on self-relatedness. *Human Brain Mapping*. doi:10.1002/hbm.25129.

38. Ataria, Y., Dor-Ziderman, Y., and Berkovich-Ohana, A. (2015). How does it feel to lack a sense of boundaries? A case study of a long-term mindfulness meditator. *Consciousness and Cognition*, 37, 133–147. doi:10.1016/j.concog.2015.09.002.

39. Shiah, Y.J. (2016). From Self to Nonself: The Nonself Theory. *Frontiers in Psychology*, 7. doi:10.3389/fpsyg.2016.00124.

40. Josipovic, Z. (2014). Neural correlates of nondual awareness in meditation. *Annals of the New York Academy of Sciences*, 1307(1), 9–18. doi:10.1111/nyas.12261.

41. Berman, A.E., and Stevens, L. (2015). EEG manifestations of nondual experiences in meditators. *Consciousness and Cognition*, 31, 1–11. doi:10.1016/j.concog.2014.10.002

42. Bauer, C.C., Whitfield-Gabrieli, S., Díaz, J. L., Pasaye, E. H., and Barrios, F. A. (2019). From State-to-Trait Meditation: Reconfiguration of Central Executive and Default Mode Networks. *Eneuro*, 6(6). doi:10.1523/eneuro.0335-18.2019.

43. Farb, N.A.S., Segal, Z.V., Mayberg, H., Bean, J., McKeon, D., Fatima, Z., and Anderson, A. K. (2007). Attending to the present: mindfulness meditation reveals distinct neural modes of self-reference. *Social Cognitive and Affective Neuroscience*, 2(4), 313–322. doi:10.1093/scan/nsm030.

44. Hasenkamp, W. (2018). Catching the Wandering Mind. Oxford Handbooks Online. doi:10.1093/oxfordhb/9780190464745.013.1.

45. Millière, R., Carhart-Harris, R.L., Roseman, L., Trautwein, F.-M., and Berkovich-Ohana, A. (2018). Psychedelics, Meditation, and Self-Consciousness. *Frontiers in Psychology*, 9. doi:10.3389/fpsyg.2018.01475.

46. Lutz, A., Jha, A.P., Dunne, J.D., and Saron, C.D. (2015). Investigating the phenomenological matrix of mindfulness-related practices from a neurocognitive perspective. *American Psychologist,* 70(7), 632–658. doi:10.1037/a0039585.

47. Raffone, A., Marzetti, L., Del Gratta, C., Perrucci, M.G., Romani, G. L., and Pizzella, V. (2019). Toward a brain theory of meditation. *Progress in Brain Research.* doi:10.1016/bs.pbr.2018.10.028.

48. Fucci, E., Abdoun, O., Caclin, A., Francis, A., Dunne, J.D., Ricard, M., … Lutz, A. (2018). Differential effects of non-dual and focused attention meditations on the formation of automatic perceptual habits in expert practitioners. *Neuropsychologia*, 119, 92–100. doi:10.1016/j.neuropsychologia.2018.07.025.

49. Fujino, M., Ueda, Y., Mizuhara, H., Saiki, J., and Nomura, M. (2018). Open monitoring meditation reduces the involvement of brain regions related to memory function. *Scientific Reports*, 8(1). doi:10.1038/s41598-018-28274-4.

50. Lehmann, D., Faber, P.L., Tei, S., Pascual-Marqui, R. D., Milz, P., and Kochi, K. (2012). Reduced functional connectivity between cortical sources in five meditation traditions detected with lagged coherence using EEG tomography. *NeuroImage*, 60(2), 1574–1586. doi:10.1016/j.neuroimage.2012.01.042.

51. Reddy, J.S.K., and Roy, S. (2019). Understanding Meditation Based on the Subjective Experience and Traditional Goal: Implications for Current Meditation Research. *Frontiers in Psychology*, 10. doi:10.3389/fpsyg.2019.01827.

52. Berkovich-Ohana, A. (2015). A case study of a meditation-induced altered state: increased overall gamma synchronization. *Phenomenology and the Cognitive Sciences*, 16(1), 91–106. doi:10.1007/s11097-015-9435-x.

53. Northoff, G. (2016). Is the self a higher-order or fundamental function of the brain? The "basis model of self-specificity"

and its encoding by the brain's spontaneous activity. *Cognitive Neuroscience*, 7(1-4), 203–222. doi:10.1080/17588928.2015.1111868.

54. van den Hurk, P.A.M., Janssen, B.H., Giommi, F., Barendregt, H.P., and Gielen, S.C. (2010). Mindfulness meditation associated with alterations in bottom-up processing: Psychophysiological evidence for reduced reactivity. *International Journal of Psychophysiology*, 78(2), 151–157. doi:10.1016/j.ijpsycho.2010.07.002.

55. Slagter, H.A., Davidson, R.J., and Lutz, A. (2011). Mental Training as a Tool in the Neuroscientific Study of Brain and Cognitive Plasticity. *Frontiers in Human Neuroscience*, 5. doi:10.3389/fnhum.2011.00017.

56. Lumma, A.L., Kok, B.E., and Singer, T. (2015). Is meditation always relaxing? Investigating heart rate, heart rate variability, experienced effort and likeability during training of three types of meditation. *International Journal of Psychophysiology*, 97(1), 38–45. doi:10.1016/j.ijpsycho.2015.04.017.

57. Tanaka, G.K., Maslahati, T., Gongora, M., Bittencourt, J., Lopez, L.C.S., Demarzo, M.M.P., … Velasques, B. (2015). Effortless Attention as a Biomarker for Experienced Mindfulness Practitioners. *PLOS ONE*, 10(10), e0138561. doi:10.1371/journal.pone.0138561.

58. Northoff, G., and Lamme, V. (2020). Neural signs and mechanisms of consciousness: Is there a potential convergence of theories of consciousness in sight? *Neuroscience and Biobehavioral Reviews*. doi:10.1016/j.neubiorev.2020.07.019.

59. Cooper, A.C., Ventura, B., Northoff, G., (2022). Beyond the veil of duality—Topographic reorganization model of meditation. *Neuroscience of Consciousness*, 2022(1), niac013, https://doi.org/10.1093/nc/niac013.

60. Hasenkamp, W., and Barsalou, L.W. (2012). Effects of Meditation Experience on Functional Connectivity of Distributed Brain Networks. *Frontiers in Human Neuroscience*, 6. doi:10.3389/fnhum.2012.00038.

61. Brewer, J.A., Worhunsky, P.D., Gray, J.R., Tang, Y.Y., Weber, J., and Kober, H. (2011). Meditation experience is associated with differences in default mode network activity and connectivity. *Proceedings of the National Academy of Sciences*, 108(50), 20254–20259. doi:10.1073/pnas.1112029108.

62. Kemmer, P.B., Guo, Y., Wang, Y., and Pagnoni, G. (2015). Network-based characterization of brain functional connectivity in Zen practitioners. *Frontiers in Psychology*, 6. doi:10.3389/fpsyg.2015.00603.

63. Mooneyham, B.W., Mrazek, M.D., Mrazek, A.J., Mrazek, K.L., Phillips, D.T., and Schooler, J. W. (2017). States of Mind: Characterizing the Neural Bases of Focus and Mind-wandering through Dynamic Functional Connectivity. *Journal of Cognitive Neuroscience*, 29(3), 495-506. doi:10.1162/jocn_a_01066.

64. Marzetti, L., Di Lanzo, C., Zappasodi, F., Chella, F., Raffone, A., and Pizzella, V. (2014). Magnetoencephalographic alpha band connectivity reveals differential default mode network interactions during focused attention and open monitoring meditation. *Frontiers in Human Neuroscience*, 8. doi:10.3389/fnhum.2014.00832 .

65. Kilpatrick, L.A., Suyenobu, B.Y., Smith, S.R., Bueller, J.A., Goodman, T., Creswell, J.D., … Naliboff, B.D. (2011). Impact of mindfulness-based stress reduction training on intrinsic brain connectivity. *NeuroImage*, 56(1), 290–298. doi:10.1016/j.neuroimage.2011.02.034.

66. Manna, A., Raffone, A., Perrucci, M.G., Nardo, D., Ferretti, A., Tartaro, A., … Romani, G. L. (2010). Neural correlates of focused attention and cognitive monitoring in meditation.

Brain Research Bulletin, 82(1-2), 46–56. doi:10.1016/j.brainresbull.2010.03.001.

67. Hernández, S.E., Barros-Loscertales, A., Xiao, Y., González-Mora, J.L., and Rubia, K. (2018). Gray Matter and Functional Connectivity in Anterior Cingulate Cortex are Associated with the State of Mental Silence During Sahaja Yoga Meditation. *Neuroscience*, 371, 395–406. doi:10.1016/j.neuroscience.2017.12.017.

68. Brefczynski-Lewis, J.A., Lutz, A., Schaefer, H.S., Levinson, D.B., and Davidson, R.J. (2007). Neural correlates of attentional expertise in long-term meditation practitioners. *Proceedings of the National Academy of Sciences*, 104(27), 11483–11488. doi:10.1073/pnas.0606552104.

69. Pasquini, H.A., Tanaka, G. K., Basile, L.F.H., Velasques, B., Lozano, M.D., and Ribeiro, P. (2015). Electrophysiological Correlates of Long-TermSoto ZenMeditation. *BioMed Research International*, 2015, 1–7. doi:10.1155/2015/598496

70. Kim, D.K., Lee, K.M., Kim, J., Whang, M.C., and Kang, S. W. (2013). Dynamic correlations between heart and brain rhythm during Autogenic meditation. *Frontiers in Human Neuroscience*, 7, Article 414. https://doi.org/10.3389/fnhum.2013.00414.

71. Saggar, M., King, B.G., Zanesco, A.P., MacLean, K.A., Aichele, S.R., Jacobs, T.L., … Saron, C.D. (2012). Intensive training induces longitudinal changes in meditation state-related EEG oscillatory activity. *Frontiers in Human Neuroscience*, 6. doi:10.3389/fnhum.2012.00256.

72. Irrmischer, M., Houtman, S.J., Mansvelder, H.D., Tremmel, M., Ott, U., and Linkenkaer-Hansen, K. (2018). Controlling the Temporal Structure of Brain Oscillations by Focused Attention Meditation. *Human Brain Mapping*, 39(4), 1825–1838. doi:10.1002/hbm.23971.

73. He, B.J. (2014). Scale-free brain activity: Past, present,

and future. *Trends in Cognitive Sciences*, 18(9), 480–487. doi:10.1016/j.tics.2014.04.003.

74. He, B.J., Zempel, J.M., Snyder, A.Z., and Raichle, M.E. (2010). The Temporal Structures and Functional Significance of Scale-free Brain Activity. *Neuron*, 66(3), 353–369. doi:10.1016/j.neuron.2010.04.020.

75. Linkenkaer-Hansen, K., Nikouline, V.V., Palva, J.M., and Ilmoniemi, R.J. (2001). Long-Range Temporal Correlations and Scaling Behavior in Human Brain Oscillations. *The Journal of Neuroscience*, 21(4), 1370–1377. doi:10.1523/jneurosci.21-04-01370.2001.

76. Hardstone, R., Poil, S.S., Schiavone, G., Jansen, R., Nikulin, V. V., Mansvelder, H. D., and Linkenkaer-Hansen, K. (2012). Detrended Fluctuation Analysis: A Scale-Free View on Neuronal Oscillations. *Frontiers in Physiology*, 3. doi:10.3389/fphys.2012.00450.

77. Bravi, A., Longtin, A., and Seely, A.J., (2011). Review and classification of variability analysis techniques with clinical applications. BioMed Eng OnLine, 10, 90. https://doi.org/10.1186/1475-925X-10-90.

78. Deco, G., Kringelbach, M.L., Jirsa, V.K., and Ritter, P. (2017). The dynamics of resting fluctuations in the brain: Metastability and its dynamical cortical core. *Scientific Reports*, 7(1). doi:10.1038/s41598-017-03073-5.

79. Escrichs, A., Sanjuán, A., Atasoy, S., López-González, A., Garrido, C., Càmara, E., and Deco, G. (2019). Characterizing the Dynamical Complexity Underlying Meditation. *Frontiers in Systems Neuroscience*, 13. doi:10.3389/fnsys.2019.00027.

80. Nair, A.K., Sasidharan, A., John, J.P., Mehrotra, S., and Kutty, B. M. (2017). Just a minute meditation: Rapid voluntary conscious state shifts in long term meditators. *Consciousness and Cognition*, 53, 176–184. doi:10.1016/j.concog.2017.06.002.

81. Gard, T., Noggle, J.J., Park, C.L., Vago, D.R., and Wilson, A. (2014). Potential self-regulatory mechanisms of yoga for psychological health. *Frontiers in Human Neuroscience*, 8. doi:10.3389/fnhum.2014.00770.

82. Lindahl, J., and Britton, W. (2019). 'I Have This Feeling of Not Really Being Here 'Buddhist Meditation and Changes in Sense of Self. *Journal of Consciousness Studies*, 26(7-8), 157-183.

83. Metzinger, T. (2003). Being no one: The self-model theory of subjectivity. *MIT Press*.

84. Metzinger, T. (2020). Minimal phenomenal experience: Meditation, tonic alertness, and the phenomenology of "pure"consciousness. *Philosophy and the Mind Sciences*, 1 (I), 7. doi: 10.33735/phimisci.2020.I.46.

85. Crick, F., and Koch, C. (2003). A framework for consciousness. *Nature Neuroscience*, 6(2), 119–126. doi:10.1038/nn0203-119.

86. Northoff, G. (2014). Unlocking the brain, Vol. 2. Consciousness. *Oxford University Press*.

87. Northoff, G., and Heiss, W.D. (2015). Why Is the Distinction Between Neural Predispositions, Prerequisites, and Correlates of the Level of Consciousness Clinically Relevant?: Functional Brain Imaging in Coma and Vegetative State. *Stroke*, 46(4), 1147–1151. doi:10.1161/strokeaha.114.007969.

88. Bauer, C.C.C., (2019). Whitfield-Gabrieli, S., Díaz, J.L., Pasaye, E.H., and Barrios, F.A. (2019). From State-to-Trait Meditation: Reconfiguration of Central Executive and Default Mode Networks. *eNeuro*, 6(6), ENEURO.0335-18.2019. https://doi.org/10.1523/ENEURO.0335-18.

89. Tononi, G., Boly, M., Massimini, M., and Koch, C. (2016). Integrated information theory: From consciousness to its physical substrate. *Nature Reviews Neuroscience*, 17(7), 450–461. doi:10.1038/nrn.2016.44.

90. Mashour GA, Roelfsema P, Changeux JP, Dehaene S. (2020). Conscious processing and the global neuronal workspace hypothesis. *Neuron*, 105, 776-798. doi: 10.1016/j.neuron.2020.01.026.

91. Dehaene, S., Charles, L., King, J.R., and Marti, S. (2014). Toward a computational theory of conscious processing. *Current Opinion in Neurobiology*, 25, 76–84. doi:10.1016/j.conb.2013.12.005.

92. Dehaene, S., Lau, H., and Kouider, S. (2017). What is consciousness, and could machines have it? *Science* 358, 486–492. doi: 10.1126/science.aan887.

93. Graziano, M.S.A., and Kastner, S. (2011). Human consciousness and its relationship to social neuroscience: A novel hypothesis. *Cognitive Neuroscience*, 2(2), 98–113. doi :10.1080/17588928.2011.565121.

94. Graziano, M.S.A., and Webb, T.W. (2015). The attention schema theory: A mechanistic account of subjective awareness. *Frontiers in Psychology*, 06. doi:10.3389/fpsyg.2015.00500.

95. Graziano, M.S.A. (2020). Consciousness and the attention schema: Why it has to be. right. *Cognitive Neuropsychology*, 1–10. doi:10.1080/02643294.2020.1761782

96. Northoff, G., and Huang, Z. (2017). How do the brain's time and space mediate consciousness and its different dimensions? Temporo-spatial theory of consciousness (TTC). *Neuroscience and Biobehavioral Reviews*, 80, 630–645. doi:10.1016/j.neubiorev.2017.07.013.

97. Tanabe, S., Huang, Z., Zhang, J., Chen, Y., Fogel, S., Doyon, J., Wu, J., Xu, J., Zhang, J., Qin, P., Wu, X., Mao, Y., Mashour, G., Hudetz, A., Northoff, G. (2020). Altered Global Brain Signal during Physiologic, Pharmacologic, and Pathologic States of Unconsciousness in Humans and Rats. *Anesthesiology*, 132:1392–1406. doi: https://doi.org/10.1097/ALN.0000000000003197.

98. Zhang, J., Huang, Z., Tumati, S., and Northoff, G. (2020). Rest-task modulation of fMRI-derived global signal topography is mediated by transient coactivation patterns. *PLOS Biology*, 18(7). doi:10.1371/journal.pbio.3000733.

Nature of Self: Yoga and Neuroscience Perspectives

References

1. Qin., P, Northoff, G., (2011). How is our self related to midline regions and the default-mode network? *NeuroImage [Internet]*. 57 (3), 1221–33. Retrieved from: https://www.sciencedirect.com/science/article/pii/S1053811911005167.

2. Davey, C.G., Pujol, J., and Harrison, B.J. (2016). Mapping the self in the brain's default mode network. *NeuroImage*, 132, 390–397. Retrieved from: https://doi.org/10.1016/j.neuroimage.2016.02.022.

3. Harrison, B.J., Pujol, J., López-Solà, M., Hernández-Ribas, R., Deus, J., Ortiz, H., et al., (2008). Consistency and functional specialization in the default mode brain network. *Proc Natl Acad Sci [Internet]*. 105 (28), 9781–6. Retrieved from: https://pnas.org/doi/full/10.1073/pnas.0711791105

4. Barrett, L.F., Simmons, W.K., (2015). Interoceptive predictions in the brain. *Nat Rev Neurosci [Internet]*. 16 (7), 419–29. Retrieved from: https://www.nature.com/articles/nrn3950.

5. Kleckner, I.R., Zhang, J., Touroutoglou, A., Chanes, L., Xia, C., Simmons, W., K., et al. (2017). Evidence for a large-scale brain system supporting allostasis and interoception in humans. *Nat Hum Behav [Internet]*. 1(5), 1–14. Retrieved from: https://www.nature.com/articles/s41562-017-0069.

6. Quigley, K.S., Kanoski, S., Grill, W., M., Barrett, L.F., Tsakiris, M., (2021). Functions of Interoception: From Energy Regulation to Experience of the Self. *Trends Neurosci [Internet]*. 44 (1), 29–38. Retrieved from: https://www.sciencedirect.com/science/article/pii/S0166223620302162.

7. Seth, A.K., Tsakiris, M., (2018). Being a Beast Machine: The Somatic Basis of Selfhood. *Trends Cogn Sci [Internet]*. 22 (11), 969–81. Retrieved from: https://www.sciencedirect.com/science/article/pii/S1364661318302079.

8. Seth, A.K., (2013). Interoceptive inference, emotion, and the embodied self. *Trends Cogn Sci [Internet]*. 17 (11), 565–73. Retrieved from: https://www.sciencedirect.com/science/article/pii/S1364661313002118.

9. Blanke, O., (2012). Multisensory brain mechanisms of bodily self-consciousness. *Nat Rev Neurosci [Internet]*. 13 (8), 556–71. Retrieved from: https://www.nature.com/articles/nrn3292.

10. Tsakiris, M., (2017). The multisensory basis of the self: From body to identity to others. *Q J Exp Psychol [Internet]*. 70(4), 597–609. Retrieved from: https://doi.org/10.1080/17470218.2016.1181768.

11. Metzinger. T., (2003). Being No One: The Self-Model Theory of Subjectivity. *MIT Press*.

12. Metzinger, T., (2020). Minimal Phenomenal Experience. *Philos Mind Sci.* 1 (I), 1–44.

13. Millière, R., Carhart-Harris, R.L., Roseman, L., Trautwein, F.M., Berkovich-Ohana, A., (2018). Psychedelics, Meditation, and Self-Consciousness. *Front Psychol [Internet]*. Retrieved from: https://www.frontiersin.org/articles/10.3389/fpsyg.2018.01475.

14. Nave, O., Trautwein, F.M., Ataria, Y., Dor-Ziderman, Y., Schweitzer, Y., Fulder, S., et al., (2021). Self-Boundary Dissolution in Meditation: A Phenomenological Investigation. *Brain Sci [Internet]*. 11 (6), 819. Retrieved from: https://www.ncbi.nlm.nih.gov/pmc/articles/PMC8235013/

15. Timmermann, C., Bauer, P.R., Gosseries, O., Vanhaudenhuyse, A., Vollenweider, F., Laureys, S., et al., (2022). A neurophenomenological approach to non-

ordinary states of consciousness: hypnosis, meditation, and psychedelics. *Trends Cogn Sci [Internet]*. Retrieved from: https://www.cell.com/trends/cognitive-sciences/abstract/S1364-6613(22)00291-1.

16. Iyengar, B.K.S., (1996). Light on the Yoga Sutras of Patanjali. *Philos East West [Internet]*. 46 (2), 291. Retrieved from: https://www.jstor.org/stable/1399412?origin=crossref.

17. Sadhguru, J.V., (2016). Inner engineering. *New York, NY: Penguin Random House*.

18. Vivekananda, S., (2019). Complete Works of Swami Vivekananda. Partha Sinha. 2784 p.

19. Varma, P.K., (2018). Adi Shankaracharya: Hinduism's Greatest Thinker. *Chennai: Tranquebar*.

20. Indich, W.M., (1995). Consciousness in Advaita Vedanta. *Motilal Banarsidass Publ*. 164 p.

21. Tononi, G., Boly, M., Massimini, M., Koch, C., (2016). Integrated information theory: From consciousness to its physical substrate. *Nat Rev Neurosci [Internet]*. 17 (7), 450–61. Retrieved from: https://www.nature.com/articles/nrn-2016-44.

22. Tononi, G., Koch, C., (2015). Consciousness: here, there and everywhere? *Philos Trans R Soc B Biol Sci [Internet]*. 370 (1668), 20140167. Retrieved from: https://royalsocietypublishing.org/doi/full/10.1098/rstb.2014.0167.

23. Baars, B.J., (2005). Global workspace theory of consciousness: Toward a cognitive neuroscience of human experience. *Laureys S, editor. Progress in Brain Research [Internet], Elsevier*. 150, 45–53. Retrieved from: https://www.sciencedirect.com/science/article/pii/S0079612305500049.

24. Seth, A.K., Bayne, T., (2022). Theories of consciousness. *Nat Rev Neurosci [Internet]*. 23 (7), 439–52. Retrieved from: https://www.nature.com/articles/s41583-022-00587-4.

25. Koch, C., (2018). What Is Consciousness? *Nature [Internet]*. 557 (7704), S8–12. Retrieved from: https://www.nature.com/articles/d41586-018-05097-x.

26. Tripathi, V., Bharadwaj, P., (2021). Neuroscience of the yogic theory of consciousness. *Neurosci Conscious*. 2021(2), niab030.

27. Dor-Ziderman, Y., Berkovich-Ohana, A., Glicksohn, J., Goldstein, A., (2013). Mindfulness-induced selflessness: a MEG neurophenomenological study. *Front Hum Neurosci [Internet]*. 7. Retrieved from: https://www.frontiersin.org/articles/10.3389/fnhum.2013.00582.

28. Brewer, J.A., Worhunsky, P.D., Gray, J.R., Tang, Y.Y., Weber, J., Kober, H., (2011). Meditation experience is associated with differences in default mode network activity and connectivity. *Proc Natl Acad Sci [Internet]*. 108 (50), 20254–9. Retrieved from: https://www.pnas.org/doi/abs/10.1073/pnas.1112029108.

29. Brewer, J.A., Garrison, K.A., (2022) The posterior cingulate cortex as a plausible mechanistic target of meditation: findings from neuroimaging. *Ann N Y Acad Sci [Internet]*. 1307(1), 19–27. Retrieved from: https://onlinelibrary.wiley.com/doi/abs/10.1111/nyas.12246.

30. Dunbar, R.I.M., (2009). The social brain hypothesis and its implications for social evolution. *Ann Hum Biol*. 36 (5), 562–72.

31. Graziano, M.S.A., (2013). Consciousness and the Social Brain. *OUP USA*. 281 p.

32. Graziano, M.S.A., Kastner, S., (2011). Human consciousness and its relationship to social neuroscience: A novel hypothesis. *Cogn Neurosci [Internet]*. 2 (2), 98–113. Retrieved from: https://doi.org/10.1080/17588928.2011.565121.

33. Northoff, G., Bermpöhl, F., (2004) Cortical midline structures and the self. *Trends Cogn Sci.* 8(3), 102–7.

34. Northoff. G., Heinzel, A., de Greck, M., Bermpohl, F., Dobrowolny, H., Panksepp, J., (2006). Self-referential processing in our brain—A meta-analysis of imaging studies on the self. *NeuroImage.* 31 (1), 440–57.

35. Overwalle, F.V., (2009). Social cognition and the brain: A meta-analysis. *Hum Brain Mapp [Internet].* 30 (3), 829–58. Retrieved from: https://onlinelibrary.wiley.com/doi/abs/10.1002/hbm.20547.

36. Grossmann, T., (2013). The role of medial prefrontal cortex in early social cognition. *Front Hum Neurosci [Internet].* 7. Retrieved from: https://www.frontiersin.org/articles/10.3389/fnhum.2013.00340

37. Li, W., Mai, X., Liu, C., (2014). The default mode network and social understanding of others: What do brain connectivity studies tell us. *Front Hum Neurosci [Internet].* 8. Retrieved from: https://www.frontiersin.org/articles/10.3389/fnhum.2014.00074.

38. Saxe, R., Kanwisher, N., (2004). The Role of the Temporo-Parietal Junction in "Theory of Mind." In: Social Neuroscience. *Psychology Press.*

39. James, W., Burkhardt, F., Bowers, F., Skrupskelis, I.K., (1890). The principles of psychology. *Macmillan London.* 1.

40. Gallagher, S., (2000). Philosophical conceptions of the self: implications for cognitive science. *Trends Cogn Sci [Internet].* Retrieved from: https://www.sciencedirect.com/science/article/pii/S1364661399014175.

41. Damasio, A., (1999). The Feeling of What Happens: Body and Emotion in the Making of Consciousness. *Harcourt Brace and Co.*

42. Damasio, A., (2003). Mental self: The person within. *Nature [Internet]*. 423 (6937), 227–227. Retrieved from: https://www.nature.com/articles/423227a.

43. Damasio, A., (2003). Feelings of Emotion and the Self. *Ann N Y Acad Sci [Internet]*. 1001 (1), 253–61. Retrieved from: https://onlinelibrary.wiley.com/doi/abs/10.1196/annals.1279.014.

44. Seth, A.K., Friston, K.J., (2016). Active interoceptive inference and the emotional brain. *Philos Trans R Soc B Biol Sci*. 371 (1708), 20160007.

45. Park, H.D., Blanke, O., (2019). Coupling Inner and Outer Body for Self-Consciousness. *Trends Cogn Sci [Internet]*. 23 (5), 377–88. Retrieved from: https://www.cell.com/trends/cognitive-sciences/abstract/S1364-6613(19)30045-2.

46. Suzuki, K., Garfinkel, S.N., Critchley, H.D., Seth, A.K., (2013) Multisensory integration across exteroceptive and interoceptive domains modulates self-experience in the rubber-hand illusion. *Neuropsychologia [Internet]*. 51 (13), 2909–17. Retrieved from: https://www.sciencedirect.com/science/article/pii/S0028393213002789.

47. Seth, A., (2021). Being you: A new science of consciousness. *Penguin*.

48. Botvinick, M., Cohen, J., (1998) Rubber hands "feel" touch that eyes see. *Nature*. 391 (6669), 756.

49. Tsakiris, M., Jiménez, A.T., Costantini, M., (2011). Just a heartbeat away from one's body: interoceptive sensitivity predicts malleability of body-representations. *Proc R Soc B Biol Sci [Internet]*. 278 (1717), 2470–6. Retrieved from: https://royalsocietypublishing.org/doi/10.1098/rspb.2010.2547.

50. Arzy, S., Overney, L.S., Landis, T., Blanke, O., (2006) Neural Mechanisms of Embodiment: Asomatognosia

Due to Premotor Cortex Damage. *Arch Neurol [Internet]*. 63 (7), 1022–5. Retrieved from: https://doi.org/10.1001/archneur.63.7.1022.

51. White, P.A., (2015) The pre-reflective experience of "I" as a continuously existing being: The role of temporal functional binding. *Conscious Cogn [Internet]*. 31, 98–114. Retrieved from: https://www.sciencedirect.com/science/article/pii/S1053810014002165.

52. Gillihan, S.J., Farah, M.J., Is self special? A critical review of evidence from experimental psychology and cognitive neuroscience. *Psychol Bull*. 131 (1), 76–97.

53. Kelley, W.M., Macrae, C.N., Wyland, C., L., Caglar, S., Inati. S., Heatherton, T., F., (2002) Finding the self? An event-related fMRI study. *J Cogn Neurosci*. 14 (5), 785–94.

54. Schore, A.N., (2003). Affect dysregulation and disorders of the self (Norton Series on Interpersonal Neurobiology). *WW Norton and Company*.

55. Kastrup, B., (2018). The Universe in Consciousness. J Conscious Stud [Internet]. 25 (5–6), 125–55. Retrieved from: https://philarchive.org/rec/KASTUI.

56. Goff, P., Seager, W., Allen-Hermanson, S., (2022). Panpsychism. In: Zalta EN, editor. *The Stanford Encyclopedia of Philosophy [Internet]*. Summer 2022. Metaphysics Research Lab, Stanford University. Retrieved from: https://plato.stanford.edu/archives/sum2022/entries/panpsychism/

57. Chalmers, D., (2013). Panpsychism and Panprotopsychism. *Amherst Lect Philos*. 8.

58. Nikhilananda, S., (2013) Drg-Drsya Viveka-An Inquiry into The Nature of The'seer' And The'seen'. *Read Books Ltd*.

59. Hanh, T.N., (2008) The Heart of Buddha's Teaching. *Random House* 306 p.

60. Austin, J.H., (1991). Zen and the Brain: The Construction and Dissolution of the Self. *East Buddh [Internet]*. 24 (2), 69–97. Retrieved from: https://www.jstor.org/stable/44361915

61. Albahari, M., (2006). Analytical Buddhism: The Two-Tiered Illusion of Self. Palgrave-Macmillan.

62. Dahl, C.J., Lutz, A., Davidson, R.J., (2015). Reconstructing and deconstructing the self: Cognitive mechanisms in meditation practice. *Trends Cogn Sci.* 19 (9), 515–23.

How Does Heartfulness Meditation Permeate Everyday Life? A Phenomenological Enquiry

References

1. Goleman, D., and Davidson, R., (2017). The science of meditation: How to change your brain, mind and body. *Penguin Random House.*

2. Siegal, D., (2007) The Mindful Brain: Reflection and Attunement in the Cultivation of Well Being. *Norton and Co.*

3. Siegal, D. (2020) Aware: The Science and Practice of Presence. *Norton and Co.*

4. West, M. (2016). *The* psychology of meditation research. *Oxford University Press.*

5. Schmidt, S. and Walach, H. eds. (2014). Meditation – neuroscientific approaches and philosophical implications., Studies in Neuroscience, Consiousness Spirituality, 2, DO!.10.1007/978-3-319-01634-4_1, *Springer International Publishing.*

6. Cortland, J.D., Lutz, A., Davidson, R.J., (2015). Reconstructing and deconstructing the self: Cognitive mechanisms in meditation practice. *Trends in cognitive sciences* 19(9).

7. Reddy, J.S.K., and Roy, S., (2019). Understanding meditation

based on the subjective experience and traditional goal: Implications for current meditation research. *Frontiers in Psychology.* 10:1827.doi:10.3389/fpsyg.2019.0187.

8. Shear, J., (2014). Some reflections on meditation research and consciousness studies copyright *Journal of Consciousness Studies* https://scholarscompass.vcu.edu/phil_pubs/3.

9. Tomasino, B., Chiesa, A., Fabbro, F., (2014). Disentangling the neural mechanisms involved in Hinduism and Buddhism related meditations. *Brain and Cognition*, 90, 32-40.

10. Finlay, L., (2011). Phenomenology for Therapists: Researching the Lived World. *Wiley Blackwell.*

11. Van't Westeinde, A., Patel, K.D., (2022) Heartfulness Meditation: A Yogic and Neuroscientific Perspective, *Frontiers in Psychology*, 13, 806131.

12. Chandra, R., (1989) Complete Works of Ram Chandra. *Toronto CA SRCM*, 1.

13. Todres, L. (2007). Embodied Enquiry: Phenomenological touchstones for research, psychotherapy and spirituality. *Palgrave Macmillan.*

14. Van Manen, M.(1997*)* Researching Lived Experience: Human Science for an Action Sensitive Pedagogy. *Althouse Press, University of Western Ontario.*

15. Bachelard, G., (1958). (tr Maria Jolas 1964) The Poetics of Space. *Beacon Press.*

16. Ponty, M. (1962). Phenomenology of Perception. C. Smith, Trans.. *Routledge.*

17. Pearmain, R. (1994) Inhabiting Space: Some reflections on embodiment and space. *Journal of the Society for Existential Analysis*, (5) 48-63.

18. Patel, K.D. (2023) Spiritual Anatomy: Meditation, Chakras, and the Journey to the Center, *2023 Balance USA.*

Bibliography

Aftanas, L.I., and Golocheikine, S.A. (2001). Human anterior and frontal midline theta and lower alpha reflect emotionally positive state and internalized attention: high-resolution EEG investigation of meditation. *Neuroscience Letters*, 310(1), 57–60. doi:10.1016/s0304-3940(01)02094-8.

Aftanas, L.I., and Golocheikine, S.A. (2002). Non-linear dynamic complexity of the human EEG during meditation. *Neuroscience Letters*, 330(2), 143–146. doi:10.1016/s0304-3940(02)00745-0.

Aftanas, L.I., and Golosheikin, S.A. (2003). Human Physiology, 29(2), 143–151. doi:10.1023/a:1022986308931.

Agrawal, P.M., (2020). Soul Science, Part-3, Samayasāra by Jain Acharya Kundakunda. *Kundakunda Jnanapith*, (1), 138-144, I.S.B.N. 81-86933-65-4.

American Psychological Association [APA]., (2020). *APA Dictionary of Psychology*. Retrieved from https://dictionary.apa.org.

Amihai, I., and Kozhevnikov, M. (2014). Arousal vs. Relaxation: A Comparison of the Neurophysiological and Cognitive Correlates of Vajrayana and Theravada Meditative Practices. *PLoS ONE*, 9(7), e102990.

Anticevic, A., Cole, M.W., Murray, J.D., Corlett, P.R., Wang, X.J., and Krystal, J. H. (2012). The role of default network deactivation in cognition and disease. *Trends in Cognitive Sciences*, 16(12), 584–592. doi:10.1016/j.tics.2012.10.008.

Arnikar, H.J., (2000). Essentials of Occult Chemistry and Modern Science. *The Theosophcal Publishing House, Chennai.*

Avvenuti, G., Leo, A., Cecchetti, L., Franco, M. F., Travis, F., Caramella, D., … Pietrini, P. (2020). Reductions in perceived stress following Transcendental Meditation practice are associated with increased brain regional connectivity at rest. *Brain and Cognition*, 139, 105517. doi:10.1016/j.bandc.2020.105517.

Bærentsen, K.B., Stødkilde-Jørgensen, H., Sommerlund, B., Hartmann, T., Damsgaard-Madsen, J., Fosnæs, M., and Green, A. C. (2009). An investigation of brain processes supporting meditation. *Cognitive Processing*, 11(1), 57–84. doi:10.1007/s10339-009-0342-3.

Baijal, S., and Srinivasan, N. (2009). Theta activity and meditative states: spectral changes during concentrative meditation. *Cognitive Processing*, 11(1), 31–38. doi:10.1007/s10339-009-0272-0.

Baron, S.E., Kose, S., Mu, Q., Borckardt, J., Newberg, A., George, M.S., Kozel, F.A., (2010). Regional brain activation during meditation shows time and practice effects: An exploratory FMRI study. *Evid Based Complement Alternat Med*, 7, 121–127. https://doi.org/10.1093/ecam/nem163 . Epub 2007 Dec 27. PMID: 18955268.

Baron Short, E., Kose, S., Mu, Q., Borckardt, J., Newberg, A., George, M.S., and Kozel, F.A. (2010). Regional Brain Activation during Meditation Shows Time and Practice Effects: An Exploratory FMRI Study. *Evidence-Based Complementary and Alternative Medicine*, 7(1), 121–127. doi:10.1093/ecam/nem163.

Barrós-Loscertales, A., Hernández, S.E., Xiao, Y., González-Mora, J.L., and Rubia, K. (2021). Resting State Functional Connectivity Associated with Sahaja Yoga Meditation. *Frontiers in Human Neuroscience*, 15. doi:10.3389/fnhum.2021.614882.

Barry, J., (1968). General and comparative study of the psychokinetic effect on a fungus culture. *Journal of Parapsychology*, 32, 237–243.

Bear, M.F., Connors, B.W., Paradiso, M.A., (2005). Neuroscience: Exploring the Brain, Enhanced Edition. *Jones and Bartlett Learning.*

Beggs, J.M., and Plenz, D. (2003). Neuronal Avalanches in Neocortical Circuits. *The Journal of Neuroscience*, 23(35), 11167–11177. doi:10.1523/jneurosci.23-35-11167.2003.

Berkovich-Ohana, A., Glicksohn, J., and Goldstein, A. (2012). Mindfulness-induced changes in gamma band activity – Implications for the default mode network, self-reference and attention. *Clinical Neurophysiology*, 123(4), 700–710. doi:10.1016/j.clinph.2011.07.048.

Berkovich-Ohana, A., Glicksohn, J., and Goldstein, A. (2013). Studying the default mode and its mindfulness-induced changes using EEG functional connectivity. *Social Cognitive and Affective Neuroscience*, 9(10), 1616–1624. doi:10.1093/scan/nst153.

Berkovich-Ohana, A., Harel, M., Hahamy, A., Arieli, A., and Malach, R. (2016). Data for default network reduced functional connectivity in meditators, negatively correlated with meditation expertise. *Data in Brief*, 8, 910–914. doi:10.1016/j.dib.2016.07.015.

Berkovich-Ohana, A., Wilf, M., Kahana, R., Arieli, A., and Malach, R. (2015). Repetitive speech elicits widespread deactivation in the human cortex: The "Mantra" effect? *Brain and Behavior*, 5(7), n/a–n/a. doi:10.1002/brb3.346.

Besant, A., Leadbeater, C.W., and Dasa, C.M.J., (1908). Occult chemistry : A series of clairvoyant observations on the chemical elements. *Theosophical Society*.

Bhikkhu, T., (1997). The Meaning of the Buddha's Awakening. https://www.accesstoinsight.org/lib/authors/thanissaro/awaken-ing.html.

Bishop, S.R., Lau, M., Shapiro, S., Carlson, L., Anderson, N.D., Carmody, J., … Devins, G. (2006). Mindfulness: A Proposed Operational Definition. *Clinical Psychology: Science and Practice*, 11(3), 230–241. doi:10.1093/clipsy.bph077.

Bousso, R., (2002). Reviews of Modern Physics, Volume 74, July 2002. *The American Physics Society*.

Braboszcz, C., and Delorme, A. (2011). Lost in thoughts: Neural markers of low alertness during mind wandering. *NeuroImage*, 54(4), 3040–3047. doi:10.1016/j.neuroimage.2010.10.008.

Braboszcz, C., Cahn, B.R., Levy, J., Fernandez, M., and Delorme, A. (2017). Increased Gamma Brainwave Amplitude Compared to Control in Three Different Meditation Traditions. *PLOS ONE*, 12(1), e0170647. doi:10.1371/journal.pone.0170647.

Brahama Kumari Pari, (2015). Holographic Universe: An introduction. *GBK Publications, Malaysia*.

Brandmeyer, T., and Delorme, A. (2016). Reduced mind wandering in experienced meditators and associated EEG correlates. *Experimental Brain Research*, 236(9), 2519–2528. doi:10.1007/s00221-016-4811-5.

Braud, W.G., (2008). Patañjali Yoga and siddhis: Their relevance to parapsychological theory and research. In K.R. Rao, A.C. Paranjpe, and A.K. Dalal (Eds.), Handbook of Indian Psychology (pp. 217–243). *Cambridge University Press India/Foundation Books*. https://doi.org/10.1017/UPO9788175968448.012.

Bréchet, L., Ziegler, D. A., Simon, A.J., Brunet, D., Gazzaley, A., and Michel, C.M. (2021). Reconfiguration of Electroencephalography Microstate Networks after Breath-Focused, Digital Meditation Training. *Brain Connectivity*, 11(2), 146-155. doi:10.1089/brain.2020.0848.

Britton, W.B., Lindahl, J.R., Cahn, B.R., Davis, J. H., and Goldman, R. E. (2013). Awakening is not a metaphor: The effects of Buddhist meditation practices on basic wakefulness. *Annals of the New York Academy of Sciences*, 1307(1), 64–81. doi:10.1111/nyas.12279.

Cahn, B.R., and Polich, J. (2006). Meditation states and traits: EEG, ERP, and neuroimaging studies. *Psychological Bulletin*, 132(2), 180–211. doi:10.1037/0033-2909.132.2.180.

Cahn, B.R., Delorme, A., and Polich, J. (2009). Occipital gamma activation during Vipassana meditation. *Cognitive Processing*, 11(1), 39–56. doi:10.1007/s10339-009-0352-1.

Carhart-Harris, R.L., and Friston, K.J. (2019). REBUS and the Anarchic Brain: Toward a Unified Model of the Brain Action of Psychedelics. *Pharmacological Reviews*, 71(3), 316–344. doi:10.1124/pr.118.017160.

Carhart-Harris, R.L., Erritzoe, D., Haijen, E., Kaelen, M., and Watts, R. (2017). Psychedelics and connectedness. *Psychopharmacology*, 235(2), 547–550. doi:10.1007/s00213-017-4701-y.

Carhart-Harris, R.L., Erritzoe, D., Williams, T., Stone, J.M., Reed, L. J., Colasanti, A., … Nutt, D. J. (2012a). Neural correlates of the psychedelic state as determined by fMRI studies with psilocybin. *Proceedings of the National Academy of Sciences*, 109(6), 2138–2143. doi:10.1073/pnas.1119598109.

Carhart-Harris, R.L., Leech, R., Erritzoe, D., Williams, T.M., Stone, J. M., Evans, J., … Nutt, D. J. (2012b). Functional Connectivity Measures After Psilocybin Inform a Novel Hypothesis of Early Psychosis. *Schizophrenia Bulletin*, 39(6), 1343–1351. doi:10.1093/schbul/sbs117.

Carhart-Harris, R.L., Muthukumaraswamy, S., Roseman, L., Kaelen, M., Droog, W., Murphy, K., … Nutt, D. J. (2016). Neural correlates of the LSD experience revealed by multimodal neuroimaging. *Proceedings of the National*

Academy of Sciences, 113(17), 4853–4858. doi:10.1073/pnas.1518377113.

Carter, O.L., Presti, D.E., Callistemon, C., Ungerer, Y., Liu, G.B., Pettigrew, J.D., 2005. Meditation alters perceptual rivalry in Tibetan Buddhist monks. *Curr. Biol.* 15 (11), R412–R413.

Chalmer, D., J., (1997). The conscious mind: In the search of a fundamental theory. Philosophy of Mind. *Oxford University Press, Revised Edition.*

Chalmers, D., Hameroff, S., Montefiore and Behar A. (2014). Abstracts of an International Conference "Towards a Science of Consciousness 2014. *Center for Consciousness Studies, The University of Arizona*, www.consciousness.arizona.edu.

Chan, A.S., Cheung, M.C., Sze, S.L., Leung, W.W.M., and Shi, D. (2011). Shaolin Dan Tian Breathing Fosters Relaxed and Attentive Mind: A Randomized Controlled Neuro-Electrophysiological Study. *Evidence-Based Complementary and Alternative Medicine*, 2011, 1–11. doi:10.1155/2011/180704.

Chan, A.S., Han, Y.M.Y., and Cheung, M. (2008). Electroencephalographic (EEG) Measurements of Mindfulness-based Triarchic Body-pathway Relaxation Technique: A Pilot Study. *Applied Psychophysiology and Biofeedback*, 33(1), 39–47. doi:10.1007/s10484-008-9050-5.

Chandra, N., Dravya Sangraha. English translation by Nalini Balbir. *Hindi Granthalaya.*

Chen, A.C., Oathes, D.J., Chang, C., Bradley, T., Zhou, Z.W., Williams, L.M., … Etkin, A. (2013). Causal interactions between fronto-parietal central executive and default-mode networks in humans. *Proceedings of the National Academy of Sciences*, 110(49), 19944–19949. doi:10.1073/pnas.1311772110.

Chialvo, D.R. (2010). Emergent complex neural dynamics. *Nature Physics*, 6(10), 744–750. doi:10.1038/nphys1803.

Chiesa, A., Calati, R., and Serretti, A. (2011). Does mindfulness training improve cognitive abilities? A systematic review of neuropsychological findings. *Clinical Psychology Review*, 31(3), 449–464. doi:10.1016/j.cpr.2010.11.003.

Chopra, D., (2019) Meta Human. *Penguin Random House.*

Close, E., (1977). The Book of *Atma, Libra Publishers*, New York.

Cohen, M.X. (2014). Fluctuations in Oscillation Frequency Control Spike Timing and Coordinate Neural Networks. *Journal of Neuroscience*, 34(27), 8988–8998. doi:10.1523/jneurosci.0261-14.2014.

Colgan, D.D., Memmott, T., Klee, D., Ernst, L., Han, S.J., and Oken, B. (2019). A Brief Report: A single case design to examine short-term intracranial EGG patterns during focused meditation. *Neuroscience Letters*, 134441. doi:10.1016/j.neulet.2019.134441.

Cotier, F.A., Zhang, R., and Lee, T.M.C. (2017). A longitudinal study of the effect of short-term meditation training on functional network organisation of the aging brain. *Scientific Reports*, 7(1). doi:10.1038/s41598-017-00678-8.

Creswell, J.D., Taren, A.A., Lindsay, E.K., Greco, C.M., Gianaros, P.J., Fairgrieve, A., … Ferris, J.L. (2016). Alterations in Resting-State Functional Connectivity Link Mindfulness Meditation With Reduced Interleukin-6: A Randomised Controlled Trial. *Biological Psychiatry*, 80(1), 53–61. doi:10.1016/j.biopsych.2016.01.008.

Csikszentmihalyi, M. (1990). Flow: The psychology of optimal experience. *New York: Harper and Row.*

Csikszentmihalyi, M. (1996). Creativity: Flow and the psychology of discovery and invention. *New York: HarperCollins.*

Davanger, S., Ellingsen, Ø., Holen, A., and Hugdahl, K. (2010). Meditation-Specific Prefrontal Cortical Activation during Acem Meditation: An FMRI Study. *Perceptual and Motor Skills*, 111(1), 291–306. doi:10.2466/02.04.22.pms.111.4.291-306.

Dean, D., (1982). Infrared measurements of healer treated water. *Roll, W.G., Beloff J, White R.A., eds. Research in parapsychology. Metuchen, NJ: Scarecrow Press*, 1983:100–101.

Dean, D. ([Doctoral dissertation]. University microfilms international, No. 8408650. Saybrook Institute) in: An examination of intra-red and ultra-violet techniques to test for changes in water following the laying-on-of-hands. 1983: 111-115.

Deane, G. (2020). Dissolving the self: Active inference, psychedelics, and ego-dissolution. *Philosophy and the Mind Sciences*, 1(I), 2. https://doi.org/10.33735/phimisci.2020.I.39.

Deepeshwar, S., Nagendra, H.R., and Rana, B.B. (2019). Evolution from four mental states to the highest state of consciousness: A neurophysiological basis of meditation as defined in yoga texts. *Progress in Brain Research*. doi:10.1016/bs.pbr.2018.10.029.

Delorme, A., and Brandmeyer, T. (2019). When the meditating mind wanders. *Current Opinion in Psychology*, 28, 133-137. doi:10.1016/j.copsyc.2018.12.006.

DeLosAngeles, D., Williams, G., Burston, J., Fitzgibbon, S.P., Lewis, T.W., Grummett, T.S., … Willoughby, J.O. (2016). Electroencephalographic correlates of states of concentrative meditation. *International Journal of Psychophysiology*, 110, 27–39. doi:10.1016/j.ijpsycho.2016.09.020.

Dennett, D., (1995). Darwin's Dangerous Idea: Evolution and the Meanings of Life, Simon and Schuster.

Dennison, P. (2019). The Human Default Consciousness and

Its Disruption: Insights From an EEG Study of Buddhist Jhāna Meditation. *Frontiers in Human Neuroscience*, 13. doi:10.3389/fnhum.2019.00178.

Dentico, D., Bachhuber, D., Riedner, B.A., Ferrarelli, F., Tononi, G., Davidson, R.J., and Lutz, A. (2018). Acute Effects of Meditation Training on the Waking and Sleeping Brain: Is it all about homeostasis? *European Journal of Neuroscience*. doi:10.1111/ejn.14131.

Deutsch, D., (1997). The Fabric of Reality: The Science of Parallel Universes and Its Implications. *Penguin*.

Devaney, K., Levin, E., Tripathi, V., Higgins, J., Lazar, S., and Somers, D. (2021). Attention and Default Mode Network Assessments of Meditation Experience During Active Cognition and Rest. *Brain Sciences*, 11(5), 566. doi:10.3390/brainsci11050566.

Dickenson, J., Berkman, E.T., Arch, J., and Lieberman, M.D. (2012). Neural correlates of focused attention during a brief mindfulness induction. *Social Cognitive and Affective Neuroscience*, 8(1), 40–47. doi:10.1093/scan/nss030.

Dissanayaka, C., Ben-Simon, E., Gruberger, M., Maron-Katz, A., Hendler, T., Chaparro-Vargas, R., and Cvetkovic, D. (2014). Information flow and coherence of EEG during awake, meditation and drowsiness. *2014 36th Annual International Conference of the IEEE Engineering in Medicine and Biology Society*. doi:10.1109/embc.2014.6944858.

Dissanayaka, C., Ben-Simon, E., Gruberger, M., Maron-Katz, A., Sharon, H., Hendler, T., and Cvetkovic, D. (2015). Comparison between human awake, meditation and drowsiness EEG activities based on directed transfer function and MVDR coherence methods. *Medical and Biological Engineering and Computing*, 53(7), 599–607. doi:10.1007/s11517-015-1272-0.

Do Buddhists Pray? *Buddhist Dharma Education Association*. https://www.buddhanet.net/e-learning/history/b_faqs.htm.

Dodich, A., Zollo, M., Crespi, C., Cappa, S.F., Laureiro Martinez, D., Falini, A., and Canessa, N. (2018). Short-term Sahaja Yoga meditation training modulates brain structure and spontaneous activity in the executive control network. *Brain and Behavior*, e01159. doi:10.1002/brb3.1159.

Doll, A., Hölzel, B.K., Boucard, C.C., Wohlschläger, A.M., and Sorg, C. (2015). Mindfulness is associated with intrinsic functional connectivity between default mode and salience networks. *Frontiers in Human Neuroscience*, 9. doi:10.3389/fnhum.2015.00461.

Dor-Ziderman Y, Ataria Y, Fulder S, Goldstein A, Berkovich-Ohana A. (2016). Self-specific processing in the meditating brain: A MEG neurophenomenology study. *Neurosci Conscious*. 2016(1):niw019. doi: 10.1093/nc/niw019. Epub 2016 Oct 10. PMID: 30397512; PMCID: PMC6210398.

Dürschmid, S., Reichert, C., Walter, N., Hinrichs, H., Heinze, H.-J., Ohl, F.W., … Deliano, M. (2020). Self-regulated critical brain dynamics originate from high frequency-band activity in the MEG. *PLOS ONE*, 15(6), e0233589. doi:10.1371/journal.pone.0233589.

Emoto, M., (2017). What is the photograph of frozen water crystals? http:// www.masaru-emoto.net/english/watercrystal.html.

Encyclopedia of Creativity. *San Diego, CA: Academic Press*, 59-70.

Engen, H.G., Bernhardt, B.C., Skottnik, L., Ricard, M., and Singer, T. (2017). Structural changes in socio-affective networks: Multi-modal MRI findings in long-term meditation practitioners. *Neuropsychologia*, 116, 26–33. doi:10.1016/j.neuropsychologia.2017.08.024.

Engström, M., and Söderfeldt, B. (2010). Brain Activation During Compassion Meditation: A Case Study. *The Journal of Alternative and Complementary Medicine*, 16(5), 597–599. doi:10.1089/acm.2009.0309.

Engström, M., Pihlsgård, J., Lundberg, P., and Söderfeldt, B. (2010). Functional Magnetic Resonance Imaging of Hippocampal Activation During Silent Mantra Meditation. *The Journal of Alternative and Complementary Medicine*, 16(12), 1253–1258. doi:10.1089/acm.2009.0706.

Ertel, S., (1994). Invited Address: Testing Sheldrake's Claim of Morphogenetic Fields. In E. W. Cook and D. L. Delanoy, eds., R*esearch in Parapsychology 1991*, *Metuchen, N. J. and London: Scarecrow Press*, 169- 192.

Faber, P.L., Lehmann, D., Gianotti, L.R.R., Milz, P., Pascual-Marqui, R.D., Held, M., and Kochi, K. (2014). Zazen meditation and no-task resting EEG compared with LORETA intracortical source localization. *Cognitive Processing*, 16(1), 87–96. doi:10.1007/s10339-014-0637-x.

Faber, P.L., Lehmann, D., Tei, S., Tsujiuchi, T., Kumano, H., Pascual-Marqui, R.D., and Kochi, K. (2012). EEG source imaging during two Qigong meditations. *Cognitive Processing*, 13(3), 255–265. doi:10.1007/s10339-012-0441-4.

Fan, Y., Tang, Y.Y., Tang, R., and Posner, M.I. (2014). Short Term Integrative Meditation Improves Resting Alpha Activity and Stroop Performance. *Applied Psychophysiology and Biofeedback*, 39(3-4), 213–217. doi:10.1007/s10484-014-9258-5.

Farb, N.A.S., Anderson, A.K., and Segal, Z.V. (2012). The Mindful Brain and Emotion Regulation in Mood Disorders. *The Canadian Journal of Psychiatry*, 57(2), 70–77. doi:10.1 177/070674371205700203.

Fenwick P, and Hopkins, R., (1986). An examination of the effect of healing on water. *J Soc Psych Res*. 53, 387–390.

Ferrarelli, F., Smith, R., Dentico, D., Riedner, B. A., Zennig, C., Benca, R. M., … Tononi, G. (2013). Experienced Mindfulness Meditators Exhibit Higher Parietal-Occipital EEG Gamma

Activity during NREM Sleep. *PLoS ONE*, 8(8), e73417. doi:10.1371/journal.pone.0073417.

Fingelkurts, A.A., Fingelkurts, A.A., and Kallio-Tamminen, T. (2015). EEG-guided meditation: A personalized approach. *Journal of Physiology-Paris*, 109(4-6), 180–190. doi:10.1016/j.jphysparis.2015.03.001.

Fingelkurts, A.A., Fingelkurts, A.A., and Kallio-Tamminen, T. (2016). Long-term meditation training induced changes in the operational synchrony of default mode network modules during a resting state. *Cognitive Processing*, 17(1), 27–37. https://doi.org/10.1007/s10339-015-0743-4.

Fingelkurts, A.A., Fingelkurts, A.A., Bagnato, S., Boccagni, C., and Galardi, G. (2012). DMN Operational Synchrony Relates to Self-Consciousness: Evidence from Patients in Vegetative and Minimally Conscious States. *The Open Neuroimaging Journal*, 6, 55–68. doi:10.2174/1874440001206010055.

Finlay, L, (2009). Debating Phenomenological Methods, *Phenomenology and Practice,* 3(1), 6-25.

Fox, K.C.R., Dixon, M.L., Nijeboer, S., Girn, M., Floman, J.L., Lifshitz, M., … Christoff, K. (2016). Functional neuroanatomy of meditation: A review and meta-analysis of 78 functional neuroimaging investigations. *Neuroscience and Biobehavioral Reviews*, 65, 208–228. doi:10.1016/j.neubiorev.2016.03.021.

Friston, K. (2018). Am I Self-Conscious? (Or Does Self-Organization Entail Self-Consciousness?). *Frontiers in Psychology*, 9. doi:10.3389/fpsyg.2018.00579.

Friston, K. (2010) The free-energy principle: A unified brain theory? *Nat Rev Neurosci* 11:127–138.

Froeliger, B., Garland, E.L., Kozink, R.V., Modlin, L.A., Chen, N.K., McClernon, F.J., … Sobin, P. (2012). Meditation-State Functional Connectivity (msFC): Strengthening of the Dorsal Attention Network and Beyond. *Evidence-Based Complementary and Alternative Medicine*, 2012, 1–9. doi:10.1155/2012/680407.

Gallagher, S. (2000). Philosophical conceptions of the self: Implications for cognitive science. *Trends in Cognitive Sciences*, 4(1), 14–21. doi:10.1016/s1364-6613(99)01417-5.

Garrison, K.A., Santoyo, J.F., Davis, J.H., Thornhill, T.A., Kerr, C.E., and Brewer, J. A. (2013a). Effortless awareness: using real time neurofeedback to investigate correlates of posterior cingulate cortex activity in meditators' self-report. *Frontiers in Human Neuroscience*, 7. doi:10.3389/fnhum.2013.00440.

Garrison, K.A., Scheinost, D., Constable, R.T., and Brewer, J.A. (2014). BOLD signal and functional connectivity associated with loving kindness meditation. *Brain and Behavior*, 4(3), 337–347. doi:10.1002/brb3.219.

Garrison, K.A., Scheinost, D., Worhunsky, P.D., Elwafi, H.M., Thornhill, T.A., Thompson, E., … Brewer, J.A. (2013). Real-time fMRI links subjective experience with brain activity during focused attention. *NeuroImage*, 81, 110–118. doi:10.1016/j.neuroimage.2013.05.030.

Garrison, K.A., Zeffiro, T.A., Scheinost, D., Constable, R.T., and Brewer, J.A. (2015). Meditation leads to reduced default mode network activity beyond an active task. *Cognitive, Affective, and Behavioral Neuroscience*, 15(3), 712–720. doi:10.3758/s13415-015-0358-3.

Gigch, J.P., (1978). Applied General Systems Theory. *Harper and Row*.

Goldin, P., Ramel, W., Gross, J., (2009). Mindfulness Meditation Training and Self-Referential Processing in Social Anxiety Disorder: Behavioral and Neural Effects. *J Cogn Psychother*. 23(3):242-257. doi: 10.1891/0889-8391.23.3.242. PMID: 25568592; PMCID: PMC4283801.

Goldsmith, E., (1990). Evolution, Neo-Darwan-ism and the Paradigm of Science. *The Ecologist*, 20 (2) 67.

Golesorkhi, M., Gomez-Pilar, J., Tumati, S., Fraser, M., and Northoff, G. (2020). Temporal hierarchy of intrinsic neural timescales converges with spatial core-periphery organization. Commun. Biol. (In Press).

Goshvarpour, A., Goshvarpour. A., Rahati. S., Saadatian. V.. (2012) Bispectrum estimation of electroencephalogram signals during meditation. *Iran J Psychiatry Behav Sci.* 6(1): 48-54.

Grad, B., and Dean, D., (1983). Independent confirmation of infrared healer effects. In: White, R.A., Broughton R.S., eds. *Research in Parapsychology. Metuchen, NJ: Scarecrow Press*; 1984:81–83.

Greeley, A.M., and William, C., M., (1975). Are we a nation of mystics. *New York Times Magazine* 26, 12-25. See also the version reprinted in Goleman et al, Consciousness.

Greicius, M. D., Krasnow, B., Reiss, A. L., and Menon, V. (2002). Functional connectivity in the resting brain: A network analysis of the default mode hypothesis. *Proceedings of the National Academy of Sciences,* 100(1), 253–258. doi:10.1073/pnas.0135058100.

Guleria, A., Kumar, U., Kishan, S.S.K., and Khetrapal, C.L. (2013). Effect of "SOHAM" meditation on the human brain: An fMRI study. *Psychiatry Research: Neuroimaging*, 214(3), 462–465. doi:10.1016/j.pscychresns.2013.06.012.

Guth, A., H., (1981). Inflationary universe: A possible solution to the horizon and flatness problems. *Physical Review D*, 23(2), 347.

Hankey, A., (2021). Following the Lucas Argument to Completion: J.R. Lucas, 18 June 1929–5 April 2020, In Memoriam. *Cosmos and History: The Journal of Natural and Social Philosophy*, 17(1), 265-78.

Hanley, A.W., Garland, E.L., 2019. Mindfulness training disrupts Pavlovian conditioning. *Physiol. Behav*. 204, 151–154.

Haraldsson, E., and Thorsteinsson, T., (1973). Psychokinetic effectson yeast: An exploratory experiment. In: Roll, W.G., Morris R.L., Morris J.D., eds. *Research in Parapsychology*, 1972: 20–21.

Harne, B.P., and Hiwale, A.S. (2018). EEG Spectral Analysis on OM Mantra Meditation: *A Pilot Study. Applied Psychophysiology and Biofeedback*, 43(2), 123–129. doi:10.1007/s10484-018-9391-7.

Harrison, R., Zeidan, F., Kitsaras, G., Ozcelik, D., and Salomons, T. V. (2018). Trait mindfulness is associated with lower pain reactivity and connectivity of the default mode network. *The Journal of Pain*. doi:10.1016/j.jpain.2018.10.011.

Hasenkamp, W., Wilson-Mendenhall, C.D., Duncan, E., and Barsalou, L.W. (2012). Mind wandering and attention during focused meditation: A fine-grained temporal analysis of fluctuating cognitive states. *NeuroImage*, 59(1), 750–760. doi:10.1016/j.neuroimage.2011.07.008.

Hasson, U., Chen, J., and Honey, C.J. (2015). Hierarchical process memory: memory as an integral component of information processing. *Trends in Cognitive Sciences*, 19(6), 304–313. doi:10.1016/j.tics.2015.04.006.

Hauswald, A., Übelacker, T., Leske, S., and Weisz, N. (2015). What it means to be Zen: Marked modulations of local and interareal synchronization during open monitoring meditation. *NeuroImage*, 108, 265–273. doi:10.1016/j.neuroimage.2014.12.065.

Hebert, R., Lehmann, D., Tan, G., Travis, F., and Arenander, A. (2005). Enhanced EEG alpha time-domain phase synchrony during Transcendental Meditation: Implications for cortical integration theory. *Signal Processing*, 85(11), 2213–2232. doi:10.1016/j.sigpro.2005.07.009.

Hernández, S.E., Suero, J., Rubia, K., and González-Mora, J.L. (2015). Monitoring the Neural Activity of the State of Mental Silence While Practising Sahaja Yoga Meditation. *The Journal of Alternative and Complementary Medicine*, 21(3), 175–179. doi:10.1089/acm.2013.0450.

Hinterberger, T., Schmidt, S., Kamei, T., and Walach, H. (2014). Decreased electrophysiological activity represents the conscious state of emptiness in meditation. *Frontiers in Psychology*, 5. doi:10.3389/fpsyg.2014.00099.

History of Ayurveda. *National Ayurvedic Medical Association*, https://www.ayurvedanama.org/history-of-ayurveda/.

Hohwy, J. (2007). Functional integration and the mind. *Synthese*, 159(3), 315–328. doi:10.1007/s11229-007-9240-3.

Hölzel, B.K., Ott, U., Hempel, H., Hackl, A., Wolf, K., Stark, R., and Vaitl, D. (2007). Differential engagement of anterior cingulate and adjacent medial frontal cortex in adept meditators and non-meditators. *Neuroscience Letters*, 421(1), 16–21. doi:10.1016/j.neulet.2007.04.074.

Honey, C.J., Thesen, T., Donner, T.H., Silbert, L.J., Carlson, C.E., Devinsky, O., … Hasson, U. (2012). Slow Cortical Dynamics and the Accumulation of Information over Long Timescales. *Neuron*, 76(2), 423–434. doi:10.1016/j.neuron.2012.08.011.

Huang, H.Y., and Lo, P.C. (2009). EEG dynamics of experienced Zen meditation practitioners probed by complexity index and spectral measure. *Journal of Medical Engineering and Technology*, 33(4), 314–321. doi:10.1080/03091900802602677.

Hudetz, A.G., Liu, X., and Pillay, S. (2015). Dynamic Repertoire of Intrinsic Brain States is Reduced in Propofol-Induced Unconsciousness. *Brain Connectivity*, 5(1), 10–22. doi:10.1089/brain.2014.0230.

Ito, T., Hearne, L.J., and Cole, M.W. (2020). A cortical hierarchy of localized and distributed processes revealed via dissociation of task activations, connectivity changes, and intrinsic timescales. *NeuroImage*, 221, 117141. doi:10.1016/j.neuroimage.2020.117141.

Ives-Deliperi, V.L., Solms, M., and Meintjes, E.M. (2011). The neural substrates of mindfulness: An fMRI investigation. *Social Neuroscience*, 6(3), 231–242. doi:10.1080/17470919.2010.513495.

Jain, S.A., (1992) Reality English translation of Sarvarhsiddhi by Pujyapad – Commentary on Tattvarathasutra of Uma Swami. *Jwalamalini Trust*.

Jang, J.H., Jung, W.H., Kang, D.H., Byun, M.S., Kwon, S. J., Choi, C.H., and Kwon, J. S. (2011). Increased default mode network connectivity associated with meditation. *Neuroscience Letters*, 487(3), 358–362. doi:10.1016/j.neulet.2010.10.056.

Jang, J.H., Kim, J.H., Yun, J.Y., Choi, S.H., An, S.C., and Kang, D.H. (2018). Differences in Functional Connectivity of the Insula Between Brain Wave Vibration in Meditators and Non-meditators. *Mindfulness*. doi:10.1007/s12671-018-0928-x.

Jao, T., Li, C.W., Vértes, P.E., Wu, C.W., Achard, S., Hsieh, C.H., … Bullmore, E.T. (2016). Large-Scale Functional Brain Network Reorganization During Taoist Meditation. *Brain Connectivity*, 6(1), 9–24. doi:10.1089/brain.2014.0318.

Jason W. Brown, drjbrown.org.

Jiang, H., He, B., Guo, X., Wang, X., Guo, M., Wang, Z., … Cui, D. (2019). Brain–Heart Interactions Underlying Traditional Tibetan Buddhist Meditation. *Cerebral Cortex*. doi:10.1093/cercor/bhz095.

Jo, H.G., Naranjo, J.R., Hinterberger, T., Winter, U., and Schmidt, S. (2019). Phase synchrony in slow cortical potentials is decreased in both expert and trained novice meditators. *Neuroscience Letters*. doi:10.1016/j.neulet.2019.02.035.

Josipovic, Z. (2013). Freedom of the mind. *Frontiers in Psychology*, 4. doi:10.3389/fpsyg.2013.00538.

Jung, C., (1974). Dreams II. Trans. by R.F.C. Hull. *Princeton University Press*.

Jung, C.G., (1960). On the Nature of the Psyche, Vol. 8 of The Collected Works of C. G. Jung, translated by R.F.C. Hull. *Princeton University*.

Jung, C.G. (1927). Collected Works, Volume 8, CW-8:180.

Kajimura, S., Masuda, N., Lau, J.K., and Murayama, K. (2020). Focused attention meditation changes the boundary and configuration of functional networks in the brain. *Scientific Reports*, 10(1). doi:10.1038/s41598-020-75396-9.

Kakumanu, R.J., Nair, A.K., Venugopal, R., Sasidharan, A., Ghosh, P.K., John, J.P., … Kutty, B.M. (2018). Dissociating meditation proficiency and experience dependent EEG changes during traditional Vipassana meditation practice. *Biological Psychology*, 135, 65–75. doi:10.1016/j.biopsycho.2018.03.004.

Karl, H., (2013). Brain and perception: Holonomy and structure in figural processing. *Psychology Press 2013a*.

Katyal, S., and Goldin, P. (2020). Long-range parietal-occipital gamma-band desynchronisation underlies meditation-induced stabilisation of perception. *PsyArXiv* Preprints. doi:10.31234/osf.io/zpxuv.

Katyal, S., Hajcak, G., Flora, T., Bartlett, A., Goldin, P. (2020). Event-related potential and behavioural differences in affective self-referential processing in long-term meditators versus controls. *Cogn Affect Behav Neurosci*, 20(2), 326-339. doi: 10.3758/s13415-020-00771-y. PMID: 31981093.

Kelso, J., Holt, K., Kugler, P. and Turvey, M. (1980). On the concept of coordinative structures. In: Stelmach, G. and Requin, J. (Eds) *Tutorials in Motor Behavior*.

Killingsworth, M.A., and Gilbert, D.T. (2010). A Wandering Mind is an Unhappy Mind. *Science*, 330(6006), 932–932. doi:10.1126/science.1192439.

King, A.P., Block, S.R., Sripada, R.K., Rauch, S., Giardino, N., Favorite, T., … Liberzon, I. (2016). Altered Default Mode Network (Dmn) Resting State Functional Connectivity Following A Mindfulness-Based Exposure Therapy For Posttraumatic Stress Disorder (Ptsd) In Combat Veterans of Afghanistan and Iraq. *Depression and Anxiety*, 33(4), 289–299. doi:10.1002/da.22481.

Klimesch, W. (2012). Alpha-band oscillations, attention, and controlled access to stored information. *Trends in Cognitive Sciences*, 16(12), 606–617. doi:10.1016/j.tics.2012.10.007.

Korponay, C., Dentico, D., Kral, T.R.A., Ly, M., Kruis, A., Davis, K., … Davidson, R.J. (2019). The Effect of Mindfulness Meditation on Impulsivity and its Neurobiological Correlates in Healthy Adults. *Scientific Reports*, 9(1). doi:10.1038/s41598-019-47662-y.

Kral, T.R.A., Imhoff-Smith, T., Dean, D.C., Grupe, D., Adluru, N., Patsenko, E., … Davidson, R. J. (2019). Mindfulness-Based Stress Reduction-related changes in posterior cingulate resting brain connectivity. *Social Cognitive and Affective Neuroscience*. doi:10.1093/scan/nsz050.

Kubota, Y., Sato, W., Toichi, M., Murai, T., Okada, T., Hayashi, A., and Sengoku, A. (2001). Frontal midline theta rhythm is correlated with cardiac autonomic activities during the performance of an attention demanding meditation procedure. *Cognitive Brain Research*, 11(2), 281–287. doi:10.1016/s0926-6410(00)00086-0.

Kuhn, T., (1962). Structure of Scientific Revolutions. *The University of Chicago Press.*

Kwak, S., Kim, S.Y., Bae, D., Hwang, W.J., Cho, K.I.K., Lim, K.O., … Kwon, J.S. (2020). Enhanced Attentional Network by Short-Term Intensive Meditation. *Frontiers in Psychology*, 10. doi:10.3389/fpsyg.2019.03073.

Kwak, S., Lee, T.Y., Jung, W.H., Hur, J.W., Bae, D., Hwang, W.J., … Kwon, J.S. (2019). The Immediate and Sustained Positive Effects of Meditation on Resilience Are Mediated by Changes in the Resting Brain. *Frontiers in Human Neuroscience*, 13. doi:10.3389/fnhum.2019.00101.

Lagopoulos, J., Xu, J., Rasmussen, I., Vik, A., Malhi, G.S., Eliassen, C.F., … Ellingsen, Ø. (2009). Increased Theta and Alpha EEG Activity During Nondirective Meditation. *The Journal of Alternative and Complementary Medicine*, 15(11), 1187–1192. doi:10.1089/acm.2009.0113.

Lal, K.N., (2014). Scientific Exploration of Jain Doctrine, Part 1 and Part 2. *Motilal Banarasidass Pvt. Ltd.*

Lamblin, M., Murawski, C., Whittle, S., and Fornito, A. (2017). Social connectedness, mental health and the adolescent brain. *Neuroscience and Biobehavioral Reviews*, 80, 57–68. doi:10.1016/j.neubiorev.2017.05.010.

Langdridge, D.(2007) *Phenomenological Psychology, Theory, Research and Method***,** Pearson Education, Harlow, England.

Laukkonen, R., Dr., and Slagter, H.A. (2020, November 17). From many to (n)one: Meditation and the plasticity of the predictive mind. https://doi.org/10.31234/osf.io/5sw6m.

Lazar, S. W., Bush, G., Gollub, R.L., Fricchione, G.L., Khalsa, G., and Benson, H. (2000). Functional brain mapping of the relaxation response and meditation. *NeuroReport*, 11(7), 1581-1585. doi:10.1097/00001756-200005150-00042.

Lee, Y.H., Shiah, Y.J., Chen, S. C.J., Wang, S.F., Young, M.S., and Lin, C.-L. (2015). Improved Emotional Stability in Experienced Meditators with Concentrative Meditation Based on Electroencephalography and Heart Rate Variability. *The Journal of Alternative and Complementary Medicine*, 21(1), 31–39. doi:10.1089/acm.2013.0465.

Lim, J., Teng, J., Patanaik, A., Tandi, J., and Massar, S.A.A. (2018). Dynamic functional connectivity markers of objective trait mindfulness. *NeuroImage*, 176, 193–202. doi:10.1016/j.neuroimage.2018.04.056.

Liou, C., Hsieh, C., Hsieh, C., Chen, J., Wang, C., and Lee, S. (2005). Studies of Chinese Original Quiet Sitting by Using Functional Magnetic Resonance Imaging. *2005 IEEE Engineering in Medicine and Biology 27th Annual Conference*. doi:10.1109/iembs.2005.1615681.

Liu, X., Jiang, A., Xu, N., and Xue, J. (2016). Increment Entropy as a Measure of Complexity for Time Series. *Entropy*, 18(1), 22. doi:10.3390/e18010022.

Lo, P., and Huang, H. (2007). Investigation of meditation scenario by quantifying the complexity index of EEG. *Journal of the Chinese Institute of Engineers*, 30(3), 389–400. doi:10.1080/02533839.2007.9671267.

Lumma A.L., Valk SL, Böckler A, Vrtička P, Singer T. Change in emotional self-concept following socio-cognitive training relates to structural plasticity of the prefrontal cortex. *Brain Behav*. March 2018, 13;8(4):e00940. doi: 10.1002/brb3.940. PMID: 29670822; PMCID: PMC5893336.

Lutz, A., Greischar, L.L., Rawlings, N.B., Ricard, M., and Davidson, R. J. (2004). Long-term meditators self-induce high-amplitude gamma synchrony during mental practice. *Proceedings of the National Academy of Sciences*, 101(46), 16369–16373. doi:10.1073/pnas.0407401101.

Lutz, A., Slagter, H.A., Dunne, J.D., and Davidson, R.J. (2008). Attention regulation and monitoring in meditation. *Trends in Cognitive Sciences*, 12(4), 163–169. doi:10.1016/j.tics.2008.01.005.

Lutz, J., Brühl, A.B., Scheerer, H., Jäncke, L., and Herwig, U. (2016). Neural correlates of mindful self-awareness in mindfulness meditators and meditation-naïve subjects revisited. *Biological Psychology*, 119, 21–30. doi:10.1016/j.biopsycho.2016.06.010.

Lutz, J,, Brühl ,A.B, Doerig N,, Scheerer H., Achermann R., Weibel A., Jäncke L., Herwig U.(2016). Altered processing of self-related emotional stimuli in mindfulness meditators. *Neuroimage*. January 2016, 1;124(Pt A):958-967. doi: 10.1016/j.neuroimage.2015.09.057. Epub 2015 October 9. PMID: 26455808.

Lymeus, F., Lundgren, T., and Hartig, T. (2016). Attentional Effort of Beginning Mindfulness Training is Offset With Practice Directed Toward Images of Natural Scenery. *Environment and Behavior*, 49(5), 536–559. doi:10.1177/0013916516657390.

Mahlberg, A., (1987). Evidence of collective memory: A test of Sheldrake's theory. *Journal of Analytical Psychology*, :23–34. https://doi.org/10.1111/j.1465-5922.1987.00023.x. https://onlinelibrary.wiley.com/doi/abs/10.1111/j.1465-5922.1987.00023.x.

Mahone, M. C., Travis, F., Gevirtz, R., and Hubbard, D. (2018). fMRI during Transcendental Meditation practice. *Brain and Cognition*, 123, 30–33. doi:10.1016/j.bandc.2018.02.011.

Marcer, P., and Rowlands P., (2017). Nilpotent Quantum Mechanics: Analog and Applications. *Frontiers in Physics* 28, 1–8. doi: 10.3389/fphy.2017.00028.

Mark 2:8; Acts 7:59; Rom 1:9; 8:16; 1 Cor 5:3-5. *Bible Gateway*. https://www.biblegateway.com.

Martínez, A. Y., Demertzi, A., Bauer, C. C., Gracia-Tabuenca, Z., Alcauter, S., and Barrios, F. A. (2021). The Time Varying Networks of the Interoceptive Attention and Rest. *Eneuro*, 8(3). doi:10.1523/eneuro.0341-20.2021.

Martino, M., Magioncalda, P., Huang, Z., Conio, B., Piaggio, N., Duncan, N. W., … Northoff, G. (2016). Contrasting variability patterns in the default mode and sensorimotor networks balance in bipolar depression and mania. *Proceedings of the National Academy of Sciences*, 113(17), 4824–4829. doi:10.1073/pnas.1517558113 .

Marusak, H.A., Elrahal, F., Peters, C.A., Kundu, P., Lombardo, M.V., Calhoun, V.D., … Rabinak, C.A. (2018). Mindfulness and dynamic functional neural connectivity in children and adolescents. *Behavioural Brain Research*, 336, 211–218. doi:10.1016/j.bbr.2017.09.010.

Matthew 3:13-17 New International Version. *Bible Gateway*. https://www.biblegateway.com/passage/?search=Matthew+3%3A13-17andversion=NIV.

McGovern, P.E., Zhang, J., Tang, J., Zhang, Z., Hall, G.R., Moreau, R.A., Nuñez, A., Butrym, E.D., Richards, M.P., Wang, C.S., Cheng, G., Zhao, Z., and Wang, C. (2004). Fermented beverages of pre- and proto-historic China. *Proceedings of the National Academy of Sciences of the United States of America*, 101 (51), 17593–17598. https://doi.org/10.1073/pnas.0407921102.

Mehta (1998) Jain philosophy: An introduction, *Bharatiya Vidhya Bhawan.*

Mierau, A., Klimesch, W., and Lefebvre, J. (2017). State-dependent alpha peak frequency shifts: Experimental evidence, potential mechanisms and functional implications. *Neuroscience*, 360, 146–154. doi:10.1016/j.neuroscience.2017.07.037.

Milz, P., Faber, P.L., Lehmann, D., Kochi, K., and Pascual-Marqui, R. D. (2014). sLORETA intracortical lagged coherence during breath counting in meditation-naÃ¯ve participants. *Frontiers in Human Neuroscience*, 8. doi:10.3389/fnhum.2014.00303.

Mishra, J., Sagar, R., Parveen, S., Kumaran, S., Modi, K., Maric, V., … Gazzaley, A. (2020). Closed-loop digital meditation for neurocognitive and behavioral development in adolescents with childhood neglect. *Translational Psychiatry*, 10(1). doi:10.1038/s41398-020-0820-z.

Mishra, S., Singh, S., Moheb, N., Khosa, S., and Trikamji, B. (2017). Changes in functional magnetic resonance imaging with Yogic meditation: A pilot study. *AYU (An International Quarterly Journal of Research in Ayurveda)*, 38(2), 108. doi:10.4103/ayu.ayu_34_17.

Mitchell, E.D., and Staretz., R., (2017). The Quantum Hologram and the Nature of Consciousness. *Consciousness and the Universe: Quantum Physics, Evolution, Brain and Mind*, edited by Roger Penrose, Stuart Hameroff, and Subhahs Kak, 82–114. Cambridge, MA: Cosmology Science Publishers.

Miyoshi, T., Tanioka, K., Yamamoto, S., Yadohisa, H., Hiroyasu, T., and Hiwa, S. (2020). Revealing Changes in Brain Functional Networks Caused by Focused-Attention Meditation Using Tucker3 Clustering. *Frontiers in Human Neuroscience*, 13. doi:10.3389/fnhum.2019.00473.

Murata, T., Takahashi, T., Hamada, T., Omori, M., Kosaka, H., Yoshida, H., and Wada, Y. (2004). Individual Trait Anxiety Levels Characterizing the Properties of Zen Meditation. *Neuropsychobiology*, 50(2), 189–194. doi:10.1159/000079113.

Murray, R.J., Debbané, M., Fox, P.T., Bzdok, D., and Eickhoff, S.B. (2014). Functional connectivity mapping of regions associated with self- and other-processing. *Human Brain Mapping*, 36(4), 1304–1324. doi:10.1002/hbm.22703.

Muthukumaraswamy, S.D., Carhart-Harris, R.L., Moran, R.J., Brookes, M.J., Williams, T. M., Errtizoe, D., … Nutt, D.J. (2013). Broadband Cortical Desynchronization Underlies the Human Psychedelic State. *Journal of Neuroscience*, 33(38), 15171–15183. doi:10.1523/jneurosci.2063-13.2013.

Nash, C., (1984). Test of psychokinetic control of bacterial mutation. *J Soc Psych Res*, 78, 145–152.

Navarro, O., Tapia-Fonllem, C., Fraijo-Sing, B., Roussiau, N., Ortiz-Valdez, A., Guillard, M., … Fleury-Bahi, G. (2019).

Connectedness to nature and its relationship with spirituality, well-being and sustainable behaviour / Conectividad con la naturaleza y su relación con la espiritualidad, el bienestar y la conducta sustentable. *Psyecology*, 1–12. doi:10.1080/21711976.2019.1643662.

Nayanar, A.C., (1975). Panchastikaya by Kundakunda, its English translation. *Bhartiya Gyanapeeth.*

Neumann, J.V., and Morgenstern, O., (2007). Theory of games and economic behavior. *Princeton university press.*

Newberg, A., Alavi, A., Baime, M., Pourdehnad, M., Santanna, J., and d' Aquili, E. (2001). The measurement of regional cerebral blood flow during the complex cognitive task of meditation: a preliminary SPECT study. *Psychiatry Research: Neuroimaging*, 106(2), 113–122. doi:10.1016/s0925-4927(01)00074-9.

Newberg, A.B., Wintering, N., Waldman, M R., Amen, D., Khalsa, D.S., and Alavi, A. (2010). Cerebral blood flow differences between long-term meditators and non-meditators. *Consciousness and Cognition*, 19(4), 899–905. doi:10.1016/j.concog.2010.05.003.

Nicolelis, M.A., Baccala, L.A., Lin, R.C. and Chapin, J.K., (1995). Sensorimotor Encoding by Synchronous Neural Ensemble Activity at Multiple Levels of the Somatosensory System. *Science*, 268 (5215) 1353-1358.

Nobel Prize. (2022). Sir James W. Black – Facts. Nobel Prize.org. *Nobel Prize Outreach AB.*

Northoff, G., Magioncalda, P., Martino, M., Lee, H.C., Tseng, Y.C., and Lane, T. (2017). Too Fast or Too Slow? Time and Neuronal Variability in Bipolar Disorder: *Schizophrenia Bulletin*, 44(1), 54–64. doi:10.1093/schbul/sbx050.

Northoff, G. (2011). Self and brain: What is self-related

processing? *Trends in Cognitive Sciences*, 15(5), 186–187. doi:10.1016/j.tics.2011.03.001.

Northoff, G. (2018). The brain's spontaneous activity and its psychopathological symptoms: "Spatiotemporal binding and integration." *Progress in Neuro-Psychopharmacology and Biological Psychiatry*, 80, 81–90. doi:10.1016/j.pnpbp.2017.03.019.

Osho. (2012). The Book of Secrets 112 Meditations to Discover the Mystery Within. *New York: Osho Media International.*

Otzi the Iceman. South Tyrol Museum of Archaeology. https://www.iceman.it/en/the-iceman/.

Pagnoni, G. (2012). Dynamical Properties of BOLD Activity from the Ventral Posteromedial Cortex Associated with Meditation and Attentional Skills. *Journal of Neuroscience*, 32(15), 5242–5249. doi:10.1523/jneurosci.4135-11.2012.

Panda, R., Bharath, R.D., Upadhyay, N., Mangalore, S., Chennu, S., and Rao, S. L. (2016). Temporal Dynamics of the Default Mode Network Characterize Meditation-Induced Alterations in Consciousness. *Frontiers in Human Neuroscience*, 10. doi:10.3389/fnhum.2016.00372.

Patel, K. (2016). The Science of Spirituality: Evolution of Consciousness. December 2016 Collectors Edition. *Heartfulness magazine.*

Penrose, R., (1989). The Emperor's New Mind: Concerning Computers, Minds and the Laws of Physics. *Oxford University.*

Pezzulo, G., Zorzi, M., Corbetta M., The secret life of predictive brains: what's spontaneous activity for? Trends Cogn Sci. 2021 June 16:S1364-6613(21)00128-5. doi: 10.1016/j.tics.2021.05.007. *Epub ahead of print*. PMID: 34144895.

Philips, S.M., (1999). ESP of Quarks and Superstrings. *New Age International* (P).

Pokharna, S.S., (2015). Quantum Field Theory, Consciousness and Jainism in Quantum Consciousness. *The International Journal for Transformation of Consciousness*, 1 (1).

Pokharna, S.S., (2021). Forty-Seven *shaktis* of Ātmā in Jainism and Analogous Ideas in Modern Science, presented at Second International Conference on Science and Jain Philosophy (ICSJP), Virtual conference, organised by Florida International University, in association with Jain Education and Research Foundation (JERF).

Pokharna, S.S., and Shah, R.B., (2022). Forty-seven powers of Aatma described in Jainism indicates its Holographic structure. The Science of Consciousness (TSC, 2022) Tucson, Arizona, Abstracts of the conference held from April 18-22 at Centre for Consciousness Studies, The University of Arizona, TSC, pp. 218-219.

Pribram, K., (1990). Prolegomenon for a holonomic brain theory. Haken H., and Stadler, M., (eds.), Synergetics of cognition: Proceedings of the international symposium at Schloss Elmau, Bavaria, pp. 150-184. *Springer-Verlag*.

Pribram, K.H., (1921) The form within: My point of view. *Easton Studio Press, LLC, 2013b.*

Pribram, K.H., (1976). Freud's "Project" re-assessed : Preface to contemporary cognitive theory and neuropsychology. *Basic Books (Gill)* https://archive.org/details/freudsprojectrea0000pribPribram.

Pujyaniya Kanji Swamy (2000). Pravachan Navneet-Bhag 4, Pujya Gurudev Shree Kanji Swamy na 47 shakti par na khas pravachno (written in Gujarati), Published by *Shree Veetrag Sat-Sahitya Prasarak Trust*.

Qin, P., Wang, M., and Northoff, G. (2020). Linking Bodily, Environmental and Mental States In the Self—A Three-level Model Based on a Meta-analysis. *Neuroscience and Biobehavioral Reviews*. doi:10.1016/j.neubiorev.2020.05.004.

Raichle, M.E., MacLeod, A.M., Snyder, A.Z., Powers, W.J., Gusnard, D. A., and Shulman, G. L. (2001). A default mode of brain function. *Proceedings of the National Academy of Sciences*, 98(2), 676–682. doi:10.1073/pnas.98.2.676.

Raichle, M.E. (2015). The Brain's Default Mode Network. *Annual Review of Neuroscience*, 38(1), 433–447. doi:10.1146/annurev-neuro-071013-014030.

Raut, R.V., Snyder, A. Z., and Raichle, M.E. (2020). Hierarchical dynamics as a macroscopic organizing principle of the human brain. *Proceedings of the National Academy of Sciences*, 117(34), 20890-20897. doi:10.1073/pnas.2003383117.

Reddy, J.S.K., and Roy, S. (2018). Commentary: Patanjali and neuroscientific research on meditation. *Frontiers in Psychology*, 9. doi:10.3389/fpsyg.2018.00248 .

Robbins, K., and Roe, C., (2010). An empirical test of the theory of morphic resonance by using recognition for Chinese symbols. *Explore*, 6, 256–262. https://doi.org/10.1016/j.explore.2010.04.001.

Robert, K., and Freeman, W.J., (2016) Cognitive phase transitions in the cerebral cortex-enhancing the neuron doctrine by modeling neural fields. *Switzerland: Springer International Publishing.*

Rodriguez-Larios, J., Faber, P., Achermann, P., Tei, T., and Alaerts, K. (2020). From thoughtless awareness to effortful cognition: alpha-theta cross-frequency dynamics in experienced meditators during meditation, rest and arithmetic. *Scientific Reports*, 10, 5419 (2020). https://doi.org/10.1038/s41598-020-62392-2.

Rom 8:9-1. *Bible Gateway*. https://www.biblegateway.com.

Root-Bernstein, R. and Root-Bernstein, M. (1999). Sparks of genius: The 12 thinking tools of the world's most creative people. *New York: Houghton Mifflin Harcourt.*

Rosenblum, B., (2011). Kuttner F. Quantum enigma: Physics encounters consciousness. *Oxford University Press*.

Sankar S.B., Nair, A.K., Jayanna K., et al. Meditation, well-being and cognition in heartfulness meditators: A pilot study. *Conscious Cogn*. 2020;86:103032.

Santarnecchi, E., Egiziano, E.D'Arista, S., Gardi, C., Romanella, S.M., Mencarelli, L., . . . Rossi, A. (2021). Mindfulness-based stress reduction training modulates striatal and cerebellar connectivity. *Journal of Neuroscience Research*, 99(5), 1236-1252. doi:10.1002/jnr.24798.

Scalabrini, A., Mucci, C., and Northoff, G. (2018). Is Our Self Related to Personality? A Neuropsychodynamic Model. *Frontiers in Human Neuroscience*, 12. doi:10.3389/fnhum.2018.00346.

Scalabrini, A., Mucci, C., Angeletti, L.L., and Northoff, G. (2020). The self and its world: A neuro-ecological and temporo-spatial account of existential fear. *Clin. Neuropsychiatry*, 17, 46–58. doi: 10.36131/CN20200203.

Scalabrini, A., Vai, B., Poletti, S., Damiani, S., Mucci, C., Colombo, C., … Northoff, G. (2020). All roads lead to the default-mode network—global source of DMN abnormalities in major depressive disorder. *Neuropsychopharmacology*, doi:10.1038/s41386-020-0785-x.

Scheibner, H.J., Bogler, C., Gleich, T., Haynes, J.D., and Bermpohl, F. (2017). Internal and external attention and the default mode network. *NeuroImage*, 148, 381–389. doi:10.1016/j.neuroimage.2017.01.044.

Schoenberg, P.L., and Vago, D.R. (2019). Mapping meditative states and stages with electrophysiology: concepts, classifications, and methods. *Current Opinion in Psychology,* 28, 211–217. doi:10.1016/j.copsyc.2019.01.007.

Schoenberg, P.L.A., Ruf, A., Churchill, J., Brown, D.P., and Brewer, J.A. (2018). Mapping complex mind states: EEG neural substrates of meditative unified compassionate awareness. *Consciousness and Cognition*, 57, 41–53. doi:10.1016/j.concog.2017.11.003.

Schoormans, D., and Nyklíček, I. (2011). Mindfulness and Psychologic Well-Being: Are They Related to Type of Meditation Technique Practiced? *The Journal of Alternative and Complementary Medicine*, 17(7), 629–634. doi:10.1089/acm.2010.0332.

Schorn, R., Tappenier, G., and Walde, J., (2006). Analyzing 'spooky action at a distance' concerning brand logos. *Innovative Marketing*, 2 (1), 45–60. https://s3.amazonaws.com/academia.edu.documents/41281873/Analyzing_Spooky_Action_at_a_Distance_20160116- 21129-akr04x.pdf.

Schwartz, S., (2017). Therapeutic intention—into the next generation. *Explore*, 13 (3), 158–162.

Schwartz, S., and Dossey, L., (2010) Nonlocality, intention, and observer effects in healing studies: Laying a foundation for the future. *Explore*, 6 (5):295–307.

Schwartz, S.A., Mattei, Brame E.J., Spottiswoode, S.J.P., (2015) Infrared spectra alteration in water proximate to the palms of therapeutic practitioners. *Explore*, 11 (2),144–155.

Schwartz. S.A., (2019). Water, Wine, and the Sacred, An Anthropological View of Substances Altered by Intentioned Awareness, Including Objective and Aesthetic Effects. *Explore*, https://doi.org/10.1016/j.explore.2018.03.010.

Shao, R., Keuper, K., Geng, X., and Lee, T.M.C. (2016). Pons to Posterior Cingulate Functional Projections Predict Affective Processing Changes in the Elderly Following Eight Weeks of Meditation Training. *EBioMedicine*, 10, 236–248. doi:10.1016/j.ebiom.2016.06.018.

Sharma, K., Chandra, S., Dubey, A.K. (2008). Exploration of lower frequency eeg dynamics and cortical alpha asymmetry in long-term rajyoga meditators. *International Journal of Yoga*. doi: 10.4103/ijoy.IJOY_11_17.

Sheldrake, R, (1981). A New Science of Life: The Hypothesis of Formative Causation. *London: Blond and Briggs*

Sheldrake, R., (1995). The Presence of the Past: Morphic Resonance and the Habits of Nature. *Rochester*.

Shetkar, R., Hankey, A., Nagendra, H.R., (2017). First Person Accounts of Yoga Meditation Yield Clues to the Nature of Information in Experience. *Cosmos and History: The Journal of Natural and Social Philosophy*, 13(1), 252-53.

Shiah, Y.J., and Radin, D. (2013). Metaphysics of the tea ceremony: a randomized trial investigating the roles of intention and belief on mood while drinking tea. *Explore (New York, N.Y.)*, 9 (6), 355–360. https://doi.org/10.1016/j.explore.2013.08.005.

Simon, R., Pihlsgård, J., Berglind, U., Söderfeldt, B., and Engström, M. (2017). Mantra Meditation Suppression of Default Mode Beyond an Active Task: A Pilot Study. *Journal of Cognitive Enhancement*, 1(2), 219–227. doi:10.1007/s41465-017-0028-1.

Singleton, O., Newlon, M., Fossas, A., Sharma, B., Cook-Greuter, S.R., and Lazar, S. W. (2021). Brain Structure and Functional Connectivity Correlate with Psychosocial Development in Contemplative Practitioners and Controls. *Brain Sciences*, 11(6), 728. doi:10.3390/brainsci11060728.

Smith, J.L., Allen, J.W., Haack, C., Wehrmeyer, K., Alden, K., Lund, M.B., and Mascaro, J.S. (2020). The Impact of App-Delivered Mindfulness Meditation on Functional Connectivity and Self-Reported Mindfulness Among Health Profession Trainees. *Mindfulness*, 12(1), 92-106. doi:10.1007/s12671-020-01502-7.

Soneji, R., Hankey, A., Sridhar, M.K., (2021). Spiritual - Scientific Yoga Based Model of Siddhi. *Shodh Sanchar Bulletin*.

Stanley, H.E., (1971). Introduction to Phase Transitions and Critical Phenomena. *Oxford University Press*.

Tagliazucchi, E., Carhart-Harris, R., Leech, R., Nutt, D., and Chialvo, D. R. (2014). Enhanced repertoire of brain dynamical states during the psychedelic experience. *Human Brain Mapping*, 35(11), 5442–5456. doi:10.1002/hbm.22562.

Tagliazucchi, E., Roseman, L., Kaelen, M., Orban, C., Muthukumaraswamy, S.D., Murphy, K., … Carhart-Harris, R. (2016). Increased Global Functional Connectivity Correlates with LSD-Induced Ego Dissolution. *Current Biology*, 26(8), 1043–1050. doi:10.1016/j.cub.2016.02.010.

Takahashi, T., Murata, T., Hamada, T., Omori, M., Kosaka, H., Kikuchi, M., … Wada, Y. (2005). Changes in EEG and autonomic nervous activity during meditation and their association with personality traits. *International Journal of Psychophysiology*, 55(2), 199–207. doi:10.1016/j.ijpsycho.2004.07.004.

Talbot, M., (2011). The Holographic Universe, *Harper Perennial*.

Tang, Y.Y., Tang, R., and Posner, M.I. (2013). Brief meditation training induces smoking reduction. *Proceedings of the National Academy of Sciences*, 110(34), 13971–13975. doi:10.1073/pnas.1311887110.

Tang, Y.Y., Tang, R., Rothbart, M.K., and Posner, M.I. (2019). Frontal theta activity and white matter plasticity following mindfulness meditation. *Current Opinion in Psychology*. doi:10.1016/j.copsyc.2019.04.004.

Tang, Y.Y., Tang, Y., Tang, R., and Lewis-Peacock, J.A. (2017). Brief Mental Training Reorganizes Large-Scale Brain Networks. *Frontiers in Systems Neuroscience*, 11. doi:10.3389/fnsys.2017.00006.

Taren, A. A., Gianaros, P. J., Greco, C. M., Lindsay, E. K., Fairgrieve, A., Brown, K.W., … Creswell, J.D. (2017). Mindfulness Meditation Training and Executive Control Network Resting State Functional Connectivity. *Psychosomatic Medicine*, 79(6), 674–683. doi:10.1097/psy.0000000000000466.

Taylor, V.A., Daneault, V., Grant, J., Scavone, G., Breton, E., Roffe-Vidal, S., … Beauregard, M. (2012). Impact of meditation training on the default mode network during a restful state. *Social Cognitive and Affective Neuroscience*, 8(1), 4–14. doi:10.1093/scan/nsr087.

Tei, S., Faber, P.L., Lehmann, D., Tsujiuchi, T., Kumano, H., Pascual-Marqui, R. D., … Kochi, K. (2009). Meditators and Non-Meditators: EEG Source Imaging During Resting. *Brain Topography*, 22(3), 158–165. doi:10.1007/s10548-009-0107-4.

Telles, S., Singh, N., Naveen, K.V., Deepeshwar, S., Pailoor, S., Manjunath, N.K., George, L., Dawn, D., and Balkrishna, A. (2014). A fMRI Study of Stages of Yoga Meditation Described in Traditional Texts. *Journal of Psychology and Psychotherapy*, 05(03). doi:10.4172/2161-0487.1000185.

Teresa (1976). Collected Work of St Teresa of Avila. *ICS Publications*.

Thompson, E., and Varela, F. J. (2001). Radical embodiment: Neural dynamics and consciousness. *Trends in Cognitive Sciences*, 5(10), 418–425. doi:10.1016/S1364-6613(00)01750-2.

Tomasino, B., and Fabbro, F. (2016). Increases in the right dorsolateral prefrontal cortex and decreases the rostral prefrontal cortex activation after-8 weeks of focused attention based mindfulness meditation. *Brain and Cognition*, 102, 46–54. doi:10.1016/j.bandc.2015.12.004.

Tomljenović, H., Begić, D., and Maštrović, Z. (2016). Changes in trait brainwave power and coherence, state and trait anxiety after three-month transcendental meditation (TM) practice. *Psychiatria Danubina*, Vol. 28, No. 1, 63-72.

Travis, F., and Parim, N. (2017). Default mode network activation and Transcendental Meditation practice: Focused Attention or Automatic Self-transcending? *Brain and Cognition*, 111, 86–94. doi:10.1016/j.bandc.2016.08.009.

Travis, F., Haaga, D.A.F., Hagelin, J., Tanner, M., Nidich, S., Gaylord-King, C., … Schneider, R. H. (2009). Effects of Transcendental Meditation practice on brain functioning and stress reactivity in college students. *International Journal of Psychophysiology*, 71(2), 170–176. doi:10.1016/j.ijpsycho.2008.09.007.

Travis, F. (1994). The junction point model: A field model of waking, sleeping, and dreaming, relating dream witnessing, the waking/sleeping transition, and Transcendental Meditation in terms of a common psychophysiologic state. *Dreaming*, 4(2), 91-104. https://doi.org/10.1037/h0094404.

Travis, F., Pearson, C., Pure Consciousness: Distinct Phenomenological and Physiological Correlates of "Consciousness Itself". *Int J Neurosci.* 1999 January;100(1-4):77-89. PMID: 10938552.

Turow, G., (2005). Auditory Driving as a Ritual Technology: A Review and Analysis, Religious Studies Honors Thesis. *Stanford University*.

Uma Swami, 'That which is' Translation in English of Uma Swami's Tattvarthasutra and combined commentaries by Pujyapad Indian edition. *Motilal Banarasidass*.

Vago, D.R., and Zeidan, F. (2016). The brain on silent: mind wandering, mindful awareness, and states of mental tranquility. *Annals of the New York Academy of Sciences*, 1373(1), 96–113. doi:10.1111/nyas.13171.

Valentine, E.R., Sweet, P.L.G., (1999). Meditation and attention: a comparison of the effects of concentrative and mindfulness meditation on sustained attention. Ment. *Health Relig. Cult.* 2 (1), 59–70. https://doi.org/10.1080/13674679908406332.

van Lutterveld, R., Houlihan, S.D., Pal, P., Sacchet, M.D., McFarlane-Blake, C., Patel, P.R., … Brewer, J.A. (2017 a). Source-space EEG neurofeedback links subjective experience with brain activity during effortless awareness meditation. *NeuroImage*, 151, 117–127. doi:10.1016/j.neuroimage.2016.02.047.

van Lutterveld, R., van Dellen, E., Pal, P., Yang, H., Stam, C.J., and Brewer, J. (2017 b). Meditation is associated with increased brain network integration. *NeuroImage*, 158, 18–25. doi:10.1016/j.neuroimage.2017.06.071.

Van Manen, M. (2014) Phenomenology of practice: meaning giving methods in phenomenological research. *Left Coast Press Inc.*

van Mulukom, V., Patterson, R.E., and van Elk, M. (2020). Broadening Your Mind to Include Others: The relationship between serotonergic psychedelic experiences and maladaptive narcissism. *Psychopharmacology*. doi:10.1007/s00213-020-05568-y.

Vivot, R., Pallavicini, C., Zamberlan, F., Vigo, D., and Tagliazucchi, E. (2020). Meditation increases the entropy of brain oscillatory activity. *Neuroscience*. doi:10.1016/j.neuroscience.2020.01.033.

von Bertalanffy, L. (1976). General System Theory: Foundations, Development, Applications (rev. ed.). *New York, NY: George Braziller*.

Vyšata, O., Schätz, M., Kopal, J., Burian, J., Procházka, A., Jiří, K., . . . Vališ, M. (2014). Non-Linear EEG Measures in Meditation. *Journal of Biomedical Science and Engineering*, 07(09), 731-738. doi:10.4236/jbise.2014.79072.

Wang, M.Y., Freedman, G., Raj, K., Fitzgibbon, B. M., Sullivan, C., Tan, W.L., … Bailey, N.W. (2020). Mindfulness meditation alters neural activity underpinning working memory during tactile distraction. *Cognitive, Affective, and Behavioral Neuroscience*. doi:10.3758/s13415-020-00828-y.

Winter, U., LeVan, P., Borghardt, T.L., Akin, B., Wittmann, M., Leyens, Y., and Schmidt, S. (2020). Content-Free Awareness: EEG-fcMRI Correlates of Consciousness as Such in an Expert Meditator. *Frontiers in Psychology*, 10. doi:10.3389/fpsyg.2019.03064.

Wolfgang, D.K., (1963). The nerves of government: Models

of political communication and control. *Free Press of Glencoe*, Vol. 90729 https://archive.org/details/nervesofgovernme0000deut.

Wong, W.P., Camfield, D.A., Woods, W., Sarris, J., and Pipingas, A. (2015). Spectral power and functional connectivity changes during mindfulness meditation with eyes open: A magnetoencephalography (MEG) study in long-term meditators. *International Journal of Psychophysiology*, 98(1), 95–111. doi:10.1016/j.ijpsycho.2015.07.006.

Xiao, Q., Zhao, X., Bi, G., Wu, L., Zhang, H., Liu, R., … Chen, Z. (2019). Alterations of Regional Homogeneity and Functional Connectivity Following Short-Term Mindfulness Meditation in Healthy Volunteers. *Frontiers in Human Neuroscience*, 13. doi:10.3389/fnhum.2019.00376.

Xu, J., Vik, A., Groote, I.R., Lagopoulos, J., Holen, A., Ellingsen, Ø., … Davanger, S. (2014). Nondirective meditation activates default mode network and areas associated with memory retrieval and emotional processing. *Frontiers in Human Neuroscience*, 8. doi:10.3389/fnhum.2014.00086.

Xue, S., Tang, Y.Y., Posner, M. (2011). Short-term meditation increases network efficiency of the anterior cingulate cortex. *NeuroReport*, 22(12), 570–574. doi:10.1097/wnr.0b013e328348c750.

Xue, S.W., Tang, Y.Y., Tang, R., and Posner, M.I. (2014). Short-term meditation induces changes in brain resting EEG theta networks. *Brain and Cognition*, 87, 1–6. doi:10.1016/j.bandc.2014.02.008.

Yale University (1999) http://chem125-.yale.oyc.webspce.yale.edu/125/history99/8occult/occult-Atoms.html.

Yang, C.C., Barrós-Loscertales, A., Li, M., Pinazo, D., Borchardt, V., Ávila, C., and Walter, M. (2019). Alterations in Brain Structure and Amplitude of Low-frequency after 8 weeks of Mindfulness Meditation Training in Meditation-Naïve Subjects. *Scientific Reports*, 9(1). doi:10.1038/s41598-019-47470-4.

Yang, C.C., Barrós-Loscertales, A., Pinazo, D., Ventura-Campos, N., Borchardt, V., Bustamante, J.C., … Walter, M. (2016). State and Training Effects of Mindfulness Meditation on Brain Networks Reflect Neuronal Mechanisms of Its Antidepressant Effect. *Neural Plasticity*, 2016, 1–14. doi:10.1155/2016/9504642.

Yogi, M.M., Tompkins, M., (1966). The science of being and art of living. *International SRM Publications*.

Yordanova, J., Kolev, V., Mauro, F., Nicolardi, V., Simione, L., Calabrese, L., … Raffone, A. (2020). Common and distinct lateralised patterns of neural coupling during focused attention, open monitoring and loving kindness meditation. *Scientific Reports*, 10(1). doi:10.1038/s41598-020-64324-6.

Yoshida, K., Takeda, K., Kasai, T., Makinae, S., Murakami, Y., Hasegawa, A., and Sakai, S. (2020). Focused attention meditation training modifies neural activity and attention: longitudinal EEG data in non-meditators. *Social Cognitive and Affective Neuroscience*. doi:10.1093/scan/nsaa020.

Zeidan, F., Martucci, K.T., Kraft, R.A., McHaffie, J.G., and Coghill, R.C. (2013). Neural correlates of mindfulness meditation-related anxiety relief. *Social Cognitive and Affective Neuroscience*, 9(6), 751–759. doi:10.1093/scan/nst041.

Zeleznikar Anton P (1997) Consciousness as Informational Phenomenalism: An Informational, Phenomenological, Philosophical, Neural and Quantum-Mechanical View. *Informatica: An International Journal of Computing and Informatics*, 21 (3).

Zhang, Q., Wang, Z., Wang, X., Liu, L., Zhang, J., and Zhou, R. (2019). The Effects of Different Stages of Mindfulness Meditation Training on Emotion Regulation. *Frontiers in Human Neuroscience*, 13. doi:10.3389/fnhum.2019.00208.

Zhang, Z., Luh, W., Duan, W., Zhou, G.D., Weinschenk, G., Anderson, A.K., and Dai, W. (2021). Longitudinal effects of meditation on brain resting-state functional connectivity. *Scientific Reports*, 11(1). doi:10.1038/s41598-021-90729-y.

APPENDICES

The Jain View on Consciousness
In the Perspective of Contemporary Physics and Neuroscience

Appendix 1: Reality from Four Different Viewpoints

- Conceptual: *dravya* (6)
    - *jīva, dharma, ddharma, ākāśa, pudgala and kāla*
- Place (*kṣetra/pradeśa*): *astikāya* (5)
    - *jīva*, *pudgala*, *dharma*, *adharma* and ākāśa
- Time (*kāla*): Interactions of *jīva* and *ajīva* 7 verities (*tattvas*)
    - *jīva*, *ajīva*, *āsrava*, *bandha*, *saṃvara*, *nirjarā* and *mokṣa*
- Actions and results (*bhāva*): 9 *padārtha* /entities
    - 7 verities + *puṇya*, *pāpa*

Appendix 2: Map of The Loka

MAP OF THE LOKA — (The Universe.)

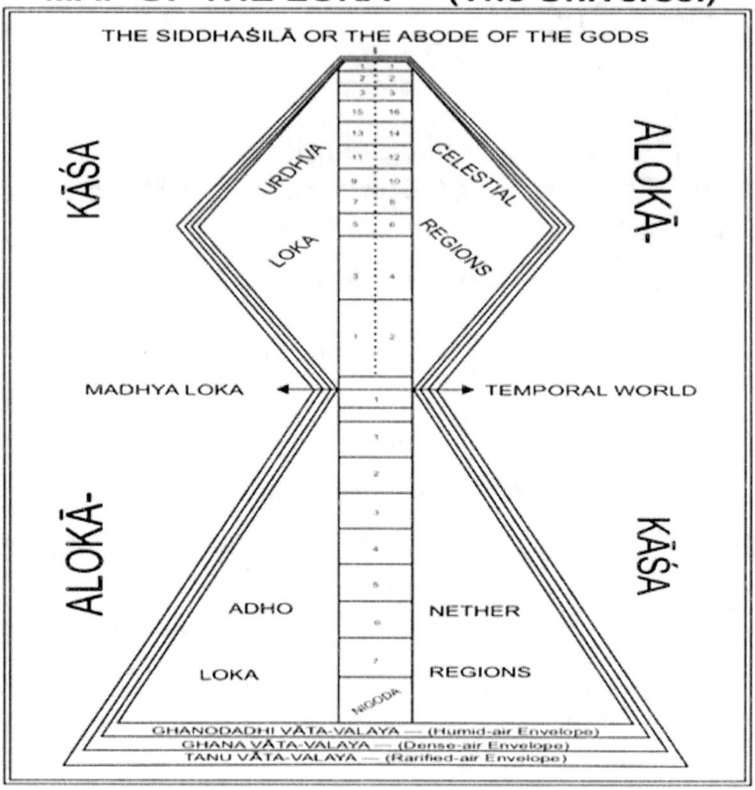

Appendix 3: Substances, Their Nature, Number, Space Occupied and Other Characteristics

#	Name	Nature	Number	Space points	Concrete	Sentient	Active	Astikāya
1.	Jīva	Knowledge, bliss	Infinite	innumerable	No	Yes	Yes	Yes
2.	Pudgala	Fusion and fission	Infinite	do	Yes	No	Yes	Yes
3.	Dharma	Supports motion	One	do	No	No	No	Yes
4.	Adharma	Supports rest	One	do	No	No	No	Yes
5.	Ākāśa	Provides space	One	do	No	No	No	Yes
6.	Kāla	Supports change	Innumerable	One	No	No	No	No

Appendix 4: Nine Attributes of Soul

Distinguishing quality	Sentient	Number: Infinite
Attribute	Empirical soul *Sansārī jīva*	Pure soul *Mukta* or supreme soul
Manif of consciousness (*upayoga*)	Intuition, knowledge due to Karmic (limited)	Just knowledge, intuition Omniscient
Lived, lives and will live *Jīvatva (prāṇī)*	Embodied, senses Life vitalities	Soul *jñātā, draṣtā*, bliss, eternal
Perceptible (*mūrtatva*)	Yes	No
Agent / Doer (*kartā*)	Of matter karmas	Of its own nature
Enjoyer (*bhoktā*)	Do	Do
Size (*svadeha parimāṇa*)	As the body it owns, elastic	Fixed < last body
Existence (*astitva*)	Everywhere in the cosmos	Summit of cosmos
Upwards movement	Nature of pure soul	Stationery

Index

C

D

E

F

G

H

I

L

M

O

P

Q

T

U

Y

Z

INDEX OF SANSKRIT WORDS